THE EPIC HISTORY OF MACARONI AND CHEESE

ARTS AND TRADITIONS OF THE TABLE

ARTS AND TRADITIONS OF THE TABLE: PERSPECTIVES ON CULINARY HISTORY

Albert Sonnenfeld, Series Editor

What We Eat: A Global History of Food, edited by Pierre Singaravélou and Sylvain Venayre, translated by Stephen W. Sawyer

Spoiled: The Myth of Milk as Superfood, Anne Mendelson

The Fulton Fish Market: A History, Jonathan H. Rees

The Botany of Beer: An Illustrated Guide to More Than 500 Plants Used in Brewing, Giuseppe Caruso

Anxious Eaters: Why We Fall for Fad Diets, Janet Chrzan and Kima Cargill

Gastronativism: Food, Identity, Politics, Fabio Parasecoli

Epistenology: Wine as Experience, Nicola Perullo

The Terroir of Whiskey: A Distiller's Journey Into the Flavor of Place, Rob Arnold

Meals Matter: A Radical Economics Through Gastronomy, Michael Symons

The Chile Pepper in China: A Cultural Biography, Brian R. Dott

Cook, Taste, Learn: How the Evolution of Science Transformed the Art of Cooking, Guy Crosby

Garden Variety: The American Tomato from Corporate to Heirloom, John Hoenig

Mouthfeel: How Texture Makes Taste, Ole G. Mouritsen and Klavs Styrbæk, translated by Mariela Johansen

Chow Chop Suey: Food and the Chinese American Journey, Anne Mendelson

Kosher USA: How Coke Became Kosher and Other Tales of Modern Food, Roger Horowitz

Taste as Experience: The Philosophy and Aesthetics of Food, Nicola Perullo

For a complete list of books in the series, please see the Columbia University Press website.

The Epic History of Macaroni and Cheese

FROM ANCIENT ROME TO MODERN AMERICA

Karima Moyer-Nocchi

Foreword by Paula J. Johnson

Columbia University Press
New York

Columbia University Press
Publishers Since 1893
New York Chichester, West Sussex
cup.columbia.edu

Library of Congress Cataloging-in-Publication Data
Names: Moyer-Nocchi, Karima author
Title: The epic history of macaroni and cheese : from ancient Rome to modern America / Karima Moyer-Nocchi.
Description: New York : Columbia University Press, [2026] | Includes bibliographical references and index.
Identifiers: LCCN 2025022873 | ISBN 9780231215312 hardback | ISBN 9780231560733 ebook
Subjects: LCSH: Cooking (Pasta)—History | Cooking (Cheese)—History
Classification: LCC TX809.M17 M68 2026 | DDC 641.82/209—dc23/eng/20250702
LC record available at https://lccn.loc.gov/2025022873

Printed in the United States of America

Cover design: Milenda Nan Ok Lee
Cover photograph: Eric Walk Wolfinger

GPSR Authorized Representative: Easy Access System Europe, Mustamäe tee 50, 10621 Tallinn, Estonia, gpsr.requests@easproject.com

To Simone . . .
who had to eat a lot of macaroni and cheese

CONTENTS

CONTENTS

FOREWORD

PAULA J. JOHNSON, CURATOR OF FOOD HISTORY, NATIONAL MUSEUM OF AMERICAN HISTORY

Macaroni and cheese—is there a dish more ubiquitous, more comforting, more evocative of home, childhood, and community than the creamy, gooey, perfectly crusty, ultra cheesy concoction we fondly call mac 'n' cheese? Have you ever wondered how such deceptively simple ingredients—pasta, cheese, butter, perhaps some milk or tomato and pinches of seasonings—can be combined to create so many versions and variations that cooks and consumers vigorously defend *theirs* as the one true recipe? And how did we get to a place in the United States where mac 'n' cheese turns up at every kind of celebration—birthdays, weddings, graduations, and holidays such as Independence Day and Thanksgiving—as well as in school cafeteria lunches, church suppers, weeknight meals, and restaurant sides? And, lest we forget, who can fully describe the wide range of packaged, frozen, and ready-to-eat servings available in supermarkets—ready-to-go casseroles for time-challenged folks. As we gaze across the mac 'n' cheese landscape that is twenty-first century America, a bigger question presents itself: where did macaroni and cheese actually come from?

This is not a trivial question. As culinary historians understand, tracing the history of foods and foodways across time and space reveals intricate threads of history—trading networks and technologies of transport, cultural diasporas resulting from conflict and disease, the influence of religion and education, and ideas about gender, race, and class that underlie relationships and fuel the dynamics of power. Karima Moyer-Nocchi has brought her historian's lens and prodigious research capabilities to the task of tracking the origins and pathways of this seemingly simple dish across time and continents to demonstrate its incredible reach and impact.

Searching through libraries and archives in Italy, France, England, and the United States, she found and now shares the documentary evidence of how the ingredients, recipes, and culinary techniques of macaroni and cheese have appeared, been adapted, and revised over the centuries and in distant locations. The documents, including official and personal writings as well as recipes, reflect the broad contexts of tradition and innovation that underlie the history of the dish, from the Italian reverence for durum wheat since the founding of Rome to the design of machines for making pasta on an industrial scale in early nineteenth-century America. She also introduces us to people—the men and women who created recipes and prepared the dish under widely different circumstances, including enslaved women in the American South and Black celebrity chefs in the modern era. The dish, we learn, is more than a recipe but an emblem of culinary knowledge and skill that continues to sustain lives and communities.

Moyer-Nocchi generously shares evidence and voices from the past, largely through archival documents and recipes. The range is astonishing, with the earliest recipe for macaroni and cheese from antiquity, 160 BCE, to a recent recipe from the American chef, cookbook author, and food television star Carla Hall. Do not rush past the recipes, as the variations provide a window into differences in the availability of ingredients, cultural preferences, and opportunistic nuances that characterize historical foodways. Additions of cinnamon, chiles, sugar, ketchup, and other special ingredients reflect social and cultural history: wealth and prestige in some contexts and community identity in others.

Moyer-Nocchi digs deeply into our mythologies about the origins of macaroni and cheese and examines our perceptions about the dish's journey to its beloved place in American popular culture and among diverse communities in the United States. Supported by documentary evidence, she sheds lights on some chapters that have been obscured for too long, for example, sorting through the details of what James Hemings, enslaved by Thomas Jefferson, really did, and probably didn't do, in terms of preparing the dish.

Finally, a relevant revelation: for a few weeks in 2024, Karima, an American who has lived in Italy for over thirty years, was our house guest while she conducted research for this book in Washington, DC, at the Library of Congress and the Smithsonian's National Museum of American History. Sharing space with a writer is never dull, and sharing space with someone writing about food history is an adventure. Evening meals were peppered with research findings and sources, interpretations of texts, and occasional forays into pasta, olives, and wine. Ironically, the one dish we never shared was . . . macaroni and cheese. In hindsight, I believe it had to do with the weather, which was intensely, insanely hot. We now know that 2024 was the hottest year on record in the United States since 1850, and the heat certainly killed my interest in diving into a bowl of hot mac 'n' cheese. However, I look forward to making the dish with Karima at some point in the future, perhaps to celebrate the publication of this marvelous work of culinary and cultural history.

THE EPIC HISTORY OF MACARONI AND CHEESE

INTRODUCTION

The historian's craft demands a delicate balance between reason and imagination—rendering the bygone both vivid and immediate without crossing over into fiction—a tightrope walk that is as precarious as it is tempting, especially when the subject matter tugs at the heartstrings of our collective memory. So it is with macaroni and cheese, a dish so deeply beloved and embedded in our cultural consciousness that separating myth from reality requires both scholarly rigor and a willingness to follow where the trail may lead.

Historical narratives serve as our time machines. With the turn of the page, they allow us to grasp the vast expanse of human experience through carefully curated journeys into the past. When we choose food as our lens, we enter into something more intimate—a connection to the lived, sensory experience that threads to the present. And this is particularly true with macaroni and cheese, a dish uniquely suited to guide us through history. This unassuming combination of pasta and cheese acts as mirror, magnifying glass, and window, reflecting our own relationships with comfort and sustenance while offering glimpses into the complex social, economic, and cultural forces that have shaped our world across time.

The story of macaroni and cheese is, in many ways, a story of evolution within constraints. For centuries, the term "macaroni" encompassed various forms of pasta, but one constant remained: Cheese was its essential companion. While modern diners might find this limiting, historical cooks found endless variation within these parameters, each iteration marking a moment in time, each recipe bearing the imprint of its creator. Only in the nineteenth century, when tomato, meat, and other sauces started gaining culinary prominence, did this cheese-centric paradigm begin to cede ground. Yet even as other sauces rose to dominance, macaroni and cheese, on a parallel track, broke away from its European parentage and began its ascent to becoming an American culinary icon.

Macaroni and cheese is unique as a vehicle for time travel in that it is a dish and not a foodstuff, and it is therefore grounded in recipes. As such, this investigation relies heavily on cookbooks as primary sources while acknowledging the scholarly debates surrounding their reliability as historical documents. Yet these culinary texts, when properly contextualized, offer invaluable insights not only into the kitchens and dining rooms of the past but also into the ongoing flow of current events.

Where documentary evidence falls silent, we must engage in what is termed *Restorative History*—a methodologically rigorous form of historical recovery and reconstruction that draws upon both primary and secondary sources to illuminate landscapes of human experience that traditional historiography has often distorted or obscured. This method of reproposing history recognizes that conventional historical narratives typically emerge from a single, dominant perspective that not only omits but also actively distorts the experiences of marginalized and minoritized peoples. Restorative History challenges assumptions that have calcified into "common knowledge" and recovers perspectives that have been systematically erased or misrepresented alongside the celebrated figures. It is not merely about filling gaps in the historical record but about questioning why those gaps exist and how they have shaped our understanding of the past.

The result is far more than a simple chronicle of a comfort food but a saga of human creativity and resilience, winding through papal halls, plantations, restaurants, and family kitchens, sailing across oceans with merchants and migrants, entangled with colonialism, industrialization, and the emergence of modern capitalism. Macaroni and cheese walks cheek by jowl with some of history's most significant developments, intersecting with issues of race, gender, and class. Its story encompasses the brutal realities of slavery, the march of technological progress, the upheavals of war, the dynamics of economic change, and the advance of scientific understanding. It inspired the human extremes of greed and love, creativity and appropriation, empowerment and oppression. As our exploration unfolds, macaroni and cheese is revealed as a lens through which we can examine the very fabric of human society. Its evolution parallels our own social transformations and contradictions from emblem of luxury to a staple of survival, and bastion of pleasure to a signpost of historical pain.

What follows is a journey into the heart of this paradox—one of careful reconstruction and measured speculation, always grounded in historical evidence but not afraid to imagine the human experiences that official records often overlook. But it is more than a story of the past; it is a celebration of enduring deliciousness aimed at captivating both the mind and the senses. To complete the experience in a more personal way, readers are invited to enter into the realm of history through the many recipes used as historical markers within the text. This is what I call "hands-on history"—a practice that uses sensory engagement as a portal into the past. The recipes included here—remapped for the modern kitchen—bring you into direct contact with history—feeling the food as you prepare it, hearing it as it bakes and bubbles, smelling the aroma as it wafts through the kitchen, and finally embodying the past as you take that first rich bite. It is not about exact replication but about surrendering to the imaginative act—yielding as the past unfolds through your senses and your creativity. That is my invitation: to explore the history of macaroni and cheese as a living thread, weaving its way from distant kitchens into your own life.

HOW DID ALL THIS COME ABOUT?

Like many creative ventures sparked by lockdown, this project began as a distraction. Italy, where I reside, was the first European country to go into lockdown in March 2020. The rules were strict but clear, and for the most part, everyone dutifully adhered. After a disheartening semester teaching online to what was often a screen of black squares—disengaged students in pajamas, if they were even there at all—I put together a course on the Italian origins of macaroni and cheese for Context Travel, which was reinventing itself during the crisis by offering intellectually upmarket virtual excursions. The series not only explored Italy but also touched upon England, France, and the American colonies and included a demonstration of sixteenth-century recipes prepared from start to finish with the help of the master artisan pasta maker Julia Griner.

Unbeknownst to me, Anna Berkes, librarian at the International Center for Jefferson Studies, had taken the course. She reached out afterward with an email of related links and references in keeping with her area of expertise. Our back-and-forth correspondence led to an invitation to give a presentation on the history of macaroni and cheese at Monticello in spring 2021—pandemic permitting. Monticello requested a stronger focus on Thomas Jefferson and James Hemings, so over the next eight months, I happily immersed myself in research. I kept Italy as the foundation while digging deeper to unearth details about England and France to trace the migration of macaroni and cheese to the American colonies. The guest lecture broadened my focus, extending into modern America and culminating in a historical dish that I prepared for the eighty attendees.

In preparation for the presentation, I was put in contact with the Soul Food scholar Adrian Miller. Our shared fascination with the history of the dish led to a coauthored article published in *Epicurious* (2022). By that point, I had also spent a couple years working on a history of pasta cookbook, a topic I cultivated extensively on my Instagram account @historicalitalianfood. In collaboration with the food photographer Eric Wolfinger, I developed a sleek proposal for the idea. But despite publishers advertising themselves as eager for innovative projects, the real-life response was that they wanted cookbooks that helped folks get dinner on the table. Since when do people buy cookbooks just to get dinner on the table? I shared my disappointment with Adrian, and it was then that I tentatively revealed that I thought there might be a book on the macaroni and cheese topic. By then, I had a well-padded archive of documentation and images. His enthusiasm encouraged me to go back to the drawing board and draft a proposal for the epic history of macaroni and cheese.

But it isn't here that I chime, "and the rest is history," because this book would not have been possible without the fellowships that supported my research. In 2023, when I signed the book contract with Columbia University Press, I received funding to study at the International Center for Jefferson Studies. My time there was dedicated almost entirely to uncovering the details of the Jefferson-Hemings issue, elaborated in chapter 4. The following year, I was honored with a fellowship at the Smithsonian's Lemelson Center at the National Museum of American History. The Smithsonian

Archive Center was a treasure trove of ephemera that deepened my understanding of American culinary history, adding layers of context to my project. That sojourn also allowed me to bask in the endless resources at the Library of Congress, a researcher's paradise. And finally, the fellowship at the George Washington Presidential Library at Mount Vernon, completed in 2025, offered an opportunity to expand the surrounding context of African American women in early American culinary history, while also deepening the analysis of James Hemings's life and its broader implications. What made this work truly complete was uncovering the connections between Washington's table and macaroni and cheese.

That final piece of research rounded out a journey that began in 2020 as a simple lockdown distraction—and evolved into a deep exploration of the history of this iconic dish.

A NOTE ON THE HISTORICAL RECIPES

The recipes in this book have been carefully chosen not only for their variety, but also because they serve as signposts on the journey this dish has taken through history. Readers may wish to follow them as armchair cooks, stirring the pots in their mind's eye, or roll up their sleeves to prepare them as sensory companions to the narrative as it unfolds from chapter to chapter. In either case, these recipes offer a tangible link to the past.

There are, broadly speaking, two valid approaches to this kind of culinary reenactment. One might engage in historical cookery as a form of living archaeology—experiencing, for example, the exertion required to hand-mill wheat, make cheese, smoke meats, dry legumes, or bake in a hearth, with historically appropriate utensils, crockery, and even architectural elements of a kitchen. That is a valuable method that offers many insights.

The archaeological path, however, can feel intimidating or overly scientific, and may discourage the broad participation that is, after all, my goal as a culinary historian. My approach is to mediate historical instructions and ingredients for the modern cook, adapting them to what can be prepared in a reasonably equipped kitchen today, even if that sometimes requires a trip to a specialty shop or market. I use the word *remapping* to describe this process. Many historical sources offer only sparse instructions, lacking weights, precise timings, or temperatures. Remapping means taking those fragmentary records and transposing them into a form that adheres to modern expectations—clear measurements, structured steps, and reliable results—while preserving their historical essence.

Yet this kind of adaptation is sometimes viewed with suspicion or even dismissed as delivering something inferior, as if it fails to be the "real" McCoy. But it is worth asking what *real* truly means when we talk about experiencing a sensory creation—whether at the table or in the concert hall.

Indeed, the analogy I like to draw comes from the world of classical music. Modern performances do not perfectly replicate those of the past: instruments have evolved, musicians and conductors bring their own interpretations, concert halls have changed, and even our listening expectations are not the same. Yet despite these changes, the music still transports listeners across time, preserving essential processes and evoking the spirit of the past—keeping it alive rather than relegating it to a museum piece.

The recipes in this book are designed to open that same kind of window onto the past: through contact with ingredients, the rhythm of preparation, the aromas rising from the stove, the appearance of the finished dish, and finally its taste and mouthfeel. Some instructions have been preserved in their historical form to help provide this experience, even if you may see ways to simplify or streamline them; you are always free to bypass those elements as you see fit. If there is anything missing, perhaps it is only the conviviality of a historical table—and that is yours to recreate.

Because cooks have their own preferences and habits, I have included both volume measures and weights. These two systems have each been calibrated to work properly within themselves: if you choose to cook by weight, follow those amounts throughout; if you prefer cups and spoons, follow those (I do not include weights for spoon measurements). While they often come close, they are not precisely interchangeable, so it is best not to mix and match between them.

Taken together, these recipes are an invitation—not to reenact the past perfectly, but to bring its echoes into your present, and to enjoy, through cooking, a richer sense of how this remarkable dish has traveled through history.

Chapter One

DIGGING IN

Ancient Antecedents

Macaroni and cheese has long been the saving grace of college dorms, soccer moms, cafeteria lines, midnight munchies, backyard barbecues, funeral wakes, and church potlucks. It is, in short, the ultimate comfort food. But macaroni and cheese isn't just a cheap, convenient crowd-pleaser. It's a cultural artifact weighted with history—one that traveled a long road before embedding itself in American life and lodging deep in the collective consciousness. It stirs strong emotions and proprietary feelings—a dish as personal as it is national—but when we dig into our dish, who would suspect the ground it's covered, or how much it might reveal about us.

For centuries, the dish has been entangled in questions of religion, class, race, and gender—far more than its humble reputation would suggest. And yet, how strange that we know so little about its true origins, its evolution, or how it became a fixture in so many national cuisines—especially, and most indelibly, in the United States. What passes for common knowledge is often based on biased accounts and pseudo-histories: narratives crafted to entertain rather than inform, thick with embellishment, distortion, and outright myth.

The time has come to honor this revered dish with a "deep history" exploration that corrects the historical record and reveals its extraordinary journey in becoming mac 'n' cheese. Our odyssey begins with an archeological exploration in ancient Rome and the all-important basic foodstuff that will make macaroni and cheese possible: wheat.

ANTIQUITY

Wheat and the Roman Belly Button

In the Roman mind, the civilized table was set with a central starch staple and accompaniments. The Romans had appropriated this concept from the Greeks—*sitos* and *opson*. They reframed this model of eating as *puls* and *pulmentarium*, respectively, their traditional, filling wheat gruel and delectable extras. Conservative Romans kept a careful eye on ratios: Overindulgence in the trimmings over the carbs smacked of immorality. Not only did they watch the ratios, but exemplary Romans exercised parsimony and restraint at the table. They looked down their noses at the Etruscans, who openly reveled in stuffing themselves.

Barbarians were even worse, surviving as they did through hunting and foraging; they spit-roasted their meat, guzzled beer, and drank milk. The Greco-Roman trinity of bread, wine, and oil, in contrast, were culturally transformed products from agricultural harvests—grain, grapes, and olives. This skillful manipulation of nature's bounty separated sheep from goats. But it was wheat, the Romans asserted, that marked their superiority over their Greek rivals, who favored that inferior grain, barley.

The centrality of wheat to the Roman identity was evident from the time of the founding of the city. Romulus, the legendary founder of Rome, is said to have carved out an underground cavity or vault, with a direct line to the underworld. The space came to be known as *mondus cerialis*, a uterine sanctuary dedicated to Ceres, the Roman goddess of grain.

The English historian W. Warde Fowler circled back many times, contemplating what purpose *mundus cerealis* might have served. He surmised that it may have been the first storehouse for the wheat seeds, the prime kernels selected for the next season's planting. The precious contents had to be safeguarded from enemies, so the opening was sealed with a slab of rock covered over in earth.[1] The location of *mundus cerialis* has been lost to us, and literary references to its whereabouts are inconsistent, but a second century BCE construction, Umbilicus Urbis Romae, the "navel of the city of Rome," may have stood over this sacred chamber as its protrusion into the external world. Thus, the navel was fittingly positioned just above the womb. Instead of choosing the heart to signify the most central and sacred position of their city, the Romans used the navel, the symbol of connection and perpetuity.[2]

Not too far from the navel, Emperor Augustus erected a symbol of similar significance around 20 BCE, the Milliarium Aureum, the "golden milestone." This was the nexus, the starting point from which all distances from the Eternal City were calculated. Its position was neither arbitrary nor aesthetic. The Milliarium, too, was a conceptual belly button nestled, as it was, among clusters of *horrea*, warehouses for wheat reserves. These were Rome's source of survival, its protective layer of fat and the placenta that would feed its ambitions. Scott Reynolds Nelson neatly encapsulates the significance of monuments like the Milliarium: "The world's pivot points are not made by proclamations or even battles; rather they stand on the foundations that underlie the roads leading to and from every empire in the world: they mark out where the people's food is and how long it takes to get it to soldiers and citizens."[3]

The golden milestone, like the Umbilicus, pinpointed two sides of the same coin—Rome's strength and vulnerability, in a word, its wheat stores.

Preservation of the Roman wheat supply was sufficiently worrisome as to warrant its own goddess. Ceres was already employed full time safeguarding against agricultural calamities affecting wheat during cultivation, harvests, and threshing. So Annona, the goddess of Rome's wheat supply, was added to the Roman imperial cult alongside the elder Ceres. Augustus, though ruling by divine right, was smart to deflect some of the responsibility for the grain cache away from himself, should times grow lean and the masses restless.[4]

Reverence for wheat oscillated between the temporal and the spiritual. It encapsulated *Romanità*, the very essence of what it was to be Roman. Its abundance or lack had the power to make or break empires. The centrality of wheat became inscribed in our culinary DNA, generating ideas of wholesomeness and well-being as well as sociopolitical ideas of entitlement and privilege. Having cast the net wide to set the stage, let's home in on the first stirrings of macaroni and cheese.

Placenta: Plating Up Nostalgia

Our story starts long before Augustus and the goddess Annona with Marcus Portius Cato, an ultraconservative, "make Rome great again" senator.

As was typical of the senatorial aristocracy, he had vast landholdings in the countryside. Part of his mission as an exemplary gentleman farmer was to convince his peers to attend to their estates and, in so doing, bring them back into the fold of solid Roman traditions. These ideals, called the *mos maiorum*, had degraded with the influx of modern ideas and foreign food. He wrote his treatise, *De agri cultura*, ca. 160 BCE, as a manual to instruct his peers on how to run their country estates, in the hope they would straighten out their values and cease dillydallying in the city.

In the book, Cato included several traditional recipes that represented the Roman culinary identity and dishes for ritual feasts. One is called *placenta*—no need for alarm: The "c" is pronounced with the voiceless velar stop /k/.[5] The word derives from the Greek *plakoenta*, indicating something that is flattened. *Placenta* was a holiday food, which invariably indicated a celebration of a religious nature. The dish is, in essence, sheets of rolled-out dough layered with cheese, the first recipe documenting the combination of the two elements. But there is an ongoing, heated, and hair-splitting debate as to whether or not those sheets can be construed as pasta. Naysayers maintain that one of the necessary characteristics of pasta, as we intend it, is that it has to be boiled. Some hesitate because the recipe contains honey, pointing to various traditional honey cakes as the descendants of *placenta*. But as we shall see, macaroni dishes, too, would be sweetened. Other scholars, however, are inclined to see the layering of dough sheets and cheese as a proto-lasagna. The proof is in the pudding.

So how's it made?

A coarse dough consisting of soaked and softened whole-grain emmer groats, durum wheat flour, and water is rolled out into flat sheets. These are oiled and left to dry flat while the filling is prepared. The filling is a mixture of fresh cheese, such as a *primo sale* or a *queso fresco*, mixed 8–1 with honey. In Cato's time, there was no concept of sugary desserts— indeed, there was no sugar—so sweetness did not relegate a dish to the dessert trolley. Rather, it was the expense of the honey that made this stand out as a holiday treat. On less celebratory days, one could satisfy a hankering for pasta and cheese with *scriblitam*, prepared just like *placenta* but without the rare and costly sweetener.[6] Indeed, honey was most often conceived of as a condiment, a foil to the saltiness of fish sauce or the acidity of vinegar. The layers of the *placenta* are assembled as onc would a lasagna: pasta, filling, pasta, repeat. Then the whole thing is wrapped in a thin crust of refined white flour and water, placed on a bed of fresh bay leaves, and baked enclosed in a preheated portable oven in the hearth. So much for the hardware of the dish. Now let us turn to the software.

A SENSUAL, GUIDED TASTING

Before looking at a recipe remapped for the modern kitchen, let's consider the experience of *placenta* from a multisensory perspective: As the dish bakes, the bay leaves release their essential oils and infuse the kitchen with floral, citrus, and peppery aromas. The leaves are actually just a hack to keep the dough casing from sticking to the baking dish, but their distinct scent is an arousing reveille. The crust will toughen up and act as a cooking vessel for the encased layers of pasta and cheese. When sufficiently heated, the fresh cheese contracts, sweating whey from the curds that provides liquid to cook the dough, which will plump up and undulate slightly as it expands. Little by little the crust acquiesces to the Maillard (browning) reaction, and the fat and honey will join forces to act upon the cheese, turning it a golden orange; some of it will seep out and caramelize. These combined processes unleash notes of toasted nuts, browned butter, baking bread, and toffee, which harmonize with the herbal aromatics. The fragrance that wafts from the dish when the lid is lifted heightens the anticipation, the nose being the first point of entry and the most primeval of our senses. As the crowd gathers, these appetitive olfactory cues trigger deep-seated memories that intensify with each repetition of the ritual meal. These memories condition expectations: Will it be as good or better than last year's? I remember when so-and-so made *placenta*—ah, hers was the best.

The mounting expectations set off by aroma mark the first stage of mouthfeel and taste. Expectancy escalates when the dish is finally displayed. The golden color makes promises about flavor, while the thick layered pasta and the weight of the warm heft in the hand (no forks yet) foretell the toothsome texture that awaits. The unctuous-creamy-sticky-sweet filling sandwiched in between plays the decadent, cheesy *opson* antagonist off the staid, whole-grain *sitos*.

The best way to enter into the evolutionary trajectory is through the experiential portal. By preparing and eating the dish firsthand, you'll gain a deeper, more complicit understanding of the role this dish plays in the history of macaroni and cheese. Once you've tried it, see how you weigh in.

PLACENTA

Serves 8

1/2 cup (100 g) whole-grain emmer (farro) or spelt—or groats if you can find them

18 oz (500 g) *primo sale* (or other unripe cheese preferably goat or sheep's milk; not ricotta, which will be too soft. A semifirm homemade paneer or queso fresco can substitute)

1 2/3 cups (225 g) fine semolina flour (*semolina rimacinata*)

3 1/2 Tbsp (50 mL) olive oil

1 1/4 cups (150 g) all-purpose or type 00 flour, plus extra for dusting

1/2 cup (1 110 mL) raw honey

10 bay (laurel) leaves (fresh if possible)

There are three components to this dish: pasta layers (tracta), crust, and filling.

If using whole grain emmer, crush the grains with a mortar and pestle or use a food processor to reduce them to the size of medium bulgur. You may be able to find ready-cut groats in shops that sell Middle Eastern or North African products. Soften the emmer groats in a small 1 cup 200 mL) warm water until very soft, about half an hour.

Place the cheese in a bowl of warm water). Over the next 50 minutes, change the water three times. If your cheese is not salty, skip this step.

Mound the semolina flour on the counter and make a well in the center. Strain the softened groats with your hands, reserving the water. Place the strained groats in the well and gradually knead the flour in, adding the reserved water as needed to form a workable but stiff dough. Knead for 5 minutes, wrap in plastic, and set aside for 20 minutes.

Separate the dough into 6 pieces of equal weight. Roll them into 22-cm (8.5 in.) rounds as thick as lasagna or a thin tortilla. These are called *tracta*. Lightly wipe the rounds on both sides with an oiled cloth. Lay them out on a drying rack or any other flat surface. Cato recommends using baskets, which may have meant racks woven to suit this purpose.

For the crust, mix the all-purpose flour with (3 1/2 Tbsp (50 mL) water. Knead for about 5 minutes. Wrap in plastic and leave to rest for 20 minutes.

Preheat the oven to 375°F (190°C) with an empty 5 qt./lt. (26 cm) Dutch oven inside.

For the filling, remove the cheese from the water and pat dry with a towel. Place it in a bowl and knead until smooth. Stir in the honey and set aside.

Flour the surface of the counter or a wooden *spianatoia* (pasta board) and roll out the dough for the crust into a 21-in. (54 cm) circle. The circle should extend 6 inches (16 cm) from the edge of the *tracta*, which will be placed in the center. On a piece of parchment paper, make a bed of well-oiled bay leaves the size of a *tracta* disk. Position the crust dough on top of the leaves. Today, the bay leaves are no longer needed to create a nonstick surface, but for the full olfactory experience they are necessary.

To put it all together, place a *tracta* in the center of the crust. Spread 1/2 cup (130 g) of the cheese and honey filling over it cover with another *tracta*. Spread another 1/2 cup of filling over it and continue. On the fifth piece of *tracta*, add the remaining filling. Cover with the sixth *tracta* and, as decorously as possible, bring the crust up around the filled layers. Remove the hot Dutch oven from the oven and carefully place the paper with the *placenta* into the pot. It is helpful if you use a bread peel or cookie sheet to assist with this move. Pierce the *placenta* with a knife 5 times. Cover and bake for 45 minutes. Then remove the lid of the Dutch oven and bake for another 15 minutes.

Once you remove the Dutch oven, place a flat plate directly on top of the *placenta* and press any air out if it has ballooned. This will help to even the form as it settles. Let it cool for 10 minutes. Then remove from pan before cutting. Serve warm, although cold leftovers are also good.

Eating for Meaning

This hearty dish is not only laden with calories but also heavy with both privilege and tradition. Eating is not, as Pliny the Younger said, just an act of filling the pot. The joy and warmth of conviviality and companions (those with whom one breaks bread) enhance the appreciation of food, impacting if and how dishes would be carried forth into the future. Cato's recipe is enormous, clearly meant for a large gathering. And it is on these occasions that the anticipation, the visual, textural, and olfactory elements of the food, the high spirits and surroundings, and the sense of continuity and belonging all meld together as a single collective memory. While these qualities are not a guarantee that any given dish will survive the fickle tastes of time, Cato's *placenta* was a likely contender to be ushered along to future generations. It was not only delicious but also a gastronomic trigger, charged with subliminal meaning forged through cumulative repetition. It was both retrospective and prospective—leading to the yearning for more. Macaroni and cheese proper was still some time away, but *placenta* was a springboard that would propel us in that direction.

There's *Tracta* and Then There's *Tracta*

While Cato used the word *tracta* for his pasta sheets, the word defies a strict definition; it seems to refer to something different depending on the period and context and the person using it. The only surviving recipe compilation from ancient Rome, dated to around 400 CE, has for convenience's sake been generically attributed to "Apicius" and is thus eponymously referred to. In keeping with our investigation, the book contains a pottage recipe with *tracta* that in its own way also lays some groundwork for macaroni and cheese. The recipe for *pultes tractogalatae* asks the cook to dry three disks of *tracta* (*tres orbicular trace siccas*), which are later crumbled into a pan of hot milk and water. Some scholars favor the claim that *tracta* functioned here as a thickener.[7] While there is an element of truth in that assertion, from a practical perspective it raises the question: Why go to the bother of making and drying *tracta* only to break it up and dissolve it? The ancients had already harnessed the ability to make wheat starch, so, in this particular instance, the use of *tracta* to make a pot of white sauce defies logic.

Granted, if one is looking for logical instruction, recipes from antiquity offer little refuge. The few instructions we are given tell us to break the *tracta* disks and put the pieces into the pot, taking care to stir so that it doesn't stick and burn; after it is cooked, salt and oil are added. There are no "untils" here (until dissolved, until thick, until the pieces have softened). But it is not unreasonable to assume that the broken pieces of dried dough would cook up like pasta and *at the same time* render a creamy sauce. Indeed, that is pasta's dual role. In Italian, the tendency of pasta to thicken sauce is a desired effect called *mantecatura.* A corresponding present-day example of pasta made from broken bits is *mille infranti.* Durum wheat macaroni, too, was sold in long tubes, intended to be broken into segments.

The pieces provided the bulk while the little shards would help thicken the sauce or soup. If only there had been an element of cheese in Apicius's *pultes tractogalatae* there would be cause for celebration, but, with no satisfaction on that count, we must press on to the Middle Ages.

MACARONI ON THE RECORD: FIRST DOCUMENTS

As a lead-in to the Middle Ages, let's go back to basics and look at the word *macaroni* itself. When does it first appear? What does it mean? Those are two surprisingly nebulous and slippery questions.

Walther von der Vogelweide and the Court of Frederick II

Numerous secondary sources trumpeting the history of pasta claim that the German *Minnesänger* Walther von der Vogelweide (ca. 1170–ca. 1230), a singer of the troubadour tradition, was the first to record the word *macaroni*. But despite repeated assertions, none cite a primary source to support the claim. A thorough research effort assisted by medievalist experts on von der Vogelweide turned up nothing.

Authors who repeat the claim state one of two things, either that Frederick II (1194–1250) (King of Sicily from 1198 and King of Italy and Holy Roman Emperor from 1220, among other titles) or the Sicilians in general *liked macaroni in a sweet sauce*.[8] Frederick, despite his central role in the powerful Hohenstaufen dynasty of Swabia, was effectively Italian, born in Jesi in the central March region to a Sicilian mother, baptized in Assisi, then, later, adopted by Lotario dei Conte dei Segni—a.k.a. Pope Innocent III.

Royal courts were the main patrons of poets and musicians, and Frederick, who excelled in both, was a generous supporter of the arts. Then, as now, entertainment and food went hand in hand. Purportedly born in what is now Italian South Tyrol, Vogelweide was the greatest singer-songwriter of his age, so it is likely that in some way he came into contact with the culinary habits of Sicilians or Frederick himself, though no record of either exists. Some documentation attests that the two men knew each other, either personally or by reputation. Frederick granted Vogelweide a fief sufficient to sustain him as a wandering minstrel. While the macaroni citation may be just another legend passed off as history, it is, regardless, worthy of note because even as confabulation, it proposes a gustatory bridge between

Cato's sweet *placenta* and the standard preparation of macaroni and cheese at the outset of the Early Modern Period.

Blessed Guglielmo Buccheri

Another macaroni reference directly related to Frederick II comes from the hagiography documenting the beatification of Guglielmo "Cuffitedda," a.k.a. Guglielmo the hermit.[9] Born to the noble Sicilian Buccheri family, he served as a young squire to Frederick. During a hunt, the boy threw himself on a wild boar to keep Frederick from harm's way. The pain from his injuries was such that he was visited by Saint Agatha, after which he decided to live out his life as a mendicant hermit. Hearsay testimony for his beatification states that one of the miracles he performed happened at a meal where the host served "macaroni or lasagne with ravioli." This reference has been greedily plucked from its context and served up as the first mention of macaroni. Let's deconstruct what really happened: While the miracle was *set* in the mid-thirteenth century, the testimony was *collected* in the fifteenth century (hence, not from direct witnesses) for the beatification ceremony that wasn't held until 1537. The testimony itself wasn't published in the *Acta santorum* until 1675. The cogs of the beatification process move slowly. While others have settled for this shaky reference, we shall push on in search of something more substantial.

Chico the Wizard

In 1964, the US Defense Department published a guidebook to Italy. In it, the author recounts one of the astounding facts they learned about pasta at the "Spaghetti Historical Museum" in Pontedassio.[10] From what they understood, "a thirteenth-century Neapolitan wizard, Ciccio the Fat, introduced macaroni. King Frederick II named the dish *maccheroni* from the Greek *magaria*, meaning food eaten at a wake."[11] Perhaps something was lost in translation? Let's take a closer look into this story.

The delight taken in mythologized food origin stories had inspired the six-time Nobel Prize nominee Matilde Serao (1856–1927) to invent a legend about macaroni called "The Wizard's Secret" (1891). Her story is set in 1220, during Frederick II's reign. It seems that in Naples, there was a mysterious wizard called Ciccio, perhaps from the Orient or maybe from Sicily, who kept pretty much to himself. Nosy people peering into his house could only glimpse him through the dirty windows standing over a stove for hours on end. Rumors spread that he was consorting with the forces of evil. In reality, as he was quite old, he was trying to concoct a dish that would immortalize his name. You can see where this is going.

After a time, he invents macaroni and *ragù*. But before he can perfect the dish, his spying neighbor Jovanella, a servant in the royal palace, steals the idea and presents it at court to Frederick. She is showered with accolades and money and becomes famous as the "angel" who invented macaroni. It doesn't end well for Ciccio. When he discovers the deception, it pushes him over the brink, and he disappears forever.

Your suspended disbelief may have faltered at *ragù*. Tomatoes would not arrive in Italy until 1544. But it is true that in the thirteenth century, the Saracens (Muslim Arabs) were active in Naples and had a bazaar in what is now the main square, Piazza Mercato, where they carried on trade with Sicily, the apex of culture at the time. So, the presence of an outcast "from the East" is plausible. However, regarding the invention of macaroni, shipments of *ittriya*, or vermicelli, from Sicily had been documented a full century before, as we shall see in the next section. This fully fictional story, the brainchild of Serao, merely intended to delight, has bizarrely been taken for fact and publicly propagated as historical documentation.

One can only hope that the Defense Department is more diligent about fact checking in matters of national security than it was about macaroni.

Ponzio Bastone and His Notary Ugolino Scarpa

Though it may seem surprising, we move up north for the first verifiable, historical record of the word macaroni in reference to pasta. While it's disheartening to debunk a beloved gastromyth, readers expecting the story of Marco Polo and his return to Venice from China in 1295 will be sorely disappointed. In fact, it is here that we put to rest that die-hard legend.

From Genoa, on the northwestern seaboard, macaroni is documented, not in a recipe or a travelogue, but in a notary's entry from 1279 of the inventory of a deceased military officer's worldly possessions. It seems Ponzio Bastone's next of kin would be heirs to a *barixella una piena macaronis*, a basket full of macaroni.[12] Although macaroni as a term had clearly proliferated from south to north, documented use of the word did not exactly go viral. We will not encounter it again for roughly another fifty years.

Over the course of the High Middle Ages, the Republic of Genoa grew to become the leading maritime mercantile power in the Mediterranean. Theirs was not merely a society of tradesmen stuffing their coffers, as the expression *Genuensis ergo mercator*, or "a Genoese therefore a merchant" would imply, but a formidable war machine on both land and sea. Wheat was the principal freight of the large Genoese sailing vessels. The extent to which control of the trade routes and food corridors carrying this precious cargo have defined power throughout history cannot be overstated. Genoa dominated shipping in the main wheat-producing areas of Sicily, Naples, Rome, Sardinia, and the hotspots along the north African coast. Through the Treaty of Nymphaeum (Greece) in 1261, they finally overcame their Venetian rivals and were able to establish a near monopoly in the Black Sea, the gold mine of the wheat trade. A vast Genoese holding called Gazaria spread over the richest ports in Crimea, Russia, Ukraine, and Romania. However, tensions in the area ran high. The capital, Caffa (Feodosija, Ukraine), was besieged by Mongols in 1343. Their secret weapon, according to a memoir by Gabriele de' Mussi, was biological warfare: Trebuchets hurled dead bodies riddled with the Black Death, a disease that was spreading in the East, over the city walls.[13]

But in 1279, Genoa was in its heyday and would not have lacked for the finest imported wheat and pasta products. As a city without agricultural hinterland, Genoa depended on trading outposts in southern Italy and Eastern Europe to supply its burgeoning population. The geographer Al-Idrisi's frequently cited observation from the mid-twelfth century of pasta exports specifies the town of Trabia, Sicily, as the point of dispatch. Although the Normans held dominion in Sicily at the time, the Genoese had resident mercantile colonies in the coastal area where Trabia is situated. Therefore, it is likely that the pasta Al-Idrisi mentions was from long-established Genoese commercial production.[14] Trade was also firmly established with Messina, Naples, and Salerno. Fourteenth-century documents show that Sardinia, another durum wheat producer, was regularly shipping pasta directly to Genoa.[15] The active northwardly transport of pasta and culinary culture was well established by the time Bastone was stationed in Genoa.

In light of Genoa's position near the end of the thirteenth century, what can we speculate about the late Bastone and his basketful of macaroni?

Social status and the consumption of pasta is a thread that follows the history of macaroni. Contrary to our idea of pasta as common and rustic, it was very much the reserve of the upper classes at this point in time. Bastone was gainfully employed in the military with enough possessions to merit a posthumous inventory; as such, dried macaroni was evidently deemed suited to his position in society. It is worthy of note that his surname indicates that he may have originally come from the southwest coastal region and thus had a cultural affinity for macaroni.

The discussion of macaroni is historically intertwined with vermicelli, as those were the two main forms of pasta that would proliferate throughout Europe. It's important to underscore at this juncture that the word macaroni was used as a blanket term for pasta of any kind, including fresh, handmade pasta of various sorts. It was all macaroni, which allows us to look at the development of the dish macaroni and cheese with a very wide lens. Hollow pasta tubes, resulting from the extrusion process, would in time come to signify durum wheat macaroni as we understand it, but the nomenclature would take centuries to evolve. I will be signposting these changes in meaning along the way. Bastone's "macaroni"—dried and stored in a basket—was, in all likelihood, hollow and made of durum wheat. We can surmise from his legacy and what we know of Genoese mercantile history that tubular, durum wheat pasta was commercially available in the northeast, appreciated by the well-to-do in the late thirteenth century, and referred to as macaroni. Now that we have looked at the first documentation of the word, we are ready to approach the question of etymology and slip down some intriguing rabbit holes.

THE MEANING OF MACARONI

The etymological origins of the word are a stab in the dark at best. In Latin, *maccare* means "to crush" or "batter," which may say something about the difficult process of grinding durum wheat into semolina. A search for Greek origins proposes *makaria*, derived from the goddess Makaria (Μακαρία), meaning "blessed," from which the Greek word for pasta, *zymarika* (ζυμαρικά) is derived. As the Greeks founded what would become the city of Naples in the eighth century BCE, it is tempting (but not advisable) to

(*continued on next page*)

(*continued from previous page*)
rub those sticks together and watch them spark into macaroni. The linguist Mario Pei asserts that "macaroni seems to have existed as far back as the eighth century. . . . A Greek lexicographer records *makaria* . . . as a food made out of dough and sauce."[16] Unfortunately, he gives no references, so it is impossible to verify this otherwise tempting assertion. Some scholars hold that a Greek barley gruel called *makaria*, while not pasta per se, is the origin of the Italian word for macaroni.[17]

For a different perspective on the word, we look to the stock character Maccus, from a form of ancient Campanian theater called Atellan farce. As marketplace entertainment, the sketches consisted of unsophisticated, poke-in-the-eye scenarios and bawdy jokes peppered with puns. Maccus, whose name may originate from the Greek term *makkoan*, meaning "to be stupid," was the most popular by far. In combination with the gluttonous character Buccus, he would develop into the Commedia dell'Arte's Pulcinella, inheriting gangly legs from the former and a potbelly from the latter. This centuries-long tradition infused the word macaroni with its connotation of silly bumpkin or bumbling fool. So, from the property sale document from 1041 listing the name "Nardus de Mari, nicknamed Macaroni," are we to understand that Nardus was a touch inept or that he liked his pasta?[18] Accordingly, the *Tuscan and Neapolitan Domestic Dictionary* defines macaroni as "figurative for a man who is goofy and lacking intellect." John Florio, in his 1611 Italian-English *Queen Anna's New World of Words or Dictionarie of the Italian and English Tongues*, provides this entry: "Maccaróne, a gull, a lubby, a loggerhead that can doe nothing but eat Maccaroni."

The Atellan plays were performed in a combination of Oscan, the now extinct local language, and Latin. Drawing from that, the term *maccheronico* in Italian denotes a literary work executed by commingling Latin and vernacular language, generally with a humorous intent. It is conceptually similar to Latin mimicry called Dog Latin (having nothing to do with Pig Latin). While there are other examples of this style, like the well-known *Carmina Burana*, combining Latin, Occitan, and German, the first publication specifically under the Macaronic banner was *Macaronea* (ca. 1488) by the Paduan poet Tifi degli Odasi. One of the principal poets in the macaronic genre was the monk Teofilo Folengo. He described his poetry as "something like macaroni, a gross, rude, rustic mixture of flour, cheese, and butter." The writing helped round out his meager earnings but, for decorum's sake, he wrote under the pseudonym Merlinus Cocaius—Merlin Cook—which may have equated the messy preparation of macaroni to debased Latin, known in Italy as *Latino di cucina*.[19] Today, in Italian, the term is used colloquially to make fun of one's inability to speak a foreign language well. The allusion to macaroni had been applied after the genre had already gelled. The word clearly conjured a vaudevillian ba-boom that captured the essence of the style.

In order to achieve comic effect and trigger that easy belly laugh, a metaphor requires a butt-of-the joke common denominator that is an immediately recognizable, cultural funny button. Besides the well-worn schtick of the theater tradition, an alternative suggestion for macaroni's satirical propensity might be its association with the piggish priest trope. A trope rarely takes off without some basis in empirical observation. For one early testimony we turn to Fra Salimbene da Parma (1221–1282), who noted in his *Chronicle* that he had never seen anyone wolf down as much lasagna with cheese as the corpulent friar Giovanni da Ravenna. The overstuffed cleric was a potent medieval tickler that still resonated in 1958 when Looney Tunes revived it in *Robin Hood Daffy*, costarring a tonsured Porky Pig as Friar Tuck. In less than seven minutes, it left us with the immortal "Ha ha. It is to laugh" and the battle cry "Yoicks! And awaaaaay!"

Giovanni Boccaccio's *Decameron*

So how was all this macaroni eaten? Before turning to culinary sources, let's make a brief foray into literature, specifically the *Decameron* (ca. 1348–1353) by Giovanni Boccaccio (1313–1375). In juxtaposition to Dante's *Divine Comedy*, the *Decameron* was nicknamed "the human comedy." It was so mired in the foibles of humanity, with no holds barred for clerics, that the fire-and-brimstone preacher Savonarola tossed it on his Bonfire of the Vanities in 1497 as a warning to pious Christians of its scandalous contents. It was included in Pope Paul IV's *Index of Forbidden Books* in 1559, and a good three centuries after its publication, it still roused the ire of the Church.

The *Decameron* tells the story of a group of friends who escape Florence for a few days while the Black Death is raging, Italian merchant ships having brought the pestilence *Yersinia pestis* along with freeloading rats, whose favorite food was wheat.[20] The friends spend their nights telling stories on assigned themes in the realms of morality, fantasy, and philosophy. On the eighth day, three of the guys riff on a story they invented about the Land of Bengodi, a utopian land of plenty. The fantasies they spin are not merely bucolic, pastoral whimsy but idealizations of high times with devil-may-care sexual mores and no need to work. It stands to follow that it's also a glutton's wonderland. In Bengodi, literally "enjoy well," with an erotic accent on "enjoy," perfection is depicted as a mountain of grated Parmesan, upon whose peak blissed-out folks perch with nothing better to do all day, every day, than make macaroni and ravioli. They prepare these delights in the style of the day: boiled in fatty capon broth. When ready, the macaroni and ravioli are rolled down Mount Cheese, picking up a good coating as they descend. To the joy of the eager townspeople, the more they gathered up, the more arrived!

While serious critical analysis of the culinary practices of a place like Bengodi may seem ill advised, there are two noteworthy points, both stemming from the food's rotatory capabilities. Picturing a flat ravioli or a macaroni elbow rolling down a hill might strain the power of one's imagination. By way of explanation, consensus holds that the Bengodi macaroni might actually be gnocchi; we will come across this again in later historical recipes. Furthermore, at this point in time, ravioli were often naked, that is, without the pasta covering. The independent food morsel that would later get tucked into a doughy wrapper was already a ravioli in its own right—even undressed. Thus, if tossed down a slope, and thereby subjected to gravitational force, they would very likely roll.

Beyond the rolling balls of macaroni and naked ravioli, Boccaccio's intention was to articulate a libidinous depiction of untethered food consumption that would elicit an immediate reaction from contemporary readers. And he chose macaroni and cheese as the vehicle to drive that concept home. The delight inherent in the dish was so titillating that it converged with both Lust and Gluttony in the realm of the Seven Deadly Sins, landing the *Decameron* on the pyre.

LIGHT IN THE DARK AGES: THE FIRST MEDIEVAL COOKBOOKS

> Whose gift do you want to become, little book? Be quick and choose a patron before you get whisked away to some filthy kitchen, your wet papyrus used to wrap tuna fish or made into a package for incense or pepper.
>
> —MARTIAL, *EPIGRAMS* 3,2

The cooking legacy handed down from ancient Rome is bleak. Good food and refined entertainment were highly valued, but the people who made that possible were by no means equally esteemed. Slaves who worked as cooks were treated with undue distain. Despite the Romans' notoriety for excess, ostentatious display was under constant fire, even necessitating a series of sumptuary laws to curb extravagance. Early Christianity adopted a similar perspective, condemning cookbooks like the one by Apicius that celebrated the pleasure of the table (i.e., gluttony), on moral grounds. Decorum precepts of the occidental court would likewise discourage interest in food, even more so the vulgarity of its preparation.[21] Thus, the Dark Ages were truly dark for cookbooks.

Historical periods, ages, epochs, and eras are usually assigned their proper names once hindsight has sharpened its focus and those who partook can have nothing to say about it. Yet, the perception of the Middle Ages as dreary centuries of darkness began with Petrarch (1304–1374), who looked woefully back on the cultural blot that spanned from the Fall of Rome to his own time period. The unprecedented advancement of ancient Rome was certainly a tough act to follow, and the control that medieval Christianity exerted over cultural and intellectual freedoms stymied creativity and discovery. In those years, there is a complete absence of cookbooks. From Apicius to the next surviving Italian cookbook, there is a breathtaking eight-hundred-year void. For culinary historians, the difficult task of speculating what might have occurred in food history during the interim is further complicated by a general lack of surviving material culture.

So why did cookbooks disappear for so long?

Culinary skills at the time were acquired through either a practical apprenticeship or the sink-or-swim method. Most aspirants were barely literate, if at all. Judging from later practices, written recipes and menus were sometimes kept with other household records as pro memoria, objects whose usefulness would quickly pass or could easily be lost. Had there been recipe compilations, they might have taken the form of personal notebooks or works by cooks for cooks, that is, inner-circle how-to manuals. Think about it: How many people have conserved the user's manual to their first computer for posterity? Tastes change and cooking methods and knowledge advance, making cookbooks obsolete in short order hence, bin fodder. Paper, such as it was, exposed to myriad grimy and greasy goings-on in the kitchen, would have soiled easily or even caught fire. How many recipes would make it to the next generation, let alone through the next hundred years? And even if they weren't tattered and stained, mightn't the next generation pitch them as stodgy examples of a bygone cuisine?

While there were certainly great chefs and fine cooks, the very concept of conceiving their writings as literature, worthy of the expense of a scribe to produce multiple copies, was a nonstarter. Had there been any cooking manuals in that eight-hundred-year interim, they would, in all likelihood, not have been perceived as having any value to posterity and would have been chucked out as worthless. But, if we return to Petrarch's gloomy perspective, perhaps there weren't any cookbooks in the Dark Ages to save. The fact is, no contemporary sources mention the existence of cookbooks. There seems to have been a collective lack of self-esteem or amour propre, as if the people in the kitchen felt they were producing nothing of lasting value; perhaps they, too, were entangled with the sin of pride.

No originals survive of the first Italian cookbooks that appeared after Apicius, only copies and copies of copies. Among those are three main anonymous texts, which, despite reworkings and cross-borrowings, resemble each other enough to be considered a family of cookbooks. So how did these particular cookbooks manage to escape the fate of the others, whose pages might have come in handy as fish wrapping? The secret is that they were included as insertions in larger texts of more grandiose purpose: theological, philosophical, literary, or medical.[22] Though some of the pairings appear incongruent (prayer and gastronomy?), that lofty textual buffer both shielded them from the garbage bin and lent a touch of prestige.[23] It also meant they enjoyed a modicum of circulation outside of Italy in refined circles of connoisseurs and professional chefs.[24]

Teasing out the evolution of the three texts to determine their order and the time in which they were written has proven both difficult and controversial. The underlying reason may be because one of the books in the family is missing, a conjecture only recently come to light through the painstaking work of the Italian philologist Anna Martellotti. She proposes that there was an original, foundational text, followed by a *liber amissus*—a missing book in Latin, which reworked the original—and a Tuscan translation version of that missing book. The other surviving text is also in Latin, a treatise again based on the original, seemingly tailored for circulation in the sophisticated, multicultural court of Frederick II in a vibrant period sometimes described as the "first Renaissance."

The recipes from what is referred to as the Anonymous family of cookbooks are international in orientation and provide insight into Italian, French, Spanish, Arabic, German, and English cooking practices. Their cosmopolitan nature reflects Frederick II's extensive dominion, his proficiency in several languages, and his own reputation in arts and letters. As an accomplished falconer, he was watchful of his diet, believing that fitness and mental acuity were paramount for mastery, but he reveled in a lively court life and was, even in his own lifetime, hailed as a "second Augustus."

That provided a context in which culinary literature might be cultivated rather than disparaged. But given Frederick's position as Holy Roman Emperor, his appreciation of fine food didn't go unnoticed or unpunished. In keeping with the times, his contemporary, Dante, wrote Frederick into Canto 6 of the *Divine Comedy* with the gluttons, destined to be pelted with stinking, freezing rain for eternity. Hellish indeed.

Exemplary Recipes from the Anonymous Family of Cookbooks

The word macaroni would mean many things to many people at different times and locations throughout history and for centuries would resist a strict definition. For a time, the basic shapes of lasagne, gnocchi, hollowed forms, and, later, tagliatelle, all fell under the macaroni umbrella. This fluid and flexible usage is an advantage that allows us to cast our net wide to accommodate a number of recipes for analysis along the medieval trajectory, as we progress toward the modern concept of macaroni and cheese. It's important to note at the outset that these macaroni recipes were not sifted out from others with different sauces. Regardless of the shape, dressing macaroni with cheese was not *a* way but *the* way to prepare it. While that may sound monotonous, the details of each recipe are uniquely nuanced, and each in its own way illuminates not only the evolution of the dish but invites commentary on the context in which it was devised. As such, the recipes that follow fit together as fundamental tiles in the larger historical mosaic, propelling us on toward the endgame of mac 'n' cheese.

The foundational text of the collection from the reign of Frederick II is called *Anonimo meridionale*, or Anonymous Southerner. Two of its recipes are stepping stones toward our target. The first concerns lasagne:

> *Affare lesagne* (To make lasagne)
>
> For whoever wants to make lasagne, take good white flour and boil it in capon broth. If there isn't enough, add more water, and put salt in to boil with it, and pour it in a tureen, and put on a lot of cheese, and strew thin strips of capon fat on top.

Cooks are busy people. The basics are given. For the rest, one had to be quick on the uptake. Measurements, cooking times, temperatures, and intuitive steps were superfluous, a waste of time and ink. Assumptions were made about what could be taken for granted with contemporary peers in mind. No one had an eye on posterity or marketing. The elusive quality may also have been a way to keep professional secrets within the inner circle of practitioners—much like early jazz players who didn't want to be recorded, fearing others could learn and imitate their style, eroding their mystique.

Here, for example, the preparation of lasagne was clearly a given—the ingredients, the method, and the way it was cut. Otherwise, if taken too literally, we have flour cooked in broth. Most likely, these were wide, medium-length flour and water noodles, like what is now called *lagane* or *sagne* in southern Italy. The specification "good white flour" is a comment on class. Contrary to our immediate assumption that historical food was rough, rustic, and toothsome, long before this, people had acquired the ability to bolt (sift) very fine white flour. But because the process of separating out the finest white flour can be likened to skimming cream from milk, the products made from it were the reserve of the upper crust of society. The aristocratic digestive apparatus was also considered more delicate and sensitive than that of peasants, thus requiring more refined foods.

The second macaroni recipe from the same book takes the gnocchi shape:

> *Affare nochi* (To make gnocchi)
>
> For whoever wants to make gnocchi, take flour and crustless bread, and put in a little water, and take eggs and mix it with that, and cut them and have them boil, and when they are cooked, take them out and sprinkle them with a lot of cheese.

The elements for Boccaccio's macaroni and cheese are already discernible: capon broth as the preferred cooking liquid, mountains of cheese, presumably parmesan as history will attest, and gnocchi, which fall under the "macaroni" umbrella at this juncture, as do the pasta sheets in the previous recipe. The luxury of discarding the bread crusts again points to upper-class sensibilities and the appreciation of soft foods. The crusts would have been recycled as sauce thickener or used to bulk out filling ingredients and not gone to waste, but the inner crumb would render unblemished gnocchi. The addition of egg would add a yellow tinge—white and yellow foods being quite in vogue at the time.

For curiosity's sake, apropos of the ravioli rolling down Mount Cheese in Bengodi, let's look at the recipe *Affare ravioli* (To make ravioli): "If you want to make ravioli, take cheese and remove the salt, and have dried grated cheese, and sprinkle it." This definitely errs on the side of brevity. The idea of removing the salt preservative from cheese can be traced all the way back to Cato's *placenta*. Most recipes throughout the history of macaroni and cheese, do not specify the type of cheese, a fact that is disconcertingly apparent in this recipe. The amount of common knowledge taken for granted between the author and his readers makes it impossible for us at this remove to get a foothold. In this case, a culinary historian would look to later cheese ravioli recipes to deduce through backtracking what these ravioli may have been like.

In fishing around for clues and connections, an interesting recipe for ravioli surfaces from a small Anglo-Norman collection in England, dated to the early reign of Edward I (1272–1307), that demonstrates the culinary interconnectedness of medieval Europe. The Normans had conquered Sicily in the eleventh century, forging an intense Norman-Arab-Byzantine intercultural mix. Following the Norman Conquest of England in 1066, the Anglo-Norman dialect developed and settled in as the language of the English court. Throw into that mix the fact that Frederick II's second wife was the Plantagenet princess Isabella of England (1214–1241). Norman is closely related to French, but the recipes in this collection have no documented French counterparts.[25] In contrast, however, there are several recipes that denote Arab influence, suggesting the anonymous Italian cookbooks written during the reign of Fredrick II as the go-between. Here is one such recipe: "Ravioli. Here is another kind of dish, which is called ravioli. Take fine flour and sugar, and make a dough; take good cheese and butter, and cream them together; then take parsley, sage, and shallots, chop them finely, and put them in the filling, and then put grated cheese on top and under them and put them in the oven."

We cannot with any certainty assume that these were boiled before being put into the oven, which for some disqualifies them as pasta. As filled pasta, ravioli also do not qualify as macaroni per se, but this recipe supports the continued appreciation of sweetened pasta, cheese, and more cheese, and it also introduces the novelty of butter in place of capon fat. Butter will become the most significant element of cross-contamination, or more generously, culinary exchange, between English and Italian foodways. Curiosity about other cultures is an irresistible force of human nature. In this instance, it led to the exportation of Sicilian foodways that someone felt were important enough to preserve on the pages of a manuscript. This act allowed people at great distances to meet, mingle, and come to know each other through the medium of food. A glimmer of light in the Dark Ages.

The second book in the series, *Libro della cocina* or *Anonimo Toscano* (Anonymous Tuscan), offers a recipe called "De le lasagne." It is similar to its predecessor but with more detailed instructions:

> On lasagne
>
> Take good white flour, add tepid water and make a thick dough: then roll it out thinly and let it rest: they have to cook in capon or other fatty meat broth: then put them on a platter with high-fat grated cheese, layer by layer as you like.

This version recognizes that a fat-forward dish is more comforting and luxurious. The type of cheese is again not specified, but the requisite "high fat" indicates the desire for a rich, creamy result. Rather than just heaping it on top, the pasta and cheese are arranged in layers. In preparing this dish, the hot, fatty broth will have thickened slightly from the residual flour on the fresh pasta, and when layered with high-fat cheese, it will melt into a silky gravy.

Here we have the Anonymous Tuscan gnocchi counterpart: "If you want to make gnocchi, take fresh cheese and reduce it to a paste, then take flour and mix it with egg yolk like you would for milliacci and get a pan with water and when it boils, put the mixture on a cutting board and throw them into the pot using a spoon and when they are cooked, put them on the board with a lot of grated cheese.

Rather than being cut into morsels, these gnocchi are made from a dough soft enough to be flicked into the pot. Cheese in the dough and additional cheese on top keep the fat and comfort levels high.

In the last book in the series, entitled Liber de coquina, we once again find the lasagne form but with several new features:

> To make lasagne, take fermented dough [sourdough] and roll out a sheet as thin as you can. Then cut it into squares that are three-fingers wide. Have salted boiling water ready and boil the said lasagne. When they are cooked, take some grated cheese. If you want, you can put together some good, powdered spices and sprinkle this powder on the cutting board. Then put on a layer of lasagne and dust again; on top another layer and dust; continue until the board or dish is full. Then eat them with a wooden stick.

Here we finally get an idea of the dimensions of lasagne. I use the plural "lasagne" instead of "lasagna" to differentiate the pasta shape from the well-known oven-baked dish. These are nowhere near the size of the sheets used to make a tray of baked lasagna; they are relatively small squares. We've lost the fat here from the fatty cooking liquid, but there is a significant development that changes the flavor profile and leads us into the next era: spices. The lack of fat shifts the burden of flavor onto the spices, but their presence was not merely about bumping up the taste. Spices made an important social statement. They were a sensually appealing expression of wealth; as such, they teetered on the razor's edge of ostentatious display and hedonism, risking accusations of Lust, Gluttony, and Pride. Spices slimly escaped condemnation owing to their medicinal qualities and utility in balancing the humors. The final suggestion in the recipe is pure gold: the very early use of a proto-fork, this one assumed to be two-pronged.

The Church exercised a heavy hand in regulating the type and quantity of food that was deemed appropriate or sinful. These permissions and restrictions were at the forefront of everyone's mind as an integral part of daily life. Cooking to satisfy human voracity for both novelty and comfort put a strain on Christian virtues. The danger was that once one had succumbed to Gluttony, Lust was sure to follow. Tertullian (155–220 CE), the early Christian author and the founder of Western theology put it so: "These two are so united and concrete that, had there been any possibility of disjoining them, the pudenda would not have been affixed to the belly. . . .

The region of these members is one and the same." As we move through time, we will see how macaroni and cheese both fit into and pushed against religious constraints.

Taking the "Evil" out of Medieval

Our exposure to the term the "Middle Ages" may have made us oblivious to its inherent snobbery. It was so named by Renaissance humanists from their superior perspective of humanity having come out of hibernation, emerging from some dank corridor in time into the light. Quite the contrary, the Late Middle Ages rivals the most active and vibrant periods in history.

Frederick II's death in 1250 was followed by the Great Interregnum, but its resolution fifty years later was merely a patch-up job. The empire, left without a central figure to bind it, splintered. Even without the loss of Frederick, fourteenth-century Europe did not lack for destabilizing forces: the Hundred Years' War, the Black Death, the Great Famine, the Little Ice Age, and the Western Schism to name a few. Aristocratic families navigated the flow of events and even profited from them by working tragedies to their advantage whenever possible. They strategically intermarried for political and economic gain and profited from power vacuums. Food was part of this momentum—not only because people had to eat but because outdoing each other was a sport in itself. Castle-hopping to maintain alliances meant bringing in tow an entourage of kitchen staff, who in their own milieu would have occasion to rub elbows with their peers in other kitchens. The eventual rivalries between the nobility played out not only on the battlefield but also in the arts. As a result of this new arena of competition, the stilted Byzantine and Gothic styles would get a jolt of life.

The Church was the main patron of the arts, however. The infusion of texture and sensuality representative of the work of the Sienese painter Simone Martini (1284–1344) found fertile ground in France when he moved to Avignon in the late 1330s, then the seat of the Holy See. The richness of his colors and grace of line were a welcome change at a time when Gothic art seemed to have lost its muse. The Black Death and Hundred Years' War put a damper on expansion, but by the late fourteenth century, the genre that would come to be known as International Gothic rippled throughout Europe. It was the beginning of globalization and would usher in the Age of Discovery.

The Church profited from the mounting hysteria that God's wrath was being visited upon the earth. The papacy responded to the spiritual angst by calling a Jubilee year. This sent hordes of bewildered believers of all classes pouring into Rome for a chance to wipe the slate clean, resetting their souls and ridding Christendom of whatever sins were causing this spate of ruination. The first Jubilee year occurred in 1300 and was followed by two more before the end of the century. Thus, even the havoc that had befallen humanity, while calamitous and devastating, inevitably resulted in mobility, migration, and the reorganization of boundaries, economies, and food corridors. As the Latin proverb goes: *Nullum malum quod prorsus omni utilitate careat* There is no evil that is entirely devoid of utility.

Events like these that form the history of humankind cannot but impact food and foodways. Food is essential to our very existence, while foodways articulate cultural identity and create affective bonds within a community. Curiously, though, reams of history have been written as if no one ever ate. By connecting the dots of the *longue durée* of food history, we come to appreciate how much more the cultural geography of food and mobility has shaped human history than borders on political maps. The fate and flourishing of macaroni and cheese remains a constant element in the flow of these events. From this perspective, it becomes more delightful than shocking to find a recipe for macaroni and cheese in an English cookery book from 1390. A brief excursion back in time will reveal how this was possible.

FROM ROME TO ENGLAND ON A PLATTER

Upon receiving his holy orders, Sigeric the Serious, Archbishop of Canterbury (990–994), traveled to Rome to retrieve his pallium, the woolen scarf embroidered with his seal of office. A member of his retinue had the foresight to leave a record of their stay and the itinerary of the return trip to England. Arduous to say the least. All roads may lead to Rome, but they were rife with bandits and perilous terrain, and, although pilgrims aspired to eat little on their spiritual trek, finding sustenance and a safe haven for the night was no small concern. All in all, it took seventy-nine days to get to their destination and eighty to return home. Rome was not the only holy site vying for pilgrims, so, in the absence of maps, information like this ensuring safe passage made the Eternal City a more appealing destination. Rome itself had little to offer by way of hospitality, even to the point of being inhospitable. On the second day, when the archbishop picked up his pallium, he had a luncheon audience with Pope John XV, but there is, sadly, no description of the food. His chronicler must have found it insignificant in comparison to the many Roman churches they visited, about which he wrote in detail.

Itineraries like this increased the traffic to Rome. However, in the first Jubilee year, the Romans were completely unprepared for the onslaught of pilgrims pouring in. Records show that various groups set up their own hostels to host their co-nationals. The next Jubilee took place in 1350, while the plague was still raging—the panic for absolution was understandable, but the consequences of contagion were catastrophic. The last Jubilee of the century was in 1390. It was scheduled ten years earlier than the standard because a ceasefire of the Caroline War phase (1369–1389) of the Hundred Years' War had been declared. Not knowing how long it would last, it was better to get while the getting was good. Somewhere within the Jubilee trajectory, with rivers of pilgrims traipsing in and out, macaroni and cheese made it to England.

The English cookbook where the macaroni and cheese recipe has been immortalized is called *The Forme of Cury* (1390). It may have been a Hundred Years' War tit-for-tat response to the extraordinary success of France's first haute cuisine cookbook *Le viandier*. For all their marvels, mysteries, and intricacies, medieval cookery books were not cutting-edge publications. Rather, they record basic outlines and alternatives for making established dishes. They contain novel preparations of foods in vogue—but already in the mainstream. That is not to say they are strictly how-to manuals. These cookbooks perennially featured aspirational dishes, intended to wow the reader or diners. The *Forme of Cury* is no different. In addition to dishes denoting what would have been "exotic" Arabic influences from the *Liber de coquina*, it includes the butter-rich "Makerouns" or "Makrows," as it is spelled in some manuscript copies.

> *Makrows:*
>
> *Tak and make a thynne foyle of dowh, and kerue it on pecys, and cast hym on boylyng water & seeþ it wel. take chese & grate hit, and butter most cast bynethen & aboue as loseyns; and serue hit forth.*

Macaroni:

Take a thin sheet of dough and cut it into pieces, place in boiling water and cook well. Take cheese and grate it and plenty of butter and put it beneath and above like lasagna sheets; serve immediately.

This takes elements from the anonymous series, in particular the layered effect mentioned in both *Anonymous Tuscan* and *Liber de coquina*, but the use of the anglicized hyperforeignism "makerouns/makrows" for macaroni denotes underpinnings of mobility, of people who had traveled, experienced, brought back, and recreated this excellent dish they felt would be a splendid addition to their own culinary landscape (see fig. 1.1).

To get an idea of the size of the English *loseyns*, we can compare it to another English recipe for *lossenges* called, "To mak loſſenges fried in lent" found in *A Noble boke off cookry ffor a prynce houssolde or eny other estately housshold*e (ca. 1468). It is a rare manuscript containing a compilation of recipes far predating its publication, the title acknowledging that this is cookery book for aristocratic homes. After making a dough of "flour knodden with faire water ſugar ſaffron and ſalt," you will then roll out a "thin foile in loſſengis the bred of your hond or leſe." So, we could say a bit smaller than the palm of your "hond"—interestingly, the same size is described in *Liber de coquina*, giving us cause to assume that this was a standard.

The Forme of Cury also contains a recipe simply called "Losyns." Here, too, there are striking borrowings from the Anonymous Italian family of cookbooks, as well as more explicit attention to detail.

Losyns:

Take good broth and do in an earthen pot. Take flour of payndemayn and make þerof past with water, and make þerof thyme foyle as paper with a roller; dry it hard and seeþ it in broth. Take chese ruayan grated and lay it in dishes with powder douce, and lay þeron loosens is ode as hole as þou myȝt, and above powder and chese; and so twyse or thryse, & serve it forth.

Losyns:

Take good broth and put it in an earthenware pot. Take bread flour and make thereof a dough with water, and make thereof a sheet thin as paper with a rolling pin; dry it until hard and boil it in broth. Take grated autumn

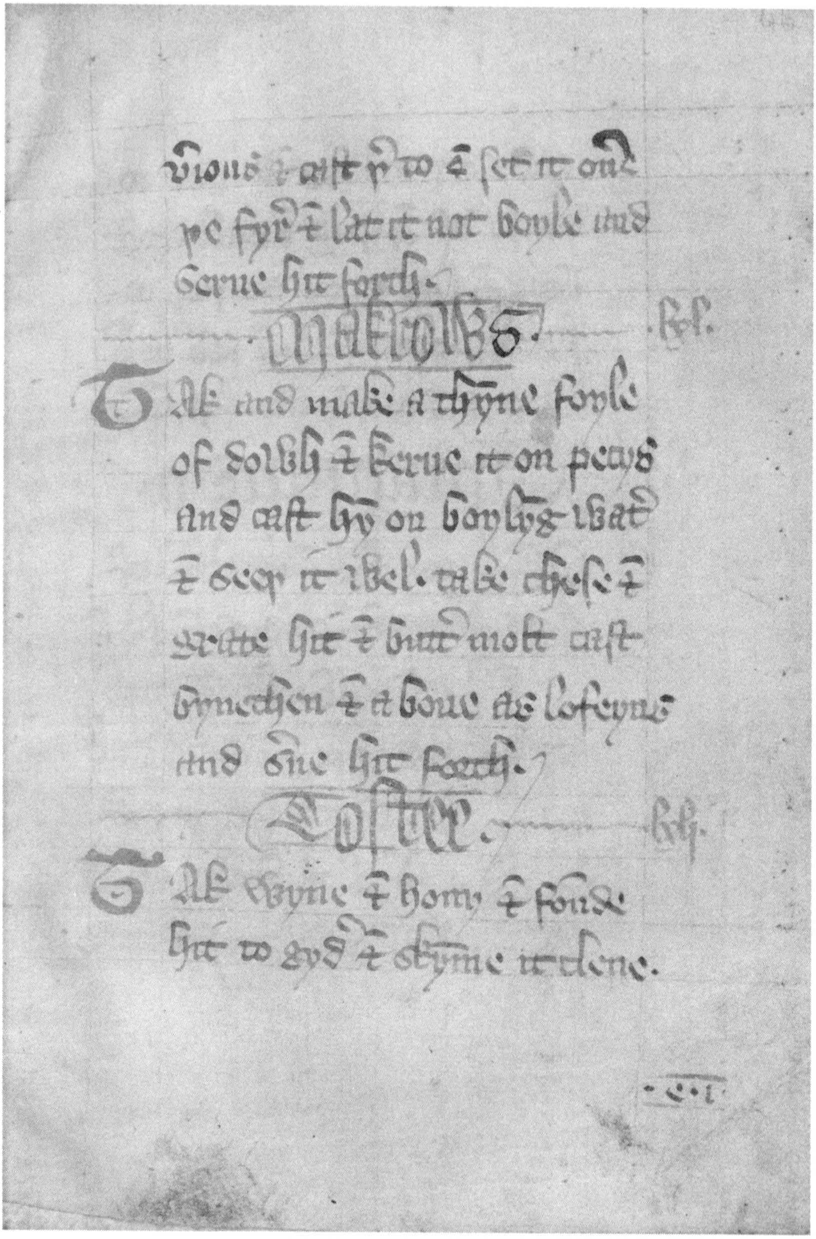

FIGURE 1.1. "Makrowns" from *The Forme of Cury* (1390). *Source*: Figure provided by the John Rylands Research Institute and Library, University of Manchester. Public domain.

cheese and lay it in dishes with sweet spice mix and put the boiled sheets on as whole as you can, and top with spice and cheese; and do so twice or thrice and serve it forth.

Of note is the specification for the type of flour: Bread flour would have been stronger.[26] Specific instructions are also given for the thickness and drying, although the part where swaths are cut from the sheet of dough was overlooked. This recipe repeats the practice of using broth as the cooking medium, thereby forgoing the need for butter. It also picks up on the sweet spice mix pairing for this dish seen in *Liber de coquina*. While parmesan was already a valued import item by this time, the specification for "autumn" cheese indicated something softer and therefore local.[27] Cheshire, too, might have been plausible as a more available and affordable alternative.

Not to venture too far afield from the macaroni category, but it is worth looking at the ravioli recipe from *Forme of Cury* to note continuities and variations in pasta and cheese-based dishes as we build toward our apogee.

Rauioles:

Take wete chese & grynd hit smal, & medle hit wit eyren saffron and a god quantitite of buttur. Make a þin foile of down & close hem þerin as tuteletes, & cast hem in boiling water, & seth hem þerin. Take note butter meltede & chese ygatede, & ley þi ravioles in dissches; & ley þi hote buttur wyt gratede chese binеþe & aboue, & cast þereon powdur douce.

Take fresh cheese and pound it well and mix with saffron and a good quantity of butter. Make a thin sheet of dough and close them therein as tartlettes and put them in boiling water and boil them therein. Take some melted butter and grated cheese and lay the raviolis in dishes; and dress them with hot butter and grated cheese underneath and on top and sprinkle with sweet spices.

Contrary to the Anglo-Norman ravioli, these are clearly meant to be boiled. Butter and cheese are protagonists, while the saffron, spices (among which sugar is included), and the expertise required indicate that this is a luxurious, highbrow dish. The English maintain butter as a near constant in their pasta adaptations, an expression from their own culinary grammar that did not originate from the Italian texts. But what goes around comes around. The Italians will adopt the English style in due time and take it to new heights.

While the recipes here represent elite dining, the reality of food consumption did not exist in a two-tiered system of rich and poor. Those producing, preparing, and serving the food were not of a single class description; if they did not work in the household itself as part of the kitchen staff, they operated directly outside, for example, as millers or cheese mongers, or in the adjacent countryside, toiling in the fields, which had its own hierarchy. Imported foods also required middlemen and curriers, more rungs on the social ladder. What ended up on the urban, upper-class plate was conceived and executed by skilled practitioners who, throughout history, were not invited to the table they served. And, finally, what was leftover systematically trickled down, recycled back into the community from whence it came. From harvest to crafting to serving and finally eating, food was the interdependent tie that bound communities together. Within that scheme, the taste of privilege could not have been unknown outside of the intimate circle of the elite table. We will examine how this cycle unfolds as the journey continues.

Chapter Two

MACARONI ON PAPAL PLATES

Come er cacio sui maccheroni. [Like cheese on macaroni. i.e. Perfection.]

—ROMAN EXPRESSION

THE ETERNAL CITY OF MACARONI

Rome Interrupted

By the Late Middle Ages, macaroni and cheese had already broken free of the confines of its country of origin. While it is true that England had come into full possession of the dish, it would be reasserted as unequivocally Italian in due time, but to do so, the Holy See had to get back to Rome. Back from where? France and the Avignon Papacy.

Four years after his election to the papal throne, Clement V (1264–1314) audaciously moved the papacy to Avignon, puppeteered by his childhood companion, the fetching Philip the Fair or, more formally, King Philip IV of France. Italian pride was bruised, but turbulent years turned into decades until the Dominican activist and mystic visionary Catherine of Siena (1347–1380) convinced Pope Gregory XI (1329–1378) that the only way to restore peace among the warring factions on the Italian peninsula was with the strong presence of papal rule in Rome. "Much of papal history in the fourteenth [century] can be understood as a series of desperate efforts by the popes to find security in a very dangerous environment. An article of faith among these princes of the church was the belief that the papacy's independence required a territorial base in central Italy."[1] Seven popes and sixty-seven years later, Gregory ended the Avignon papacy and brought the Curia back to Rome. It was a tight political squeeze, as he had expansionist ambitions of his own.

Shortly after Gregory arrived in Rome, however, he was ready to return to Avignon. But that was not to be. At forty-nine years of age, Gregory died before arrangements for the move could be set in motion. So, it was out of the Avignon papacy and into the Western Schism (1378–1417), fostering a mayhem of anti-popes and their partisan allegiances. When the crisis came to a head, there were three sitting popes. The Church was about to implode. Following formal deliberation in Germany, two abdicated in support of the elected incumbent Martin V (1369–1431), but the French papacy refused to acquiesce, preferring to fizzle out slowly rather than bow out gracefully. *Habemus papam.*

Oddo Colonna, a.k.a. Martin V, was born into one of the oldest, wealthiest, and most powerful families in Rome. He was not chosen by chance. The Eternal City that Martin inherited was in shambles. The population had dwindled to about seventeen thousand, an anarchic ghost town compared to its glory days. Small wonder the popes had been reluctant to leave the opulence and order of Avignon.

Martin waited two years before taking up residence in Rome. But once he did, he went against his own ascetic inclinations and started pouring money, much of it his own, into laying the foundation for the Roman Renaissance. It set off a chain reaction of one-upmanship among the cardinals of investing, constructing, and patronizing the arts. The restoration of refinement and civility signaled that Rome was once again open for business, and the hordes came pouring in. Rome reestablished itself as a cosmopolitan city, attracting all professions of people from all over Europe. Germans represented the largest group of foreign-born residents.

Early Days: German Macaroni for Romans

Despite Martin's unhurried return to Rome, he had set about hiring his staff immediately after receiving the papal appointment. Records show that on November 20, 1417, the clergyman Johannes de Bockenheim was taken on as the *cocum communis palaccii apostolici et juravit*, that is, he was sworn in as the common cook (read: executive chef) of the apostolic kitchen.[2] He was but one of a preponderance of Germans in the new Curia. His duty was overseeing the food service for the various residents and visitors to the papal court, the *coquina communis*, as opposed to the *coquina oris*, the food destined for the pope's mouth. To put a fine point on it, Bockenheim did not cook for the pope's table in any capacity. He remained in Martin's employ until the pope's death in 1431. Then, as was customary, the incoming pope installed a new kitchen entourage of his choosing, and Bockenheim was dismissed. He retired having secured a tidy nest egg over the years through his ecclesiastical ties.

Around the time of his retirement, Bockenheim wrote a cookbook, a curious little manual that proved to be much more than a window into medieval cookery. It is a socioculinary manifesto. His *Registrum coquine* is a slim volume in Latin (sort of) of about seventy-five recipes written most likely with the intention of passing on the benefit of his experience.[3] The recipes themselves are mere sketches, meant for contemporaries who knew their way around the kitchen. Accustomed as he was to a cosmopolitan environment, Bockenheim knew that writing in Europe's lingua franca would assure accessibility to a wide range of readers. As a cleric, he knew that Latin would elevate the value of the work, though his was, shall we say, macaronic. But what makes the collection singularly invaluable is that most of the recipes are followed by a brief dictum stating what category of person that particular dish would be suited to, thereby leaving posterity with an incomparable cultural perspective of the milieu he operated in. Some of his prescriptions delineated classes, from the aristocratic hierarchy to rustics, or occupations from clerics to courtesans. Most often, however, the recommendations specified nationality, a good number of them, perhaps not surprisingly, labeled "right for Germans." Accordingly, he considered the following macaroni recipe to be right for Romans:

> Cheese soup:
>
> Take breadcrumbs and put them in a dish, and put aged, grated cheese on top, with sweet spices: and then put on another layer of bread, and another of cheese and spices, until the dish is full; and then take fatty broth, and put it on top; and then put on another layer of bread and cheese with spices as before. And this is what the Romans call macaroni.[4]

At first glance, one might wonder how often Bockenheim actually mingled with the Romans.[5] But if we look closer, the elements of this critical mass align with what had become something of a medieval modus operandi: a layered wheat-based carb graced with a gentle spice mix, pungent cheese, and a flavorful fatty broth. Though he has egregiously overlooked the low-hanging fruit—macaroni—one could bridge his breadcrumb layers with the breadcrumbs in traditional gnocchi without undue strain on the imagination. Strewing them out in layers mimics the technique seen in previous recipes. Bockenheim has clearly heard about Roman macaroni; he just underestimated the importance of the main ingredient. Though it may be lacking in salivation factor, his "Cheese soup" does raise the question: So, what *was* Roman macaroni?[6]

Macaroni in Rome and Roman Macaroni

The dish called "Roman macaroni" rides the wave of the Roman Renaissance and introduces a novelty to the macaroni family: cut noodles, or tagliatelle. These *fettucce*, or ribbon pasta, will completely upstage the lasagne shape, which fades silently into the background. The new player first appears in the cookbook collection ascribed to Martino da Como, a.k.a. Maestro Martino, from the mid-fifteenth century. Like the Anonymous cookbooks, this collection involves copies, versions, and reworkings. To simplify, I will refer to Martino as the representative author and *De arte coquinaria* (On the Art of Cooking) as the text.[7]

At any given point during the Middle Ages, formally written recipes documented fashionable dishes that had enjoyed a modicum of success and were worth making again. The impetus for committing a known recipe to paper was principally twofold: instruction for initiates and exemplary best practices from an authoritative voice. Naturally, cookbooks would include signature and innovative dishes alongside the perennial tried and true, but as history would reveal, "Roman macaroni" was not just canonical; it was a sort of proving ground where chefs showed off their culinary prowess. Martino is the first to document the recipe in 1465. His instructions show signs of advancement in the genre, though measurements are not given. The recipe has clear continuity with the past, maintaining the fatty broth, unspecified cheese, and the spice mix, but significantly provides an alternative for the many meatless days on the Christian dietary calendar, discussed in detail later in the chapter.

ROMAN MACARONI: *PER FARE MACARONI ROMANESCHI*, HISTORICAL VERSION

Take good flour, add water and roll it out thicker than you would for lasagne and wrap it around a rolling pin [*bastone*] and pull out the pin and cut the dough as wide as your little finger so that it is like ribbons or strings and put it to cook in fatty broth or water depending on the times and be sure the broth or water is boiling when you put them in. And if you cook them in water, put some fresh butter in and a little salt and when they are done plate them with good cheese and butter and sweet spices.

REMAPPED VERSION

Hearty chicken broth:
1 1/4 pounds (500 g) chicken wings and/ or backs (scrappy bits with skin, bones, and cartilage)
1 Tbsp butter
1 carrot
1 onion, peeled and halved
1 stalk celery
1 bunch parsley
1 1/2 tsp salt
6 1/3 cups (1.5 L) water
[dough]
3 1/4 cups (400 g) type 0 or all-purpose flour
3/4 cup (150 mL) warm water (more or less to make a stiff workable dough)
2 Tbsp butter
1 tsp spice mix (see below)
3 1/2 oz (100 g) parmesan cheese, grated

[Broth] Brown the chicken pieces in butter in a large pot. Add the carrot, onion, celery, parsley, salt, and water. Bring to a boil and cover. Simmer on low for 1 hour. Do not skim off the fat.

[Macaroni] Mound the flour on the counter and make a well in the center. Add half of the water and work it into the flour with pinching motions. Keep adding water until you have a stiff but workable dough. Use a little more water, if needed. Knead the dough vigorously by hand for 5 minutes. Cover with a bowl and leave for an hour.

(*continued on next page*)

(*continued from previous page*)

On a floured surface, roll out the dough into a circle that is 2 mm (1/8 in.) thick. This is best done with a long rolling pin called a *matterello*. Generously flour the surface of the dough and loosely roll the dough over the rolling pin. Remove the rolling pin. Cut ribbons the width of your pinky finger. Shake them out. Dust with flour if they seem sticky.

Bring 4 cups (1 L) of the broth to a boil in a large pot. Add the pasta and reduce heat to a low boil. There should be enough broth to cover the pasta. If the liquid gets too low while cooking, add more. The flour will create gravy. When cooked to taste, remove from heat; add the butter and spice mix. Add the cheese and mix well. The cheese will thicken the sauce further. If it is too dry, the cheese will clump. Plate and serve with more cheese on top.

Spice mix (there will be some left over for other occasions)

2 tsp ground cinnamon
1/2 tsp ground cloves
1/2 tsp ground ginger
1/2 tsp ground nutmeg
1 tsp ground grains of paradise (or 1/2 tsp aromatic pepper and the ground seeds of one cardamom pod)
1/2 tsp ground saffron
1 tsp sugar [also considered a spice at this time]

For best results, make from whole spices ground in a coffee grinder.

This dish was lavish enough to grace the table of the high clergy or shall we say, it graced the table of the high clergy despite its lavishness? What we can safely speculate about Martino is that he was originally from the Como area and that he acquired his skills in the kitchens of the far north. There are indications that he spent time in the court of Naples, adding a southern dimension to his experience. It was undoubtedly by reputation that he was taken on as chef to one of the Church's most powerful cardinals, Ludovico Trevisan (1401–1465), an unabashed epicure, renowned for sumptuous banquets held at his Roman residence. Oblivious to the looming specter of sin, these princes of the Church avidly indulged their appetites. "The cardinals' hedonistic dispositions often blurred the line between their own lives and the kind of life they recommended for good Christians."[8] Grandiloquence at the table was willfully brazen. It was a lifestyle intended to punctuate class and rank, delineating the haves and have nots, and macaroni and cheese was on their menu.

A signpost recipe in the evolution of tubular macaroni from *On the Art of Cooking* is Martino's "To make beautiful Sicilian macaroni," a handmade, hollow pasta meant to be dried for storage. We know that macaroni had long been part of the Sicilian heritage, but it is here that we have explicit instructions on how to make and serve it. The recipe calls for the very best refined white flour to be mixed with egg white and rose water, the culinary cologne of the age.[9] While Roman-style macaroni is akin to fettuccine, Sicilian macaroni starts with dough cut into "sticks" (strips) as "thin as straw" that are then positioned under an iron rod and rolled with both hands so as to wrap around the rod. Remove the rod and you have a hollow piece of macaroni. The effort expended to craft half a mouthful of food may seem an unbalanced output of labor to product, but the meticulous attention to shaping that intrigues the eye and follows through with a satisfying mouthfeel make macaroni a delight. As such, Martino's instructions are more than just an aide-memoire; they lean toward purposeful elucidation of how to achieve artisan-quality macaroni.

He follows up with instructions to dry this pasta—under the sun in August when the moon is waxing—drawing on biodynamic agricultural folk practices. That way, he assures us, it will last two or three years. To withstand storage, this macaroni, which was not a durum wheat product, would presumably have been rather sturdy and thick. This might explain the stupefying cooking time of two hours. Like its Roman counterpart, Sicilian macaroni is cooked in fatty broth or buttered water—in accordance with the dictates of the Christian dietary calendar—and served with copious amounts of cheese and a finishing sprinkle of sweet spice mix.

Macaroni's Latin Moves

The significance of Martino's work might have gone the way of splatter-stained notebooks had it not been for the man who plagiarized nearly his entire opus; this was when plagiarism, a common practice, was a form of admiration. The quality of Martino's writing indicates that he had a modicum of education and may have trained as a cleric, but his manuscript was in vernacular Italian, or *volgare*, and was intended for circulation among other culinary practitioners. His admirer, on the other hand, transplanted *On the Art of Cooking*, almost verbatim, into a self-help lifestyle manual for *illuminati* (read: progressives) written in Latin.

It was one thing for Martino to write a cookery manual for his ilk and quite another for a well-educated humanist of modest standing in the court to commit words to paper celebrating the enjoyment of food. Such an act required strategic jockeying around moral systems and foes. While few limits were placed on the sensual satisfaction derived from admiring a work of art or yielding to the joy of music, taste (and its companions smell and touch) was a base, visceral sense bound to animalistic hunger, thus needing to be tamed.[10] Conservative detractors eagerly awaited the opportunity to squash radical upstarts—particularly epicureans. That is the fray that Bartolomeo Sacchi (1421–1481), referred to hereafter by his nickname, Platina, threw himself into when he wrote *On Right Pleasure and Good Health* (ca. 1472), covering gastronomy, nutrition, sleep, exercise, and human relationships. Platina was an abbreviator, a privileged secretarial post in the papacy. Despite his advantageous position, Platina's subversive literary activities and humanist views had already landed him in prison more than once, and a book about self-care and good food might have secured the final nail in the coffin. He tested the waters early on looking for support in a sheepish letter to Cardinal Piccolomini, referring to his "little book" about a "greasy and sordid subject," "dry," "unpolished," and "full of imperfections," etc. . . . Piccolomini was unmoved by his prostrations, so it was back to square one. Finding a powerful patron to dedicate a book to was not only an honorary gesture; it was a kind of insurance policy. And given Platina's audacious topic, it was essential.

Platina's search found purchase with Cardinal Roverella. The cardinal must have appreciated how attention to one's physical well-being might also benefit the soul and not, therefore, constitute an unholy alliance. *On Right Pleasure* (initially printed anonymously) was dedicated to Roverella and thus paved the way for its general acceptance among high-ranking ecclesiastics, give or take a few malcontents. But because it was written by a man of letters, in Latin, and perceived as both ecumenical and practical, it would reach into homes, minds, and libraries that Martino's cookbook would never have touched . . . and with it his recipes for macaroni. *On Right Pleasure* was the first cookbook ever printed with that vulgar contraption called the printing press, which exponentially changed the availability and affordability of books.[11] From Platina's exquisite Latin, eighteen editions were published between 1470 and 1541, in addition to over twenty translated editions over the next one hundred years in various vernacular languages, including Italian and German, but mostly French. The word on macaroni had broken new ground. In 1516, an unauthorized reworking of Martino's opus appeared under the name Giovanni de Rosselli—likely a fictional invention. Among its contents was the recipe for hollow Sicilian macaroni, which would cross linguistic and cultural borders once more when the book was translated into English in 1598. Through the circulation of *Epulario, or The Italian Banquet*, the dish entered the English culinary imagination during a wave of fervent Italophilia.

The Renaissance Master Chefs

CRISTOFORO DI MESSISBUGO

When Roman macaroni surfaces again, it is in full Renaissance regalia and has traveled quite a distance from Rome, showing that Roman macaroni was not only a local phenomenon. Cristoforo di Messisbugo (d. 1548) was not a chef but a steward, overseer of everything having to do with food—from the kitchen staff to the dining linens. He worked for the D'Este household in Ferrara and often had dealings with the Gonzaga court in Mantova, both in the northeast. Having received favor from Charles V, Holy Roman Emperor (1500–1558), he ascended into the ranks of the nobility and took a wife suited to his acquired station. Whether or not his version of Roman macaroni is a reflection of his gentility is debatable, but he does take the dish to sublime heights.

The dough combines flour, eggs, the inner crumb of a soft white bread roll that has been soaked in rose water, and just a touch of sugar.[12] His *sfoglia* is rolled out thickly and cut into finger-width strips. The mouth-watering anticipation of gorgeously plump, wide noodles deflates when he says they should look like a mass of intestines. They are tossed into a hearty, fatty broth and finished with what had (or would) become the gold standard: cheese, sugar, and cinnamon. If it is not a "meat day," the pasta can be boiled in water or milk, and in any case with butter and salt.

Another macaroni dish Messisbugo proposes for a fasting day is "How to make 10 plates of macaroni." Here macaroni was essentially gnocchi, which would continue to fall under the macaroni umbrella for at least another 150 years. These, too, were made with white bread rolls and flour mixed with egg to render a soft yet sturdy dough. Chestnut-sized balls were rolled one by one against the back of a cheese grater to imprint a decorative pattern on one side and leave a hollow indentation on the other that would cup the sauce. Boiled in water, they were finished with a generous slathering of butter and the triumvirate of cheese, sugar, and cinnamon.

Serving up satisfying dishes that met the requisites for religiously dictated meatless days was a fundamental part of the chef's responsibilities, though sumptuousness was formally frowned upon. These sanctioned recipes and ingredient substitutions were duly earmarked in cookbooks into the early twentieth century. The fact that macaroni and cheese fulfilled the criteria of being both delicious and meatless not only kept it on the menu but encouraged its proliferation. Here are some insights into the details of fasting in the Roman Catholic tradition.

MACARONI AND CHEESE AND MORTIFICATION OF THE FLESH

> It is sometimes necessary to check the delight of the flesh in respect to licit pleasures in order to keep it from yielding to illicit joys.
>
> —AUGUSTINE OF HIPPO (354–430), *THE USEFULNESS OF FASTING*

Discipline of the flesh through modifications in the diet operated on three basic levels: not eating, delayed eating, and selective eating. The pangs and cravings that surfaced were an occasion to take stock and align the spirit with the ultimate suffering of Christ in the hope of redemption. But people, being naturally averse to discomfort and restriction, would seek out ways to comply while attenuating the anguish. On that count, macaroni with cheese met with the formal requirements while gratifying the palate's longing for savor.

Year-round fasting was observed on Friday, with Wednesdays and/or Saturdays included in some jurisdictions. While some groups such as monastics were subject to stricter fasting rules throughout the year, the population as a whole was expected to adhere to the principles of moderation and avoidance to degrees according to the season. Advent, the period prior to Christmas, was strikingly austere compared to present custom, but the major fast for all was Lent, a forty-day period first decreed in 325 at the Council of Nicea. At its peak, a third of the calendar year was punctuated with days of dietary observance.

Abstaining from meat is conceptually straightforward, but why was meat singled out as the taboo food? Before the ascendancy of Christianity in the Roman Empire, meat was strongly associated with the rituals of traditional Greek and Roman sacrifice. Early Jewish and Christian texts reveal that there was a certain ambivalence about meat consumption, given its association with idolatry. Fish was exempt from these concerns because it was not among the products offered in pagan temples. The choice to forgo meat was later repackaged by St. Thomas Aquinas (1225–1274) as an act of contrition mirroring the Lord's sacrifice of his flesh.

For monks, the early years of Lenten fasting prescribed a single meal after 3 P.M.—the ninth hour of the Divine Office (Officium divinum) called "nones"—consisting of bread, vegetables, and watery beer or wine. Around the ninth century, they complained that the stringent regimen left them too weak to fulfill their daily duties. The break from fasting had already been moved from vespers (6 P.M.) to nones, but, to appease the hangry ascetics, it was changed to midday. It is from this shift that we get the English word "noon" for 12 P.M.

The Roman Catholic Church's position on dairy was less clear cut. Dairy foods were not associated with the "cuisine of sacrifice," but, as highly prized animal derivatives, they were suspect. In defense of dairy, one might point to the martyr narrative of St. Perpetua (ca. 200) in which God appears as a good shepherd offering milk to his chosen ones. Seventh-century records exist of monks taking milk during Lent. By the thirteenth century, dairy was a hot topic that St. Thomas felt he must put to rest in the *Summa theologiae*. Foods that are the most pleasing to the palate are prone to stir lust. As animal foods, including dairy and eggs, are closer to the likeness of humankind than fish and vegetables, he concluded that unchecked indulgence would result in a buildup of "seminal matter" and weaken one's will to resist the baser appetites.

(*continued on next page*)

(*continued from previous page*)

In the northern countries, no meat, no cheese, and no butter left people with empty larders. Butter deprivation hit particularly hard. A plea advanced by the Saxon prince-elector Ernst (1441–1486) to Pope Nicholas V for permission to use butter to make their traditional stollen was denied. Five popes later, in 1490, permission was finally granted in the infamous *Butterbrief*, but it only applied to the prince's household. Martin Luther (1483–1546), a man who liked his food, railed against the measure: "Eating butter, they say, is a greater sin than to lie, blaspheme, or indulge in impurity." It was easy for the Romans to dispense with butter as they had olive oil. The Germans, on the other hand, were forced to sustain themselves on imported oil that the Romans "would not use to grease their shoes." Not coincidentally, the countries reliant on butter as their main source of fat would break with the Catholic Church in the sixteenth-century Protestant Reformation.

Though fast-day regulations varied in degrees, through the Renaissance, Lent meant strict fasting—one meal per day of bread, vegetables, and wine or beer (plus a morning and/or evening snack as needed). Good Friday was a "Black Fast"—no food was allowed from the evening of Maundy Thursday to Holy Saturday. As for the other fasting days, St. Thomas says, "The custom varies among different people, and each person is bound to conform to that custom which is upheld by those among whom he is dwelling. Hence Jerome says 'Let each province keep to its own practice, and look upon the commands of the elders as though they were the laws of the apostles.' "

Thus, it is not a contradiction to find Martino and Messisbugo's macaroni boiled in milk with butter and doused with cheese for a fasting day, whereas recipes like "Almond junket," a fake cheese made with almonds, were for Lent. For the desperate with disposable income, dairy indulgences could be purchased as part of the systemic merchandising of grace.

It was perhaps not so much the empty stomach that tormented the faithful as the perception of privation. Macaroni dishes, unctuous with butter and thick with cheese, were a godsend that satiated body and soul without technically breaking the rules—so long as expressions of enjoyment were suppressed. A fifteenth-century German Benedictine manuscript shows that the even monks purposefully set aside costly, delectable foodstuffs to consume during the Lenten period.

The power of macaroni and cheese to circumvent culturally imposed regulations on appetitive impulses is illustrated in a short story in *Porretane* by the humanist writer Giovanni Sabadino degli Arienti (1445–ca. 1510). The vignette is set in post-pestilent Bologna in 1388 and draws upon the ever-popular "gluttonous priest" trope to elicit Three Stooges–type laughs. The scourge that had ripped through the area left only three survivors at the abbey of Saint Proculo. One Friday, "a day of passion" (i.e., suffering), the cook (coincidentally German?) set out a big pot of lasagne noodles with cheese in the refectory.[13] The tempting aroma immediately short-circuited Abbot Dionisio's forbearance. Taking advantage of a moment alone, he grabbed a handful of the steaming, cheesy pasta and quickly stuffed it in his mouth. As Father Domizio and Father Martino enter, the abbot starts to sputter. Tears stream down his face as he surreptitiously tries to choke back the scalding food. Domizio instinctively throws a glass of white wine on him to quell the crisis.

The abbot, drenched in wine, swallows and explains that he had been momentarily overcome with emotions, thinking about the bygone days before the plague had decimated their brotherhood when all had enjoyed a hearty dish of macaroni and cheese together. Involuntarily commiserating, Domizio, too, reaches for a handful of the hot pasta. In so doing, he suddenly realizes why the abbot was teary-eyed. Martino follows suit, spoon (interestingly) in hand, to see what's going on. Wide-eyed, he spits the food out and throws the contents of the pot in the abbot's face, who now has more lunch on him than in him.

The cultural taboo of nipping a bit before sitting down to a meal may be lost on moderns, whose etiquette is more relaxed. In the monastic setting, the brothers would have sat together and said a solemn prayer before silently taking in the allotted sustenance. Voracity, particularly on a fasting day, would have been reprimanded with penance. Such is the potency of macaroni and cheese. The abbot ordered up another pot.

DOMENICO ROMOLI

Despite the unflattering nickname "Greasy Bread," Domenico Romoli (no dates available) was a Florentine of notable culture and learning. Like Messisbugo, he was a household steward. He had worked in the service of several aristocratic families as well as for Pope Leo X (1475–1521), son of Lorenzo de' Medici. This was a golden age in Rome, and the pope entertained in grand style, flanked by his *amiche* Beatrice Ferrarese and Lucrezia da Clarice. Epic quantities of food were served in interminable courses. The primary purpose was to dazzle; eating was the happy consequence. The leftovers were later distributed in a trickledown system to the eagerly awaiting populace. Such arrangements helped temper rebellious sentiments at a time when agitators such as Luther were stirring up trouble.

It may very well be that Romoli's signature version of Roman macaroni, "*Maccheroni alla Romana*," inscribed in his book on stewarding, *La Singolare Dottrina* (1560), had graced the papal table. His was a no-frills, weakly bound dough, made with just flour and milk—either goat or cow's. No fussy soft rolls, eggs, or rose water. He uses the word *tagliolini* in the cutting instructions but specifies that they should be wider—so, in effect, fettuccine. They are boiled in salted water, not broth, drained, and then mixed with cinnamon-coated grated cheese "more hard than fresh" and however much sugar suits your fancy. It's a dry, clumpy dish. Not exactly the height of elegance. But as the chef Bartolomeo Scappi adroitly points out, a head chef worth his salt should be able to slip into the role of steward, but being a steward does not mean you can cook.

Bartolomeo Scappi

Elements of his predecessors' Roman macaroni were recycled into the sublime interpretation by Bartolomeo Scappi (1500–1577), private chef to both Pius IV and V. By this time, the Golden Age had been eroded by the aftershock of the sack of Rome and the relentless disruption of the Protestant Reformation. Grounded in the austerity of the Catholic Counter-Reformation, neither of Scappi's employers took much interest in food. Pius IV (1499–1565) was a fierce supporter of the Inquisition and established the Roman *Index of Forbidden Books*. The printing press had opened the floodgates to the proliferation of uncensored information, and staunching the flow with an *Index* was a fool's errand. Pius V (1504–1572) was a strident traditionalist and infamously grim (he had made discharging the papal court jester a top priority upon ascending the throne). Few mourned his passing after his brief six-year reign, as the draconian shadow he cast over Rome had made him immensely unpopular. He was sickly and fanatical about fasting and penance, which must have been a great professional disappointment for a chef with Scappi's virtuosity.

FIGURE 2.1. "Working the dough" detail from *Opera* (1570), by Bartolomeo Scappi. *Source*: Public domain.

To the pope's credit, though, he financed the publication of Scappi's magnum opus called *Opera*—or Work (1570).

Opera is divided into six sections. Scappi's four unfilled pasta dishes are in the second section, called "Meat Day Dishes," as they contain eggs and cheese and are boiled in meat broth. The Church had, by this time, been forced to soften their stance on butter. The Lenten section has one macaroni dish, which is worth examining by way of comparison. It is called "Several ways to make & cook macaroni for Lenten days." The dough is a humble mixture, half flour, half breadcrumbs, moistened with boiling water and olive oil, rendered more colorful (and expensive) with saffron. It takes a good fifteen minutes of kneading to work it into a dough suited to making "Gnocchi, that is, macaroni." Here again, the nuggets are rolled over the back of a cheese grater. The classic Lenten condiment to replace the cheese and butter is an *agliata* sauce. It is made with cloves of garlic, walnuts, pepper, and breadcrumbs pounded in a mortar and moistened with hot water then finished with a dusting of cinnamon. Sugar was allowed though not encouraged. Should you prefer, a stiffer version of the dough can be rolled into sheets to fashion rectangular strips of macaroni. As an alternative dressing he proposes another Lenten standard, the *salsa verde*, made of parsley, spinach shoots, sorrel, burnet, arugula, mint, pepper vinegar, and breadcrumbs. This is his signature take on a sauce that had been around since at least the Middle Ages.

The first of Scappi's four pasta recipes in the "Meat" section he calls "tagliatelle," even though the noodles are nearly identical to Martino's Roman macaroni. Scappi reserves that honorific title for his own magnificent "*Maccaroni alla Romanesca*." Though one can only speculate, Scappi may have knowingly built upon his predecessors, leveraging crustless white bread, eggs, sugar, and rose water from Messisbugo, and goat's milk from Romoli. He experiments with cheese, adding both a soft, unctuous buffalo-milk cheese called *provatura*, local to Rome, and a hard cheese for pungency, presumably parmesan. Broth is the standard cooking liquid, but he says you can use water so long as there is a big pot of it and it is well salted. His Roman macaroni is layered, following the centuries-long practice. The two cheeses, sugar, cinnamon, and knobs of butter are laid out between strata of cooked tagliatelle. The final touch of sophistication is a generous splash of rose water. Then, harkening back to Cato, the dish is baked until golden, achieving similar flavor accents that arise from baking. Here's the recipe for the modern kitchen.

MACCARONI ALLA ROMANESCA: ROMAN MACARONI

Serves 6

4 1/4 oz (120 g) crustless Italian bread from a loaf 2–3 days old, cut into chunks

1 2/3 cups (400 mL) goat's milk

1/4 cup (50 g) sugar

3 1/4 cups (360g) type 0 flour (or all-purpose)

4 large egg yolks

7 Tbsp (100 g) salted butter

1/4 cup (50 g) sugar

1 tsp cinnamon

1/2 cup (50 g) grated parmesan

12 1/2 oz (350 g) *mozzarella di bufala* (buffalo-milk mozzarella), sliced thin

4 Tbsp (60 mL) rosewater

Soak the bread in a cup (250 mL) of goat's milk for half an hour. Mix the sugar with the flour and mound on the counter, making a well in the center. Squeeze the milk out of the bread so that it is moist but not dripping. In total it should weigh about 8 oz (225 g). Crumble the bread into the well.

Beat yolks slightly, pour over the crumbled bread, and combine the two with your hands.

Little by little, mix the flour into the egg and bread mixture and knead the dough for 10 minutes. Adjust with flour or milk to form a dough that is springy and pliant, not sticky or stiff. Wrap in plastic and leave to rest 30 minutes. Then flour the work surface and roll out the dough so that it is 1/8 in. (3 mm) thick. Let it dry slightly.

Using either a knife or a specially made rolling pin with blades called a *mattarello tagliapasta*, cut the dough into noodles that are about 1/4 in. (5 mm) wide. This dough is not suited to folding and cutting as one normally would with a *sfoglia*.

Lay the cut noodles on a floured towel or a drying rack and leave to rest, uncovered, for 1-5 hours.

Preheat oven to 375°F (190°C).

Bring a pot of salted water to a boil. In a large skillet, melt the butter. Combine the sugar and cinnamon in a bowl. Butter the bottom of a non-stick baking dish and dust lightly with one-fourth of the sugar and cinnamon mixture. Sprinkle one-fourth of the grated parmesan on top to create a thin layer. This will

(*continued on next page*)

(*continued from previous page*)
create the desired crust when baked. The pan size should allow for three layers of pasta, about 4 in. (10 cm) deep in total.

Toss the pasta into the boiling water and cook for about 5 minutes, testing for doneness. Historically, the pasta would be cooked until soft. Drain the pasta, transfer to the pan of melted butter, and toss.

Place one-third of the pasta in the prepared baking dish. Top with one-fourth of the mozzarella slices, 1 Tbsp rose water, and another one-fourth of the sugar and cinnamon mix and parmesan. Build two more layers in the same way and top with the last tablespoon of rose water and the remaining cheese.

Bake for 30 minutes. Tent lightly with foil if it starts to brown. Remove from the oven and leave it to rest for 10 minutes. Serve hot.

From our modern perspective, the pairing of sugar with cheesy pasta is curious if not jarring. This would be the moment to refer back to the honey-laced *placenta* and the reference to Frederick II's purported penchant for macaroni with a sweet sauce. The heady experience of sugar on macaroni was well expressed by the humanist writer Ortensio Lando, addressing someone who would soon alight in Sicily: "And [there] you will eat such macaroni, whose name derives from the word blessed: customarily cooked with fat capons and fresh cheese strewn all over, oozing with butter and milk, and then topped with a generous handful of sugar and cinnamon, the finest to be found; oh, my! How my mouth waters just remembering it."[14]

Sugar inherited honey's reputation as a health-promoting source of energy. In his *Treatise on the Nature of Foods* (1583) the physician Baldassare Pisanelli lauds sugar as "not as warming as honey . . . but easier on the stomach, lungs, and chest than honey. It goes wonderfully with all dishes except tripe, because when sprinkled on top, it makes it stink like freshly dumped cow's dung. It soothes the throat & chest, just as sugar candies do for a scratchy throat."

The use of cinnamon predates the Roman Empire, but as it proliferated, its origins and cultivation were kept shrouded in mystery. Pliny the Elder (23–79) unmasked those stories as tall terroir tales, purposely fabricated to keep prices high. Then, as now, a good food story added to its allure. He also notes that the early traders exchanged the spice for luxury items like glass and bronzeware, clothing, and all manner of jewelry—just one more trade route, Pliny sneers, prompted by women's vanity. The gastromyths about cinnamon persisted into the Middle Ages. Those stories were buoyed up by its association with nobility and claims of its medicinal and aphrodisiacal properties. Both sugar and cinnamon were main ingredients in Nostradamus' (1503–1566) love potion jam recipe, a bizarre twelve-ingredient philter. If you managed to source the blood of seven male sparrows bled via the left wing, a requisite for the potency of the concoction, proceed thus: Put a dab of the jam in your mouth and kiss the woman (aphrodisiacs were intended for heterosexual men) who has caught your fancy, and, if the potion has been properly prepared, she will wantonly abandon her virtue. If not, you were not attentive in your ministrations.

While the efficacy of Nostradamus's prescription is a big pill to swallow, it is true that both sugar and cinnamon have dopaminergic effects, that is, they are mood boosters. Albeit without the benefit of molecular science, our forebears may have intuited the impact cinnamon also has on metabolism, slowing the breakdown of carbohydrates and modulating the use of sugars for energy. The Roman physician Paulo Zacchia (1584–1659) edges near that idea in his treatise *Lenten Victuals—Where it is Taught How to Get through Lent without Ruining your Health* (1637). He paints a rather disconcerting picture of the effects macaronis have on the organism—the thicker and harder they are, the more noxious—causing colic, difficulty urinating, bloating, indigestion, kidney stones, and melancholy. At one end of the macaroni toxicity continuum are gnocchi and, at the other, thinly rolled lasagne. He recommends both sugar and cinnamon as remedies for these ills, so, in the spirit of "Let food be thy medicine and medicine thy food," putting them on pasta was not only delicious but medicinal.[15] Cinnamon and sugar were hardly restricted to macaroni; they were ubiquitous seasonings, very much like salt and pepper are today. The difference is that cinnamon and sugar were terrifically expensive, so much so that they were kept under lock and key. Hence, those who could afford them flaunted them—though, one hopes, not on tripe.

Like Martino, Scappi also has an entry for Sicilian macaroni, though he makes no allusions to Sicily. He descriptively calls it "To make a dish of macaroni with an iron rod" or *maccaroni a ferro*. The dough is a stiffer, sweeter version of his Roman macaroni and is brightened with saffron, perhaps reminiscent of the color of durum wheat pasta? Here, too, this macaroni is specifically meant to be dried and stored. In a pinch, it's a handy alternative to Roman macaroni and meant to be cooked the same way: fatty meat broth or milk with butter, layered with plenty of cheese and butter—and, of course, sugar and cinnamon.

As was common practice with cookbooks, a section of *Opera* was allocated to menu planning. "*Maccaroni alla Romanesca*" is listed on the bill of fare described as "Dinner for a fasting day in the aforementioned month of December which can be served as the prandial meal with four sideboard, & four kitchen courses served on thirteen plates, with thirteen table attendants & thirteen platers." The first two courses consist of cold dishes from the *credenza*, or sideboard. All in all, twenty different nibbles are included to get started: salads, dried fish dishes, savory pastries, olives, and pickled fish. The meal intensifies when the "kitchen courses" of hot food are rolled out. All four of these courses are brought out in succession headed up by fish pies, the coveted fish head, fish soup, almond pudding, stuffed calamari pastries, pike bits with *agliata*, naked ravioli, pressed tuna with sugared anise, and snail soup. Then come several kinds of roasted and grilled fish: mullet, orate, tuna, eel, more soups, eel stew, and eel pie. The third course is yet more fish and seafood but this time marinated, fried, and encrusted: sardines, tuna, trout, mullet, calamari, along with several kinds of grapes, olives, green frittatas, and sweet and sour spinach. The fourth and final hot course from the kitchen offers a bit of respite from the onslaught of fish headed up by our Roman macaroni. Let's consider the company it keeps in the overall scheme:

- Roman macaroni topped with cheese, sugar, and cinnamon
- *Bianco mangiare*: or "whitedish", made with red gurnard (fish) topped with sugar and grated apple[16]
- Crayfish pottage
- Large eels stewed with lamprey reduction, served in its own gravy
- Stuffed, cut side-down hard-boiled eggs
- Bolognese cabbage soup with cheese bits
- Naked ravioli *alla Lombarda* topped with cheese, sugar, and cinnamon
- Shelled snail pastries, fifty per pastry
- Large, stuffed calamari in pottage
- Split chickpea soup

Roman macaroni leads the lineup of this "comfort course," or the *entremets*, unimposing, soft foods and warming soups meant to ease the passage from carousal feasting toward the soporific denouement.

To cap the event, the third sideboard (cold food) course is brought out. This was a mixed bag of savory and fruit pies, raw and stewed truffles, grilled oysters, several varieties of apples and pears, roasted chestnuts, marzolino and parmesan cheeses, sweet, whipped cream, wafers, and mini doughnuts. At this point, the soiled tablecloth is removed, and the event draws to a close. Water bowls and clean serviettes are passed around for handwashing. Sugar-coated fennel seeds to ease digestion are laid out with candied fruit, aromatic toothpicks, and bunches of flowers tied with silk. Despite the absence of meat in this mortification-of-the-flesh meal, one is hard pressed to discern the burden of restraint, abstinence, and humility.

THE ITALIAN RENAISSANCE CEDES TO THE GRAND SIÈCLE

While the established model for preparing macaroni remained sacrosanct through the seventeenth century, some noteworthy details surfaced. In his book on stewarding (1638), Antonio Frugoli pontificates on the qualities of foods and lists "macaroni, vermicelli, tagliatelle and particularly those doughs worked in Sicily" under the heading *Pasta azima*, meaning unleavened dough, thereby differentiating it from bread dough. While this is literally true, his choice of terminology is curious because it carries a highly religious charge. It is closely associated with both Jewish matzah and Roman Catholic *azymes*, the communion wafer. The attention given to distinguishing between leavened and unleavened doughs also evokes one of the main sacramental schisms between Roman and Orthodox Catholics: the latter celebrate the Eucharist with leavened dough. So, it is interesting that he should position pasta, having nothing to do with religious practices, under that heading.

Frugoli praises the versatility of pasta for both fasting and meat days. For the latter, he suggests using Sicilian-style macaroni—prepared according to standard with cheese, sugar, and cinnamon—as a flavorful topping for poached fowl such as duck, chicken, or capon, to liven up an otherwise insipid dish. Since broth was so frequently called for, kitchens were often left with an abundance of boiled poultry. This method of plating had been popular for decades, typically involving handmade lasagna-style pasta layered over the meat and smothered in a cheesy gravy. Frugoli's suggestion marks a shift: now tubular macaroni is being used in this traditional context.

Looking to Bologna and the grand *cucina emiliana*, renowned for its pasta and rich cuisine, you might expect to find macaroni showcased with fanfare. Nothing of the sort. In his book for gentleman farmers managing a country estate (1644), Marquis Vincenzo Tanara (?–1667) mentions it in passing in a section dedicated to breadcrumbs, saying that if you mix flour, breadcrumbs, and water together you can make morsels that "are called *strozzapreti* [priest chokers], macaroni, or, by us, gnocchi." Significantly, they are cooked in milk and dressed in cheese and butter, but no cinnamon or sugar is used. In his index or "Table of Notable Things" at the back of the book, macaroni wasn't deemed notable enough to mention. Likewise, Tanara's contemporary and fellow Bolognese Bartolomeo Stefani, chef to the crème de la crème of the aristocracy, did not include a single recipe for macaroni and cheese in any form in his *L'Arte di ben cucinare* (1662).

However, lesser known among the seventeenth century Bolognese chefs is Giuseppe Lamma (no dates available), who at the end of his career had cobbled together a lifetime of menus, notes, and recipes into an eight-volume opus (ca. 1684), of which only two have survived the ravages of time. One of the extant recipes is similar to Roman macaroni, although the dough presents yet another personal spin: refined white flour, egg yolks, and butter. The procedure is also unique: Roll the dough up on the pin and cut it lengthwise, so that the dough falls away from the pin in a stack. Then cut it into thin strips, like short tagliatelle. Keeping that shape in mind, consider his illuminating note in the recipe: "In Genova this pasta is called *crecette* [corzetti?]. In Emilia-Romagna called *crosetti and croxetti*, while the Bolognese call it lasagne." His instructions are surprisingly detailed: The pasta is cooked in boiling salted water, and he even specifies draining it in a colander; it is put in a bowl, and tossed with butter, cinnamon, pepper, and, surprisingly, Lodigiano—a hard cheese from Lodi considered the forerunner to Grana Padano—apparently preferred over the locally available parmesan. The pasta is then piled into a baking dish, topped with extra butter, cheese, and cinnamon (but no sugar), and baked.

Antonio Maria Dalli (d. 1710), a Bolognese contemporary to Lamma and pastry chef to the Duke of Parma and Piacenza, gives us a priceless bit of information in his *Piciol lume di cucina* (1701). The recipe "Sicilian pasta soup" starts with the line "This [pasta] you buy at a shop, and it is called Sicilian because that is where it originates." This indicates that hollow macaroni, recognized as Sicilian, was a store-bought product, presumably machine extruded durum wheat, and commercially available in a dried form. Given his employer's status, it was also the reserve of the few. Notably, Dalli, too, preferred cheese from Lodi, and forgoes the sugar. Soon after publication, Dalli received his calling and quit the food business to become an Augustinian hermit.

End of an Era

The last of the great Italian stewards of the Baroque period was Antonio Latini (1642–1696). Orphaned at the age of five; he went to work as a servant to survive. As a youth, he trained in Rome as a cook and had already worked his way up to steward by age twenty-eight. All in all, his vocation took him to twenty-five different locations before he settled in Naples. His opus, *Lo Scalco alla moderna* (1692), though steeped in the Renaissance tradition, was not stagnant and showed glimmers of leaning into the current trend favoring the aromatics of fresh herbs over spices. He was writing on the cusp of the French vanguard; therefore, unlike his successors, he escaped being held to their standards. While he is not a trailblazer, he is credited with having laid the first foundations of what would become Neapolitan cuisine, not the least of which is the first recorded tomato salsa, albeit as a dressing for meat, not pasta. Cookbooks at this time were becoming cultural commodities, exalting what Stefani called in his subtitle "this praiseworthy profession." No expense was spared in producing *Lo Scalco*, and Latini would later be knighted for outstanding mastery of his craft.

Latini reveled in macaroni and cheese. He revives lasagne, the sheets the size of the palm of your hand, adorned with a riot of cheeses: parmesan, caciocavallo, provola, and pecorino Pugliese. The layers are buttered and topped with the inevitable. To avoid unpleasant clumping, he cleverly mentions serving it on a hot water plate (see fig. 2.2). A water plate is a brilliant construction with a base like a baking dish and with a decorative plate affixed to the top. A small spout protrudes from one side into which boiling water is poured just before serving. In finer homes, the kitchen may have been some distance from the dining room. The serving plate would have been brought out at the scheduled moment in the course of the meal along with several other dishes. If diners were taking the meal at a leisurely pace, the pasta and cheese would have become unpleasantly cold. With such a profusion of cheese in Latini's signature dish, a heat source was essential.

FIGURE 2.2. Example of a water plate. *Source*: Personal collection. Public domain.

He follows up with four different kinds of gnocchi, Sardinian gnocchetti soup, and naked cheese ravioli, all predictably dressed and seasoned. He also mentions using macaroni and cheese, in any form, as a top layer to this baked duck recipe: "Duck [stuffed with] beef *piccatiglio*, bone marrow, raisins and pine nuts, parboiled calf brains finely minced with aromatic herbs and spices, and [the duck's] pre-baked liver and entrails, finely minced, with squash and candied citron peel, and other noble ingredients, bound with beaten eggs." While Frugoli suggests macaroni and cheese in a Hamburger Helper sort of way to liven up lackluster poultry, Latini assigns the pasta a supporting role, cloaking a capricious stuffed duck.

WHAT'S CATHERINE DE' MEDICI GOT TO DO WITH IT?

By all appearances, it would have been safe to bet that Scappi had posited Italian cuisine center stage on the world's gastronomic stage from whence it would flourish, but that was not the case. In due time, the French would overtake the Italians and assert their culinary hegemony for the next three hundred years. The force behind their climb to the top is often attributed to the marriage of Catherine de' Medici (1519–1589) to Henry II in 1533 in a story that unfolds much like this: The daughter of one of the richest and most powerful families in Italy translocates to France, bringing in tow her well-articulated Italian tastes, favorite recipes, Italian delicacies, a fork, and a full entourage of culinary specialists. The latter assume the helm in the kitchens of the reigning king, Francis I, give French cookery a jolt *à l'italienne* and, from that spark, the great tradition of haute cuisine would skyrocket. Italian cuisines would fall into the shadows and kowtow to French dictates until the end of the nineteenth century. The end.

Culinary historians have picked apart this greatest of gastromyths time and time again—Loïc Bienassis and Antonella Campanini having done so with surgical precision—and yet it lives on.

What's odd is that this wasn't an Italian sour grapes story trumped up by sore losers to soothe their bruised egos. It was of *French* devising. As macaroni is a player in this transitional story, smoothing out this kink in history will allow us to proceed into the next chapter on the right footing.

In Her Day

No contemporaries in France or Italy ever mentioned anything related to Catherine de' Medici and food except that she had a voracious appetite. At a wedding reception, the Queen Mother reportedly ate so much she wanted to die and twice wandered off to disgorge.[17] Italian ambassadors in France remarked on her rotundity and the abandon with which she ate. However, records of household staff contain no names—not even Frenchified versions—of Italian cooks.[18] Granted, there are few chefs and cooks from the royal court whose names remain for posterity, but all those who do are French. In contrast, a Frenchman by the name of Jean Duval, a.k.a. Maestro Giovanni, appears in the 1536 archives as private chef to Pope Paul III.[19]

Given the ironic but nonetheless deep-seated abhorrence for luxury, it is odd that the 1574 poison-pen pamphlet *Marvelous discourse on the life, actions, & behavior of Catherine de Medicis, queen mother: which recounts the methods she used to surprise the government of the realm of France & ruin the state therein* never ventured into the Lust-Pride-Gluttony avenue, which would have fit perfectly into their arsenal of accusations.[20] The text is an unabashed, anti-Italian, misogynistic character assault seeking to unveil the queen as calculating, devious, and perverse. Her image as culinary corrupter would mature in due time, but for now the seeds of Catherine the Black Queen were being sown.

At the same time, as Giovanni Battista Rossetti intimates in the preface to his book *On Stewarding* (1584) there had been a perceptible passing of the baton, or rather scepter, from Italy to France and Germany: "I praise the Germans and the French . . . for the way they prepare dishes. They are truly unequaled connoisseurs when it comes to meats and fish, in addition to myriad doughs and sauces.[21] The use of these things they learned from our chefs in Italy, but they added noble refinement and raised them up to the height of perfection."

The influential Italian teachings he speaks of were likely sourced from Platina's *On Right Living*, which between 1505 and 1586 went through sixteen translated editions in France alone, thanks to mass output made possible by the printing press. Scappi's *Opera* also circulated in France, though not in French. But nowhere is Catherine's arrival in France implicated as a catalyst for the loss of Italian preeminence.

Delayed-Onset Myth Making

The French "discovery" of their debt to Italian cuisine would materialize about 130 years after Catherine's death, though she is still cast as a harbinger of evil. The pattern of the food myth about her that would persist for some time comes from the oddest of sources: the police commissioner Nicolas Delamare's chapter called "Seasoning" in his 1719 *Traité de la police*.[22] This is the basic outline:

1. The ancient Romans spread their customs in Gaul, and/or the Italians, having learned the way of the ancient Romans, brought them into France.
2. The Middle Ages are completely left out of the story.
3. French kings imposed laws to stanch the culture of luxury and excess imported by Catherine de' Medici and other hedonistic Italians.
4. Xenophobia: Once vexing foreign ways have taken over, alas, there is no turning back.
5. The pupil (France) surpasses the teacher (Italy).

With the convenient removal of the Middle Ages from history, Catherine's arrival becomes the tipping point that visited the burden of luxury on France. Her vulgar appetites, and that of all Italians by way of association, ran contrary to whatever idea the French had constructed about their true virtues. Early-eighteenth-century moralists got considerable mileage out of Catherine as the cause of their descent into the clutches of luxury.[23] The idea to blame her and her ilk for the fraying of French mores had been fomenting since her reign, and it was pummeled into the origin story of French cuisine. At best, it is a backhanded compliment, a snide recognition of French indebtedness to Italian culinary foundations.

There was pushback from those who refused the Italian master and French apprentice computation. In 1742, Adrien-Maurice de Mairault launched his rebuttal: "It is claimed that it was the Italians who taught the art of fine cuisine to the French. . . . But judging by modern Italian cuisine, it seems to me that ours is not indebted to the lessons of Italy, regardless of all the cookbooks they published in the fifteenth and sixteenth centuries."[24] But as Bienassis and Campanini point out, the grounding of this counter-argument is as shaky as the claim it seeks to refute.

The story snowballed within France. When Denis Diderot (1713–1784) elaborated the idea in his monumental *Encyclopédie* (1751), the acrid vision of Italians, cooks, cookery, and Catherine as the epicenter was punctuated even more:

> Apicius made rendering food delicious into an art. This art spread in Gaul: our first kings knew the consequences and stopped them; and it was only under the reign of Henry II that crafty cooks started to become important men. It is owing to that crowd of pleasure-loving Italians who followed Catherine de Medici to the court. Things since then have only gotten worse; & we can say with near certainty that there subsist in society two sorts of men, on the one hand are our domestic chemists [i.e., cooks], working incessantly to poison us; & on the other are our Doctors, who cure us; the difference being that the former are much more sure of themselves than the latter.[25]

Unbeknownst to Diderot, his publisher secretly edited out all of the parts that risked inciting political controversy and may have rewritten some sections in accordance with the statecraft of the day. Regardless, the *Encyclopédie* was considered an authoritative publication and its contents unimpeachable.

Changes in Perspective

While other eighteenth-century writers ran with the "Black Queen" trope, Pierre-Jean Baptiste Le Grand d'Aussy proposed a more reasoned explanation to support the Italian legacy story. In his three-volume study of French food (1782), he hypothesized that it was the Italian Wars (1494–1559) that had provided the window of opportunity.[26] For six decades, the French Valois kings and the Spanish Habsburgs vied for control of Italy. Over those years, tens of thousands of Frenchmen entered Italy—wars, as ever, being fertile ground for the exchange of both foodstuffs and foodways. The lived experience of the sheer numbers of soldiers and occupiers moving in and out of Italy over an extended time span was more likely to stimulate a national culinary transformation than the arrival of the fourteen-year-old orphaned Catherine, who had hitherto lived under the protective custody of the Church. Arriving in what was already the European center of culture with her own kitchen staff, or insisting that one be installed according to her specifications, would have been unthinkable if not an outright insult. She was there as a political chess piece in the Italian Wars, an arrangement brokered by her cousin Gulio de' Medici, a.k.a. pope Clement VII.

From d'Aussy's more equitable perspective, exchanging culinary ideas was a time-honored practice; no matter how one's forefathers might have prepared a dish, the next generation would add to it whatever had come along that was to their liking—even if they didn't like the people who brought it. Apropos of macaroni, d'Aussy digs back further in time and leaves us with this historical gem: "The long wars that our nation suffered through in Italy under Charles VIII, Louis XII, and Francis I brought with it an introduction to various stews and preparations which were adopted. Among these are the lasagnes and the macaroni and the other doughs whose use spread among us in the sixteenth century."[27]

The statement positing macaroni in France in the sixteenth century can be supported with historical evidence. First, two copies of the *Liber de coquina*, discussed in the previous chapter, had been commissioned at the beginning of the fourteenth century for the private library of the gastrophile Jean du Valois, Duke of Berry (1340–1416), testimony to the interest the French nobility took in the food of their southern neighbors.[28] Platina's *On Right Living* was first translated into French in 1505 with the title *Platine en Françoys*, indicating that even before translation, Platina (and consequently Martino's recipes) had already become a household name.[29] In reference to the Italian Wars, in 1494, Charles VIII marched into Naples with twenty-five thousand men and claimed the crown without a battle. His successor, Louis XII, conquered Milan in 1500 but lost the claim to Naples. Francis I came to power deadlocked between opposing forces. His main nemesis was Charles V, Holy Roman Emperor and ruler of Spain, Austria, and parts of France, and his perennial enemy, Henry VIII of England, whose great ambition was to take France. In search of an ally, Francis set up an alliance with the Ottoman Empire under Suleiman the Magnificent, a pairing that scandalized the Christian world. After a torrent of victories and losses, Henry II of France would be forced to give up all claims to Italy. In 1559, Henry died after a commemorative celebration joust during which he took a lance in the eye. Catherine, thereafter, would rule as queen regent of France.

Twisting History

In 1807, Catherine as the evil queen was given a makeover in a bit of historical acrobatics. This next excerpt is from "*Introduction à l'histoire de la gourmandise*" in the periodical *Journal des gourmands*, at a time when *gourmandise* meant gluttony and *gourmand*, glutton. It starts by ruminating on the same well-worn legacy structure, but watch for the turnaround:

> The Italians were the first to collect the remains of Roman cuisine, like those of belles-lettres and all the arts; it was the Italians who introduced us to this science. . . . At first it met with resistance and persecutions; several of our kings tried to prevent its propagation through edicts: finally it triumphed over the laws under Henri II. And in the footsteps of Catherine de Medici, cooks from beyond the mountains came to settle in France. This is but one of the many debts we owe to this illustrious queen, who was, . . . in all her person so agreeable, kind-hearted, the essence of refinement, affable, that nothing could be more delicate, graceful, stately, and worthy of the rank of king.[30]

The journal was founded by Alexandre Grimod de La Reynière (1758–1837), one of the most influential voices in modern French culinary culture. With this article as a springboard, the Catherine's mythology would grow throughout the nineteenth century, adding lists of specific foods, recipes,

FIGURE 2.3. "The Macaroni Eater": seventeenth-century ceramic plate. *Source*: Courtesy of the Fondazione Museo Internazionale delle Ceramica in Faenza.

and even names of their Italian originators, but none was anchored in historical fact.[31] The *Encyclopédie du dix-neuvième siècle* (1846), for example, explicitly states that vermicelli and macaroni were introduced into France by the Italian ambassadors' entourages, inaccurately referencing, albeit with laser precision, the *Mélanges tirés d'une grade bibliothèque . . .* (1779), vol. III (p. 86) as their source, which does not mention pasta in any form.

The first to systematically refute Catherine's legacy story was Jean-François Revel in 1972. But by then it had been enshrined in the culinary bible *Larousse Gastronomique* (1938). While you could edit misinformation out of a book, removing it from the national collective conscience would have been more difficult than changing the French retirement age. Italy latched onto the story and elaborated details at the slightest provocation.

It is a classic example of what Roland Barthes called modern mythologies, stories that undergo reconceptualization and fossilize as groupthink. In this case, Bienassis and Campanini surmise, "It offers relative intellectual comfort: thanks to it, the history of French cuisine has a logical starting point, and easily datable birth certificate. It simplifies reality and illuminates gray areas."[32] We will encounter this phenomenon again.

But now we are ready to move on to France.

Chapter Three

THE FRENCH CONNECTION AND ENGLISH REFLECTION

> Those who have more leisure to study what they shall eat and drink, require something more in their food, than what is barely wholesome or necessary; their palates must be gratified with rich sauces and high-seasoned delicacies.
>
> —*LONDON MAGAZINE*, 1755

APPRECIATION AND APPROPRIATION

Gearing Up for Frenchification

Over the course of the sixteenth century, the revised French rendition of Platina's 1474 culinary and lifestyle treatise, *Platine en françoys* (1505), would go through twenty-one editions. It was not merely a translation but an expanded, updated version, containing so much additional commentary that it doubled the length of the original work. The French perspective was seamlessly worked in and showed hints of the impending shift away from spices and toward fresh local ingredients. The combined forces of continuity with the past alongside a modern, distinctly French outlook kept the book and Martino's pasta recipes in circulation.

The first French-language cookbook to feature macaroni and cheese was *Ouverture de cuisine* (1604), published in Belgium. The author, Maistre Lancelot de Casteau (d. 1613), had one foot planted in medieval foodways, but the other was decidedly on the move toward a more cosmopolitan and daring repertoire. De Casteau had cooked his way to fame and wealth as chef to three successive prince-bishops, the rulers of Liège during a period of prosperity in Belgium. The Low Countries and Italy were mercantile powerhouses with robust trade routes facilitating their common interests, both material and cultural. In particular, they were both leading textile producers—Italy's silk and other luxury fabrics complementing the Low Countries' high-quality wool and linen—commodities that bolstered their position in Europe as trade barons. Diplomatic ties, banking networks, and a vested interest in art tightened the bond. As a propertied man in a thriving city, de Casteau held the privileged title of burgher. Given his status, *Ouverture* is a useful window to the culinary pulse of these larger northern cities, where select Italian dishes were part of the clamor for splendor. His pasta entries include *raphioulles* (beef ravioli), *rafioule* (naked spinach ravioli), and *agnoilen* (seemingly *agnolini* but actually gnocchi), and finally we come to "*Pour faire maquaron*": "Make a dough with eggs & butter, & make large sheets of the stiff dough, & cut into strips the size of three fingers, & cut them as you would tripe, & put to boil like raviolis [from the recipe above: boiled in water, drained, moistened in the plate with fatty broth], & fill a plate putting melted butter, parmesan & cinnamon thereupon, well mixed together: & serve thus, putting again a little cinnamon thereupon."

Besides the typical insider shorthand, the methodology and unique mode of expression suggests that de Casteau had witnessed the preparation of the dish firsthand and jotted down his understanding of it, rather than copying it from another source. The tripe analogy was, and would remain, his own personal aide-mémoire. *Ouverture* was written toward the end of de Casteau's career; as such, it documented recipes that had been in vogue for quite some time. Notably, even though the Dutch and Belgians were ramping up their colonial involvement in the sugar trade, making it more available, and expense was no issue to de Casteau's employers, there is no sugar in this recipe. Perhaps it had something to do with the tripe. Regardless, it was quite an innovative departure for the times and a signpost of the shifting tides.

As early as 1660, the growth potential for macaroni in the Netherlands was deemed high enough to prompt a certain Isaac Benedetto Fuine van Savoyen to take a bold step: bypass the middleman and produce pasta locally. He obtained a patent for a product "which is very much used in Italy, called *fideli* and macarony."[1] Had the macaroni been handmade, there would be no need for a patent; therefore we can assume that van Savoyen was setting up a commercial extrusion apparatus, which is easier said than done in a climate so ill-suited to the manufacture of dried pasta. The extruder would have looked similar to what is shown in fig. 3.1.

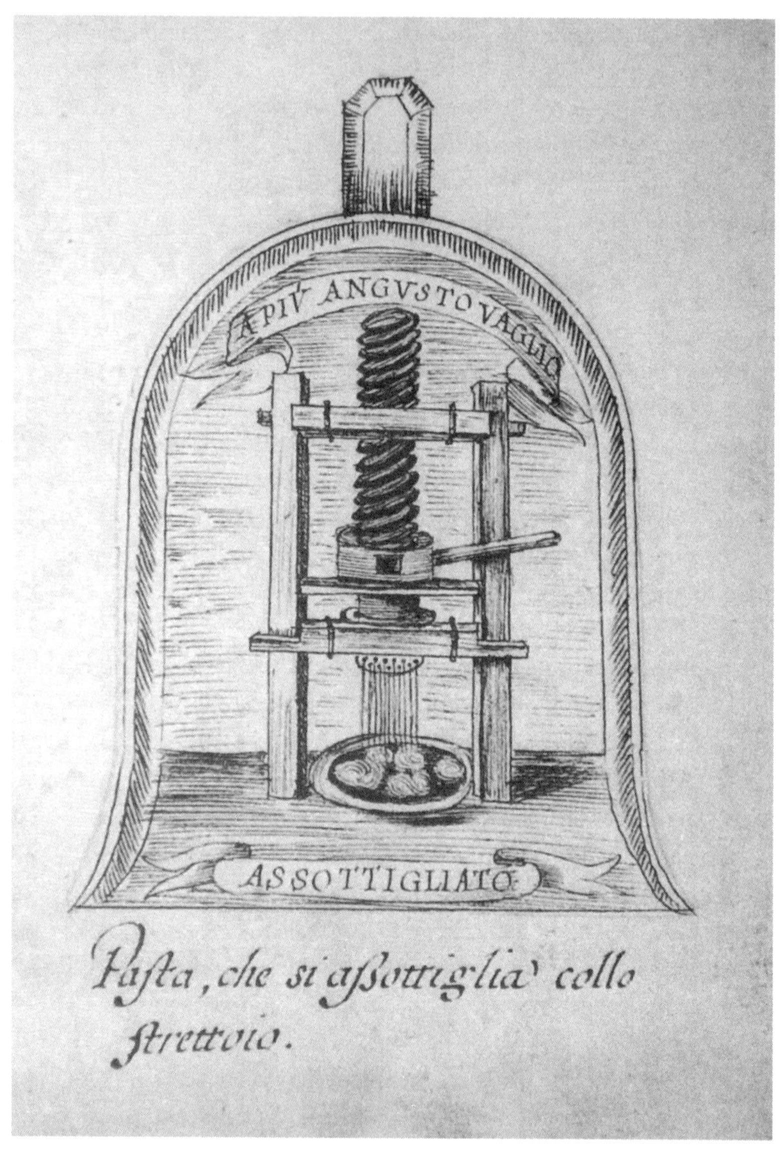

FIGURE 3.1. Pasta extruder (1638), Niccolò Cini. The figure forcing dough through a die is used along with the heading "A più angusto vaglio—Assottigliato" to symbolize how life's trials shape and refine us. *Source*: Accademia della crusca. Public domain.

The French Assume the Helm

In France, there had been a long silence on the cookbook front. After *Le viandier* (ca. 1300), little of note was published in the subsequent centuries and nothing on macaroni. Despite the popularity of *Platine en françoys*, French publishers failed to see the marketing potential in something as trivial as cookery books—the paradox being their reluctance to hazard the risk unless success was guaranteed. Like the hare and the tortoise, the Italians busied themselves with a prolific output of distinguished tomes, but when the French reappeared on the culinary stage with *Le cuisinier françois* (1651) by François Pierre, a.k.a. "Sieur de La Varenne" (1618–1678), it was cataclysmic. The disruption put France on a pedestal and reordered the status quo across Europe.

The maverick publisher Pierre David gambled on the fact that the book would be entering the market with no competing titles. As he says in his foreword, he counted on the cultured people of Paris to appreciate that food was not merely a medicinal corrective but an essential element of a refined lifestyle, one of the many qualities that set France apart on the world stage. He voiced his hope that the provinces would follow the Parisian lead, after which all other nations would surely "be bitten by the desire to fall in line." This was not just David's humble opinion but the echo of established conviction.[2]

David also banked on La Varenne's standing as *chef de cuisine* in the household of a marquis. As the marquis was also a lieutenant general, La Varenne often accompanied him on military campaigns, as one's personal cook did, picking up tips and tricks of the trade from place to place. For a cook, these field assignments were ideal occasions for exchange and comparison, forging "we eat—they eat" concepts and identities. A fish understands more distinctly what water is once it has been swept up on the beach.

David's gamble paid off handsomely. *Le cuisinier françois* quickly became the bible of French cookery, and, as he predicted, the success rippled throughout Europe, firmly planting the French flag in the center of culinary culture. Other publishers followed suit, keen to cash in on what was now a surefire investment. Some simply pirated La Varenne's book, producing multiple versions, and others came in the guise of pretenders who were quick to denigrate La Varenne as yesterday's news.[3]

La Varenne's repertoire does not include a straight-up macaroni and cheese recipe per se. However, there are two vermicelli pottage recipes that are building blocks to the reconceptualization of our dish outside Italy.[4] The first recipe is in the "Lean" section, and the second is in the "Lenten" section. Presumably, Lean should be less stringent than Lenten, but oddly, that is not the case:

> Lean Vermicelli pottage
>
> Peel five or six onions & chop them, and boil them in water & butter. Once cooked, strain them through a linen filter & in this bouillon cook the vermicelli & season with salt and pepper; once cooked, take your bread & garnish it, then serve.
>
> They can also be cooked in milk.

> Lenten Vermicelli pottage
>
> Cook them [the vermicelli] in some water or milk. Once cooked & well seasoned, take some out to fricassee & with the rest make a pottage with butter, salt, pepper and an onion stuck with cloves, then dress & serve.

The Lenten vermicelli recipe strains the imagination no matter how many times you read it: On one hand, we have a pasta cooked fricassee style with a creamy sauce, and on the other, a pasta soup infused with clove and onion, very much like the Lean recipe. Were the two meant to end up in the same pot? And might that final note to "dress" mean with cheese?

Fricassee was one of the most important developments in French culinary history. Its origins trace back to medieval times, but it became a standard in French cookery in the seventeenth century. Broadly speaking, a fricassee involves sautéing ingredients in butter and creating an emulsified sauce, typically bound and thickened with egg yolks or a roux of flour cooked in fat then combined with a liquid. As eggs were not sanctioned during Lent, a roux would have been the default.[5] The resulting sauce would be velvety smooth, a different mouthfeel than the dense and textured sauces achieved with earlier thickening methods relying on breadcrumbs, almonds, or pulverized foods. Such delicate liaisons required the controlled heat of a masonry cooking stove called a *potager*, which had proliferated in the finer French households by this time.

The conspicuous absence of sugar and cinnamon, replaced by salt and pepper, cannot have escaped notice. Sugar features in a mere 5 percent of the book's savory dishes and cinnamon in less than 1 percent, in direct contrast to the dictates of the previous five hundred years. What phenomenon toppled such a stalwart tradition? Two crucial factors were at play: market dynamics and shifts in mentality.[6]

In 1599, the Dutch set off for the Spice Islands with the intention of breaking the Portuguese monopoly on the spice trade. Within two years, they established a foothold and formed the formidable Dutch East India Company. The period 1635–1690 marked its "golden age," during which the quantity of spices imported into Europe doubled. In an unforeseen turn of events, availability and subsequent affordability tarnished their allure.

There were plenty of new, exclusive luxury items vying for attention, such as chocolate, coffee, tea, distilled alcohol, and tobacco—all more potent drugs than cinnamon and sugar. Indeed, the medicinal use of spices to balance the humors was (gradually) being brought into question, undercut by a Christianized approach to healing. The rebellious Swiss physician Phillip von Hohenheim, a.k.a. Paracelsus (1493–1542), spearheaded the transition, advocating the interconnectedness of body, spirit, and nature as central to God's divine plan. His approach emphasized natural remedies that had been placed at man's disposition by divine providence as the solution to healing. This departure from canonical medicine would meet with fierce reproach, but his empirical back-to-nature ideology resonated in ways that would eventually transform the table.

Nature Runs Its Course

Nicolas Bonnefons, the author of the groundbreaking *Jardinier françois* (1651) and *Les délices de la campagne* (1654), explicitly describes the culinary shift away from the monotonous mishmash, or *cuisine de confusion*, as he termed it, to *le goût naturel* (natural taste) or *le vrai goût* (true taste). Both La Varenne and Bonnefons advocated for the delicate style of cookery, an approach that had been gaining momentum in France for some time, although not explicitly documented as such.

According to this unilateral philosophy of taste, spices were seen as unnatural, masking the true essence of foods, whereas delicate, silky sauces and herbal aromatics complimented and potentiated their flavors. Bonnefons argued that spices had hitherto been applied by rote to every dish, rendering one dish indistinguishable from the next. In contrast, the

French approach of using herbs and sauces relied upon case-by-case assessment to exalt the qualities inherent in each.[7] This philosophical shift liberated macaroni and cheese from the sugar and cinnamon merry-go-round and propelled it toward a creamier, saucier, Frenchier elegance.

The delicate style should not be mistaken for down-home cooking or bourgeois cuisine. Bonnefons was a noble wannabe. His role as *valet de chambre* in the royal household positioned him to ascend to the lower ranks of hereditary nobility. Although his post was no sinecure or "money for rope," it did afford him ample time to pursue his combined interest in food and gardening. As an influencer of sorts, Bonnefons's promotion of the delicate or natural style resonated with other aspirants seeking to emulate the refined lifestyle of elites. The Sun King, Louis XIV, a man who loved his spices, meat, and a heavily laden table, was having none of it, but the delicate style prevailed even without his adherence. Just as the Renaissance was lauded as a move from the dark into the light, so too would the delicate style of cookery shake off the monotonous shackles of its predecessors and squarely establish France as the indisputable gastronomic leader.

FRENCH CUISINE AND THE ENGLISH TABLE

> We too can send for *niceties* from *Rome*:
> To please your tastes will spare not pains nor money,
> Discard *Sirloins*, and get you *Maccaroni*.
>
> —DAVID GARRICK, *VIRGINIA. A TRAGEDY* (1754)

When La Varenne's *Le cuisinier françois* was translated into English in 1653, it stood in sharp contrast to culinary currents in England, and the English struggled to grasp it.[8] They were curious but confused. Giles Rose's translation of the anonymous classic *L'escole parfait des officers de bouche* (1661) into *A Perfect School of Instructions for the Officers of the Mouth* (1682) was meant to cater to the demand for modern French techniques. However, the dizzying details left all but seasoned professionals bewildered with, for example, twenty-six methods for folding a napkin.

But finally, the entrepreneur chef François Massialot produced a volume that systematized French cuisine in a way that eased its passage into kitchens across the Channel. By the time Massialot's landmark tome *Le cuisinier roïal et bourgeois* came along in 1691, translated into English as *The Court and Country Cook* in 1702, *le goût naturel* had become the defining characteristic of French cuisine. For the most part, Massialot had relegated cinnamon to the pastry section and did away with all other spices except nutmeg and cloves, which appeared frequently in savory dishes. The only recipe he has as a lead-up to our macaroni is again a pottage made with vermicelli, clearly drawing upon earlier Italian recipes of fowl draped in a macaroni and cheese mantle. It is an odd mix of the old and the new: A boiled capon is heaped onto broth-soaked toast, in turn covered with a mound of vermicelli, then topped with grated Parmesan, oh, and . . . cinnamon. Bread, fried in lard to a deep brown, crowns the dish, and the whole is doused with mutton gravy and lemon juice. Diners might have been hard-pressed to discern *le goût naturel* in this particular option.

Among the earliest English advocates of French trends is Sir Kenelm Digby (1603–1665), a diplomat, courtier, philosopher, scientist, and avid foodie. A devout Roman Catholic and Francophile, Digby had close, albeit conflictual, ties with the Stuart monarchy. Knighted by James I, he held a position of influence in Charles I's Privy Council and served as chancellor to Queen Consort Henrietta Maria, Charles's French Catholic wife. As a young man, Digby had spent three years in the French court, which likely impacted his tastes.[9] After the Restoration, he retained influence in the court of Charles II, so his loyalties ran deep in both spheres.

With the consent of Digby's son, a collection of his papers with culinary notes and recipes was posthumously published in 1669 as *The Closet of the Eminently Learned Sir Kenelme Digbie Kt. Opened*.[10] "Closet" was a beguiling word used in domestic titles, intimating an exchange of secrets among confidants. Digby's *Closet* discloses five versions of the French mainstay *potage de santé* (healthy soup). One version, adapted from a "very *Valetudinary*" (hypochondriacal) French acquaintance, is a restorative pottage chock full of foraged and cultivated greens, cooked with veal and a whole chicken, then seasoned with herbs and the customary onion stuck with cloves. The vegetables will vary according to the season, he says, but vermicelli is a good addition any time of year. This marks the first mention of vermicelli in an English-authored cookbook, although the word had already circulated among English readers through John Florio's 1598 Italian–English dictionary, with the food itself plausibly in modest circulation at that time. Presumably, Digby is referring to an imported product, as were La Varenne and Massiolot—available in France as well as England. Vermicelli would dominate as the preferred form of pasta for a time, owing perhaps to the visual appeal of the delicate strings in an age that also associated such refinements with sound digestive practices.

Macaroni was built to travel. Sir Hugh Plat (1552–1608) gave it his highest recommendation in *The Jewel House of Art and Nature* (1594), a compendium of domestic innovations and scientific curiosities. He praised pasta as a lightweight, practical food—agreeable to "any reasonable stomach, and serveth both for bread and meat"—ideal for long voyages. It offered variety to the mariner's monotonous fare and served as insurance against the lack of fresh provisions. Cheap and durable, it would "last two or three years sound and sweet if it bee kept dry."

What sets Plat's account apart, however, is not just his endorsement but the inclusion of what is, to date, the earliest known printed image of an extrusion press for pasta. Equipped with a sophisticated lateral crank and internal cogs, the design signals larger-scale production rather than domestic use, underscoring just how far macaroni had already traveled—both literally and technologically—by the end of the sixteenth century.

Patrick Lamb

Another name aligned with the Stuart monarchy, having served in the kitchens of Charles II, James II, William and Mary, and finally Queen Anne, was Patrick Lamb (ca. 1650–ca. 1709). His posthumously published cookbook, *Royal Cookery; or, The Complete Court-Cook* (1710), is an exaltation of the gastronomic bounty of England, whose "chief Aim was to represent the Grandeur of the Engliſh Court and Nation. . . . I mean thoſe of publick Regales made on the more ſolemn Occaſsions of admitting Princes to their Thrones, Peers to their Honours, Ambaſſadors to their Audience, and Perſons of Figure to the Nuptial-Bed." Other countries, like France and Italy, will by comparison "lament their own Barrenneſs whenever they reflected on the Fleſh-Pots they left behind them [in England]."

Despite the nationalistic preamble, the better part of Lamb's recipes were from the French canon. The opening recipe is "Soupe Santé the French way," followed by "*To make* Soupe-Santé, *after the* Engliſh Way." The first recipe sprawls across three pages, while the second recipe occupies a single page, a cultural commentary in and of itself. Among the soups is also "*To make* Soupe Vermiſelly," reminiscent of Massialot's pottage. Vermicelli is cooked in veal and fowl broth, flavored with a clove-studded chunk of bacon, and thickened with a walnut-sized ball of butter mixed with a spoonful of "flower." A boiled chicken is placed on a platter of bread soaked in that same broth, and the vermicelli is poured into the dish before finishing with a lemon garnish.

With Lamb we forge a strong link to the American colonies. The food historian Gilly Lehmann argues that Lamb was most likely the "first of the star chefs" in England, a reputation that would have echoed in the colonies. However, his connection to the New World colony of Virginia went by way of tobacco. Despite James I's open revulsion for the stuff, reinforced in his *A Counterblaste to Tobacco* (1604), he eventually cottoned on to its potential for revenue through a state monopoly. Lamb's grandfather was granted dividends from the sale of tobacco at all of the royal palaces and places of residence of the court; subsequently, Charles I followed suit with Lamb's father, and in due time Lamb himself inherited this lucrative sideline.[11]

It was by then a family interest that spanned generations and continued on with Lamb's son. Given this close relationship with Virginia, and the colony's close cultural and political bond with England, it is reasonable to speculate that his cookbook, which went through three editions in England, might have circulated in the royalist households of the south interested in maintaining (or attaining) a sense of English refinement.[12]

Edward Kidder

The master pie maker Edward Kidder (1665–1739), a contemporary of Lamb's, operated on a decidedly different strata of society. His *Receipts of Pastry and Cookery, for the Use of His Scholars* first appeared as handwritten manuscripts that accompanied his popular cookery courses at his schools in London.[13] Several of these survive, the earliest dating back to 1702.[14] The text later came out in printed form for commercial distribution in 1720, serving the dual purpose of cookbook and advertisement for his school.[15] Kidder's courses appealed to young women sent by employers or those looking to acquire skills to enter into domestic service. Likewise, "ladies" could be taught privately at home, presumably to increase marriageability. Publication allowed the general public, who otherwise could not attend his course, to benefit from his expertise.

Kidder was a respected authority, and his recipes were frequently plagiarized throughout the eighteenth century; in one case the book was lifted in its entirety.[16] One of Kidder's recipes, "Brown Pottage Royale," was also copied into an anonymous, handwritten family cookery manuscript in

(*continued on next page*)

(*continued from previous page*)
Virginia, begun ca. 1700, and may even predate the commercial publication of *Receipts of Pastry*. This supports speculation that fame of Kidder's book had spread to the colonies at the same time it was in vogue in England.[17] "Brown Pottage Royale" includes "vermachelly" cooked in a broth reduction, heaped onto gravy-braised duck parts posited on darkly toasted slices of dried French rolls. The main feature was accompanied by slivered palates, cockscombs, meatballs, and lamb sweetbreads, classic French accoutrements, all of which had been stewed with the duck. Colonists aspiring to make this recipe would have required the pasta. Vermicelli soup became a regular feature in English cookery, along with impressionistic spellings, like Charles Carter's "Pottage *of* Vermajelly *with* Capon" from *The Complete Practical Cook Or, A New System of the Whole Art and Mystery of Cookery* (1730). Kidder's recipe was later riffed in Susannah Carter's *The Frugal Housewife, or Complete Woman Cookbook* as "To make Vermicelli Soup." This popular British publication circulated in the colonies, prompting a local (thus cheaper) reprinted edition published in Boston in 1772 with engravings by Paul Revere. Yes, that Paul Revere. Macaroni was listed on the August Bill of Fare suggestions, unfortunately without an accompanying recipe.

Eliza Smith

The first English cookbook ever published in the American colonies was Eliza Smith's *The Compleat Housewife: Or, Accomplish'd Gentlewoman's Companion*, first published in London in 1727, with the American edition issued in 1742. She ushers in vermicelli in the section entitled "BROTHS &c. for the SICK" with the delightful "To make Broth of a Knuckle or Scrag of Veal." It is a vermicelli soup with hawthorn shavings, mace, and clove. "If the patient be coſtive, boil in it a quarter of a pound of currants, and ſweeten it with *Liſbon* ſugar." Scrag, in case you are wondering, is neckbone. Knuckle and scrag would become a standard go-to preparation for vermicelli for the next century.

Lamb and Kidder may have made names for themselves, but it was French cooks who were in demand among the English grandees. In 1728, the Earl of Chesterfield, then ambassador to the Netherlands, wrote for advice on acquiring a Frenchman who was "a master chef of superior genius, who should be able not only to execute but invent delectable and perfect delicacies."[18] He had been through plenty of merely competent cooks so would settle for nothing less than Paris's top chef. Vincent La Chapelle (1690–1745) came highly recommended as "the phoenix of modern-day cuisine."

He was in Chesterfield's employ, traveling through Portugal and Spain, when he wrote *The Modern Cook*, later published in London in 1733. The title is meant to announce that Massialot's time had come and gone and that a new voice in culinary culture had landed. Self-assured though he was as a chef, he humbly adds, "Being a Foreigner, the *Engliſh* Reader will, I hope, excuse the Defects in my Style, which however, I believe, will be plain enough to thoſe who are ever ſo little converſant in Cookery."

The last book of this three-volume opus presents a bizarre contraption that goes by the name "*A Maſcaronis Pye, the* Italian *way*." It starts off with the time-honored method of boiling the macaroni in fatty capon broth. But then it meanders on an adventure through boned pigeons stuffed with forcemeat, wrapped in bacon, and stewed in milk, cooked together with additional bacon and veal slices, all infused with a fragrant cinnamon stick. An unctuous pomade of beef marrow pounded with butter, parmesan cheese, and cinnamon is slathered over the crust lining a deep baking dish. Finally, the macaroni appears, creating a bedding in which the cooked pigeons and meats are nestled. The pie is then filled with a creamy capon and parmesan gravy. It's all suspiciously reminiscent of French-style pigeon pie. In the body of culinary literature that precedes *The Modern Cook*, there is nothing to support this pie as being "*the* Italian *way*." Curiously, the recipe that follows, "A Maſcaronis Pye in Meager" (for a "lean" day), is not tagged "*the* Italian *way*"—though it is nearly identical to Bartolomeo Scappi's macaroni pie from 1570. It seems that macaroni and cheese had been appropriated and was entering the public domain.

A MASCARONIS PYE IN MEAGER

BOIL your Maſcaronis in Water with a little Salt. When boil'd, drain them and let them be cold. Take as much Parmeſan as you pleaſe, pound it and mix it with good Cream. Your Pye being form'd and pretty deep, put in the bottom of it a Laying of freſh Butter, then a Layering of Maſcaronis, over which you put five or ſix Spoonfuls of your Parmeſan in Cream, ſtrow it with pounded Cinnamon. Do the ſame over and over again, till your Pye is filled up.[19]

Here are the remapped instructions for La Chapelle's all-purpose savory short crust:

1 1/2 cups (350 g) salted butter, cold and cut into small cubes
5 1/3 cups (650 g) flour
2 eggs, cold
Cold water
4 cups (500 g) macaroni
1 2/3 cups (400 mL) cream
7 oz (200 g) grated Parmesan, plus an additional 2 oz (55 g)
10 tbsp (150 g) cold butter, sliced
1 tsp cinnamon, freshly ground

Cut the butter into the flour and salt in a food processor so that bits are still visible. Mix the eggs with 1/4 cup (50 mL) cold water and pour into the running food processor until just combined. Divide the dough into three parts. Let rest 2 hours. Roll out one of the portions to line the bottom of a 9-inch (24 cm) springform pan and a smaller one for the top crust, and a long strip fitted to the height and circumference of the pan. Refrigerate.

Preheat oven to 350°F (180°C).

Boil the macaroni to al dente in salted water. Mix the cream with the parmesan. Begin by layering a third of the butter into the pie shell, followed by a third of the macaroni, a third of the parmesan cream, and cinnamon. Repeat with two more layers. Spread the additional Parmesan over the top. Position the top crust and cut a 1-inch hole in the center. Bake for 1 hour and 30 minutes. Cool 15 minutes before serving.

The Plain and the Pilfered: Hannah Glasse

Originality is nothing but judicious imitation.

—VOLTAIRE

Hannah Glasse (1708–1770) was having none of this fussy French business. In *The Art of Cookery Made Plain and Easy*, she railed unapologetically against the bother and expense it incurred as a forthright demonstration of her parsimonious English values. Her book, she avowed, was "not wrote in the high polite stile" and was a protest against "the Blind Folly of this age that they would rather be imposed on by a French Booby than give encouragement to a good *English* Cook. . . . If Gentlemen will have *French* cooks, they must pay for French tricks." Her rantings were nothing new, merely an echo of others before her. William Harrison (1534–1593), in his *Description of Elizabethan England* (1577), blames the gluttony and frivolousness of his contemporaries on the craftiness and wiles of French cooks: "In number of dishes and change of meat, the nobility of England (whose cooks are for the most part musical-headed Frenchmen and strangers) do most exceed." Musical-headed. Quite a low blow.

Embracing French cookery was fraught with conflict. The dilemma was not just political but a question of different lifestyles. The English gentry were less concerned about courtly pomp and display at the table than their French counterparts. The value placed on the genteel lifestyle of the English squire in the countryside or the sensible thrift of urbanites played out in food choices and cooking styles. Yet as the American author and renowned historical cookbook collector Elizabeth Robins Pennell wryly observed, patriotism does not begin in the stomach, at least not for the English. Despite Glasse's apparent unwillingness to acknowledge how deeply French style and practice had penetrated English culinary culture, she herself includes many recipes tagged "the French Way."

In response to the general consensus that Glasse's work represents the bedrock of British cookery, Pennell, writing in 1903, begged to differ: "I do not mind admitting that no other treatise on cookery owes its reputation so little to merit, and so much to chance. It was popular in its own day, I grant you. The Biographical Dictionary says that, except the Bible, it had the greatest sale in any language. . . . But almost all the eighteenth-century books shared its popularity,—only the Biographical Dictionary has not happened to hear of them."[20]

She also points out the promiscuous recipe "sharing" among those authors: "The diligence with which the authorities upon cookery in the eighteenth century borrowed one from the other, without word of acknowledgment, ought to have kept the law courts busy."[21] Indeed, Glasse had helped herself to 342 of the 972 recipes in her first edition (1747), claiming them as her own. A rival author, Ann Cook, dedicated the entire sixty-eight-page introduction to her book *Profeſſed Cookery* (1754) to a recipe-by-recipe takedown of Glasse, exposing her as an incompetent imposter.

In her refusal to kowtow to the fashion for luxury imports, Glasse provides a recipe for homemade vermicelli, which is essentially thin egg noodles. Technically, vermicelli was an extruded then dried durum wheat product; here, Glasse jerry-rigged a sieve to produce a similar effect. Her recipe, calling for only yolks and flour, is akin to the thin Piemontese pasta *tajarin*:

> To make *Vermicella.*[22]
>
> Mix Yolks of Eggs and Flower together in a pretty ſtiff Paſte, ſo as you can work it up cleverly, then roll it as thin as it is poſſible to roll the Paſte. Let it dry in the Sun; and when it is quite dry, with a very ſharp Knife cut it as thin as poſſible, and keep it in a dry Place, it will run up like little Worms, as Vermicella does; though the beſt way is to run it through a coarſe Sieve, whilſt the Paſte is ſoft. If you want ſome to be made in haſte, dry it by the Fire, and cut it ſmall. It will dry by the Fire in quarter of an Hour. This far exceeds what comes from abroad being freſher.

Just how dry a sheet of dough lying in the sun should be is perilously unclear, and the "easy" alternative of forcing dough through a sieve in lieu of an extrusion mill seems an exercise in exasperation. It is difficult to resist exhuming Samuel Johnson's misogynist dinner-party witticism about Glasse: "Women can spin very well; but they cannot make a good book of cookery."

In her recipe "A Vermicella Pudding, *with* Marrow" (bone marrow), she clarifies that the flattened sheet should dry only until to the point where you can roll it up and cut it without it breaking. "*To make a* Vermicella Pudding" appears in the third edition (1748). It includes a pound of her handmade vermicelli, a pound of butter, and ten eggs, but neither of the puddings contains cheese. She's not keen on cheese and only included it in five recipes, three of which are "rabbits" (rarebits), a dish that will later cross paths with macaroni and cheese. Her preference is for cheshire.

Despite the book's success, in 1754, Glasse was forced to sell the copyright to clear her exorbitant debts; three years later, however, she ended up in debtor's prison and largely disappeared from public record. Under new management, the appendix in the 1767 edition was expanded to include a series of foreign (to England) dishes, one of which was "Chickens and turkeys dreſſed after the Dutch way." Somehow, the reincarnation of the familiar boiled fowl with vermicelli and its outdated finishing of cinnamon and sugar had become Dutch. In the 1778 edition, actual macaroni makes its first appearance in soup form, but there is no cheese. The book expands further in 1791 to include monthly menu suggestions (something Glasse had been dead against), and a savory macaroni tart is listed but, alas, with no corresponding recipe. The households of Benjamin Franklin, George Washington, and Thomas Jefferson all reportedly had a copy of Glasse's cookbook.

Where Can You Buy Some Decent Macaroni?

La Chapelle had no need to stoop to making his own macaroni. In a subsequent pie recipe that features chicken and macaroni, he makes a point of saying, "Then get some *Italian* Maſcaronis" (italics original), clearly referring to the dried, imported product. Would hollow durum wheat macaroni have been widely or even reasonably available? A clue comes from the 1737 self-help guide *The Whole Duty of a Woman, or, An Infallible Guide to the Fair Sex: Containing Rules, Directions, and Observations, for Their Conduct and Behavior Through All Ages and Circumstances of Life, as Virgins, Wives, or Widows . . . and Receipts in Every Kind of Cookery.*[23] The only recipe with pasta is "A Vermicelli Soop," unremarkable insofar as it was filched directly from Patrick Lamb. More to the point at hand is a noteworthy list of provisions under the heading "Things to be provided when any Family is going into the Country for a Summer": "Nutmegs, Mace, Cinnamon, Cloves, Pepper, Ginger, *Jamaica* Pepper, Raiſins, Currants, Sugar Lisbon, Sugar Loaf Lump, Sugar double refin'd. Prunes, Oranges, Lemons, Anchovies, Olives, Capers, Mangoes, Oil for Salads, Vinegar, Verjuice, Tea, Coffee, Chocolate, Almonds, Cheſnuts, French Pears, Sagoe, Truffles, Morels, Macroni [*sic*], Vermicelli, Rice, Millet, Comfits, and Piſtachoe Nuts." This short list of the staple necessities for a summer getaway contains precious few native English items. The fact that both macaroni and vermicelli made the cut indicates that for the sort of family that could afford summer sojourns the supply of macaroni was reliable, knowledge about cooking it was widespread, and it was pleasing enough to be included as an essential.[24] But underlying its *desirability* was a cultural trend advanced during the Georgian era (1714–ca. 1837), as we shall see.

Entries in household manuscripts for macaroni and cheese begin in this time period, leaving clues for culinary sleuths, such as the one by a Lady Farkland from 1750. Right away, the title "Macaroni / The Italian Way" presumes an awareness of national nuances, although what she calls the Italian way was actually the English way. She specifies "pipe macaroni" meaning commercial, long-form tubular pasta, a distinction used to differentiate it from other pastas. After boiling in salted water and straining, she suggests pressing the macaroni on a cloth to dry it warning readers, "But don't break the pieces." Put it in a baking dish and mix with butter, heavy cream, and parmesan cheese. Top with more cheese and bake.

In a macaroni recipe by the English publican William Verral (1715–1761) in his self-published *Complete System of Cookery* (1759), there is a simple but revealing headnote. Verral was a second-generation pub owner, but in the kitchen, he was a Francophile, taken with their systematic sophistication. His father, owner of the White Hart Inn, had sent William to formally apprentice under the tutelage of M. Pierre de St.-Clouet, the maître d'hôtel or steward of the duke of Newcastle. Verral combined his publican knowhow with his training to create a Franco-Anglo hybrid cuisine to challenge Glasse's vitriol and bridge the divide.

Verral's two macaroni recipes lead one to wonder how well the master and his apprentice understood each other. Both entries are uniquely baffling but invaluable for their historical insights. All of Verral's recipe titles were bilingual or, more precisely, a semblance of French with puzzling English translations. Thus, we have, "Des macarons a la creme. Macaroons with cream." Despite appearances, he does actually mean macaroni. A dubious start, but it's the opening line of the recipe we are after: "Theſe are to be had at any confectioner's ſhop in London, and the newer they are the better."

Dried macaroni was no ordinary commodity but a boutique item that was sold at confectioners, specialty spice shops, and salters (trading in salt and salt-cured goods). However, it was in the many "Italian warehouses" that its mystique was curated. In a literal sense, these were shops selling Italian wares—but more to the point, grocers targeting a highbrow clientele seeking fine imports. Initially, they were run by enterprising Italians who saw an opportunity to cash in on the growing interest in Italian goods and culture—art, fashion, food, wine, literature, and music—stoked by the glamour of the Grand Tour. The shopping experience in such locations was groomed to evoke participation in that beau monde. Bartho (Barto) Valle, proprietor of London's leading Italian warehouse, "had been able to propose his own notion of gentility through what Eric Hobsbawm has defined as the 'invention of tradition.' The 'Old Italian Warehouse' was probably opened in 1749 but had created the myth of its early eighteenth-century origin. Valle portrayed himself as a descendent of a culinary dynasty for which, in reality, he was the founder."[25] This caricature of Italian-ness was fantasticated to match the romanticized expectations of his English customers and smooth over potential xenophobia (see fig. 3.2).

FIGURE 3.2. *Barto Valle's Italian Warehouse*, by Thomas Rowlandson. Valle was also a purveyor of elixirs, but the marked box of macaroni at the upper right in a single word makes a statement about the nature of the shop and the man. *Source*: Courtesy of the London Museum.

While Verral's word to the wise regarding the manufacture date may seem to echo Glasse's tongue in cheek remark that her pasta recipe "far exceeds what comes from abroad being freſher," there is a subtle difference: Verral is commenting on the quality of commercial dried macaroni, while Glasse is comparing homemade noodles to store-bought pasta. Drying durum wheat pasta in the eighteenth century required experience and precise climatic conditions, one of the reasons that pasta production met with little success outside of Italy. As macaroni products gained in popularity, less scrupulous pasta companies let protocols slip in order to meet demand. But even conscientious manufactories could not control weather conditions. What does one do with kilograms of subpar macaroni when demand is up and trade is brisk? This kept rigorously made artisan pasta highly priced—and the reserve of the well-to-do. It behooved fancy grocers to source well to keep their custom. Apparently aware of the freshness issue, G. Pastorini, of the Two Civet Cats and Olive-Tree shop, specifies "new Maccaroni" in a 1759 ad in *The Public Advertiser*. Competitors followed his lead.

Verral's "Macaroons with cream" is one of many examples of the net bifurcation macaroni had undergone throughout Europe under the influence of the French and English. The once androgynous sweet and savory macaroni of the Italian Renaissance split into two distinct tracks: One is a sweet pudding, cousin to rice pudding (whose ancestry may lie in the bizarrely popular "whitedish"—*blancmange, biancomangiare*), and the other, macaroni and cheese.[26] For contemporaries who might be confusing the sweet version of macaroni with the well-known French treat macarons, Veral clarifies: "This is not what we call macaroons of the ſweet biſcuit ſort, but a foreign paſte, the ſame as vermicelli but made very large in compariſson to that."

The second macaroni entry in Verral's *Complete System* is a macaroni pie with a faux crust—just a rim of dough around the lip of the dish akin to a dickie. The macaroni is first boiled and then stewed in gravy, with a squeeze of lemon, bringing the dish into fricassee territory. True to his mission to instruct the reader on French fundamentals, Verral concludes with allusions to the mother and daughter sauces, béchamel and mornay. Let's have a look:

> Des macarons au Parmeſan. Macaroons with Parmeſan cheeſe.
>
> For this too you muſt boil them in water firſt, with a little ſalt, pour to them a ladle of cullis, a morſel of green onion and parsley minced fine,

pepper, ſalt and nutmeg; ſtew all a few minutes, and pour into a diſh with a rim as before, ſqueeze a lemon or orange, and cover it over pretty thick with Parmeſan cheese grated very fine, bake it of a fine colour about as long a time as the laſt, and ſerve it up hot.

The French ſerve to their tables a great many diſhes with this ſort of cheeſe, and in the same manner, only ſometimes with a ſavory white ſauce.

Despite Verral's efforts to reconcile the English-French divide, *Complete System* was given a tepid reception and he did not live long enough to see it through to a second edition.

AN IN-THE-WEEDS DIGRESSION FOR LANGUAGE GEEKS

Lexicographers took some time to find etymological and orthographical terra firma and may have perpetuated the confusion. John Florio's 1598 *Queen Anna's New World of Words, Or Dictionarie of the Italian and English tongues* sets us off on the right path: "MACCARÒNI a kinde of paste meate boiled in broth, and drest with butter, cheeſe, and ſpice." By 1611, he's made an adjustment in the cooking liquid: "a kind of meat made of round pieces of paſte, boyled in water and put into a dish with butter, ſpice and grated-cheeſe upon them."

In *A Dictionarie of the French and English Tongues* (1611), the entry for macaroni is under "MACARONS: little fritter-like bunnes, or thicke Loſenges compounded of sugar, Almonds, Roſewater, and Muske, pounded together, and baked with a gentle fire; alſo the Italian *Macaroni*; lumps, or gobbets of boyled paſte ſerved up in butter, and ſtrewed over with ſpice, and grated cheeſe." Gobbets, from the Old French *gobet*: piece, mouthful, or lump.

The renowned Italian dictionary *Vocabolario degli accademici della Crusca* (1729–1738) defines "Maccheroni" as "a food of note made of wheat flour paste thinly rolled out in sheets and cooked in water." Here is the sub-entry: "Thicker than macaroni water, is said about a man of little intellect."

(*continued on next page*)

(continued from previous page)
Followed by the expression "tossing cheese on macaroni," meaning the ultimate pairing.

The first edition of Samuel Johnson's (1709–1784) dictionary (1755) has only "MACAROON, [*macarone, Italian*], a coarse, rude, low fellow; whence *macaronick* poetry in which the language is purposely corrupted." By the tenth edition in 1792, editors have added "a kind of ſweet biſcuit made of flour, almonds, eggs, and ſugar." The 1812 edition, "improved by the best authorities," adds this entry: "MACARONI [*macarone*, Ital.] A fop; one who dresses fantastically; one who follows every ridiculous mode of dress," a definition we will explore later, but still, no joy. After many revisions, the work is entirely overhauled in 1818 by Reverend Henry John Todd. His entry for macaroni repeats Florio's 1598 definition and adds, "A favorite dish among the Italians; and now common, in our own country, at dinners; a sort of vermicelli." Surely to the chagrin of the French, under MACARO'ON he has the same "kind of sweet biscuit" but adds the following brackets: "[from the Italian word; whence *macaron*, Fr.]."

Richard Rolt, seeking to enlighten fellow merchants, compiled *A New Dictionary of Trade and Commerce* (1761), but apparently he did not trade in macaroni. "MACARONI, or *Macaroon*. A delicious cake paſste, or ſweetmeat, made with the flour of rice, being ſomewhat thicker than the little finger. There is a great trade made of this paſte in all parts of Italy: but, in general, all the paſtes made of this rice flour are called farinelli."

Though succinct to the point of confusion, the French stepped up to the plate in the *Dictionnaire portatif de cuisine* (1772): "A sort of Italian paste which is cooked in a pot of broth, made with flour and cheese." A copy of this dictionary was among the culinary works in Thomas Jefferson's collection.

The stately *Dictionnaire de l'Académie française* didn't acknowledge macaroni until its fourth edition in 1776: "MACARONI. A word borrowed from Italian. Paste made with flour, cheese, & some other ingredients, made into soups & other dishes. Only used in the plural." And the example they give is "*De bons macaronis*"—Some good macaroni.

A 1797 English dictionary with Spanish translations starts off with "MACAROONE. "a courſe, rude, low fellow," followed by "a kind of ſweet biscuit made of flour, almonds, eggs, and sugar." But tucked at the bottom as a subscript comes the clearest definition yet: "A paſte made of flour and water, and formed in the ſhape of the barrel of a large quill." Quite an evolution from gobbets.

In his 1769 annotated translation of Louis Francois Henri de Menon's *Les soupers de la cour ou L'art de travailler toutes sortes d'alimens* (1755), B. Clermont underscores the dubious quality of imported macaroni. The obvious translation of the title should be "Court Suppers, or The Art of Working All Sorts of Foods, to Serve on the Best Tables, Following the Four Seasons," but Clermont preferred the hammering *The Professed Cook; or, The Modern Art of Cookery, Pastry, and Confectionary, Made Plain and Easy. Consisting of the most approved Methods in the French as well as English Cookery. In Which the French Names of all the different Dishes are given and explained, whereby every Bill of Fare becomes intelligible and familiar*. The title is longer still, but this suffices to get the gist. His target audience was the English Francophile, eager not only to walk the walk but talk the talk. For the purposes of a food historian, his translation of the recipe "*Macaroni*, entremets" is both enlightening and deceptive. The French original has a headnote for readers unfamiliar with macaroni, literally translated as "This is a paste that comes to us from Italy. The best is found in the Spice shop in Prouvaires St." Clermont, on the other hand, gives us:

Macaroni: An Italian Paſte.

> The French Author names in what ſtreet the beſt is ſold in Paris; but I ſshall not take upon me to be ſo affirmative for London; it is however neceſſary to obſerve, that it is very apt to be muſty, which is very eaſily found out by ſmelling, and ſo of all Italian Paſte in general.

CHEESE AS YOU PLEASE: KEEPING IT LOCAL

After telling readers where they can get the pasta, Menon goes on to give a simple recipe for macaroni and cheese: "Cook it well as you would rice in a fatty broth until it is well cooked and thick; add some grated gruyere cheese; place it in the dish; put on some fine parmesan and gruyere and brown it in the oven until the sauce has reduced" (translation mine). Clermont makes a rather quick business of it: "It is to be boiled in good Broth; when it is very tender and thick, mix ſome Parmeſan Cheeſe with it, or *Gruyere*, put it upon the Table-diſh, and colour it with a Salamander."

A critical eye will have noted that Clermont's translation presents gruyere as an option rather than the main cheese, overlooking a key turning point. Originally a Swiss cheese, the French had been producing their own version for centuries by this time. From a practical standpoint, it would have been cheaper and easier to obtain on the French market and perhaps more amenable to the French palate. Gruyere's appearance in print in conjunction with macaroni and cheese marks a noteworthy shift. Menon had made his mark with the cookbook *La cuisinière bourgeoise* (1746). In a field dominated by male cooks catering to the upper class, he made the daring move to write this cooking manual specifically for a female readership: women who were either managing their own middle-class kitchen or cooking for a bourgeoise family—untitled gentry sufficiently well off to afford a female cook but not affluent enough to have the coveted male chef.[27] Although *Court Suppers* speaks to a higher economic strata, the choice of gruyere is still a social statement about affordability and accessibility, in addition to putting a decidedly French accent on the dish.

Here's a slow-motion view of Menon's basic macaroni recipe: As the pasta plumps and softens in the meat broth, it soaks up the savory flavors and releases starch into the broth, thickening it. Gruyere cheese is then added to this concentrated gravy. It is milder than parmesan and has a lower melting point, rendering a macaroni and cheese that is not just creamy but luxuriously gooey. It will bubble nicely in the oven and form an unctuous golden crust. So, whether or not gruyere made a political or patriotic statement, it was a welcomed boon to the macaroni and cheese profile. Given Menon's dominance as the culinary authority of his age, his stamp of approval on gruyere gave others the confidence to use it, and eventually it came to characterize French-style macaroni and cheese.

The final deviation mentioned in Clermont's translation is the salamander, sometimes referred to as a hot shovel or, less frequently, a cheese iron. A salamander is a metal disk with a long handle that is heated in glowing embers until red hot. It is then placed over the baking dish or pot to brown (sometimes scorch) the top of the food. In essence, a manual broiler, one of the hacks of yesteryear—a practical solution in times when ovens were not commonplace. And even if you had one, you weren't going to fire up the oven just to brown your macaroni.

In "Macarony Soop," again from Menon's *Court Suppers*, Clermont puts his own spin on the cheese selection in the addendum. The recipe unfolds like this: After boiling the macaroni in broth, it is arranged in a baking dish in alternating layers with grated parmesan. A bit of extra broth is ladled on, and the dish is set to stew slowly in the hearth. Once fully cooked, more broth is added as needed, and the salamander is put to work. It is important to note that "soup" in this context did not necessarily imply a soupy result but rather that the method at some stage involved boiling in broth.

At the end of the recipe, Clermont offers this personal observation for his English readers: "N.B. I have had this done with mixing good mild Cheſhire Cheeſe, to ſave Parmeſsan Cheeſe; it anſwered very well." He too chose to swap out part of the expensive imported cheese for a local one, introducing yet another nuance to the flavor and texture profile. This adaptation, issuing from a culinary authority, would encourage the spread of macaroni and cheese in areas where the price of parmesan was prohibitive.

Menon moves macaroni and cheese from simple to superlative in the ultrachic "*Tourte de Macaroni au Zéphir*." Even the title exudes loftiness, referencing the Greek god of the gentle western wind, Zephyr—a nod not to gassy inconveniences but to the airy quality of the crust. The preparation involves layering two disks of puff pastry, one atop the other. While baking, they will puff up and create a cavity. The fully baked top crust is carefully cut away and the cavity filled with macaroni.

For the filling, macaroni is boiled in rich broth with a dollop of bacon grease. When it has reduced and thickened, grated parmesan is added to make a creamy, cheesy sauce. After loading the decadent mixture into the flaky pie shell, it is doused with a ladleful of beef coulis (gravy). Finally, the pastry dome is placed on top and voilà! A spectacular sight and tantalizing dish. Taking a cue from Clermont, I have recreated the recipe for you using both parmesan and cheddar—and it answered very well![28]

Menon's success as a cookbook writer was unparalleled in his day, with his works going through multiple editions for more than one hundred years. On the wings of such success, they would have made easy passage to the American colonies—in fact, Thomas Jefferson gifted a French edition, the one dedicated to ladies, to his daughter Martha.

TOURTE DE MACARONI AU ZÉPHIR

Makes one small *croute*

2 7-inch (18 cm) disks of homemade puff pastry, each .4 inches (1 cm) thick

1 egg, lightly beaten

1 Tbsp flour

2 cups (225 g) long-form macaroni broken into small pieces

2 cups (500 mL) rich quality beef broth

1 Tbsp bacon grease

2 1/2 oz (60 g) parmesan, grated

2 1/2 oz (60 g) sharp cheddar, grated

1 cup (250 mL) brown beef gravy

Cut a hole in the center of one of the pastry disks, leaving a 1.5-in. (3-cm) border. Brush a 1.5in. (3 cm) edge around the outer perimeter of the uncut disk with some of the egg yolk and place the dough ring on top. Flour the inside of the hole. Take the internal cutout and roll it out to 7 inches (18 cm) and score decoratively. Brush the ring layer with the rest of the egg yolk and place the rolled-out disk on top. Refrigerate 1 hour. Freeze 15 minutes. Preheat the oven to 430°F (220°C).

Move the pastry from the freezer directly to the oven. Bake 10 minutes and reduce the heat to 375°F (190°C). Bake until golden brown, approximately 45 minutes. Remove and cut away the top crust. Pull out any doughy layers from inside. Cool completely.

Boil the macaroni in broth and bacon grease on medium high until soft. There should be some broth in order to make the sauce. Off heat, add the cheese and toss to combine until the cheese has melted. Spoon the mixture into the crust, pour a ladleful of hot gravy over the top, cover, and serve. [For the best result, cook the base and the lid separately.]

The inclusion of alternative cheeses in two household manuscripts from 1765 adds further evidence of the tendency to adapt and adopt. One from Ireland titled "To drefs Macherony" starts with the instruction "Wash your macaroni very well," a clear indication that it is imported durum wheat macaroni, a product sold in bulk and covered with surface dust and dirt. Once cooked, the recipe gives a choice of "Parmisan" or gloucester cheese. It is stirred over the fire with a half pint of cream and finished with a salamander.[29]

The second manuscript, penned by a professional scribe, contains a "doublet," meaning, the same entry put in twice. The first is called "Mackerony Cheese" and the second "Maccarony Cheese." (The spelling would take another century to work itself out.) Both call for "Two Ounces of the best Gloucester Cheese, 4 Ounces of Cheshire." The grated cheeses are pounded in a mortar with two or three eggs along with "White Wine" in the first recipe and "Sack [sherry] or Mountain Wine" in the second. The thick cheesy mass is poured over cooked macaroni and in comes the salamander. One supposes that the eggs would be partially cooked upon contact with the hot macaroni. While there is a lack of protocol ingredients, such as broth, butter, cream, and parmesan, they are still recognizably macaroni and cheese. Besides radically changing the flavor and texture profile, both gloucester and cheshire cheeses have a naturally occurring orangey tinge, adding a novelty to the mix: color, a topic we will explore further in the next chapter.

Historic Macaroni and Cheese Haters

The aversion to parmesan cheese is expressed in no uncertain terms as early as 1673 in the treatise by John Ray (1627–1705) based on one of his observations while traveling in Italy in the early 1660s. Ray was a parson-naturalist—clerics who, like Paracelsus, attempted to bridge the gap between science and theology, asserting that the very complexity of the natural world was proof positive of God as the creator. In his description of pasta, he maintains a detached, scientific stance: "*Paſte* made into strings like packthread or thongs of whit-leather (which if greater they call *Macaroni*, if leſſer *Vermicelli*) they cut in pieces and put in their pots as we do oat-meal to make the *meneſtra* or broth of, much eſteemed by the common-people. Theſe boil'd and oil'd with a little cheeſe ſcraped upon them they eat as we do buttered wheat or rice. The making of theſe is a trade and myſstery; and in every great town you ſhall ſee ſeveral ſhops of them." It is only when discussing the cheese that he breaks character: "They ſcrape or grate *Cheeſe* upon all their diſhes even of fleſh, accounting that it gives the meat a good rellifh; which to thofe that are unaccuftomed makes it rather naufeous or loathfome."

In the book documenting his extensive travels in Italy, the French cartographer Albert Jouvin de Rochefort recounted his repulsion for both macaroni and the cheese. His enjoyment of the white wine he had in Genoa turns sour as he describes the food:

> I ate a strong potage called *Maccaroni*, or *Vermicelli*, common in all of Italy. It is made from durum wheat shaped like slender rods or rather like earthworms by way of a small mill, needed to draw out the stiff dough. They serve it to you at the table after cooking the food in a pot; you are obliged to put a grated cheese on it which is made in the mountains expressly for this. But those who are not accustomed to this strong-tasting potage cannot eat it without being inconvenienced by this paste, which is only half cooked, though the Italians exclaim their delight with the words, *Maccaroni bene mio*. Macaroni my love.

His countryman Jean Batiste Père Labat (1663–1738), a Dominican monk, published his own encounter with the dish in his 1730 travelogue. He warns his French readers not to confuse macaroni with macarons, explaining that it is a food made with dough of the finest flour but without leavening. The stiff dough is forced through a mold with holes, and the result is called macaroni. "The consumption they make of pasta in Italy is surprising. Those who have not left the old ways prefer bread to macaroni." He describes how it is prepared in broth and seasoned with a bit of cinnamon or pepper, but he says he waved away the usual addition of cheese, as he couldn't stomach the taste, try as he might. As his travels in Italy wore on, he found it so repugnant that, toward the end of his stay, he took to calling it a "detestable dish" owing to the pungently disagreeable cheese. He had come across several "Manufacturers of *Macaroni & Vermicelli*" in San Remo, a town in northwestern Italy very near Nice. Notably, he remarks that it had already spread to Provence and "has been introduced into Paris where it has also started being used." Labat can be credited as the first to sound the warning: "When the pasta is fresh & well made, it is white, and they yellow with age, & take on a disagreeable odor."

FIGURE 3.3. *Still Life with Plate of Macaroni* (Natura morta con piatto di maccheroni) (ca. 1750), by Giacomo Nani. *Source*: Courtesy of Archivio fotografico Palazzo Reale di Napoli/Ministero della Cultura.

MACARONI ON THE MOVE

He wore upon his head a macaroni hat about the size of a small tea saucer.

"VICE IN ITS PROPER SHAPE" (1789), ISAIAH THOMAS, WORCESTER, MA

The idea that a young man's education was complete when he had traveled to the continent to bask in the cultures of France and Italy—or, for the adventurous few, even Greece—was not entirely new when, in 1660, it became formalized as "The Grand Tour." While some would push on to Naples, for most the ultimate destination was the Eternal City. There, in theory, their days were spent buzzing from monument to gallery to ancient ruins. However, like students today on a semester abroad, some Grand Tourists slogged through the heavy burden of imposed cultural enrichment, lacking the sensitivity and intellectual acuity to appreciate the opportunity their parents had bankrolled. They preferred playing cards, going to parties, and the *dolce far niente*—whiling away the time. This did not stop those who had done their tour of duty from flaunting their superiority through affected mannerisms and extravagant attire, accessories, and wigs—accoutrements picked up on the continent. It was the eighteenth-century equivalent of a T-shirt that reads "I went on the Grand Tour (and you didn't)."

In order to underscore and overstate their exclusivity, they formed the "Macaroni Club" in 1764, which grew into a veritable subculture with distinct characteristics. "Macaroni" was a metonymic symbol condensing the entire experience abroad into the quintessential Italian food they had so frequently encountered in Rome and Naples.[30] The name was also a parody of the Beefsteak Club, an exclusive gentleman's club that feted comradery, hearty living, and the glory of a good steak.[31] In contrast, members of the Macaroni Club were a pack of notoriously obnoxious, privileged young men. They deliberately paraded their ostentatious behavior and dress to stir the envy of less fortunate wannabes. As the circle widened and fell into the clumsy hands of uninitiated imitators, it became an object of grotesque mockery. The entertainment value therein inspired songs, plays, and poems along with a large collection of cartoons and illustrations lampooning them in every possible guise (see fig. 3.4).

A popular magazine writer from the period rendered a colorful origin story, "The macaronis are the offspring of a body, a many-headed monster in the Pall-Mall, produced by a demoniac committee of depraved taste and exaggerated fancy, conceived in the courts of France and Italy, and brought forth in England."[32] In 1770, the *Oxford Magazine* took a satirical stab at them: "There is indeed a kind of animal, neither male nor female, a thing of the neuter gender, lately started up amongst us. It is called a Macaroni. It talks without meaning, it smiles without pleasantry, it eats without appetite, it rides without exercise, it wenches without passion."

"Macaroni" was used to express a phenomenon that had taken root centuries before as the "English Italianate." Writing in 1564, Roger Ascham appropriated the term with a negative slant, fueled by the English proverb *Inglese italianato è diabolo incarnato* (the English Italianate is the devil incarnate).[33] He cautioned parents that without a rigorous chaperone, all those young men, so eager to get to the continent, would fall prey to the

FIGURE 3.4. "A Macaroni French Cook" (1772): one of a large collection of caricatures depicting the macaroni fashion phenomenon, most of which are attributed to the satirical artist Philip Dawe. The print was issued by Mary (née George) and Matthias Darly, who published numerous macaroni-themed cartoons in the 1770s. *Source*: Courtesy of the Prints and Photographs Division, Library of Congress. Public domain.

lax morals of company who had not benefitted from a regimented English upbringing. The fear was palpable. George Gascoigne, in a verse epistle from 1572, likewise warned that young men of an impressionable age were susceptible to adopting Italianate costume and manners, a posturing they proved loath to abandon once they arrived home.[34]

The playwright Ben Jonson made the earliest association between mannerisms and actual macaroni in *Cynthia's Revels; Or, The Fountain of Self-Love* (1600). Someone in the play describes a character in an upcoming theatre production: "He doth learn to make strange Sauces, to eat Anchovies, Maccaroni, Bovoli, Fagioli, and Caviare, because he loves 'em; speaks as he speaks, looks, walks, goes so in Cloaths and Fashion: is in all as if he were moulded of him." The type exhibits other habits, such as "frequenting a dancing School, and grievously torturing strangers with Inquisition after his grace in his Galliard. . . . He treads nicely like the Fellow that walks upon Ropes; especially the first Sunday of his Silk-stockings."

Macaroni culture and fashion sailed across the Atlantic as both tangible and intangible cargo from Europe. As early as 1769, "maccaroni waistcoats" are seen advertised in *Rind's Virginia Gazette*. Referring to someone as a Macaroni became commonplace, met with say-no-more immediacy. Despite the higher financial investment, young American men also participated in the Grand Tour, mingling in the same circles as their European counterparts.[35] Popular theater productions imported to the colonies from England and France frequently featured the Macaroni, a stock character built upon the lace handkerchief-carrying fop of Restoration theater with roots in antiquity. The phenomenon itself was nothing new, and would go by many other names—gallants, bloods, bucks, beaux, fribbles, dandy, exquisites, and swells. It was a cultural counterpoint, akin to today's queer culture and the "Noodle Boy" aesthetic.

Regardless of where one's politics fell, colonists still looked to Europe as the last word in culture and made a concerted effort to emulate their betters to fend off the country yokel label. It was a losing battle. So long as Americans sought European approval, belittling them for their perceived shortcomings would be irresistible. And how better to mock them than through the graceless Macaroni caricature, Yankee Doodle Dandy—the hapless sod who thought sticking a feather in his hat could mask his backwardness? Taking the knife by the handle, the ditty was turned into a patriotic anthem. Through its many interpretations and manifestations, the concept of the Macaroni had thoroughly permeated eighteenth- and early nineteenth- century society, adding to the visibility and desirability of the foodstuff from which it had arisen. Indeed, the first advertisement for macaroni imports into the American colonies appeared in New York in 1772, coinciding with the fashion craze. What began as a trickle would expand into a steady stream of shipments along the Eastern Seaboard. Macaroni had landed.[36]

Colonial FOMO

Americans relied heavily on British and, to a lesser extent, French cookbooks as a resource to keep abreast on what to eat, how to cook it, and how to serve at table. Fear of being out of fashion drove book sales. By the end of the seventeenth century, most people in Virginia were native born and, as the wealthy landowner and historian Robert Beverley (1667–1722) noted in *The History and Present State of Virginia* (1724), "the gentry pretend to have [insist on having] their Victuals dressed and served up as Nicely as at the best Tables in London."

Achieving European culinary standards rested most often in the skilled hands of enslaved cooks and the network of household domestics, as well as the ancillary bondspeople charged with dairying, animal husbandry, cider making, and the like. The historian Kelley Fanto Deetz suggests that "the currency of proper food was so important that the teaching of basic reading became essential to guarantee culinary delight."[37] Beyond keeping pace with the latest trends, it was the day-to-day reliance on the flow of family meals that made the cook indispensable to the tranquility, health, and overall well-being of the household.

One of the most popular cookbooks circulating in the colonies was *The Experienced English Housekeeper* (1769) by Elizabeth Raffald (1733–1781), a practical manual that appealed to the middle classes, along with Hannah Glasse's anti-Gallic *Art of Cookery*.[38] Perhaps not coincidentally, while Macaroni culture was hitting its stride, Raffald includes the recipe "*To dreſ* Macaroni *with* Permaſent Cheeſe," which would go on to become one of the most enduring and repeatedly plagiarized versions of macaroni and cheese: "BOIL four Ounces of Macaroni 'till it be quite tender, and lay it on a Sieve to drain, then put it in a Toffing Pan, with about a Gill of good Cream, a Lump of Butter rolled in Flour, boil it five Minutes, pour it on a Plate, lay all over it Permafent Cheefe toafted; fend it to the Table on a Water Plate, for it foon goes cold."

Raffald was an exceptionally industrious woman. In addition to the many pies she had her hands in—from her cooking school to a confectionery shop to her main profession as housekeeper—she reputedly also had sixteen daughters. Her recipe for macaroni and cheese reflects her pragmatic, no-nonsense approach, but it was by no means budget fare. Macaroni and parmesan were still luxury import items; she uses quality cream, not milk, enriched with the clever English thickening method of butterballs rolled in flour to bypass making a roux. The top is browned, and she duly recommends the water plate (see chapter 2) to keep it from congealing.

For a time, her interpretation of macaroni and cheese seemed to be set in stone, with few daring (or bothering) to challenge it. Instead, direct rip-offs and thinly veiled versions of her recipe would reappear in numerous cookbooks without so much as a wink of acknowledgement to her.[39] The incessant plagiarism of her recipe can be ascribed to five factors: 1) The recipe was easy to execute; 2) it was English with no French pretense or upper-class bravado; 3) Raffald had proven herself in the market; 4) she was not a high-profile male chef, so it was like borrowing a recipe from a neighbor lady; and 5) stealing was faster than reinventing the wheel. Richard Briggs's nearly verbatim "*Macaroni a la Parmazan*" in *The New Art of Cookery* spread the recipe in Philadelphia in 1792 and Boston in 1798. Raffald's macaroni and cheese became so ubiquitous that variations of it found their way into numerous family recipe collections, spanning both English and American households over the following century. Such monotony ensued that it was refreshing to happen upon a family recipe like the one below with reminiscences of Raffald but also a dash of originality and a French nod.

To make Maccaroni.

Take about half a Handfull of Macaroni, boil it till it is tender, take 5 or 6 Spoonfuls of Cream; the Yolks of 3 Eggs; put this into the Stew Pan & shake it up together till as thick as a Fricassee; put it in ye Dish & put some old cheese over it in very thin Slices & brown it with a Salamander.

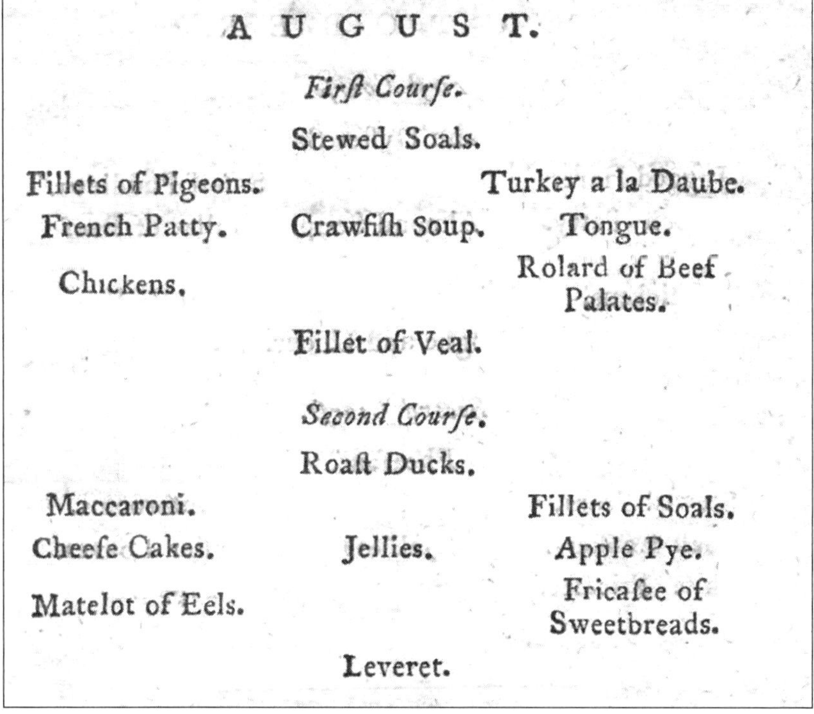

A U G U S T.

Firſt Courſe.

Stewed Soals.

Fillets of Pigeons. Turkey a la Daube.

French Patty. Crawfiſh Soup. Tongue.

Chickens. Rolard of Beef Palates.

Fillet of Veal.

Second Courſe.

Roaſt Ducks.

Maccaroni. Fillets of Soals.

Cheeſe Cakes. Jellies. Apple Pye.

Matelot of Eels. Fricaſee of Sweetbreads.

Leveret.

FIGURE 3.5. A trendy bill of fare from E. Spencer's *The Modern Cook: And Frugal Housewife's Compleat Guide to Every Branch in Displaying Her Table to the Greatest Advantage* (1782). Macaroni was featured on menus as both a first and second course offering, keeping company with a wide variety of dishes throughout the calendar year. *Source*: Public domain.

One wonders how big her hands were, or how many people she intended to serve.

By 1795, the time had come for *The New Experienced English Housekeeper*. The byline "Written purely from her own experience" may have even been true, judging from the macaroni recipe. The "authoress" Sarah Martin had figured out that the English favorite, stewed cheese—a rich sauce thickened with egg yolk—was well suited to macaroni. For those who fancy it, she suggests putting the macaroni on toast before pouring on the cheese sauce. which marries the concept of Welsh rarebit to macaroni and cheese.

MACARONI ON TOAST WITH STEWED CHEESE

5.5oz (150 g) long-form macaroni, broken into short lengths
3 Tbsp (45 g) butter
1 1/2 cups (355 mL) heavy cream
3 large egg yolks, beaten lightly
3 thick slices of buttered toast
3 1/2 oz (100 g) sharp cheddar, grated ([it would have been orange at this time in England])
Salt to taste

Cook the macaroni in boiling salted water until soft. Drain and put back in the pan with 1 Tbsp of the butter.

For the sauce, heat the cream in a small saucepan until it is simmering but not boiling. Then slowly whisk the cream into the yolks in a small bowl. Pour the mixture back into the pan and heat gently, stirring with a wooden spoon until thick (about 4 minutes). Off heat, stir in the rest of the butter and cheddar. Prepare the buttered toast.

Heap macaroni onto the toast. Pour over the hot cheese sauce and serve immediately. Salt to taste.

Meanwhile, Back in Italy

A role model for the Macaronis may have been the infamous womanizer, bad boy, and aristocratic wannabe Giacomo Girolamo Casanova (1725–1798). His parents were both actors, and while they were moderately successful, they did not frequent the upper crust circles that Casanova aspired to—although it would later come to light that his biological father may have been a nobleman.[40] They did see to his education and, according to Casanova's colorful memoirs, he went on to receive a degree in law. In a brush with fate, he was on hand to save the life of a nobleman who, out of gratitude, granted Casanova a lifetime allowance which, to put it prosaically, saved his bacon. Casanova curated his life to socialize with the VIPs of the day, eventually rubbing elbows with such luminaries as Rousseau, Mozart, and Benjamin Franklin, among others. However, his reputation for imprudent behavior grew, racking up a list of improprieties that eventually landed him in a Venetian prison in 1755 for libertinism, owing most notably to his numerous affairs with married women and open disregard for religion.

The prison was rather top tier as far as jails go, but confinement is never pleasurable, particularly for one as restless as Casanova. To make matters worse, he had no idea when his sentence would end, so he set about orchestrating his escape. The inmates in this holding facility were afforded certain privileges and could lodge requests for items from outside. They were even given a small petty cash allowance, which played into Casanova's scheme.

He had requested access to the larger room adjacent to his own so that he could get some exercise, his cell being rather cramped. There he happened upon an iron door bolt, which got him thinking. He could befriend his fellow inmate Marino Balbi, the friar incarcerated in the attic room above his, and ask him to chip away a hole in the floor with the bolt, through which Casanova could enter his cell and escape through a window onto the roof.

In order to discreetly pass the bolt to the friar, he devised a ruse involving the prison guard, Lorenzo. He requested a copy of the recently published Bible, a hefty tome in which he could conceal the bolt inside the spine of the book, and have it presented to the cleric as a gift. As a further distraction, he also requested the fixings to make the friar a platter of macaroni and cheese. The brief snippet below from his memoirs offers a glimpse of Italian macaroni. It was swimming in butter, but the dairy-based or fricassee-style sauce was not the Italian Way. Here is Casanova's account of the escapade: "Lorenzo appears with a big boiling pot of macaroni. I melted butter on the stove and spread grated cheese out onto the plates. Then, with a slotted spoon, I filled each with a layer of macaroni, butter, and cheese and I kept on until the friar's dish was full and the butter flowed up to its rim. I carefully put this platter on the book, taking care that the butter didn't spill over." Lorenzo was duped, and the plan came off without a hitch, or almost did. In their escape, the two men scurried onto the roof and entered back into the building from another window. A passerby saw them but assumed they were visitors who got trapped in the building. He alerts the superintendent who comes to escort them out through the front door.

Seizing the opportunity, Casanova flees for Paris. Unable (or unwilling) to quell his impetuous nature, his adventures continued unabated until his death in 1798. In a curious twist of fate, a butter-laden dish of macaroni and cheese had played a part in solidifying Casanova's status as a legend in his own time.

Chapter Four

JEFFERSON, HEMINGS, AND THE MACARONI MYTHOLOGIES

Few periods in the history of macaroni and cheese present such a dense thicket of gastronomic mythology as the Jeffersonian age. We have thus far traced the trajectory of macaroni and cheese from its Italian roots to England and France and have firmly established its arrival into the American colonies. It was only after macaroni and cheese had become well entrenched in the American pantry in the twentieth century that origin stories pointing first to Thomas Jefferson and later to his enslaved chef James Hemings hit the mainstream. Through repetition and unchecked flourishes, a paradigm or groupthink emerged that became impenetrable, preventing facts and informed speculation from breaking through the calcified layers.

You may be familiar with aspects of the tales: Jefferson, while ambassador to France, went to Italy or sent someone there to purchase a machine to extrude macaroni and had it shipped to the United States.[1] Some claim the machine broke or was not durable.[2] Others say that he designed a macaroni machine to be built at Monticello from observations in Italy.[3] It is also said that Jefferson, devoted to French cookery, even cooked with Hemings and brought back a recipe for making macaroni (and cheese) from France (or Italy), where he had lived for a time, as it was unavailable in the United States.[4] The famous "Macaroni pie" may ring a few bells, attributed variously to Jefferson, James Hemings, or Peter Hemings, but never the more likely suspects: Honoré Julien or Edith Fossett.[5] The pie, it seems, was a hit and the rest is history.[6] Other tellings include the supposed original

James Hemings recipe, either explicitly or through insinuation.[7] Subsequently, attribution for the introduction and popularization of the dish in the United States transferred onto James Hemings, overshadowing the complex and tragic story of a fascinating figure in African American history by burying his legacy in macaroni.[8]

FIGURE 4.1. Budweiser advertisement disseminating misinformation. *Source*: *Saturday Evening Post*, March 22, 1948. Public domain.

What follows here is a painstaking unveiling based on the historical record and material culture, shedding light on what can be reasonably speculated, separating out fact from what must be put to rest as wishful thinking, and uncovering overlooked aspects in the Jefferson-Hemings narrative as it intertwines with macaroni and cheese.

Early Years: Acquiring a Taste for French Cuisine

Thomas Jefferson had an undeniable penchant for macaroni and cheese, a dish which, by then, was transitioning from food fashion to culinary fixture in England and France. One of the most frequently cited quotations about Jefferson's affinity for French food comes from the fiery populist Patrick Henry. He chided his sometimes friend, sometimes foe for having returned to Virginia so Frenchified that he "abjured his native vittles in favor of French cuisine." His clipped quip glossed over the complex underpinnings driving Jefferson and other culinary Francophiles.

Jefferson was a great admirer of French style and refinement, British philosophy, science, and political thought, and Italian art and architecture. He felt that selectively importing the best Europe had to offer was akin to sowing seeds of culture on American soil, where it could be nurtured in a more fertile environment. From this perspective, the burgeoning nation was not an underling mimicking its betters but a strategist acquiring the means to emerge as a world leader. France set the bar for good taste, and, as La Varenne's publisher Davide had predicted, other nations saw the light and fell in line. Virginia underwent such a cultural awakening around 1725, after which ignorance about French cuisine, etiquette, and table service came at a social cost: "No hostess would wish to risk the family standing by being seen as lagging behind with respect to fashion. To do so would have been tantamount to an admission that the family had fallen on hard times or was unsophisticated. If such an event occurred, the status of the husband, not to mention the family, would suffer. . . . By serving such fashionable foods, currently in vogue, a hostess, not only flattered her visitors, but also demonstrated the correct decorum for the dining table."[9]

Jefferson's acculturation to French cuisine and fine wines began when he was an impressionable young man studying at the College of William & Mary. His sharp intellect so impressed William Small, his Scottish-born professor of natural philosophy, that he was invited to join the Friday dinner gatherings hosted by Royal Governor Francis Faquier at the Governor's Palace in Williamsburg.[10]

Faquier's father, a French Huguenot, was among the many who emigrated to Britain with the exodus following the revocation of the Edict of Nantes in 1685, an event that placed this sizable Protestant community in danger. With a successful career as a financier in London, he went on to become director of the Bank of England, bequeathing his substantial fortune to his son. When Faquier the younger received his gubernatorial appointment in 1758 and made the trek to Virginia, it's plausible that French cuisine was the default dinner fare given his wealth and background. The kitchen at the Governor's Palace would have been kitted out with a stew stove, a fixture long used in France, essential for executing the intricate dishes that accompanied an array of imported wines.

It was quite an enlightening experience for a young man. In keeping with Jefferson's inquiring mind and growing appreciation of fine dining, he very likely endeavored to explore the inner workings of a French-style kitchen in a prominent home. This may account for the sketch he made in the 1760s, envisioning the kitchen he planned to construct in the South Pavilion of his future home in Monticello.

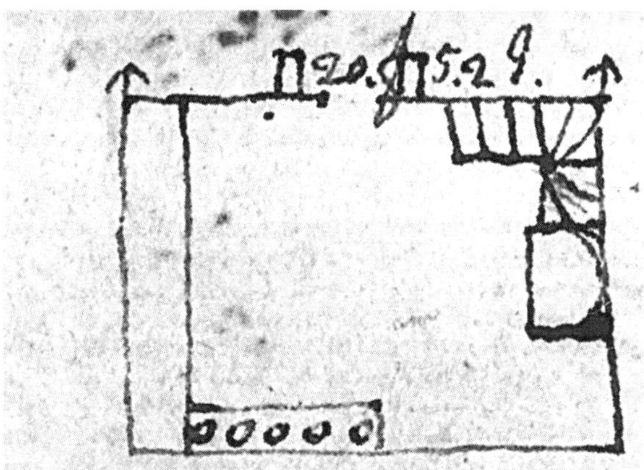

FIGURE 4.2. Jefferson's thumbnail sketch of the placement of the stew stove in the Monticello kitchen, what the French called a *potager*. *Source*: Courtesy of the Huntington Library. Public domain.

FIGURE 4.3. Detail of a stew stove from Bartolomeo Scappi's *Opera*, 1570. *Source*: Public domain.

Archaeologists believe that the five circles in the floor plan represent a stew stove. Recent excavations showing evidence of a very early stew stove seem to confirm this theory. Such an innovation in colonial America would have been a mark of sophistication. A second stove was erected atop the original in later years. It is unlikely that the second installation was a new and improved model as the concept had changed little since the first illustration in Bartolomeo Scappi's *Opera* (1570) (see fig. 4.3).

It is, in essence, a long brick structure akin to a kitchen counter. The cooktop is fashioned by leaving a series of square apertures in the masonry, each fitted with a cage-like receptacle set inside. These iron baskets cradled embers, which served as the heat source shoveled in from the fire in the hearth. Once the glowing embers are in place, a breathable mesh, perforated metal plate, or iron grate is positioned on top and you are ready to cook. With experience, a good degree of control could be achieved by putting more or less fuel in the cage structures and replenishing as needed.

Pans could easily rest on the surface and be removed or manipulated quickly without stooping. The cook had more control over stew stove pans, which did not require elongated handles or legs (hence the name "spider pans"). Nonetheless, stew stoves did not replace hearth cooking. It was not until the widespread adoption of wood-burning and eventually gas stoves that hearth cookery became obsolete—and a sign of backwardness. All affluent households in the Chesapeake region were also equipped with ovens, although for standard everyday baking, the Dutch oven with nubby legs was preferred.

The kitchen in Jefferson's design may reflect the setup of the facility in which Ursula Granger, Monticello's first known enslaved cook, labored. Jefferson had begun work on his home in Monticello in 1768 and moved into the construction site in 1770. In 1772, he married the twenty-three-year-old widow, Martha Wayles Skelton, and the newlyweds lived in the South Pavilion, the only habitable part of the house at the time. Soon after her arrival, Martha specifically requested that Ursula be acquired as their cook and domestic manager, a testament to her firsthand knowledge of her skill and reliability. Ursula played a vital role in the management of Monticello, so much so that Jefferson would later write he knew of no one more capable and trustworthy than her. She came to Monticello with her children, and efforts were later made to procure her husband, George, who would become the only Black overseer at the estate.

In an oral history narrative taken many years later, Ursula's son, Isaac, recounted that Mrs. Jefferson would go down to the detached kitchen to read recipes to his mother, as was common practice. Quite possibly, the cookbook referred to was Hannah Glasse's *The Art of Cookery Made Plain and Easy*. In Isaac's recollection, Jefferson himself only ventured into the kitchen to wind the clock. Ursula ran a full-scale kitchen, juggling that with her duties as housekeeper, laundress, and dairymaid. Isaac noted that even when the Jeffersons were alone, there were never fewer than eight dishes in the main meal, and sometimes even more.

THE MACARONI ENCOUNTERS

Philip Mazzei at Large in Virginia

In 1773, a fortuitous encounter occurred when the Italian Filippo (a.k.a. Philip) Mazzei (1730–1816) disembarked upon the shores of Virginia with the intention of setting up a company dedicated to cultivating European grapes for making wine in America. While residing in London, he had been in involved in the import-export food business, dealing in wine, macaroni products, olive oil, candied fruit, and silk. In 1765, he established one of those Italian warehouses stocked with fine imported goods but operated behind the scenes, as retail was beneath his station. "I did not wish to expose myself to being called Philip the Shopkeeper. . . . I would not let myself be seen in the shop, and I did not want it to bear my name either."[11] A social climber, Mazzei had ingratiated himself into London's high society by offering his services as a language instructor to a wealthy and culturally inclined clientele. Among the distinguished elbows he rubbed were Benjamin Franklin's, one of the Americans who encouraged the enterprising Italian to go there to try his fortunes.

During a visit to Williamsburg on governmental business, Jefferson caught wind of Mazzei's arrival and ambitious plans. Intrigued by the prospect of producing European quality wines on American soil, Jefferson set out straight away to meet him. In short order, Mazzei and his band of ten Italian laborers were occupying a 150-acre allotment of Jefferson's land. The two gentlemen became close associates. As both appreciated the civility of the table, Mazzei likely found Jefferson a receptive companion with whom to share the delights of his country's cuisine, which may have acquainted him with macaroni and cheese. The Italians even made an impression on Isaac Granger (see fig. 4.4). Looking back over the years, he remarked that never before had he seen people make and eat so much food.[12]

Political Office in Richmond

When Jefferson became governor of Virginia in 1779, the Governor's Palace, where he had so memorably dined with the *partie carrée*, was in a dilapidated state. The decision to take up lodgings in Richmond, which would officially become the capital in 1780, was a wise move because the residence would be tragically ravaged by fire in 1781, marking the end of an era.[13] Among Jefferson's retinue were the brothers Robert, James, and Martin Hemings, enslaved men who served as liveryman, personal valet, and butler, respectively.[14] He also brought Jupiter Evans and his twenty-one-year-old wife, Sukey, as cook.[15] Ursula, however, remained at Monticello.

FIGURE 4.4. Portrait of Isaac Granger Jefferson (1775—ca. 1850). *Source*: Courtesy of Special Collection, University of Virginia Library. Public domain.

Compared to Williamsburg, Richmond was still a fledgling town but large enough to warrant clubs and societies dedicated to fostering cultural and scientific pursuits, as well as a local newspaper, a theater, and taverns. Taverns were not mere watering holes but the heart of social life in colonial cities, gathering places where people discussed politics, debated current events, spread news, and fomented subversive activities—all made merrier with good food and drink. The temptation to draw parallels with social media would not be unfounded.

One such tavern keeper was Serafino Formicola, hailing from Naples and previously in the service of the Doge of Venice. Initially, he was the maître d'hôtel (butler) to the Scotsman John Murray, the fourth earl of Dunmore (1730–1809) and the last royal governor of Virginia (1771–1776)). In June 1773, we find an order placed in Williamsburg on Lord Dunmore's account for a shipment including fifty pounds of macaroni, twelve large cheshire cheese rounds, and two dozen double gloucesters.[16] Given this documentation, it is plausible that his kitchen was turning out the popular dish called macaroni and cheese. Dunmore fled Virginia at the outbreak of the American Revolutionary War in 1776.[17]

At the height of the war in 1779, Formicola and his wife, Matilde, set up a tavern in Williamsburg. By 1781, the situation was untenable, prompting them to relocate their business in Richmond. This burgeoning town was a bustling, multicultural trading center, abuzz with the comings and goings of merchants from distant lands. While Formicola likely offered the customary French and English fare, dishes from his native Italy may also have found favor with his clientele.[18] The predilection for these three cuisines, coupled with Formicola's own origins, strongly suggests that macaroni and cheese could have graced his menu. His establishment attracted a diverse array of male patrons, such as Dr. Johann David Schoepf (1752–1800), surgeon to the Hessian troops of the British army during the war. Schoepf left us this vivid vignette: "I stopped at the Tavern Formicola, which was naturally much crowded at that season. Every evening there came generals, colonels, captains, senators, delegates, judges, doctors, clerks and gentlemen of every weight and calibre to sit around the fire, drink, smoke, sing and swap anecdotes. Very entertaining, but Formicola's not being a spacious house, I found the crowd embarrassing."[19] "Embarrassing" here means packed in so tight as to be cumbersome.

Jefferson would have been in his element among such ebullient company. From ledger entries in his *Memorandum Book*, we know for certain that he frequented Formicola's tavern on two occasions in May, just before circumstances forced him to flee in June 1781. General Benedict Arnold and General Charles Cornwallis were rampaging through Virginia on a mission to seize the capitol and capture its governor. Events culminated in

October with the Siege of York, effectively marking the end of the American Revolutionary War. When Jefferson came out of hiding, we once again find a ledger entry for money spent at Formicola's tavern in December 1781. Even George Washington, once retired, sought lodging at "Formicalo's [*sic*] Tavern, where by invitation I dined with the Judges of the General Court," in April 1786.[20] Might they have given a thought to ordering the macaroni and cheese?

CALLED TO FRANCE

In 1782, Martha Jefferson died due to postpartum complications. Jefferson withdrew from public service, mourning a wife with whom he had shared a happy marriage and family life. Martha left behind three daughters: Patsy (Martha), Polly (Maria), and Lucy. Despite his loss, Jefferson was also confronted with a professional opportunity.

That same year, he was approached for the third time to step in as Minister Plenipotentiary of the United States to the Court of Versailles; he acquiesced. The assignment offered an opportunity to distance himself from painful memories by immersing himself in the cultural vibrancy of France that so captivated his curiosity. The United States was navigating the "Critical Period," when delegates struggled to establish government under the Articles of Confederation. The founding fathers would ultimately restructure their entire concept of government, but Thomas Jefferson would play no direct role. He would be in Paris replacing Benjamin Franklin, who had spent nine years there securing diplomatic relations with France. But by 1784, at the age of seventy-eight, the once indefatigable statesman was ready pack it in and head home.

In the period between accepting the diplomatic post and leaving for Paris, Jefferson faced the task of choosing who among his "servants," as he called his enslaved workers, would accompany him. He was accustomed to traveling with "Bob" (Robert Hemings), who on occasion alternated with his younger brother "Jame" (James Hemings,1765–1801), who had been his riding valet on the journey to the Continental Congress in Philadelphia in 1783. This provided ample opportunity to spend time in close proximity with the eighteen-year-old and assess his acuity, reliability, and their compatibility.

In the months leading up to his departure for Paris, Jefferson had Robert trained as a barber, a reliable and even profitable line of work for a man of

African descent then, giving him the means to build a measure of independence. Evidently, Jefferson had no intention of bringing Robert to Paris. It was James who would be summoned to accompany him.

Finding James Hemings

In a letter dated May 7, 1784, Jefferson delegated his protégé, William Short, to find James and instruct him to make his way posthaste to Philadelphia—adding that he would be going to Paris for "a particular purpose." The fact that James had to be sought out indicates the freedom of movement he was afforded. He was finally located in Richmond, where he had hired himself out as a riding valet to a Mr. Henry Martin. The historian Annette Gordon-Reed, expert in the genealogy of the Hemings family at Monticello, provides a valuable context:

> The young man was living in Richmond, having gotten a place to stay on his own and found work that paid enough for him to support himself—not only to get housing but also to rent a horse for travel. He, like his brothers, knew how to ride and did so routinely. Horses were symbols of power and prestige in Virginia. Most enslaved people, and poor whites, walked to their destinations, sometimes for miles. Hemings, atop a horse, actually saw the world from a different perspective, and was seen in a particular way by the people whom he passed on the road.[21]

The occupation of valet was prestigious, its status contingent upon the standing of his employer. In the extreme, referring back to Bonnefons (see chapter 3), such proximity to nobility could put one in line for a noble title. Such was the case of Norborne Berkeley, the fourth Baron Botetourt, who was granted the position of royal governor of Virginia in 1768, the result of having been Lord of the Bedchamber to George III. The role originally included valet duties and later evolved to be the exclusive confidant to the sole man in power.

William "Billy" Lee, George Washington's personal valet, is an example within the context of American slavery, his position underscoring the multifaceted and contradictory nature of such roles. Lee's unwavering loyalty led him to accompany Washington even after his physical infirmities prevented him from adequately executing his duties. He was featured in three portraits with Washington and granted freedom in Washington's will. However, this must be viewed alongside the stark reality of the power imbalance, denial of basic human rights, and lack of personal freedom and agency inherent in enslavement.

For James Hemings, the position played out on two parallel tracks. In Jefferson's household, he was a bondsman, ultimately subject to the demands of his master. Yet in the service of Henry Martin, James Hemings was an employee. The very fact that he needed to be located suggests that he had secured the position himself and did not need to clear it or check in periodically—though he did need to be accessible. It allowed him to utilize a skill set that gave him a sense of identity; he may even have come recommended. Upon hearing that he had been recalled to Monticello, Hemings had to abandon the job. In a letter to Jefferson, Martin praised Hemings as "very careful and assiduous. Immediately upon hearing your intention I put him under the direction of Mr. Short."[22] At the age of nineteen, Hemings was earning a living wage. He could leave the post if it didn't suit him or if he found better employment elsewhere. While the specter of enslavement was ever present, the taste of freedom was also palpable.

Now Hemings had been summoned to go to Paris for the "particular purpose" of receiving training in the French culinary arts. Not only was there nothing in his background to suggest he had any inclination toward cooking or even the slightest interest in culinary pursuits, nothing indicates that he had any experience whatsoever in the kitchen. Yet, it was Jefferson's *ne plus ultra* to have a French-trained chef in his kitchen, just as he had wanted European-quality wines at Monticello. In the same way that Robert may not have chosen to become a barber, so too was James given no choice about his vocation. What Jefferson did know is that the two men traveled well together; James was dependable, and among the enslaved people of Monticello, Jefferson singled him out as having chef potential.

How this man, remarkably well traveled and independent for one so young, felt about being uprooted from the modicum of selfhood he had managed to construct within the strictures of slavery is a topic that has been largely unexplored. Today, Hemings is cast as having been a culinary prodigy, whose talent was innate. Some authors assume, or even assert, that part of his duties at Monticello included kitchen work and that Jefferson had spotted his talent. Quite a stretch for a man who only went to the kitchen to wind the clock.

Faced with the prospect of leaving behind his occupation as a valet—a manly profession associated with dignity and status—for the onerous life tucked away in a kitchen—perceived as women's work, rife with cadaverous tasks, fumes, grease, grime, and heat—what might James Hemings have chosen? Like it or not, he was going to France.

THE PARIS YEARS

Training and Understudy

Thomas Jefferson's official role in Paris was as minister plenipotentiary, akin to what we would now call an ambassador. The mandate did not have an official termination date. Benjamin Franklin, Jefferson's predecessor, stayed nine years in the position, and there is an indication that the expected tenure was seven years.[23] In light of this, Jefferson anticipated staying long enough to warrant enrolling his daughters in school and having Hemings trained in French cookery. Jefferson, his eldest, Patsy, and Hemings went ahead to get settled in Paris. The two younger daughters would be sent for in due time.[24]

Upon their arrival, they were shocked to discover how unfashionable their clothes were. In a letter to a friend, Patsy recounted, "I wish you could have been with us when we arrived. I am sure you would have laughfed, for we were obliged to send immediately for the stay maker, the manumaker [dressmaker], the milliner and even a shoe maker, before I could go out."[25]

On hand to ease their entry into society was one of the few Parisians Jefferson knew personally, François-Jean de Beauvoir, marquis de Chastellux, an intellectual and major-general in the French army—another who had frequented Formicola's Tavern (while there, he spoke to the proprietor exclusively in Italian, hoping it might shave a few louis off the price of his dinner).[26] Although an American diplomat would not have needed a local to grease the wheels, Chastellux intervened to get Patsy into boarding school and may also have facilitated the arrangement for Hemings to apprentice under the *traiteur*, or caterer, known only as Combeaux.

Hemings fell ill for a period after their arrival but was fit enough to begin his training in December 1784. For the duration of the year-long course, all of the meals at the Hôtel de Langeac, their townhouse on the Champs-Élysées, were provided by a caterer, presumably Combeaux. Upon completion, Combeaux was paid the balance of what he was owed for his services. In January 1786, there was a change in the kitchen regime. A large sum of money, recorded in the ledger under "kitchen expenses," was allocated to equip the kitchen.[27] A cook, presumably French and possibly a woman, was hired to take charge. Hemings worked under her, putting his newly acquired skills into practice. During this time, he studied briefly with a pastry chef.[28] By August 1786, the kitchen staff was complete with the addition of a scullion, or *garçon de cuisine*, a boy to fetch, clean, and generally pick up the slack.

In January 1787, Jefferson writes, "gave James *etrennes*, [a tip] of 12 francs," the new monetary system that would slowly replace the *livre*.[29] One franc was roughly twenty to twenty-five livres at the time, and the cook's monthly wage was forty-eight livres plus a sizable Christmas bonus. In that same month, seventy-two livres are spent "for James's apprenticeship with Patissier."[30] Mastering pastry was the pinnacle of French cookery.

Jefferson Leaves for a Period of Travel

Jefferson embarked on a tour of southeast France and northwest Italy at the end of February 1787, after which the cook was dismissed. Although there would be no activity in the house for some time, James Hemings unofficially took charge of the kitchen at the Hôtel de Langeac. In April, we find Philip Mazzei at large in Paris. Whether by request or on his own initiative, he kept an eye on Jefferson's residence. On his watch, a situation arose prompting him to write Jefferson an urgent letter to alert him that Hemings had overstepped his bounds. Before delving into the contents of the letter, some backstory may help put the actions of Mazzei into perspective.

The wine venture never came to fruition, but in the meantime, Mazzei had wormed his way into American politics. In his memoirs, he recalls a scene during the war years, when the Virginia Assembly put the prospect of abolishing slavery up for debate. The anecdote presents a window into Mazzei's character as well as a disturbing reflection on a pivotal event in history:

> Jefferson declared that he did not go in for palliative remedies; . . . that he would move for abolishing slavery entirely since both humanity and justice demanded it; that to keep in bondage beings born with rights equal to our own, and who differed from us only in color, was an injustice, not only

> barbarous and cruel, but shameful as well while we were risking everything for our freedom. . . . Mr. George Mason and I were the only ones to dissent. I said that I ardently desired to see that come to pass as soon as possible, that is, as soon as circumstances permitted. But in the existing situation, such a step seemed too risky to me, there being twice as many blacks as whites.[31]

Mason pointed out that they would need to be educated or "the first use they would make of their freedom would be to do nothing, and that they would become thieves out of necessity." Once they had been taught reading, writing, and arithmetic, those who deserved it could be freed.[32]

In later years, Mazzei pitted himself against Franklin, bent on proving he was incompetent and thus unfit for office. Franklin detested him. In an uncharacteristically panicked letter to Madison, Jefferson said, upon hearing that he might encounter Mazzei, "I tremble at the idea. I know he will be worse to me than a return of my double quotidian head-ach. . . . His coming will be attended with evil."[33]

Hemings in Conflict with Mazzei

We learn in Mazzei's letter to Jefferson that Hemings was in contact with "the Cook of the Prince of Condé," who served as the chef at the Château de Chantilly for Louis Joseph de Bourbon. The chef had set up a ten-day training session between James and *one of his apprentices*.[34] This bit of information has been repeatedly misinterpreted due to an inaccuracy in the modern translation of Mazzei's letter from Italian into English.[35] It would lead the reader to believe that Hemings took the course *with* the prince's chef, when in fact he hadn't. While this brings an error to light, it does not detract from the fact that Hemings was keeping high-status company in his new vocation, indicative of the level of his accomplishments and aspirations. He was proactive in furthering his education above and beyond what he had been required to do, a demonstration of his personal drive to hone his skills to master French cuisine.

The instructional itinerary entailed one day in the city, five days in the country, and another four once they were back in the city—all at the exorbitant price of twelve francs per day.[36] One suspects the chef and his apprentice knew who was footing the bill. Mazzei didn't get wind of it until after the fact and took it upon himself to raise objections for what he perceived as indiscretion and insolence. Feeling cornered and perhaps apprehensive given Mazzei's agitation, Hemings said that he only learned of the cost once he was already in the country. As Gordon-Reed points out, that level of instruction aligned with the sort of expenditure Hemings knew Jefferson was willing to pay for quality, such as their lavish accommodations in a fashionable part of Paris.[37] The instructor rebutted that he had been up front from the beginning. Regardless, Mazzei reprimanded Hemings for not having abandoned the course upon their return from the country. In the midst of the haranguing, the apprentice, apparently guided by the scent of money, tried to cut a deal: he would take James on for a hundred francs a month for a year, or two hundred francs monthly for a shorter period. Mazzei recommended cutting their losses by paying the cook off with fifteen livres. More cryptic, however, is Mazzei's other recommendation: to keep with the plan wherein "the Prince's cook will continue on the old basis, when the Prince is in Paris, and make arrangements to take him [presumably James] to Burgundy for that session of Parliament."[38]

We are left with some questions: What was the old basis? How long had they had this arrangement? How and why had it come about? Jefferson responded from Marseilles a month later. Following a long preamble of niceties, he gets to Hemings. On principle, he can't see shelling out even the fifteen livres: "Should he not shew that some person has been fool enough to give him half a guinea a day?" Rather than faulting Hemings, his irritation lies in being taken for an idiot by a swindler. He agreed that the proposed "deal" from such a man was out of the question and concludes, "These however are only my grumblings, for I suppose I must finish by paying." As for the coda involving the prince's chef, Jefferson concurs that they should proceed with "leaving him to the antient cook."[39] What that entailed we may never know.

While there are no further payments in the ledger for cooking instruction, based on the commentary above it would be reasonable to speculate that Hemings was receiving some sort of exposure to aristocratic kitchens, learning from professional cooks as they churned out the gastronomic wonders of the age, one of which, at that time in Paris, was macaroni and cheese. Culinary arts at this level in France were a man's world, a domain of creative expression and authority, with a hierarchy based on merit and due diligence. Hemings had entered into the ranks of that exclusive group of men, finding purpose and a renewed sense of agency. Profiteers like the apprentice and meddlers like Mazzei were types one had to navigate in life. More to the point is that even in France, Hemings was actively pursuing goals that would edify his identity and sense of self-worth—just as he had been accustomed to doing in Virginia.

His horizons had limits, though—limits he could free himself of at any moment if he so chose. Slaves brought into France had to be registered. He was not. As such, Jefferson was breaking the law. Any enslaved person seeking to remove the shackles had merely to jump through the hoops of bureaucracy, and it would be granted. But in balancing the uncertainties that freedom held in comparison to the indignities of bondage, the young James Hemings evidently did not feel ready to take the leap. Not yet.

In mid-April, the Italian leg of Jefferson's journey began. Throughout his travels, he wrote copious notes, mostly about the landscape and agriculture of each area. Not once does he mention macaroni, let alone having seen it made. However, toward the end of April he was in Rozzano, a dairying area on the outskirts of Milan, where he observed the making of Parmesan cheese.[40]

CHEESE CORNER

Throughout the history of macaroni and cheese, the overwhelming majority of recipes did not specify the type of cheese used. The historical overview indicates that prmesan cheese was the default, in accordance with Italian practice. However, the popularity and internationalization of macaroni and cheese inevitably led to variations in cheese due to availability, affordability, and taste.

It is likely that much of the cheese circulating in Europe under the name "parmesan" was actually *granone lodigiano*, a cheese tradition dating back to at least the twelfth century. It was the keystone in the now obsolete grana genus—a formulation that originated from a processing error by distracted monks. By heating the milk twice, they discovered how to produce a highly compact cheese with very low moisture, whose salt content assured a long shelf life. The process was refined in the Middle Ages in the central regions of northern Italy. The long aging produces a granular, crystalline, crumbly texture and intense flavor. The milk comes from specific breeds, and the quality of the milk is determined by their environment. Mentions in the

Middle Ages of this family of cheeses references Milan, Parma, Piacenza, and Mantua while Lodi is considered the oldest area of production. But was the cheese commonly referred to as parmesan really from Parma? Or had it become a catchall term for grana cheeses?

A notarized document from 1254 in Genoa chronicles the commercialization of *caseus parmensis*, while the first indications of export abroad come in 1389, coinciding with the "Makerouns" recipe. By the seventeenth century, both in Italy and abroad, parmesan had become genericized, prompting the duke of Parma, a man who saw dairying—not wheat fields—as the stronghold of prosperity, to reverse the trend. In a decree enacted in 1612, he mapped out the area of parmesan cheese production, making fraudulent use of the name even more lucrative. By then the genie was out of the bottle. It would not be until 1951 that a clear distinction between grana lodigiano (which would become grana padano) and Parmigiano Reggiano would be established and later written into law.

There were profits to be made if someone could come up with a way to produce parmesan-style cheeses in the American Colonies. Among his myriad wild ideas, Benjamin Franklin remarked in 1769, "If I could find in any Italian Travels a Receipt for making Parmesan Cheese, it would give me more Satisfaction than a Transcript of any Inscription from any old Stone whatever." A Scottish doctor by the name of Leith relayed his firsthand observations of the process to Franklin, who disseminated the information in *Lloyd's Evening Post* in December 1773.[41] His opening statement is most revealing: "The Parmesan Cheese is not made at present in the neighbourhood of Parma, but is solely the produce of the State of Milan, and especially of the country betwixt Placentia and Milan; that made near Lodi is the most esteemed. The following account is given from an observation of the whole process, as conducted at a considerable Farmer's on the road to Lodi."

Jefferson, too, set out to study the trade secrets of parmesan cheese, taking a day trip to Rozzano, on the outskirts of Milan. His diary entry for April 23, 1787, reads "Rozzano. Parmesan Cheese. It is supposed this was formerly made at Parma, and took its name thence, but is not made there now. It is made thro all the country extending from Milan 150 miles. The most is made about Lodi." Notably, this cheese was also colored slightly, with saffron, a quarter ounce to seven brenta (20 gallons/76 liters) of milk. It would have lent an ever-so-slight tinge of yellow.

The puzzling assertion that parmesan is not made in Parma is further complicated by the statement that it is made everywhere in a 150-mile

(*continued on next page*)

(*continued from previous page*)
(240 km) radius, a distance that would also include Parma. Notably, however, at the time of his observation, Jefferson hadn't read Franklin's article.

The Reverend Charles Clay wrote to Jefferson requesting information about his trip to Rozzano to see the parmesan production, as he intended to attempt manufacturing it in Virginia, indicating he sensed a potential market. Jefferson responded, "For tho' it has been tried without success in other parts of Europe, it may answer here. There must be some part of America correspondent to Lombardy where this cheese is made."[42] Twenty years later, John Skinner wrote to Jefferson, wanting to publish the parmesan papers in his new weekly periodical *American Farmer*, still convinced it could be produced on US soil.

While the production of parmesan remained elusive, Americans had successfully replicated versions of English cheeses from Cheshire and Cheddar on their home turf, and this would be a decisive factor in the future of macaroni and cheese. The Yanks imported not only British cheesing know-how but also the deceitful orange coloring that had become standard practice. Cows that fed on the lush green grasses of these areas produced milk with high beta-carotene. As the cheese aged, an orange hue came through, the hallmark of quality cheese. Crafty cheesemakers would skim off the cream and add coloring or perk up the tint when pastures were less fruitful. Orange became synonymous with quality to such an extent that even producers of naturally white cheese were forced to add color.

The English merchant Josiah Twamley, writing in 1787, tells us that in the olden days this was achieved with turmeric, red sandalwood, marigolds, and hawthorn buds, but moderns in his day and age used annatto, which "is much the beſt colouring that ever was found out." The Spanish were the first to import annatto from South America. Druggists also made a concoction they called Cheeſe-colouring. While purists criticized the practice as unwholesome, Twamley defends it, saying, "It is of a very rich fattening nature, and improves Cheeſse to a great degree, in quality, as well as colour; I never met with any Cheeſs ſo exquiſite, that had not been colored with it, as I have of that which hath," yet without denaturing the taste or smell. In the first cookbook by an American, *American Cookery or the Art of Dressing Viands, . . . Adapted to This Country, and All Grades of Life* (1796), the author Amelia Simmons, a domestic servant, begs to differ: "Deceits are uſed by ſalt-petering the outside, or colouring with hemlock, cocumberries or ſafron, insuſed into the milk; the taſte of either ſupercedes every poſſible evaſion." Coloration later graduated from deceitful to criminal with the introduction of red lead.[43]

In October 1787, James Hemings formally enters the ledger as chef, at the monthly wage of twenty-four livres.[44] It has been noted that the previous cook earned twice as much, insinuating that Hemings's lower pay marked his standing as a bondsman and, more pointedly, his race. While that may be true, it must also be weighed against the possibility that the previous cook's higher wage included a standard allowance for living off-premises, as those who lodged elsewhere often received extra pay. In fact, in 1790, when Jefferson requested that his French household manager, Adrien Petit, enter his service in the United States, he explicitly stated that Petit's wage would be reduced since room and board would be provided—eliminating any separate housing supplement. Jefferson also asked Petit to bring a good supply of macaroni and parmesan cheese.[45]

THE "MACARONI MACHINE" PAPER TRAIL

An undated document in Jefferson's hand in the Library of Congress collection stands at the heart of much of the confusion. It has variously been assumed to be a diagram of the macaroni extrusion machine that Jefferson brought back to the United States; the machine he designed and had built at Monticello; or a drawing of the machine that Short, who had become Jefferson's secretary in Paris, described to him following his trip to Naples—or indeed, all three. A closer look at the related documentation will reveal that none of these assumptions are true.

"It is in Naples, Genoa, Marseille, & Paris where they make the most pasta, & where it is best prepared," said Paul-Jacques Malouin (1701–1778) in his book *Description and Details of the Art of Milling, and of Pasta and Bread Making: with a Brief History of Bakeries, & a Dictionary of These Arts* (1767 first ed., 1779 second ed.). Malouin was the physician to the queen and later to the dauphin (a position he purchased, as one did), but he also credited himself with having introduced the macaroni industry to Paris.[46] *Description* is the first-ever treatise on pasta-making, and Jefferson purchased a copy during his sojourn. Benjamin Franklin may have been the one who brought it to his attention, as the book was also in Franklin's personal library.[47] It contains an elaborate etching of an industrial-sized machine and a series of dies with holes of various sizes, as well as a close-up diagram of the holes for hollow macaroni (see figs. 4.5 and 4.6). Jefferson's undated document bears a striking resemblance to the illustrations in *Description* suggesting it as a plausible source. The same diagram was printed in *Recueil*

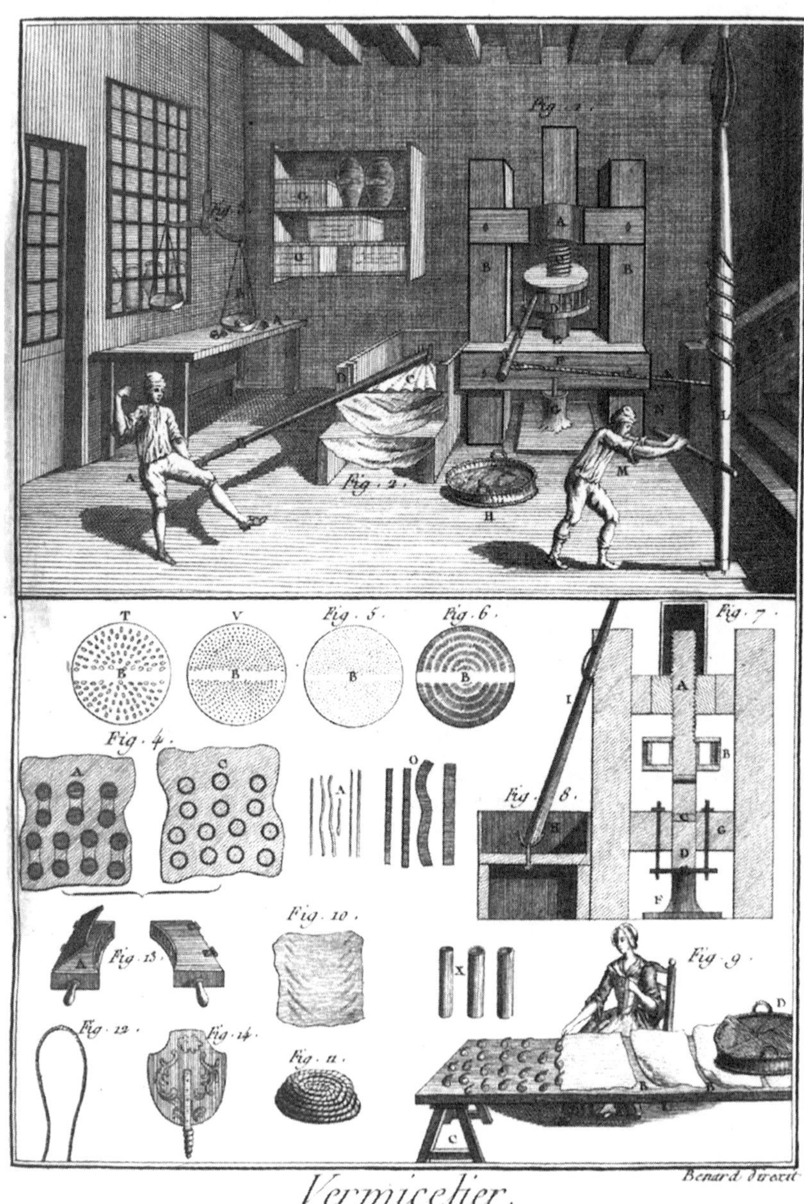

FIGURE 4.5. Diagram detailing pasta production from Malouin's treatise on the so-called "white arts"—milling, bread, and pasta. It was engraved under the direction of Robert Bénard, who had collaborated on Diderot's *Encyclopédie*. *Source*: Public domain.

de planches de l'encyclopédie: Encyclopédie mèthodique arts et métiers mécaniques, vol. 8 (1787), which was also in Jefferson's personal library.

Malouin's treatise on industrial pasta-making is long-winded and convoluted. There are bold passages of inaccurate information about the nature of wheat and flour—a reflection of best intentions in the Age of Enlightenment. Despite reputedly rusty French-language skills, Jefferson did a commendable job at distilling the meandering text on pasta to a concise one-page summary. In addition to the similarities between Jefferson's diagram and the original illustration, there is one particular passage in the summary that unmistakably echoes *Description*. Throughout the section dedicated to pasta, Malouin draws frequent comparisons between bread dough and pasta dough: "You have to convert the semolina into dough to make vermicelli, macaroni, lasagne, etc. It is good to have a piece of the last dough to add leaven when kneading the semolina. You could do without it if you don't have it; dough keeps better when

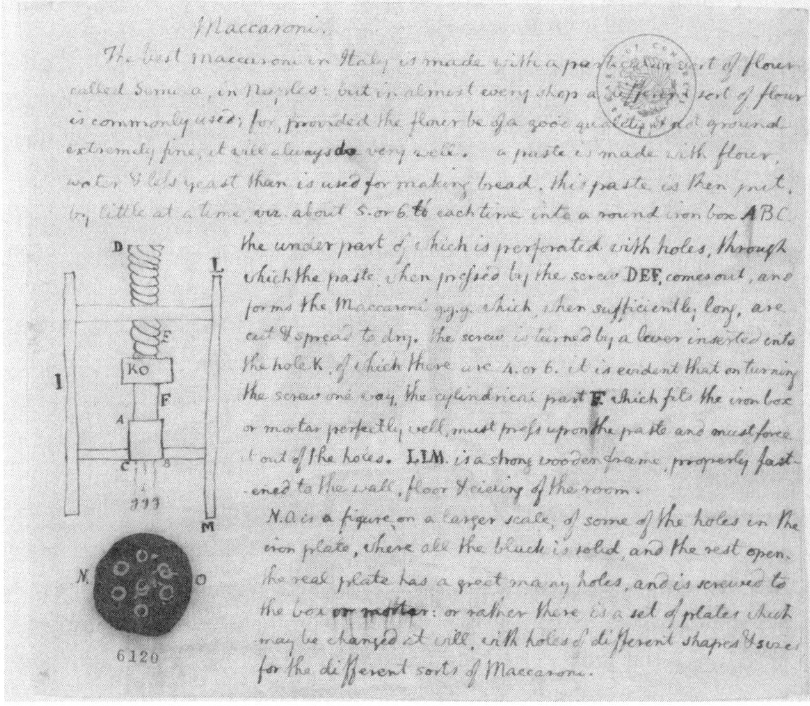

Maccaroni.

The best maccaroni in Italy is made with a particular sort of flour called Semola, in Naples: but in almost every shop a different sort of flour is commonly used; for, provided the flour be of a good quality & not ground extremely fine, it will always do very well. a paste is made with flour, water & less yeast than is used for making bread. this paste is then put, by little at a time, viz. about 5. or 6 lb each time into a round iron box ABC the under part of which is perforated with holes, through which the paste when pressed by the screw DEF, comes out, and forms the Maccaroni g.g.g. which when sufficiently long, are cut & spread to dry. the screw is turned by a lever inserted into the hole K. of which there are 4. or 6. it is evident that on turning the screw one way, the cylindrical part F. which fits the iron box or mortar perfectly well, must press upon the paste and must force it out of the holes. LIM. is a strong wooden frame, properly fastened to the wall, floor & cieling of the room.

N.O. is a figure on a larger scale, of some of the holes in the iron plate, where all the black is solid, and the rest open. the real plate has a great many holes, and is screwed to the box ~~or mortar~~: or rather there is a set of plates which may be changed at will, with holes of different shapes & sizes for the different sorts of Maccaroni.

FIGURE 4.6. Thomas Jefferson's drawing of a macaroni machine and instructions for making pasta (undated). *Source*: Courtesy of the Manuscript Division, Library of Congress. Public domain.

it's made without any sort of leaven. . . . In Provence, Languedoc & Genoa commonly the Vermicelli makers do not use leaven as some do in Naples & in Paris."[48] He carries on at length about leavening in pasta dough, but humbly concedes that pasta-making took a backseat to bread-making as the French make the best bread in the world. Jefferson nutshells the windy passage as "A paste is made with flour, water & less yeast than is used for making bread."

In mid-September 1788, more than a year after Jefferson's trip to southern France and northern Italy, he sends a letter to Short, who had come to Europe as his secretary. While Short was on tour, Jefferson asked if he could do him a favor when he got to Naples. He explains that there is "a round piece of metal," the essential piece to be fitted into an iron mortar for making pasta. To make it crystal clear, he draws a picture that is identical to the one on the undated document and says, "This iron is thus formed where all the black is solid." He then clearly specifies, "I would wish to have one of these irons the smallest (as to diameter) that is ever used, but with holes for macaroni of the common size." As for the apparatus itself, he says, "I have no occasion for the mortar, because we can easily make that."

Not until February 11, 1789, did Short write back confirming he had procured the "mould for making macaroni," the "mould" being the perforated die. It was not the industrial size but a smaller, easily shippable version that "had been sent to gentlemen in other countries," so it was apparently a popular item. Short had the piece sent to an intermediary, Stephen Cathalan, who would notify Jefferson upon its arrival. At this point, Jefferson had started to plan for a return trip to the United States but was waiting for formal permission to leave.[49] But before the piece could arrive, Jefferson was ready to leave Paris. He writes to Cathalan in August 1789 to send the "maccaroni machine" to Short, who was now in Paris acting as his chargé d'affaires during his absence. This is the first reference to the die as a "machine," hitherto referred to as an "iron" or "mould." At the time Jefferson was writing, the word "machine" could signify parts—levers, wheels, screws, etc.—and fell under the heading *simple machines*. When assembled into an apparatus, they became *compound machines*.[50] Cathalan responds affirmatively in September 1789.

Jefferson's departure has been attributed to multiple factors, not the least of which was the French Revolution and the need to attend to his long-neglected estate and family affairs. Regardless, he assumed that he would return to Paris.[51] It was not until the end of October that conditions aligned for Jefferson to set sail; traveling with him were James Hemings, his sister Sally Hemings, who was pregnant, and Jefferson's daughters, Patsy and Polly.

Given Sally's condition, Jefferson could have alleviated himself of a scandal that would damage his political and social standing by setting her and James up in Paris, where James had connections and a viable skill—and where they would be free. Gordon-Reed explains, "History, and his philosophe friends of the moment, would have recorded that Jefferson (breathing the rarefied air of Enlightenment France) so identified with the Freedom Principle that he let go of two of his own slaves. He would have been a veritable hero. Instead of doing that, Jefferson insisted on setting up an arrangement with a young woman that he knew could easily result in a houseful of children whose existence would be easily tied to him."[52]

Though there is no documentation to support any bargaining between Jefferson and the Hemingses, the brother and sister had options and would surely have weighed them up before agreeing to go home. James had left as a teenager and would be returning as a man. In the United States, he would be a big fish in a small pond, one of the few men with formal training in French cookery. In 1789, Paris was becoming increasingly dangerous, with riots, bread shortages, and violent protests shaking the city. It is understandable that Hemings, facing the uncertainty of revolution, might have chosen to leave rather than risk being caught up in the chaos. But perhaps he chose to return simply out of a desire to be back in the country that, for better or worse, was home.

Shortly after alighting on the shores of Virginia, Jefferson received news that he had been appointed secretary of state under the newly elected president, George Washington. He did not want the job. He tried to beg off but acquiesced in the end, not only as his civic duty but also perhaps because the prospect of leaving again for France meant straining personal ties. With the turmoil in Paris rapidly escalating, Jefferson sent word that he would be vacating Hôtel de Langeac and wished to have all of his belongings shipped. Continuing with the investigation into the "macaroni machine" paper trail, we find nothing even remotely similar mentioned on what is referred to as the Grevin packing list, the meticulously detailed inventory of each crate of Jefferson's possessions. It did, however, contain a full battery of copper pots and pans for use with a stew stove, two cases of macaroni, and a quarter wheel of cheese.

Resuming Life in America

When Jefferson accepted the appointment as secretary of state, he clearly expressed his reservations and hinted at the possibility of not serving out the full term. Accompanied by James Hemings, who assumed the role of steward in addition to his duties in the kitchen, Jefferson moved to the seat of the central government in New York. Petit would soon arrive from France to take up the position as maitre d'hôtel. Jefferson and Hemings lived in closer quarters with fewer pastimes, no family, and a smaller staff. The account book seems to tell the story of interdependence, a new dynamic in which for "the first time he served as a paid employee to him in their native land."[53]

As tensions with Alexander Hamilton reached a peak, Jefferson began to see the escape clause set out at the beginning of his tenure as a viable option. The most famous of their disagreements centered on the management of the nation's debts and the permanent location of the seat of government. In June 1790, during a meeting referred to as the "dinner table bargain," Jefferson, Hamilton, and James Madison convened over a clandestine meal in Jefferson's New York residence, where the men managed to come to a compromise. Hemings would have been the attendant chef, but, unfortunately, the extant documentation of the event failed to consider the crucial role of the evening's bill of fare. Therefore, we cannot know if macaroni and cheese had been a determining factor in softening Hamilton's resolve, but we do know that the food stuff itself would have been available, as imported macaroni had been advertised in New York newspapers for the last twenty years (see chapter 3). Regardless, the US capitol would be moved temporarily to Philadelphia, conveniently closer to Monticello.

Hemings and Jefferson settled into their residence in Philadelphia. Here, the question arises as to why, once again, Hemings did not claim his freedom, this time under the Gradual Abolition Act of 1780. The law mandated emancipation for slaves whose owners took up formal residence in the city for more than six months. Hemings had resided for stretches of time in the city exceeding six months. Why, too, did Jefferson not send him periodically to Monticello, driven by the same angst that prompted Washington to illegally send his enslaved workers to and from Mount Vernon? The loophole was that delegates to the government were exempt, as *residing* in Philadelphia was not the same as *being a resident* of Pennsylvania. While it was no Mecca, Philadelphia of 1790 was a comparatively safe oasis with networks of support and strong abolitionist leanings. Before Washington's term was up, two of his domestics would run away. One of those was the chef Hercules Posey.

Washington's decision to bring the enslaved cook Hercules Posey to serve as chef in his presidential household may have had less to do with culinary skill than with his distaste for Mount Vernon's hired washerwoman and cook, Mrs. Lewis. He shuddered at the thought of anyone catching sight of that "dirty, unpleasant woman" in the President's kitchen.[54] While in New York, Washington had encountered the refined skill of Jefferson's French-trained chef. As the nation's head of state, where every detail conveyed authority, he could not allow himself to be outshone. Posey more than fit the bill and came to be known in Philadelphia as quite the dandy, spending his extra earnings from selling the kitchen remnants and household leftovers on finery.[55] Indeed, with his fashionable clothes and a gold-handled walking stick, contemporaries would have pegged him as a Macaroni.

The President's House was just three blocks away from where Jefferson and Hemings resided. Though Jefferson and Washington would eventually have a bitter falling-out, these years saw them working closely and with mutual respect.[56] For Hemings and Posey, given the parallels, they must have encountered each other regularly. They would have participated in official events together, shopped at the same markets, and kept the same company with both free and enslaved Philadelphians of African descent. The complete lack of references documenting their interactions has left a gaping void in culinary history. The same holds true of Petit. The two men collaborated in the kitchen (Petit specializing in pastry), had French as their common language, and, by virtue of their training, approached cookery with the same exacting French standards—a caliber of collaboration that not only suggested an amicable and productive partnership but also ensured the work retained its male tenor.

Before the end of Washington's first term, Jefferson had had enough, although he reluctantly agreed to stay on until the end of 1793. Here, a couple more clues appear on the macaroni machine paper trail. In a letter to his friend, George Gilmer, a fellow Virginia plantation owner and his personal physician, Jefferson says, "I had indeed hoped by this time to have been with you. But it seems I must stay here a little longer in penance for my sins." That was followed by this curious addition: "This will give you the start in your manufactures of porter and maccaroni, in which however I shall certainly attempt to rival you."[57] Medicine and macaroni may seem strange bedfellows, but remember Malouin was also a doctor. Jefferson took a house in the country a short distance from Philadelphia and started sending his belongings back to Monticello. The die surfaces again in Petit's list of "superfluous furniture," furniture being a French false cognate for "supplies," so, essentially a crate of unnecessary items. On the list is "*une moule a Macaroni*," a macaroni mold or die.[58] If Jefferson still intended to build that macaroni extruder, Gilmer would beat him to it.

The country retreat was a balm for Jefferson, and it ultimately may have saved all of them from yellow fever as it swept through Philadelphia in late summer 1793—though country life did not seem to appeal to Hemings or Petit. Petit had reached a breaking point and decided to return to France. For Hemings, a young man who had spent the formative years of his adult life in the hustle and bustle of city life, the pastoral life may have seemed numbingly boring. Still a bachelor, unencumbered by family obligations that might anchor him, the prospect of their imminent return to the secluded house on the hill in Virginia brought Hemings to a crossroads. It was against this backdrop that he finally requested his freedom.

The gravity of the request was underscored in the formal document drawn up by Jefferson, dated September 15, 1793.

> Having been at great expence in having James Hemings taught the art of cookery, desiring to befriend him, and to require from him as little in return as possible, I do hereby promise and declare, that if the said James shall go with me to Monticello in the course of the ensuing winter, when I go to reside there myself, and shall there continue until he shall have taught such person as I shall place under him for that purpose to be a good cook, this previous condition being performed, he shall be thereupon made free, and I will thereupon execute all proper instruments to make him free. Given under my hand and seal in the county of Philadelphia and state of Pennsylvania this 15th day of September one thousand seven hundred and ninety three.

There have been many interpretations about the tone and content of this promissory agreement. Does the opening line imply the sting of perceived ungratefulness, or is Jefferson paving the way for a mutually fruitful outcome by reminding Hemings of his indebtedness? As they returned to Monticello for the month of October to wait out the epidemic, this turn of events would change the dynamic of their relationship.

When it was safe to return to Philadelphia, Jefferson and Hemings temporarily took rooms in Joseph Mussi's house. Hemings was relieved of duties because Mussi's Milanese chef prepared Jefferson's meals. Did he make macaroni and cheese? One of the reasons Jefferson knew Mussi was because he dealt in fine Italian food imports, evidenced from an order placed in 1790. But more to the point, on December 17 there is a ledger entry: "Pd. Delany duties on Maccaroni. 7."[59] Two days later there is a payment for 16 1/2 pounds of cheese. Possibility becomes probability.[60]

After withdrawing from public life to Monticello, Jefferson writes a lengthy letter filled with advice to James Monroe, who is serving as minister plenipotentiary in Paris. He included a request to ship books from his French bookseller and a while-you're-at-it "supply of 20 or 30 lb of Maccaroni."[61] Eight years would pass before placing another order, which may suggest he was sourcing it through other avenues, such as import shops or even local manufacturers. The other option was making them by hand in the time-honored way.

With everything Jefferson had on his plate, the fact that he had taken the time to pen a recipe called "Nouilly a' maccaroni" bespeaks a true passion. But why both noodles and macaroni? To unravel that, let's first look at the recipe itself alongside the original document (fig. 4.7).

NOUILLY A' MACCARONI

6 whole eggs
2 wine glasses of milk
2 lb (900 g) flour
A little salt

work them together without water and very well.
roll it then with a roller to a proper thickness.
cut it into small pieces which roll again with the hand into long slips, & then cut them to a proper length.
put them into warm water a quarter of an hour. drain them. dress them as Maccaroni.
but if they are intended for soups they are to be put into the soup & not into warm water.

Nouilly. a' maccaroni
6 eggs. yolks & whites
2 wine glasses of milk
2 lb of flour
a little salt
work them together without water, and very well.
roll it then with a roller to a proper thickness.
cut it into small peices which roll again with the hand into long slips, & then cut them to a proper length.
put them into warm water a quarter of an hour.
drain them.
dress them as Maccaroni.
but if they are intended for soups they are to be put into the soup & not into warm water.

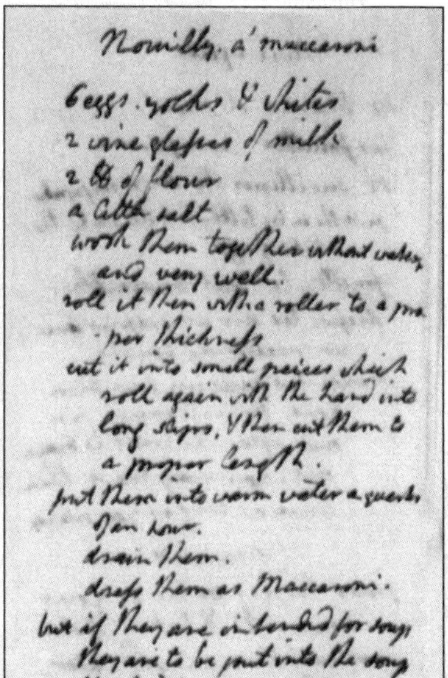

FIGURE 4.7. Thomas Jefferson's handwritten recipe for macaroni. *Source:* Courtesy of the Library of Congress. Public domain.

The ingredients and initial instructions are clear, though the massive quantity of dough, enough to serve at least ten people, poses quite a challenge. After rolling the mass out into a sheet (whatever "proper thickness" is), we are then instructed to cut it into smaller pieces of an unspecified size. Here lies the real puzzle: How exactly are we to roll the small pieces by hand—and what are "slips"? Before answering that, let's revisit Malouin's instructions for homemade macaroni.

He starts with flour, eggs, and water, *optionally adding cream*. He first describes rolling out the dough for vermicelli, synonymous with noodles: "C'est ce sue l'on nomme des *Nouilles*," a word Jefferson anglicized as "Nouilly." He transitions directly into cutting slices of dough, two to three "lines" wide for lasagne, emphasizing that in homes *this pasta is called macaroni*. However, these strips of pasta, when cut to the proper length, are then *rolled again by hand* "with a sort of a large needle to make macaroni." These instructions for rolling bits of dough on a metal rod to render hollow pasta had been standard practice for centuries.

The text would pose a challenge for native French speakers, even more so for one unaccustomed to such kitchen maneuvers. In Jefferson's rendition, "slips" is likely a reference stemming from his familiarity with and lifelong interest in plants and gardening. In that context, slips are twigs cut from plants for the purpose of grafting. Hence, "she's just a slip of a thing," meaning a slim woman. But a glaring question remains: Was the absence of the "large needle" or rod to shape the macaroni an oversight?

While it is plausible that Jefferson referred to Malouin for the procedure, the ingredient measurements came from another source. Some presume these details came from Jefferson's French cook, but in the absence of documentation there is no reason to rule out Hemings as the source. When Jefferson's recipe was transcribed into the family cookbook curated by his granddaughter, Virginia Jefferson Randolph Trist (1801–1882), she renames it "Noodles to thicken the soup." For her, "slips" are flat noodles that are two inches long and a quarter of an inch wide. If they are to be used for macaroni, they are to boil for quarter of an hour. Apparently, they were rather thick.

James fulfilled his end of the agreement and trained his brother Peter, five years his junior, in French cookery, and on February 5, 1796, he was formally released from bondage. On February 20, before departing from

MONTICELLO MACARONI

With an eye on the fashion of the day for preparing macaroni in France, I present you with the composite historical recipe I cooked and served as part of a guest lecture and demonstration in Monticello in 2022.

Serves 6

4 cups (450 g) type 00 or all-purpose flour
3 extra-large eggs (160g shelled)
1/3 cup (100 mL) whole milk
1/4 tsp salt
1/2 cup (125 mL) salted, cultured butter
1/2 cup (125 mL) heavy cream (36 percent milkfat)
7 oz (200 g) gruyere cheese, grated
3 1/2 oz (100 g) parmesan cheese, grated
Fresh ground black pepper, to taste
For the topping:
Sourdough breadcrumbs toasted in butter

Mound the flour on the counter and make a well to accommodate the eggs and milk. Whisk the eggs, salt, and milk together and pour into the well. Mix carefully, pinching the flour into the liquid. When it has formed a paste, use your hand and a bench scraper to work the dough together. Knead 5–8 minutes until smooth and elastic. The dough should be stiff but easy to work. Wrap it in plastic and set it aside for an hour.

Roll out the dough into a slab about 1/8 in. (3 mm) thick. Cut that into strips about 1/4 in. (6 mm) wide, the width of a chopstick, and 4 in. (10 cm) long. Flour the work surface, take each strip, placea metal rod or wooden skewer on top and roll it back and forth to create a hollow piece of pasta and remove the rod. Don't worry if it is not a perfectly closed tube. Set aside and repeat. Cut the pieces in half. Flour them to prevent sticking.

Preheat the oven to 350°F (180°C).

In a small saucepan, melt the butter in the cream on low heat. Bring a large pot of salted water to boil and add the pasta, initially stirring lightly to separate the pieces. Cook until al dente and drain quickly. In a large bowl, toss with the warm cream and butter and then the cheeses until well incorporated. Pour the mixture into a baking tray. (The dish can be prepared up to this point a full day in advance and kept refrigerated.) Sprinkle with buttered breadcrumbs. Bake 20–25 minutes until bubbly. Tent with foil if it is browning too much.

Monticello, James prepared an inventory of the kitchen items. The closest we get to a final hint of the macaroni relic from France is this listing: "3 past cuting moulds." Interpreting this as the mysterious macaroni machine requires an extraordinary stretch of the imagination, though some have rubbed those sticks together.

We hear no more of the macaroni machine. Jefferson did not bring a macaroni machine from France or Italy, nor he did not have one built at Monticello.

The ledger reveals that on February 26, 1796, Hemings was given the equivalent of three months' pay as a sendoff. He left Monticello with ten years' experience as a chef. Instead of repairing to Richmond, where he had family, contacts, and the reassurance of a large Black community, he headed to Philadelphia. He had only been away for two years, and finding employment in the Francophile city should not have proven difficult with his unique skills. However, as was often the case with former slaves, newfound freedom manifested as wanderlust, and James, too, seemed to eschew laying down roots. Jefferson, having returned to Philadelphia as vice president, met up with him there and wrote to his daughter Polly, expressing concern about his restlessness—relieved, however, that rumors of his excesses in drink were unfounded.[62]

Eventually, Hemings ended up in Baltimore, but any employment he took was tentative, as he maintained a gentleman's agreement with Jefferson. He was no longer at his former master's beck and call but remained open to offers should something come up. And something did indeed come up. Jefferson was elected the third president of the United States in 1801 and required a chef at the newly built President's House. As had happened in the past, Jefferson got word out that he was looking for James. He attempted initial contact through Francis Say, a former employee now residing in Baltimore. Say, desperate for work, prevailed upon Jefferson to give him permanent employment. But, being averse to Say's drinking, Jefferson persuaded him that it was inconvenient. Regarding Hemings, Say responded, "He has made mention again as he did before that he was willing to serve you before any other man in the Union but sence he understands that he would have to be among strange servants he would very much obliged to you if you would send him a few lines of engagement and on what conditions and what wages you would please to give him with your own hand wreiting."[63]

Three days before receiving Say's reply, Jefferson had also written to the Baltimore hotel owner William Evans: "You mentioned to me in conversation here that you sometimes saw my former servant James, & that he made his engagements such as to keep himself always free to come to me. Could I get the favor of you to send for him & to tell him I shall be glad to receive him as soon as he can come to me?"[64] Jefferson seems assured that based on past conversation, his offer would fall well. It was not based on self-flattery but on wishes expressed openly by Hemings.

Evans carried out the task immediately. Hemings answered that he was under obligation with a man named Peck and could not get free for a few days. When Evans pressed him to be more specific, Hemings said he would think it over and get back to him that evening. He did not. After a second solicitation, Evans reported back "that he would not go untill you should write to himself."[65]

From Hemings's perspective, the second request from Jefferson may have landed as an insult, as he had already responded to Say. Such is the confusion that can arise with letters. His reluctance to reply through go-betweens and his insistence on negotiating man to man were arguably triggered from recollections of Jefferson's past habit of sounding the call to come back home. Jefferson was a great delegator and frequently called on others to do his bidding, part of a system in which he, too, did the bidding of others. The job represented what could have been the pinnacle of Hemings's career. Jefferson's confidence in Hemings was absolute, as was his belief that James knew he would be paid fairly and have free rein. In what Gordon-Reed describes as a "masterpiece of Jeffersonian control and subtlety, all the more so because he probably figured that Hemings would actually see the letter," Jefferson writes again to Evans:

> I suppose I saw in the difficulties raised by James an unwillingness to come here, arising wholly from some attachment he had formed in Baltimore; for I cannot suspect an indisposition towards me. I concluded at once therefore not to urge him against inclination, and wrote to Philadelphia, where I have been successful in getting a cook equal to my wishes. . . . I would wish James to understand that it was in acquiescence to what I supposed his own wish that I did not repeat my application, after having so long rested on the expectation of having him.[66]

Under pressure to set up his domestic staff, Jefferson hired Honoré Julien, a Frenchman who had by then been working in the United States for ten years. Julien had left France during the upheaval of the French Revolution (1789-1799), drawn to the United States, where French culinary skill all but guaranteed prestige, prosperity and the propagation of macaroni and cheese.[67] He had previously served George Washington in Philadelphia, alongside chef Hercules Posey and the noted tavernkeeper Samuel Fraunces. Consistent with Jefferson's usual practice, the entire matter of Julien's appointment was handled through intermediaries. Jefferson and Hemings resolved their misunderstanding, but it was too late to take James on at the President's House. Neither he nor Julien could be expected to play sous chef to the other. In August, during the government's recess, Hemings returned to Monticello with his salary doubled. He left in September when Jefferson returned to Washington. At the end of October, news of Hemings's death reached Jefferson. Once again, he wrote to Evans. Of all the mechanisms for exercising emotional restraint, the brief letter opens with comments about a sea bass (rock fish) and proceeds thus: "It was indeed a remarkably fine one and I pray you to accept my thanks for it. A report has come here through some connection of one of my servants that James Hemings my former cook has committed an act of suicide. As this whether true or founded will give uneasiness to his friends, will you be so good as to ascertain the truth & communicate it to me."[68] The response affirming the rumor came four days later. "I made every enquiry at the time this melancholy circumstance took place, the result of which was, that he had been delirious for Some days previous to his having committed the act, and it was the General opinion that drinking too freely was the cause."[69]

ENSLAVED WOMEN COOKING AT THE PRESIDENT'S HOUSE

Over the span of his presidency, Jefferson brought only three enslaved people from Monticello to work in the kitchen—all trained with Julien in the art of French cookery. The first to come was a fourteen-year-old named Ursula, a child who was herself three months pregnant when she arrived in September 1801. She was the namesake of her grandmother Ursula Granger, who had been brought to Monticello years earlier at the request of Martha Jefferson. In light of this, she may have been chosen for sentimental reasons.[70] Other than the distinction of having the first child born in the President's House, the arrangement was less than optimal for the kitchen, and Ursula was sent home shortly after giving birth in March 1802. Given her condition, she may not have participated in one of the most misrepresented macaroni events of the Jeffersonian age: the macaroni pie.

The Infamous Macaroni Pie

Jefferson entertained three evenings a week, hosting gatherings that brought together diverse members of the government for conversation and conviviality in a less formal setting. Manasseh Cutler, a Federalist representative of Massachusetts, left us with the details of one of the dinners he attended with about twelve other invitees:

> Feb. 6, Saturday. Dined at President's . . . Dinner was not as elegant as when we dined before. Rice soup, round of beef, turkey, mutton, ham, loin of veal, cutlets of mutton or veal, fried eggs, fried beef, a pie called macaroni which appeared to be a rich crust filled with the strillions of onions, or shallots, which I took it to be, tasted very strong, and not agreeable. Mr. [Meriwether] Lewis told me there were none in it; it was an Italian dish, and what appeared like onions was made of flour and butter, with a particularly strong liquor mixed with them. Ice cream very good, crust wholly dried, crumbled into thin flakes; a dish somewhat like a pudding—inside white as milk or curd, very porous and light, covered with cream sauce—very fine. Many other jimcracks [frivolities], a great variety of fruit, plenty of wines, and good. President social. We drank tea and viewed again the great cheese.[71]

The cheese he is referring to is the "Mammoth Cheese," a tribute of allegiance from the citizens of Cheshire, Massachusetts, spearheaded by the Baptist clergyman John Leland (1754–1841). It was a behemoth weighing in at 1,235 pounds (560 kg) and bearing the Jefferson motto: "Rebellion to tyrants is obedience to God." The accompanying tribute letter makes a point of underscoring that "the Chees was produced by the personal labor of Freeborn Farmers, with the voluntary and cheerful aid of their wives and daughters, without the assistance of a single slave."[72] In accordance with Jefferson's personal policy to not accept gifts while in office, he paid two hundred dollars for it. With the expiration date looming on such a bounteous quantity of cheese, the February 6 macaroni pie may even have been made with it.

Modern studies on cheese aversion show that 12 percent of people experience a revulsion for cheese that is measurable in an MRI scanner. They perceive its pungency as decay, a trait that runs in families.[73] As with the macaroni and cheese haters in the previous chapter, Cutler may have been reacting to odiferous cheese rather than critiquing the overall quality of the dish. Or perhaps Cutler's disgust had a political edge. In order to make the "big cheese," Leland implored the Cheshire cow owners to contribute a quart of milk per day—so long as the cow in question *was not a Federalist*, "lest it should leaven the whole lump with a distasteful savour." Milk from Cutler's cows would have been turned away. Cutler's comment about the appearance of the pasta as "strillions of onions" indicates that the macaroni in question was tagliatelle-style noodles rather than tubular pasta, and that not only were his politics conservative but so were his culinary horizons. The "rich crust" worthy of mention may have been a Menon-style puff pastry. February would have been an optimal month to keep the butter cold between foldings. Cutler should have been so lucky.

This event is often touted as the macaroni and cheese "shot heard round the world," when it spread from sea to shining sea, or, in today's parlance, its viral moment. But we know that the dish had been on a steady course of increasing popularity long before this occasion. The influence of French culinary trends was already deep-seated and widespread in Early America. While the presence of macaroni and cheese on the president's table undoubtedly conferred his stamp of approval—given Jefferson's fondness for the dish, it likely appeared frequently on the presidential bill of fare. However, there is no evidence that stands up to the rigors of historical scrutiny pegging Philadelphia, Washington, or Monticello as macaroni and cheese epicenters from whence waves of increased use radiated. While one-upmanship at the table is a sociological fact that spans history, so, too, was homogeneity and adhering to norms. Macaroni and cheese was a standard in the repertoire of dishes crafted by classically trained French chefs, who coordinated the menu in collaboration with the French maitre d'hôtel. However, Cutler was most certainly *not* going to spread the word about macaroni and cheese, a dish he found decidedly repugnant, and no one else who attended the many dinners Jefferson hosted was even interested enough to comment.

Edith Hern Fosset

For the remainder of the Jeffersonian macaroni history, credit must be given to Edith Hern Fossett, who, based on the massive orders for macaroni from Italy, appears to have made more macaroni and cheese than any of the other cooks or chefs who ever passed through Jefferson's kitchen. She had been summoned to Washington in September 1802, and for six years apprenticed in French cookery under Honoré Julien. Her sister-in-law Frances (Fanny) Gillette Hern would join her in 1806.[74] "Edy" returned to Monticello at the end of Jefferson's presidency in 1809 to assume the role of chef. Initially, Julien accompanied her to assist setting her up in the kitchen, replacing Peter Hemings, who moved on to specialize in cider, for which he gained some renown. Julien left to open a fine foods retail and cookshop in Washington, DC, where he sold the usual luxury goods, including macaroni.[75] He also continued to apprentice young African Americans in the art of French cookery.[76] Upon Jefferson's death, Edith Fossett moved to Ohio. Her grandson went on to become one of the most prominent caterers to the wealthy families of Cincinnati, carrying on recipes from the White House and Monticello.[77]

THE MACARONI DENOUEMENT

There was something inherently delightful about hollow macaroni tubes, or Naples macaroni, as it came to be called in the eighteenth century. Perhaps it was the mystery of their formation or the succulent way the tubes held a creamy cheese sauce in their inner recesses. The fact that they were a foreign specialty item that required some effort (and money) to obtain certainly added to their allure. To acquire the genuine article, Jefferson inquired with his man in Marseille, Stephen Cathalan, in May 1803; the order for fifty pounds of "Naples maccaroni" was filled by an export company in Genoa in December. The goods arrived in New York at the end of March 1804, from whence they were shipped to Washington. The wait certainly raised the anticipation.

In 1807, Jefferson jotted a note on a shipping notice for his latest order from Italy (eighty pounds of parmesan cheese and sixty pounds of macaroni): "Note. Sartori, at Trenton sells his Maccaroni in boxes of 25 lb each at 4. D the box." John B. Sartori may have been on Jefferson's radar as he had served as US consul at Rome from 1797 to 1801. In 1802, a lengthy ad in the Philadelphia newspaper *Aurora General Advertiser* announced his latest endeavor:

Vermicelli & Macaroni

> THE subscribers having at considerable expense established at Lamberton, near Trenton, New Jersey, a manufactory of Vermicelli and Macaroni, for which purpose they imported the necessary apparatus, and procured the most experienced workmen from Italy, beg leave to inform the public, that they will constantly have for sale a large quantity for exportation or home consumption, at reasonable prices; besides its being fresher they warrant it equal to any imported.

This was the first American macaroni "manufactory." Sartori provides a long list of shops carrying his product from Boston to Savannah, including several in Virginia. Jefferson was not yet desperate enough for the domestic product. However, the Embargo Act of 1807, signed into law by Jefferson, found him writing a panicked letter in July 1807, fearing his own legislation would impede future shipments. He orders fifty pounds of macaroni and three hundred bottles of Montepulciano wine through his merchant, coupling two of his great passions. By November 1808, while the embargo is still in effect, he breaks down and orders two boxes of macaroni from Sartori in Jersey.

The following year, Jefferson retired, and Edith Fossett became the chef at Monticello. Jefferson wrote to his specialty grocer in Richmond recommending they stock Sartori's macaroni, making it easier for him to procure. In response, they informed him that there was a macaroni dealer in Richmond, a Mr. Le Forest, who imported from Italy, but he charged four times more than Sartori. The Embargo Act was repealed in 1809 and replaced by the Non-Intercourse Act. These trade restrictions, combined with the rising tensions that ultimately led to the War of 1812, made it nearly impossible to get orders through to France.

Finally, in 1815, Jefferson turns once again turns to Cathalan. After a lengthy description of the wines he requires, he says, "To these I add 50 lb of Maccaroni, an article not to be bought in the United states." It seems that Sartori was not up to snuff, and Le Forest was too rich for his blood.

Indeed, for the genuine article through his man in Marseille, he paid ten dollars for fifty pounds. At this point it is a steady stream. Another order was placed in 1816—again for wine and "maccaroni." This time it only took six months to arrive. In 1817, the order is increased to a hundred pounds. In macaroni and cheese terms, that is about five hundred servings. For some years, the orders no longer included cheese. Another hundred pounds was ordered in both 1818 and 1819, meaning that Edy was serving up great quantities of the stuff.

With Catalan's retirement, Jefferson began dealing with a new exporter. In both 1820 and 1821 he orders 50 pounds, specifying in both instances, "those of Naples preferred if to be had." He must have regretted ordering so little because he increased the order to seventy-five pounds in 1822. In 1823 and 1824 he increased again to eighty pounds and by 1825 was back to a reassuring hundred pounds. The order for a hundred pounds arrived slightly over that quantity. It was registered in the 1826 inventory as 113 lb.[78]

While we must relinquish the stories claiming that James Hemings or Thomas Jefferson introduced, disseminated, or popularized macaroni and cheese, or at best treat them with skepticism, the nation's founder did continue to eat macaroni and cheese with gusto to the very end of his life on July 4, 1826, fifty years to the day after the adoption of the Declaration of Independence.

MACARONI AND CHEESE: MYTHOLOGIES AND LEGENDS

Traditions fulfill the human need for a sense of purpose and belonging. Collectively, groups consciously or subconsciously select factual data, stories, artifacts, and practices from the past to shape and define the identity of their community. These elements are sifted out and repurposed to construct a heritage narrative, delineating the criteria for inclusion and reinforcing the common values among adherents. So long as they are not presented as absolute truth, culturally inspired storytelling, legends,

(continued on next page)

(*continued from previous page*)

and mythologies are effective vehicles through which social ideals are expressed and handed down. But, within our striving to create meaning lies the tendency to indulge in the creation of what the British historian Eric Hobsbawm famously termed "invented traditions," which, when left unchecked and uncontested, can fossilize into groupthink, rendering them impervious to critical examination.

The philosopher Roland Barthes frames the phenomenon of the modern mythology succinctly: "It abolishes the complexity of human acts, giving them the simplicity of essences. It does away with all dialectics and organizes a world which is without contradictions because it is without depth. It establishes a blissful clarity: things appear to mean something by themselves."

Attempts to Give Credit Where Credit Is Due

It isn't clear precisely how and when the Thomas Jefferson–centered macaroni myth shifted to James Hemings, but evolution offers a glimpse into how historical narratives can shift over time. As far as we know, the tale begins in 1938 with Marie Kimball's *Thomas Jefferson's Cook Book*, where she boldly claims that Jefferson was the first to bring macaroni to the United States and more vaguely that he had a classically trained enslaved cook named "James Hastings" whom he later freed. By 1954, this cook's name appears correctly as "Hemings" in the African American academic journal *Phylon*, though he is only mentioned in passing as an "expert cook" without deeper exploration of his culinary contributions.[79] Many Americans may have first learned of Hemings's French culinary training through a brief mention in a 1963 *Cosmopolitan* article. The piece stated outright that the two men cooked together and noted Jefferson's bringing back macaroni and parmesan but stopped short of any claims of either man's influence in popularizing the dish.[80]

A story linking Hemings to macaroni may have begun circulating on the tailwinds of the cultural and intellectual momentum of the Harlem Renaissance, which laid the foundation for overtly political Civil Rights Movement. The chef and cookbook author Leonard E. Roberts (b. 1916) had experienced both of these decisive eras. It is in his book *The Negro Chef* (1969) that we hear elaborated praise of James Hemings:

> In the middle of the 1700's our third President, Thomas A. Jefferson, brought back from France a Negro as his servant. His name was James Hemming. Hemming was not only a servant, but a first class chef,

schooled in the art of French cuisine. He and Jefferson concocted the great continental cuisine of France and made some of our most glamorous American dishes. At Monticello and the White House, they introduced ice cream, macaroni, spaghetti, Savoye, cornbread stuffing, waffles, almonds, raisins, vanilla and many more dishes and foods to America. James Hemming and other of Jefferson's servants from these two great houses handed down to generations of Negro and white families alike the repertory of the American table.[81]

Roberts's version of the story carries the ring of authenticity—not in the sense that it is factually accurate but insofar as it is stated with a conviction that is more than personal. It seems to capture a story that had been in circulation before this version made it into print in his self-published book. The misspelling of Hemings's name, and the sweeping claims about the culinary impact of his and Jefferson's experience in France, suggest Roberts was drawing from a popular narrative that may have been widely shared, containing details that had not previously appeared in print.

Despite its informal origins, Roberts's account gained scholarly legitimacy, notably in the seventh volume of the *New Encyclopedia of Southern Culture on Foodways*, where his version of the Hemings story serves as a quotable source for the article on Jefferson himself.[82]

By 1994, in the cookbook *The African-American Kitchen*, various elements of the story had been corrected but other embellishments added. This headnote, for example, implies that there was an actual Hemings recipe:

James Hemings, President Thomas Jefferson's black slave chef, was among the first cooks in America to serve macaroni. His recipe was fairly simple:

Break macaroni into small pieces, there should be two cupfuls, and boil in salted water until tender. Grate 1/4 pound of cheese and mix with the same amount of butter. Stir into the macaroni and bake in a moderate oven until the cheese is thoroughly melted.

While Hemings did not leave a recipe for macaroni and cheese, this approach to the dish might have been typical of the time. It would be interesting to compare this with Louis Fresnaye's 1802 recipe for macaroni pudding (see chapter 5). It is plausible that these two men had had dealings, as they both would have been in Philadelphia during Jefferson's tenure as secretary of state.

(*continued on next page*)

(*continued from previous page*)

The description further on in the book conjures an attractive picture of a Hemings-Jefferson collaboration together with some hasty history: "Together Hemings and Jefferson created dishes that introduced an exciting new cuisine to America. . . . Hemings creatively combined the elements of French cuisine with American cooking. For Jefferson and his guests, he prepared macaroni, cornbread stuffing, waffles, and ice cream, unusual dishes at that time. . . . You could say Hemings cooked his way to freedom. In 1793, Jefferson signed a document that emancipated Hemings if he promised to train a new chef for Monticello."

Similar "signature" recipes with elaborated historical notes linking James Hemings to the iconic American dish would be echoed by myriad others seeking to "correct" the historical record. Gastro-tales such as these snowball into modern mythologies, which by definition resist dismantling once ingrained in the public consciousness. The beloved dish macaroni and cheese came to represent the tangible, take-home aspect of the story of Hemings as a forgotten hero. By consuming the food with directed awareness, one can commune with and embody the poignant narrative of his resilience. Hemings as the creative spark behind the popularity of macaroni and cheese in the United States was presented to the public in no uncertain terms through articles with titles such as "You Can Thank James Hemings, the Enslaved Chef of Thomas Jefferson, for the Mac and Cheese on Your Table—The truth behind America's favorite cheesy pasta dish" (2022).

While the motivation behind bringing James Hemings's story into the public forum is commendable, as it pays homage to his contribution to early American culinary history, elevating him as a hero in African American history, the continued insistence on macaroni and cheese as the crux of his legacy is a foreclosure on the opportunity for wider inquiry and eclipses the substantial role that African American women across generations played as innovators and expert practitioners. Advocates seeking to exalt his achievements now default to macaroni and cheese due to its pervasive—though purely speculative—association with him. The perpetuation of this association inevitably detracts from Hemings's complex backstory and the broader implications of his experiences from enslavement to freedom as a multiracial man of African descent in antebellum United States.

Disheartening as it may be, in the absence of an actual Hemings macaroni and cheese recipe, our only recourse is to imagine the sumptuous macaroni and cheese that this able chef, with years of training in Paris and a specialization in fine pastry, might have produced.

Chapter Five

THE NEW WORLD ORDER

Macaroni's Triangular Transformation

On the CHARACTER of a GENTLEMAN
. . . Love is my god, beauty is my passion, macaroni is my diet, music is my pastime, verse is my delight, and my motto amor vincit.

—NEW-YORK DAILY GAZETTE, SEPTEMBER 21, 1790

THE PIES HAVE IT

Serving up cheesy macaroni in a pie shell combines both homey charm and an air of elegance. This double-carbohydrate fusion first manifests in writing in a Bartolomeo Scappi creation in 1570. By the close of the eighteenth century, it had settled in Scotland, tucked into a hot water pastry crust. The Scots, whose climate and appetites were well-suited to such fare, would warmly usher macaroni pie into their national cuisine. The zeal for Scotch pie helped ease macaroni pie into the cultural fold, though excessive coaxing can't have been necessary. For city dwellers, the main ingredient seemed to be readily available. Hugh Campbell's Shop in Edinburgh first announced its stock of "leaf and pipe macarony" in the *Caledonia Mercury* on March 9, 1767, sparking a steady stream of advertisements thereafter.

Vincent La Chapelle's "*A Chicken Pye with* Italian *Maſcaronis*," may have inspired Mrs. Frazer's "*A Macaroni Pie*," though the difference in title reveals where her priorities lie. Her cookbook, *The Practice of Cookery, Pastry, Pickling, Preserving, &c.* by "Mrs. FRAZER, sole teacher of these arts in Edinburgh" (1791), marries Scottish pragmatism with gastronomic flair. She starts by making a hearty broth with the skin and carcass of a roasted chicken, seasoning it with white pepper, nutmeg, and cayenne. Notably, this marks the first documentation of cayenne in our dish, keeping in mind

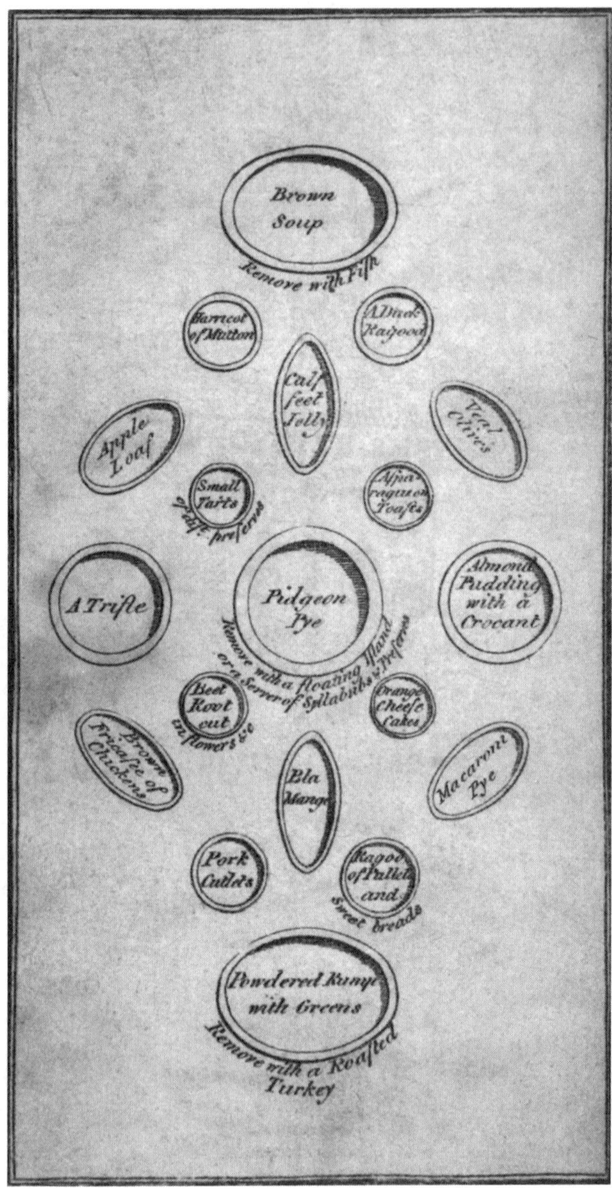

FIGURE 5.1. Menu planner from Mrs. Frazer's *The Practice of Cookery*, showing macaroni pie in a late-eighteenth-century Scottish meal composition. *Source*: Public domain.

that actual practice precedes publication, often by decades. The macaroni is cooked in this spicy stock, absorbing the liquid until the pasta is plump and the liquid reduced to a thick gravy. This mixture is layered into the dough-lined baking tin with an equal weight of cheese—either parmesan or double gloucester. First, the cheese: "Lay ſome of it into your ſhape, then ſome of your macaroni, with bits of butter above it, then a lair of the ſlices of the fowls, and repeat this till the whole is exhauſted." A swath of dough was positioned on top, with the edges tightly sealed to prevent seepage. To serve, it was released onto a platter, adorned with a generous sprinkling of grated cheese. These freestanding pastries, known as 'raised pies,' were baked in molds with removable sides and false bottoms, allowing the encasement to be lifted out intact. The forms came in various shapes—often oval or round, and occasionally boat-like. Impressive as they were, the bravura lay in not sacrificing deliciousness for spectacle. A macaroni pie would fall into the category of a "made dish"—not the main event, but a showpiece that required multiple steps and skillful assembly.

Frazer contrasts this showpiece with "*A diſh of Macaroni*" for less formal occasions. Here the macaroni is cooked in milk. Once it has reduced and thickened, a "half a mutchkin of cream" is added, with white pepper as the sole spice.[1] The rim of the tin is adorned with an ornate dickie crust of puff pastry, the unfulfilled promise of a proper pie, a common decoy that aligns with Verral's example (see chapter 3). Here, again, cheese equaling the weight of the dry macaroni is set out in layers, each one separated by pats of butter. After piling the last layer high with cheese, the whole is anointed with butter. Creamy, caloric comfort. The pie is baked in the oven for half an hour. A similar filling packed into a hot water crust would in due time be hailed as one of the culinary identity markers of Scotland in the venerable company of haggis—some creative cooks have even incorporated both into the same dish.[2]

The English cook and tavern owner John Mollard has a similar raised macaroni pie in his cookbook with the strikingly familiar title, *The Art of Cookery Made Easy and Refined* (1801). "*Raised Macaroni Pie*" starts with a pre-baked hot water crust. Inside, layers of creamy parmesan "stewed macaroni" alternate with chicken fricassee, a touch of French elegance. Mollard fails to let his reader in on what "stewed macaroni" is in the first edition but rectifies the error in the 1802 revised edition. Note that his macaroni is noodles and not tubes.

To stew Maccaroni.

Boil a quarter of a pound of riband macaroni in beef stock till nearly done; then strain it and add a gill of cream, two ounces of fresh butter, a tablespoonful of the essence of ham, three ounces of grated parmezan cheese, and a little cayenne pepper and salt. Mix them over a fire for five minutes then put it on a dish, strew grated parmezan cheese, over it, smooth it with a knife, and colour with a very hot salamander.

Cayenne appears once again. The call for the essence of ham was not an isolated oddity. The intensely flavored drippings or deglazed juices from the crusted-over pan of a roasted ham was something savvy cooks would store in the cellar for just such occasions.[3] But there were also purpose-built recipes. Strip what remains of a leftover baked ham from the bone and beat it to a pulp with a rolling pin; then, pan-fry to heighten the flavor. Add herbs and pepper and stew slowly over the fire in half a pint of beef stock. Press the liquid out, and you have ham essence. The umami impact of this elixir was apparently worth going to such lengths. Maria Eliza Rundell (1745–1828) assures us, "A little of this is an improvement to all gravies."[4] Mollard's raised pie finds its way onto the first course of his November menu sampler, accompanied by a water souchet (a thin fish soup), stuffed pickled tongue, vegetable ragout, chicken "bershamelle," slices of fried cod in oyster sauce, pork cutlets with fried potatoes, and a medley of cauliflower and green beans.

The early Scottish cookbook dynasty, headed up by Elizabeth Cleland (1755), Susanna MacIver (1773), and her successor, Mrs. Frazer (1792), was followed in 1809 by Mrs. Nourse. These cookbooks were fruit of their experience as teachers at their Edinburgh cooking schools for young ladies and used as textbooks, a practice carried on from Edward Kidder. Mrs. Nourse has a macaroni pie modelled on Mrs. Frazer's that inexplicably loses the cheese. Perhaps it was an oversight. In the 1813 edition, to our relief, we find another pie recipe called "*To Dress Macaroni*" in which reason (vis-à-vis cheese) has been restored. The macaroni is boiled in water then cooked again in cream. The water bath came recommended more and more, not only to precook the pasta but to insure it was free of bugs, dirt, and any impurities lodged in the tubes, not to mention the infamous foul odors. To season, Nourse chooses mace and "made mustard"—so, not the powdered variety. The addition of mustard was built on the popular classic Welsh rabbit, or rarebit, as it is now called, and would become a common feature. Macaroni and cheese and rarebit recipes were often placed in close proximity in cookbooks as pertaining to the same wheat and cheese culinary concept.

Timbale: Raising the Bar

The pride of French culinary arts, Marie-Antoine Carême (1784–1833), started his ascent to fame as a *tourier*, a pastry apprentice tasked with folding dough to make puff pastry. While not the inventor of the technique, he brought it to new heights, both literally and figuratively. By the age of thirty-one, his fame had spread throughout Europe, earning him the moniker "The king of cooks and the cook of kings." It was then that he published his masterwork on pastry, which included a raised macaroni pie called "Timbale de macaroni à la Milanaise."

In the headnote, Carême extolled the raised pie as an excellent way to present macaroni and cheese, though one must be meticulous with the ornamentation. Indeed, the intricacy of his crusts reflects his other great passion, architecture. The macaroni filling, while sumptuous, played second fiddle to the ornate edifice that housed it. He makes a point of emphasizing "true Italian macaroni" because the French-made pasta products that dominated the market were considered inferior, as they were not made of pure semolina. For one pound of dried pasta, he used one pound of parmesan cheese and half a pound of butter, seasoned only with salt and mignonette pepper. The cooked pasta was then combined with the cheese, butter, and seasonings in a saucepan, aided by a bit of gravy to fend off stringiness.[5]

In 1822, Carême published two volumes of menus, a retrospective treatise detailing his philosophy and past performance in Paris, Saint Petersburg, London, and Vienna. Macaroni and cheese in various forms (timbales, pottages, and simple *macaroni lié au parmesan*) featured prominently as fare deemed worthy of dignitaries and notables. The principles espoused in Carême's work stood as the epitome of culinary culture, ensuring France's continued status as the unrivaled gastronomic leader and the enduring legacy of macaroni and cheese as a noteworthy dish.

Though he may have been a master theoretician, Carême would not be remembered as an able cook.[6] André Viard (1759–1834), Carême's elder and contemporary, was both and left us with a timbale whose filling was quintessentially French, accommodated in an inspiring construction.

TIMBALE DE MACARONI

1 cup (235 g) cold butter, cubed
3 cups (350 g) flour
1/3 cup (100 mL) cold water
1 tsp salt
3 eggs

8 oz (225 g) macaroni
1 onion stuck with two cloves
1 tablespoon (15 mL) plus 4 1/4 tablespoons (60 g) butter
4 oz (120 g) Gruyere, grated
3 oz (90 g) parmesan, grated
1/4 tsp (1 mL) freshly ground pepper
1/4 tsp nutmeg
1/2 cup (125 mL) heavy cream
Buttered breadcrumbs and Parmesan for topping

Cut the butter into the flour by hand or pulse in a food processor. In a small bowl, mix the water, salt, and eggs then pour into the butter and flour, mixing until just combined. Form into a ball and let the dough chill one hour in the fridge. Bring it to room temperature, cut it into strips, and roll those into ropes to spiral inside a well-buttered springform baking tin. Refrigerate while you prepare the macaroni.

Bring a pot of water to a boil with the first amount of butter, onion, and macaroni. Boil until soft. Drain and put back in the pot with the rest of the ingredients. Stir on low until the butter is melted.

Fill with crust with the macaroni mixture, sprinkle with equal amounts of breadcrumbs and grated Parmesan and bake 75 minutes at 350°F (180°C).

SUPPLY AND DEMAND IN THE NINETEENTH CENTURY

Manufacturing macaroni in North America was a venture capitalist's dream. John B. Sartori, for one, had no intention of being a small-time pasta-maker with local distribution. In the first years of the 1800s, he set up a network of wholesale and retail outlets throughout the United States.

Sartori's advertisements boldly asserted unsubstantiated claims, the ends apparently justifying the means: "recommended by all physicians who have tried it, as gratifying the taste of those in health, and proving beneficial to the convalescence of the sick."[7] A wordsmith he was not. His ambition was to make macaroni as popular in the fifteen states of the Union as it was in "Southern parts of Europe, and the East and West Indies."[8] The Indies? We'll circle back to this.

The Embargo Act of 1807, though predicated on good intentions, proved disastrous for the young nation. It was an attempt to steer clear of the Napoleonic Wars and maintain neutrality while Britain and France had at it. The cessation of trade was not just a diplomatic move. American seamen on merchant ships were being "impressed"—forcibly conscripted—into the British Navy, as the Crown was short of able hands. But stepping back from the fray had devastating effects on the economy. In 1808, Sartori's name surfaced again, as the legislation was ruining his business. His solicitor filed a petition to the government, "praying on account of the spoilation," to be given permission to export his product. Permission denied.[9]

In March of 1809, the act was repealed, and Sartori once again made the news. The article, "Manufacture of Vermicelli and Macaroni, in the U. States," in the *Richmond Enquirer*, reveals that macaroni products had for years been produced in the country for export, specifically naming the West Indies, where it had become a remunerative trade item in exchange for rum, coffee, and sugar. Demand for macaroni was also high in other French and Spanish colonies of the Americas and the East Indies, where the English were actively expanding their dominion. Sartori may have been the kingpin among the exporters, but there were "several smaller establishments, for the preparation of these nutritive articles, in New York and elsewhere."[10] Despite their arts and parts—imported workmen and machinery—these manufacturers relied on soft, American-grown wheat to contain costs, which could not compete with the quality of semolina, a hard wheat. In an attempt to explain in terms Americans could relate to, the article oversimplifies it: "Semolina is a coarse or harsh powder, which bears the same relation to wheat, that hominy or rather grits bears to maize."[11] Without giving trade secrets away, Sartori assures the public that "he overcame this difficulty, and made his pastes so good, that in 1805, they were pronounced in Havana equal to those of Italy."[12] Again, the West Indies. Was Spanish-dominated Cuba setting the bar? Jefferson had tried Sartori's wares during the embargo crisis but went back to imported macaroni as soon as it became possible. Granted, he had high standards, acquainted as he was with the genuine article.

Competitors, like Joseph Anastasi in New York, went so far as to claim his domestic product was superior to the import, playing the freshness card as a lure: "As he is constantly manufacturing from the best flour, therefore it is not liable to the many disadvantages incurred by long keeping." This downside would continue to plague commercial macaroni. Warnings like Eliza Acton's, "Ingredients . . . should be fresh and of good quality, particularly Italian pastes of every kind (macaroni, vermicelli, &c.), as they contract, by long keeping, a peculiarly unpleasant, musty flavour," would make locally produced macaroni an attractive option and allow more families access to the hitherto highbrow Macaroni Club.[13]

Sartori had thirty-five thousand dollars' worth of macaroni stocked and ready for shipment at the outset of the Embargo Act. Forced to rely on domestic sales alone, he suffered a 99 percent loss—or so he claimed in his plea to Congress in 1808. He maintained that his revenue for that year had been estimated in the range of ninety thousand dollars—500 percent of the price of the raw materials. Macaroni was a lucrative business. Regardless of the quality, the market potential was astronomical. Enterprising Americans were eager to get a piece of the pie.

English cheese-making had gone the same route and been successfully replicated in New England, importing the denominations of origin, Cheshire and Cheddar, along with the corresponding practices. The dairy-minded focus of the Dutch made the importation of cattle a priority, introducing them into New Netherlands in 1625. By 1650, a missive from the colony's governor proclaimed that there was no longer a need to import them as "they can be got at a reasonable price from the Dutch, and principally among the English, who have plenty of them."[14] Further south, the Carolinas came to be known as "cattle country." Their livestock had been purchased from Barbados, the Bermudas, Virginia, and New York.[15] The evergreen pastures of the Carolinas meant that "an Ox is raised at almost as little expence as a Hen is in England."[16] The Carolinians "that understand it make as good butter and cheese as most in England."[17] The instructions on how "*To Make a* Chedder-*Cheeſe*," in the Williamsburg edition of Eliza Smith's *Compleat Housewife* (1747), assumed it was commonplace to have twelve cows on hand. And that may not have been far off the mark. By the 1790s, the quality and output of American cheddar was so high that producers found themselves in the paradoxical position of exporting it back to its country of origin. It flourished in the British marketplace owing to its consistent quality at an affordable price, making it very likely that imported, orange cheddar was finding its way into English macaroni and cheese. American cheesemakers were singing Yankee Doodle Dandy all the way to the bank.

Also Known as "Pie": Bajan Macaroni

Wherever colonialization takes root, the contours manifest with relative predictability. Colonizers endeavor to replicate the standards of material culture and conventions they deem suited to their station, settling into a comfortable lifestyle while capitalizing on local resources. In the British West Indies, superimposing that fantasy onto reality and establishing a plantation economy required exploiting large numbers of people across various forms of servitude—from enslaved Africans, Indigenous Caribbeans, and Native captives from North America, to numerous indentured Irish, Scots, and later South Asians. The triangular trade routes between the Americas, Europe, and Africa ensured a steady influx of goods and laborers at a pace that would allow colonizers to achieve a satisfactory degree of verisimilitude to live the dream. Eyewitness accounts marveled at the extravagant feasts that inspired the expression "as rich as a Barbados planter."[18]

Thus, barring incidental divergences, the same culinary values and de rigueur dishes that traversed the Atlantic from France and England to the North American colonies were exported to the Caribbean. Within this context, the trajectory of macaroni and cheese mirrored the path of prestige, desirability, and subsequent popularization that it had in other areas where English and French cuisines were replicated. Moreover, the products and foodways of the New World that had piqued the interest of the Old World since the time of Columbus would circuitously find their way to the West Indies in various European recipes.

In procuring involuntary labor, some slave traders targeted specific African regions where populations demonstrated an acumen in agriculture and husbandry that aligned with New World markets.[19] The great majority of people forcibly taken from Africa were first brought to the West Indies and Brazil, and most of the enslaved who were transported to the United States had either descended from people brought to the Caribbean or been transferred from there. Many US plantation owners also had landholdings in the area or relatives who did.[20] Some of the captured individuals destined to become cooks in the United States might have undergone a form of "breaking" in way stations in the West Indies—a period of processing to coerce them into compliancy before moving them on to their final destination. In this scenario, European recipes, locally modified in the hands of enslaved cooks, may have been disseminated across a broader geographical range. Despite the decimation of the Carib, Arawak, and Taíno populations, those remaining would have likely interacted with Africans, introducing their own culinary influences, which came together as Afro-Indigenous cuisine, notable among which was the use of chilis, a key element in this exchange.[21]

Generation after generation, the hands responsible for recreating these European cuisines—that is, those charged with meeting the standards and expectations of masters and mistresses—were primarily enslaved women of African descent. The Slavery Abolition Act of 1833, which phased out slavery in the British Empire over a five-year period, did little to impact this de facto aspect of domestic servitude. As such, Black women continued to command the kitchen. It was under the watch of generations of these authoritative cooks that our dish underwent reinterpretation and regimentation and would eventually emerge as an expression of Caribbean cuisine.

Evidence of macaroni aboard ships traveling to the Caribbean can be traced back to Sir Francis Drake and Sir John Hawkins' fateful voyage in 1596, whereupon the crew was fed "victuells for sea service devised by Mr Hugh Platte," (see chapter 3).[22] From the intricacies of Sartori's plight, suffered as a result of the economic fallout from the Embargo Act, we know that substantial shipments of macaroni were exported to the area from the United States and likely from Europe as well. Macaroni and cheese would go on to become a staple throughout the West Indies, notably in Trinidad and the Bahamas, but even more markedly in Barbados. There, it is a fixture in their national cuisine, known as Bajan macaroni pie—or just "pie"—although in this iteration, there is no pie crust.

The Wikipedia page for the general concept "macaroni pie" previously suggested that it was first created in Barbados and subsequently spread across the Americas during the slave trade era, eventually making its way back to Europe. While this misconception has since been deleted and rectified, the Barbadian version of macaroni and cheese does draw attention to the fluidity of culinary currents during the eighteenth and nineteenth centuries, occasioning an invitation for a closer look. Indeed, this is not a simple case of adding a few native ingredients to impart a local twist to an imported dish. Nor is Barbadian macaroni and cheese the "fusion" of two cuisines. The novelties represent a nuanced adoption of flavors selected over time from a panorama of options and influences, resulting in an assemblage that is undeniably macaroni and cheese and distinctly Barbadian (or Caribbean).

Let's explore some of these details of exchange by taking a look at a composite recipe of Bajan macaroni pie.

BAJAN MACARONI PIE

11 oz (300 g) long, pipe-style macaroni; *mezzani* format is best
4 1/2 Tbsp (65 g) butter
1 small onion, grated
1 clove garlic, finely chopped
1 small sweet red pepper, very finely chopped
1 1/2 cups (375 mL) evaporated milk
1 egg, lightly beaten
1/4 cup (60 mL) ketchup
1 Tbsp dry English mustard (or prepared)
Heat to taste: cayenne, Scotch bonnet, Caribbean curry powder, or Bajan pepper sauce
1 Tbsp (15 mL) fresh thyme
1 tsp (5 mL) white pepper
10 oz (330 g) + 4 oz (120 g) extra sharp orange cheddar
Buttered breadcrumbs for topping (optional)

Other commonly used ingredients: tomato paste, allspice, nutmeg, mayonnaise, paprika, parsley, onion powder, garlic powder

Often served with gravy or stew.

Preheat the oven to 375°F (190°C). Butter a 9 × 9-in. (23 × 23 cm) baking dish.

Break macaroni sticks into 3-in. (7 cm) lengths over a bowl to collect the shards. Boil them in a pot of salted water until al dente. Heat the butter in a

(*continued on next page*)

(continued from previous page)
skillet and sauté the onion, garlic, and red pepper. In a large bowl, combine that mixture with the evaporated milk, egg, ketchup, mustard, thyme, white pepper, with heat to taste. Then add the macaroni, stir, and pour all of it into the prepared dish, gently pressing it into the dish. Top with the cheese and breadcrumbs and bake for half an hour.

Having surveyed numerous versions of macaroni and cheese in the previous chapters, the distinctive elements in the Barbadian recipe stand out, allowing for a comparison to past practice. While these adaptations arguably came into play over the course of the eighteenth and nineteenth centuries, the precise details of their integration remain speculative. By taking a retrospective look at various elements of the modern recipe, we can connect some historical dots to more fully appreciate how Bajan pie may have come to manifest in its present form.

Unpacking Bajan "Pie"

MACARONI

The most prevalent packaging for macaroni exportation at that time was long form. Whether they were bucatini or the larger mezzani, Barbadian tradition maintains a preference for the long pipes, linking the dish to its distant past. Throughout the nineteenth century, recipes frequently instructed the cook to break the macaroni or cut it after boiling. Breaking it leaves the ends jagged, a telltale characteristic of Bajan pie. Native Barbadians nostalgically recall breaking the macaroni as a childhood task. Bajan baked macaroni is meant to be rather solid so that it can be served in neat squares. The longer tubes lend themselves to creating that desired consistency. While many practitioners today have adopted elbows, they were not an option at the time. With the advent of US manufacturing, cheaper, fresher macaroni became readily available, encouraging the diffusion of the dish and entrenching it ever more deeply in local culture.

DAIRY

Despite Britain imperiously nicknaming Barbados "Little England," the country had no dairy industry, and cheese had always been imported. Agricultural pursuits were focused on sugar cane cultivation and its by-products. In the mid-nineteenth century, innovations in the cheddar industry ushered in mass production, leading to a veritable boom. Lower prices and increased availability made cheddar the preferred choice for macaroni. The distinct flavor of sharp cheddar remains nonnegotiable for Bajan pie traditionalists.[23]

In Bajan pie, evaporated milk is the default. Experimentation to lengthen the shelf life of milk began in the first half of the nineteenth century in Europe. By 1856, Gail Borden had patented his condensed milk and bottled it for commercial distribution from the Borden Milk Factory in Wolcottsville, New York. During the American Civil War, it rose to prominence as a way to supply milk to soldiers. Increased demand led to canning, which proved more reliable for shipping. When the sweetened version hit the market in 1885, the original became "evaporated milk" while the viscous, sugary newcomer retained the name "condensed milk" to avoid confusion. Evaporated milk was not only cheaper and more storable, but it was sometimes the only option; removal of 60 percent of the water also made it comparatively creamier, contributing to one of the other essential characteristics of Bajan pie: ooze. Proper preparation should yield a consistency conducive to cutting discrete blocks or slices—but straight out of the oven, there must also be some creamy give. Blocks, yes, bricks, no.

Evaporated milk would become the most economical and accessible option for recreating the dish, although its codification into the recipe likely coincided with the surge in consumption during World War I and II. These global conflicts prompted experimentation with its culinary possibilities, coaxing gastronomy from practical constraints. In the case of Bajan pie, there is yet another factor at play. At the intersection of practice, taste, and memory, use of this ingredient, originally borne out of necessity, has been repackaged as a tradition. Evaporated milk is now considered the standard, and variations are met with a raised eyebrow.

In the more recent history of the dish, a margarine called Mello Kreem occupied a similar coveted position. This orange-colored hydrogenated fat product was strategically marketed as the epitome of true Caribbean taste. It was cheaper than butter, had a longer shelf life, and was sometimes the only possible option. The ad campaign for its Trinidadian counterpart initially played upon imperialist status. Golden Ray margarine imparted "that good cooking-butter flavour," or, as the package proclaimed, "real French flavour." Following independence from Britain, it went native with the slogan "Adds that rich Creole flavour," a direct appeal to the Black community.[24] After transitioning to zero trans fats, the brand rebounded with "The secret of rich Caribbean flavour," aiming for a more inclusive message. This strategy pushed an association between the taste of the product and cultural pride. Even though "golden" margarine was a culinary latecomer, manufacturers tried to force-feed it as a ready-made tradition. In macaroni and cheese, it boosted the incandescent orange color, which had come to signify goodness. Today, while some remain loyalists, most prefer butter.

KETCHUP

The desired orange cast in macaroni and cheese was also achieved through ketchup, a distinctive element unique to Barbados. Its use on other islands depends on how closely the cooks adhere to the Barbadian model. The overwhelming importance that sauces called ketchup once held in the English kitchen has long since faded, but there was a time when walnut or mushroom or any number of other popular ketchup blends were pantry staples. In the time before refrigerators, recipes tried to outboast each other about the shelf life of their concoction—unlikely as it was that a batch would make it to the twenty-year expiration date some claimed. Ketchups were built to last.

They satisfied the human craving for piquant stimulation amid blandness, hitting all the taste sensors with combinations of vinegar, salt, sugar, spices, and the mellowing umami of fermentation. Tomato ketchup, one of the few remnants of this tradition, was actually a latecomer. Yet today, this one type is so singularly ensconced that we dispense with mentioning the tomato. Two New York manuscripts dating back to the 1780s feature recipes for tomato ketchup, seasoning the "love apples" with allspice (also called Jamaican pepper), mace, and whole pepper.[25] In 1804, James Mease, a scientist and horticulturist in Philadelphia, noted the extensive use of love apple catsup among the French. However, as the food historian Andrew F. Smith observed, "ketchup" was not a French culinary term. He speculates that what Mease had observed were the French Creole practices of those who had taken refuge in Philadelphia after the Haitian slave revolt.[26] Thus, given their ubiquitous use of tomato ketchup, it had clearly been in the Caribbean for some time. Mease published a ketchup recipe of his own, though, to put it kindly, cooking was not one of his many accomplishments.

The first tomato ketchup–like recipe to reach the United States in a cookbook was neither American nor original but a copy of a copy. Let's unpack that. Despite a heavy workload, the eccentric head of the York Lunatic Asylum, Alexander Hunter (1729–1809), found time to put out the peculiar *Culina famulatrix medicinae: Or, Receipts in Cookery* (1804), which included a recipe called "Tomata sauce"—essentially a tomato ketchup. It was a perky concoction, spiked with capsicum vinegar, garlic, and ginger. Hunter believed that a competent physician should be familiar with cookery, but his recipes, while couched in his own brand of witty erudition, were fruit of other minds.[27] The same recipe would be published a decade later in Maria Eliza Rundell's revised *A New System of Domestic Cookery: Formed Upon Principles of Economy, and Adapted to the Use of Private Families throughout the United States*.[28] The edgy inclusion of cayenne in this ketchup hinted at the emerging penchant for hot sauce. Europeans were thrilled about the prospect of chili peppers. Unlike black pepper, chilis could be grown nearly anywhere and at minimal cost. Ironically, accessibility became a point of contention. "With chili available to every peasant, strong spices and high flavors could no longer be the prerogative of the tables of the prominent."[29]

CHILIS

Chili peppers became a divisive issue in the nineteenth century, denounced by moralists who claimed they had no nutritive value and, like tobacco, were both a physical menace and a sign of moral decay among their adherents.[30] But the killjoys would not prevail, and cayenne became a popular addition to macaroni and cheese in the nineteenth century. However, in the Caribbean, the preference leans toward the decidedly pungent species *Capsicum chinense*, commonly known as Scotch bonnet.

The colloquial term's origin may be linked to a category of Scottish hat called a bunnet. Among these is the "blue bonnet," a common head covering that came to be associated with Jacobite allegiance. This connection harks back to the time when Barbados and other regions were claimed in the name of James Stuart, under whom the crowns of England and Scotland were unified. Colonization would begin during the reign of his son Charles I. Notably, Earl Dunmore, governor of the Bahamas from 1787 to 1796, who we met in the last chapter, was depicted wearing a blue bonnet in his portrait, as was his father before him, the gesture of a proper Scotsman. A later variant of the bunnet is the "tam o' shanter," popularized after Robert Burns's poem of the same name was published in 1791. The reason for the name is that the way the fabric flops over the brim of the hat is reminiscent of the shape of the pepper.

Regardless of the similarity in shape, the adoption of this anglophone reference to an indigenous botanical would only have occurred in a context where it conjured an immediate image for the speakers. Indeed, Scots numbering in the thousands journeyed to the Caribbean in the nineteenth century, some staying on permanently.[31] However the term eased into the language, it was already in common use in 1839 when Thomas Young arrived there on a mission for the British government. He was lucky to have arrived at all. The old Scotch mariner at the helm had accosted him one day and said, "We sha'na hae ony luck this voyage, sir! A cat has been killed on board and we set sail on a Friday." Doleful tidings, indeed! But Young did make safe passage, and in his writings on the Caribbean's diverse array of fruits and vegetables he specifically identified Scotch bonnet peppers.[32]

Chilis originated in South America and are indigenous to the West Indies, but the multidirectional ebb and flow of culinary currents that would lead to their use in macaroni and cheese are best conceptualized as incremental cofactors rather than singular events. In Barbados, one of the favorite ways to enjoy this pungent fruit is through the local hot sauce, made of Scotch bonnet peppers, vinegar, mustard powder, garlic, onion, salt, brown sugar, and turmeric, all the elements of a ketchup. It is often in this form that it adds a signature kick to Bajan pie.

THE FIRST AMERICAN PUBLICATIONS WITH MACARONI AND CHEESE

Macaroni: a sweet, very thin, tubular biscuit.

—"COOKERY: TERMS USED IN FRENCH AND ENGLISH COOKERY," IN *THE EMPORIUM OF ARTS & SCIENCES*, PHILADELPHIA (1813)

First Stop: Philadelphia

We can rather quickly bypass Richard Briggs's *The New Art of Cookery, According to the Present Practice*. It was published in Philadelphia in 1792, based on his 1788 London edition. His "Macaroni a la Parmazan" was lifted directly from Raffald's 1769 recipe, which was already in circulation. So much for "new art" and "present practice." Though the author was long since deceased, a new printing of Raffald's *English Housekeeper* would appear in Philadelphia six years later.

Newspaper advertisements dating back to the 1770s affirm the presence of an import network to satisfy Philadelphians' demand for pasta.[33] From a 1795 ad in the *Aurora General Advertiser*, it appears that it could also be had ready-made by the French pastry chef Chrétien Simonet, who offered "excellent Italian macaroni" alongside the many meat dishes and desserts in his upmarket cookshop in Philly.[34] But it is his countryman, the émigré Louis (Lewis) Fresnaye, who more firmly secured his place in our history. Fresnaye was a pasta manufacturer and vendor, though the specifics of his operation, such as whether or not he had an extrusion press, made his pasta by hand, or sold imported macaroni is unclear. What we do know is that he had a leaflet printed in 1802 with two recipes for macaroni and cheese, most likely as a how-to incentive to promote his wares, an early example of marketing that foreshadowed brand-name recipe booklets.

The title is "To make Soup of Vermicelli, Maccaroni and other kinds of Paste." Despite the term *soup*, the consistency of the end result is thick and buttery. He starts with a meat-based recipe, saying it can also be made with milk, butter, and cheese: "In this manner that it is very salutary and nutritive for persons of a weak stomach, and in a weak and debilitated state of body and is much used in the Italian Hospitals. This dish may well be substituted in the place of meat especially in the hot seasons of the year, when too great use of meat is prejudicial to health."

Although the distinction between sweet pudding macaroni and savory macaroni with cheese had been forged about a century earlier, Fresnaye refers to his second recipe as a pudding, despite no clear indication in the ingredients or method delineating it as such. However, as the first documented Franco-American macaroni and cheese recipe, it deserves elaboration for the modern kitchen. Fresnaye gives a bare bones version and an alternative "delicate" version; both options are included in the recipe below.

The first cookbook by an American (or Americans) to mention macaroni is *The Universal Receipt Book* (1814), published in New York by "A Society of Gentlemen." It includes instructions for hand-making macaroni noodles alongside a comparative description of the Italian tubular variety. The expanded edition (Philadelphia, 1818) adds a recipe for "Paris receipt for making the famous Camarani Soup"—a rich, layered dish of macaroni and parmesan interspersed with layers of minced vegetables, fowl liver, and aromatic herbs and spices.

FRESNAYE'S MACARONI PUDDING

3.5 quarts (3 L) water or 1 quart (1 L) milk

1/2 tsp salt

1 lb (45 g) long-form macaroni, broken into thirds

5.5 oz /1 1/3 cup (175 g) parmesan or "other good cheese"

1/2 cup (115 g) butter

1/2 cup (125 mL) beef gravy - optional finish

Bring salted water or milk to a boil then add the macaroni. If using water, strain the pasta when just cooked. Mix the cooked macaroni with the cheese and transfer to a 10-in. (26 cm) baking dish. Melt the butter and pour it over the macaroni while it is still warm. Place in a hot oven until it starts to brown. Finish with an optional ladleful of hot beef gravy.[35]

British Publications in the United States

Publishers in Philadelphia and Boston snapped up Maria Eliza Rundell's 1806 runaway success *A New System of Domestic Cookery*, publishing (or pirating) it for the US market. Originally prepared for her daughters, Rundell, at the age of sixty-one, entrusted the manuscript to her friend, the renowned Scottish publisher John Murray. As a woman of breeding, she opted for the genteel attribution "by A Lady" on the title page, eschewing explicit authorship. Rundell was shocked when she saw what a right mess Murray had made of her work and insisted on corrections and a reissue. The 1810 revised and enlarged edition expanded the macaroni and cheese recipes from one to four. This new version caught the attention of a New York publisher and hit the US market in 1814.

The dreary title "Macaroni as usually served" inexplicably finds itself in the "Sweet Dishes" section. It is a straightforward procedure: boil in milk or broth, add butter, cheese, an extra layer of the same on top, and bake in a Dutch oven. The second recipe, "Another way," has us boiling the macaroni in milk *and* broth then adds an egg yolk and a daring spoonful of cream. Butter and cheese as usual, brown with a salamander. The final recipe, "Another," goes heavy on the cheese. After boiling in broth infused with mace, the macaroni is mixed with generous amounts of an unspecified cheese, placed in a baking dish, and covered with breadcrumbs. But wait. Before placing the dish in a Dutch oven, douse with melted butter. Now, bake.

The outlier is "Macaroni Soup," suspiciously on its own in the "Soup" section. It starts off predictably enough: macaroni cooked in "good stock." But then there's a clever hack. Half of the macaroni is taken out and put to boil with more meat broth "till you can pulp all the macaroni through a fine sieve." The resulting macaroni cream is poured back in the saucepan with the spared macaroni then combined with actual cream and a good bit of Parmesan cheese. Serve with the crust of a French roll. Isn't it odd, though, that a nearly verbatim recipe was in Mrs. Smith's *The Female Economist: Or, A Plain System of Cookery: For the Use of Families*, whose first three editions were also published in 1810?

Might "Macaroni Soup" have been one of the recipes John Murray slipped in when he published the 1810 enlarged edition? In Rundell's struggle to regain the publishing rights to her book, Murray dug his heels in, citing his personal contribution to the expanded edition—doubtfully the result of pottering about in the kitchen.[36] Regardless of the creaming technique's origins, other authors would glom onto this novel thickening method.[37] It must have created quite a stir as one author (another "Lady,") felt compelled to snip, "It is folly to make these pastes [dried pasta] into thickenings, as ground rice, fine flour, or potato starch answer as well, at so much less expense."[38] But what better source to filch recipes from than *New System*, the bestselling cookbook of the first half of the nineteenth century? Given Rundell's reticence to have her identity revealed, and the promiscuous borrowing of recipes, it was folly not to. Rundell's authorship was finally disclosed in connection with her achievement after her death in 1828, when it was entered into the British *Dictionary of National Biography*. She was one of only two women deemed worthy—the other was Hannah Glasse.

The prize for the most eccentric cookbook author of the early nineteenth century goes most decidedly to Dr. William Kitchiner (1775–1827), evident in the title *Apicius Redivivus: or, The Cook's Oracle* (1817). His name does not grace the title page; he prefers to underscore his qualifications in the tagline: "The result of actual experiments instituted in the kitchen of a physician for the purpose of composing a culinary code for the rational epicure (etc.)." The part about being a physician was actually a lie, but it was an apparently inconsequential detail as the book enjoyed resounding success. He was most likely inspired by the vibrant Alexander Hunter (mentioned previously regarding ketchup), an actual medical doctor who had trained in Scotland, as Kitchiner also claimed to have done. Hunter's *Culina famulatrix medicinae* (literally, Cookery, the handmaid of medicine) was signed thus: Ignotus. Hunter's macaroni recipes are all borrowed, but in a witty postscript to the umpteenth replica of Raffald's recipe he takes the sixteenth-century French physician Carolus Stephanus to task. Stephanus had proclaimed that macaroni was indigestible and only suited to manual laborers and peasants, to which Ignotus replied, "The frequent use of it at genteel tables does not seem to confirm his opinion."[39]

Kitchiner's publishers felt they should tone down the *Apicius redivivus* pomposity to get on board with the prevailing buzzword in cookbooks: economy. By the time the 1822 expanded and revised fourth edition hit London, the title had been tweaked to be more marketable: *The Cook's Oracle: Containing Receipts for Plain Cookery on the Most Economical Plan for Private Families*. The nineteenth century witnessed a rapidly changing socioeconomic landscape propelled by industrialization and a growing middle class—the prime target for cookbooks. This demographic was rigidly status conscious but inclined toward no-nonsense thrift, foresight, precision, and utility.

In the same year that the new edition was published, the old version was coming off the presses in Boston. Kitchiner had broken into the American market. Success in the United States spurred the Boston publishers to release the latest edition the very next year. It is in this expanded edition that macaroni debuts.

As self-appointed oracle, Kitchiner generously dispensed his advice and commentary. Here are his pearls on macaroni: "The usual mode of dressing it in this country [England] is by adding a white sauce, and Parmesan or Cheshire cheese, and burning it; but this makes a dish which is proverbially unwholesome: but it's bad qualities arise from oiled and burnt cheese, and the half dressed flour and butter, put into the white sauce." His attempt to mend the error of their ways resulted in "English way of dressing Maccaroni," which is little more than a downgrade of Raffald's macaroni. He starts by boiling the macaroni in milk or broth, which is nothing new. The white sauce is bypassed entirely, and the pasta is dressed with butter and cheese (Parmesan or Cheshire) then topped with an additional layer of cheese. Wary of the scorching salamander, he suggests using a Dutch oven to lightly brown the top. Though his prowess as an oracle certainly did not shine through in this recipe, his entire macaroni treatise was brazenly copied word for word in M. Radcliff's *A Modern System of Domestic Cookery* (1824), which also graced us with the cocktail "Macaroni cordial." Kitchiner had his followers, but also his critics. One, particularly intent on unmasking him as an imposter spewed, "It is written in a vain-glorious, assuming style, and filled with gasconading vulgarisms and obsolete pedantry. The attempts at wit are ludicrously heavy and unsuccessful."[40]

Kitchiner's second macaroni entry, though not particularly cheesy, is historically relevant. It came to his attention on the recommendation of an unnamed "Grand Gourmand" residing in the fashionable Grosvenor Square of Westminster, a tidbit that would have piqued the attention of contemporary readers. During a gastronomic tour of the Continent, the discerning gentleman sampled numerous dishes, concluding that "Maccaroni Pudding," or *Timballe de Maccaroni*, was the most noteworthy addition to his cook's repertoire. It is an English-style steamed pudding, so the airs about gourmands on gastronomic tours may have been as fictitious

FIGURE 5.2. The vainglorious Dr. Kitchiner, author of *The Cook's Oracle* and the *Art of Invigorating and Prolonging Life*, although he would die at the age of fifty-two. *Source*: Public domain.

as Kitchiner's degree in medicine. It is a long-winded recipe for what is in essence a rich custard with macaroni, cheese, and bits of minced fowl breast and ham. The finishing touch is gravy, a concept imbued with connotations of indulgence. This is the only instance of this recipe in the cookbook corpus to date. However, it remarkably appears two years later, nearly verbatim, in Mary Randolph's *The Virginia House-wife.*

The First American Macaroni and Cheese Recipes by an American

The family history of Mary Randolph (1762–1828) sheds light on the interconnectedness of the First Families of Virginia but is also the basis for speculation about the American legacy of macaroni and cheese. Her mother, Anne Cary (whose mother was also named Mary Randolph), married her first cousin, Thomas Mann Randolph. When Mary's paternal grandfather, Colonel William Randolph, died, Peter Jefferson, Thomas Jefferson's father, became the executor of the Randolph estate in Tuckahoe. Peter had been a close friend, and his wife, Jane Randolph Jefferson (whose sister was also named Mary Randolph), was William's cousin. Thus, Peter and Jane moved their four children—including a two-year-old Thomas—to Tuckahoe, where they took charge of the plantation and acted as guardians to the orphaned Randolph children from 1744 to 1752. When the Jeffersons returned to their own plantation, Shadwell, near Charlottesville, they maintained relations with the Randolphs, as prominent families did. The trip was a full day's journey away, but given the vast open spaces, proximity was relative. Their genealogies are far more complex than this, with a mind-boggling repetition of names, but their bloodlines would cross once again when Mary Randolph's younger brother, Thomas Mann Randolph Jr. (1768–1828) married Martha (Patsy) Jefferson, his third cousin, in 1790—immediately after the Jeffersons and Hemingses had returned from Paris. Mary Randolph herself had, at the age of eighteen, married her cousin once removed, David Mead Randolph (1760–1830), making her Mary Randolph Randolph.

The newlyweds took up residence at David's family plantation, Presquile, where they had eight children, four of whom survived to adulthood. Mary assumed the traditional role of the Virginia housewife, entertaining frequently and earning a reputation as an exemplary hostess. They were the Revolution Generation, whose formative years were in lockstep with the birth of a nation, crossing the threshold to a promising future. The

Randolph dynasty had for over a century been well placed in politics and, on Thomas Jefferson's recommendation, George Washington followed suit, appointing David as US marshal in Virginia. It was an opportunity for Mary and David to change residence—both of them suffered from constant malaise due to the noxious fumes emanating from the swampland of their plantation. Their new home in Richmond was christened Moldavia, a combination of their names (Molly being Mary's nickname).

However, no sooner had Jefferson taken office as president than he removed David Randolph from his post, accusing him of jury-packing. In retaliation, Randolph, who had always opposed Jefferson politically, became more vocal in his criticism. The dissention backfired. It not only derailed his career but also disgraced the family, and their fortunes quickly dissipated. In 1807, Mary opened a boardinghouse to make ends meet, while her husband left for England to find investors for his inventions. He wouldn't return for eight years. We hear news of their plight in a letter from Martha to her father: "Sister Randolph has opened a boardinghouse in Richmond, but she has not a single boarder yet. her husband is gone to England upon some mercantile scheme with barely money to defray his expenses. the ruin of the family is still extending itself daily."[41]

In 1819, the Randolphs retired to Washington. Their finances had never recovered, so the ever-resourceful Mary set about compiling recipes drawn from her diverse experiences from plantation mistress to society hostess to boardinghouse keeper. It culminated in the publication of the first edition of *The Virginia House-wife* in 1824. Her style is essential and expedient, lauded by some, like the Early American culinary historian Karen Hess, as being, "of admirable simplicity of concept, clearly expressed, and full of perceptive observations."[42] The culinary historian Leni Sorensen believes that Randolph's "bossy directness" may have been targeting the young wives of elite Virginia families pushing further southwest, who may for a time have had to make do without an experienced enslaved cook. A brass-tacks cookbook would have been a welcome companion.[43]

While generally singing Mary Randolph's praises for her contribution to American history, Hess is dismissive of the macaroni recipe. In her discussion of Randolph's borrowings from other cuisines, she derogatorily refers to it as uninteresting, "a prototype for the limp factory macaroni and processed cheese that was to spread like a plague over the country." Given the parade of macaroni and cheese recipes that preceded *The Virginia House-wife*,

Randolph's recipe neither benefited from best practices nor improved upon her predecessors. In the unlikely event that she passed through the Monticello kitchen, she would have encountered French-influenced chefs, from James and Peter Hemings to Edith Fossett. And yet nothing in her recipe commends itself as having stemmed from that tradition, reinforcing the improbability that it arose from the Monticello chefs. Others speculate that it might have been passed on to her via Jefferson's granddaughters. But if the family cookbook later compiled by Virginia Jefferson Randolph Trist is any indication, the only recipe even vaguely related was an adaptation of the "Nouilly" recipe that Jefferson had scrawled in France. Nevertheless, Mary Randolph's macaroni and cheese recipe stands as a milestone in culinary history—the first to be published by an American woman in the United States.

Macaroni

Boil as much macaroni as will fill your dish, in milk and water till quite tender, drain it on a sieve, sprinkle a little salt over it, put a layer in your dish, then cheese and butter as in the polenta [referring to the recipe before this one: slices of cold corn mush layered with butter and cheese], and bake it in the same manner [slices of cheese on top then into a hot oven for 20–30 minutes].

Except for the layering, there is little difference between this and Kitchiner's lackluster rendition. Perhaps it's a coincidence. But it is in her 1825 edition that we find an unmistakably "borrowed" version of Kitchiner's macaroni pudding, even spelling it as he did with the double "c." Whereas he pontificates at length, Randolph manages to distill his recipe down to a single run-on sentence:

Maccaroni Pudding

Simmer, half a pound of macaroni in a plenty of water, with a table-spoonful of salt, till tender, but not broke—strain it, beat five yelks, two whites of eggs, half a pint of cream—mince white meat and boiled ham very fine, add three spoonful of grated cheese, pepper and salt; mix these with the maccaroni, butter the mould, put it in, and steam it in a pan of boiling water for an hour—serve with rich gravy.

Plagiarism was par for the course in cookbooks. Mary Randolph was neither the first nor the last. However, the addition of eggs, considered one of the hallmarks of southern-style macaroni and cheese, is erroneously attributed to Mary Randolph as an American innovation. Likewise, the ham in this recipe has been interpreted as her creative fusion of Virginian and Old World cookery. But readers here know better.

Mrs. Margaret Dods, from the Scottish lineage of rational culinary practitioners, also helped herself to Kitchiner's recipe in *The Cook and Housewife's Manual* (1826). Dods was a no-nonsense woman. Having once been forced to endure a tedious lecture on the science of cookery filled with curious trivia and philosophical musings, she reportedly burst out, "Let us to the wark! What business ha'e thae lang ink-horn-tailed words wi' teaching wives to make a Cock-a-leekie?"[44] Despite her protestations over pretense, she tarted up the recipe title, calling it "Parisian Macaroni Pudding" and, like Kitchiner, added a revelatory postscript: "This, by gourmands of high taste, is considered as out of sight the best modern preparation of macaroni; sweetened dishes of this paste being considered by them as only fit for boys and women." Actually, the taste for sweetened macaroni we first encountered in the thirteenth century would linger on for quite some time—apparently the fault of women and boys who just couldn't let go.

The second edition of *The Virginia House-wife* was sent to Jefferson with the single line, "Will you permit me my dear Sir to offer a copy of a book which my necessities compelled me to publish, and which I shall be much gratified to know meets with your approbation," a subtle reminder that that she and her husband had not recovered financially, and Jefferson's approval would help the success of the book.[45] In his reply, Jefferson employs illeism, a third-person rhetorical device, and follows up with a literary exercise in feigned appreciation with overtones of condescension: "Th Jefferson returns his thanks to mrs Randolph for the valuable little volume she has been so kind as to send him. it is one of those which contribute most to the innocent enjoyments of mankind, and which give us the useful instructn how to employ to our greatest gratification the means we may possess, great or small. a greater degree of merit few classes of books can claim. with his thanks he prays her to accept the assurance of his high respect and esteem."[46]

James Madison also received a copy of the "little volume," which at 250 pages was actually a rather substantial output. Flummoxed, he stumbled somewhat through his thank-you letter, which he dictated to his wife,

FIGURE 5.3. Early American fine silver macaroni servers. *Source*: Public domain.

Dolley. Indeed, one does wonder why the book wasn't sent directly to Mrs. Madison, known far and wide for her hospitality. He may in fact be saying just that in the last line:

> DEAR MADAM
>
> The copy of your little Volume accompanying your letter of the 17th instant, came duly to hand; & I am very sensible of the politeness to which I owe the favor. Of the value of its precepts on paper I cannot undertake to judge: when reduced to practice on the table, the question will be less beyond my pretentions. But altho' I cannot decide on the merit of the Author by the book, it is a case in which I think myself very safe in reversing the rule, & infering the merit of the publication from the pen from which it proceeds. In this confidence I anticipate the welcome reception that will be given to it by better judges than myself.[47]

THE FRAUGHT ART OF SOUTHERN HOSPITALITY

The acclaimed reputations of the Dolley Madisons and Mary Randolphs of the South were directly commensurate with the exceptional abilities of Black chefs, cooks, and the extended network of enslaved domestic labor. However, the plantation mistress came to the role with little to no preparation in managing a home.[48] Young wives were expected to morph into adept managers, running the household by virtue of the fact that they were women.[49] But the aura of Southern gentility that would become legendary was created by those tasked with carrying out the actual work. Over the course of the century leading up to the Civil War and the Emancipation Proclamation, the dishes that nourished the families and impressed the guests were predominantly crafted by African American women. These women had inherited the culinary knowledge and experience from generations before them, and they in turn passed on this wealth of expertise to the next generation. Along the way, each cook left her mark in terms of timing, method, ingredients, and mode of presentation—a continuous process of honing, refining, and establishing best practices.

These kitchens were the crucible wherein the essence of Southern hospitality was refined. It was there, in the authoritative hands of African American women, that the perception of macaroni and cheese as a European dish gradually fell away and its American identity began to take shape. The appropriation process was one of naturalization or transference rather than misappropriation; the dish was not wrested away and implanted with a foreign flag but was seamlessly eased into the cultural fabric elsewhere. Charles Ball casts light on appropriation from a different angle in the autobiographical narrative *Fifty Years in Chains: The Life of an American Slave* (1859): "I was never acquainted with a slave who believed that he violated any rule of morality by appropriating to himself any thing that belonged to his master if it was necessary to his comfort. . . . The slave reasoned differently, when he took a portion of his master's goods to satisfy his hunger, to keep himself warm, or to gratify his passion for luxurious enjoyment."[50] It was especially the case when, "in tracing things from cause to effect, the slave attributes all that he sees in possession of his master to his own toil."[51] From that perspective, both the material and cultural appropriation of the bounty of the slave owner's table, including macaroni and cheese, could be interpreted as an act of moral justice in taking what is due—luxurious enjoyment ranking as fundamental to human well-being as food and shelter. It was, in a word, vindication.

Even in Early America, appreciation of Southern hospitality extended beyond just the grandes dames to include the African American female cook. Despite laboring under the conditions of bondage, the head of the kitchen was fully aware that the family's sustenance and social standing hinged on the excellence of her ministrations. While the householders also recognized her importance, any reverence was fraught with contradictions. A skilled cook was indispensable; her talents were both desired and incongruent with subordination, placing those who exploited her services in a predicament. This esteem, coupled with the threat it posed to institutionalized power dynamics, played out in the idealized image of the cook and housekeeper embodied in the archetypal "mammy" figure.

The enshrinement of this two-dimensional caricature in popular culture belies a troubling reality of depersonalization and commodification. "Mammy" was standardized in physical appearance, attire, intelligence, and personality, and her cooking aptitude reduced to a racial stereotype.[52] Nostalgia for this antebellum myth lingered well into the twentieth century, conveniently locking in the notion that Black women were tireless cooks who labored happily for low wages. The institution of this asexual, subservient, and loyal bastion of caregiving established a model for saintliness that made mortal women, by comparison, perpetually inadequate or, conversely, open to attack as assimilationists participating in their own oppression. "Mammy" was a lose-lose wager, effective in quelling what the cultural studies scholar Doris Witt noted as "individual and collective fears about threats to white patriarchal power in a volatile social order."

"Mammy" stands as a conspicuous symbol of disempowerment, deeply rooted in Americana. But beneath the layers of characterization lies an essential contribution that demands recognition. Beyond the icon and the detriment caused by its portrayal, enslaved African American women cooks made invaluable contributions that cannot be overlooked. Besides providing free labor, they offered something French chefs could not: a taste of home. Their cooking resonated with food memories associated with comfort, nurturance, and familiarity, qualities that transcend mere culinary skill. While the French-trained cook embodied meticulous competence, adherence to codified recipes, and an arsenal of exacting techniques—in a tradition largely dominated by men—the home-trained African American cook brought a unique mix of culinary expertise to the table. She mastered a repertoire of French, English, and American dishes on her own terms, integrating local foodways and elements from her cultural heritage.[53] Cooks, of course, come in varying degrees of ability and sensitivity, but the experienced Black female cook was not second best to the male French-trained cook; she stood on her own merits, possessing skills that conferred status on the household. However, the division of the two was not so clear-cut. As part of the fallout from the French Revolution, many culinary specialists emigrated, settling in New York, Trenton, Philadelphia, Charleston, Baltimore, Richmond, and Washington, DC. In addition to cooking in private homes, restaurants, and cook shops, they also took on apprentices, spreading the knowledge and appreciation of French cookery.

The surfeit of want ads in late eighteenth- or early nineteenth-century newspapers is testament to the high demand and centrality of Black women as kitchen labor. This one in the *Louisville* (Ga.) *Gazette* (February 19, 1799) is typical:

Wanted to Hire,

A NEGRO WENCH, who can Cook, Wash and Iron; for such a one, generous Wages will be given.

Far fewer were the ads selling; however, these examples draw attention to the allure of European cookery skills:

FOR SALE
A Young Healty
Negro Wench

ABOUT two and twenty years of age, with her two children. She understands house keeping perfectly, and is a pretty good Cook, partly in the French fashion. [etc.] *Albany Centinel* (September 21, 1798).

For Sale,

A Negro WENCH, about 33 years old, a complete Cook in the French and English style, a washer, ironer and clear starcher [etc.] *Charleston City Gazette* (March 18, 1818).

For Sale.

ONE negro Women, 30 years of age, [. . .] she is a tolerable French cook and Seamstress. *Augusta Chronicle* (May 5, 1819).[54]

Navigating this historical narrative presents a dilemma regarding acknowledgement: balancing the imperative to give due credit with the need to challenge the assumption that cooking was inherently any woman's calling, irrespective of skill, in a context devoid of choice. However, focusing on victimization denies agency and erases their fortitude and defiance from the historical record.[55] At the same time, it is crucial to be wary of idealizing what the historian Rebecca Sharpless identified as the "common trope, in which the supposedly exotic, 'other' African American woman, cooks by innate ability while the supposedly more intelligent, rational, white woman empiricized her work."[56] Grappling with this "herstory" demands a highly nuanced critical eye—one that honors the significant contributions of these women while acknowledging the constraints imposed by the circumstances of their time and yet remains watchful of the tendency to mystify rather than recognize.

Chapter Six

PASTA, POWER, AND PROGRESS

From the Elite to the Everyday

Give us some mustard and make us some macaronis.
Donnez.nous de la moutard. Faites-nous du macaroni.

—*A MANUAL, CONTAINING THE EXPRESSIONS MOST USED IN TRAVELING, IN ENGLISH AND FRENCH—BOSTON* (1817)

THE GOLD STANDARD IN TURBULENT TIMES

The nineteenth century proved a key transitional period in the macaroni story, a time of turbulence, riddled with fluctuations in prosperity, social reckoning, and the ever-present specter of violence. Seismic shifts reverberated across nearly every sphere of life—from the halls of power to agricultural fields, from ideological awakenings to technological innovations and dietary discoveries. Though often at odds, these forces intertwined and set the stage for macaroni manufactory to emerge as a prime industry in the United States and, consequently, for the ascendancy of macaroni and cheese as an American food icon.

The era was punctuated by a series of economic catastrophes fittingly termed "panics." They traversed international borders, upending stability and sending shockwaves that rippled through increasingly interlocked global markets. The Panic of 1819 fired the first salvo, leaving in its wake a renewed emphasis on preparedness and frugality in the domestic sphere. Women would come to the fore as the authoritative voice in the emerging field of domestic science. Though consumers still clung to notions of elegance, hospitality, and status, the most pressing concern was far more pragmatic: getting a decent, affordable meal on the table.

Yet even as budgets tightened, French cookery remained the gold standard for culinary values. Louis Eustache Ude (1768–1846), who had apprenticed in the royal kitchens of Versailles, emerged as a self-styled ambassador of culinary arts to the English-speaking world. Credited with introducing haute cuisine to London, Ude walked a precarious tightrope, simultaneously denigrating the English for their unrefined palates—"unable to judge anything in cookery beyond boiled chicken"—while commanding the highest chef's salary of his day. His opus, *The French Cook* (1813), went through thirteen editions, and it crossed the Atlantic to become the first book on French cookery published in the United States.[1] *The Illustrated London News* hailed it as "the standard work in the science of cookery."

Ude's contribution to the macaroni narrative lay in his clarification of browning techniques. His "Macaroni with Parmesan Cheese," a classic French rendition featuring butter, cream, parmesan, and gruyere, called for the use of a salamander to achieve the perfect golden crust, insisting that the oven would make the butter unpleasantly greasy—a point that divided cooks for years to come.

Ude's grandiloquent style may have been aspirational, but it did not square with the turbulent times. Into this gap stepped an author identifying only as "An English Physician" with his practical compilation *French Domestic Cookery*, aptly subtitled *Combining Economy with Elegance and Adapted for the Use of Families of Moderate Fortune* (1825). In the "prefatory remarks," the good doctor acknowledged Ude's merits, but tsks that such works were beyond the means of the English middle class. Odd, then, that one of his three macaroni and cheese recipes was lifted from Ude's oeuvre. Another borrowing is a macaroni timbale from the classic of French bourgeois cookery, *La cuisinière de la campagne et de la ville* (The Town and Country Cook, 1818) by Louis-Eustache Audot (1883–1870). The American Eliza Leslie (1787–1858) latched onto the coattails of these successes with *Domestic French Cookery* (1832), an adaptation and translation of selections from the revised *La cuisinière de la campagne et de la ville* (1827).[2]

Leslie herself was born into a so-called "family of moderate fortune" in Philadelphia. Her father, a watchmaker, was reportedly on friendly terms with Thomas Jefferson and honored him by christening one son Thomas Jefferson Leslie and a daughter Martha. After her father's death, Eliza and her mother ran a boardinghouse to make ends meet—a detail she carefully omitted in her writings, perhaps concerned it would tarnish her reputation.[3] Building on the success of her first publication, *Seventy-Five Receipts . . .* (1828), Leslie embarked on the French translation. The selected recipes are "described in such a manner as to make them intelligible to American cooks, and practicable with American utensils, and American fuel." She included nothing that required French equipment or training and excluded recipes that were obsolete "in a country where provisions are abundant," and where respectable folks "can obtain better articles of food than sheeps' tails, calves' ears &c." While Americans wanted to keep up with their European counterparts, they wanted to do so on their own terms. The "Maccaroni" is a bare bones pasta, butter, and cheese—baked then crusted over with "a red-hot shovel." The only adjustment she made was to switch water for the broth as a cooking medium. Though it removed an element of flavor, the pragmatic choice was more American. The second entry was "Maccaroni Pie," the same one that the English physician had lifted from Audot.

While Leslie aimed to make French cuisine accessible to American kitchens, other authors believed the real priority for American housewives was stretching pennies, not perfecting sauces. Two cookbook authors professing to be the voice of true parsimony and humility were Lydia Maria Child (1802–1880) and Caroline Gilman (1794–1888).

Child's title says it all: *The Frugal Housewife. Dedicated to Those Who Are Not Ashamed of Economy* (1828). In her fire-and-brimstone introduction, she snubbed Leslie and her ilk with a backhanded compliment: "The writer [Child] has no apology to offer for this cheap little book of economical hints, except her deep conviction that such a book is needed. . . . Books of this kind have usually been written for the wealthy: I have written for the poor. I have said nothing about *rich* cooking; those who can afford to be epicures will find the best of information in the 'Seventy-five Receipts.' "[4]

Gilman's *The Carolina Receipt Book or Housekeeper's Assistant* (1832) struck a similar chord. As the first known charity cookbook, compiled to raise money for the local Unitarian Church, headed by her husband, it bridged the gap between New England thrift and Southern practicality.[5] Gilman, a native of Boston who had crossed paths with Child before transplanting to Charleston, aimed her "little work" squarely at "that class of female readers, who, like herself are engaged in the cares and duties of rearing a family."[6] Her mission was "to avoid giving any precepts that may violate the principles of a sound economy, and not multiply unnecessary or trivial directions."[7] Neither Gilman nor Child included a recipe for macaroni in their cookbooks. Their American reality had no room for such fare.[8]

PLATE 1 Placenta, *De agri cultura*, Cato, 160 BCE.

PLATE 2 Makerouns or makrows, *Forme of Cury*, ca. 1390.

PLATE 3 Roman macaroni, *Libro de arte coquinaria*, Maestro Martino de Rossi, 1465.

PLATE 4 A Mafcaronis Pye in Meager, *The Modern Cook*, Vincent La Chapelle, 1733.

PLATE 5 *Tourte de macaroni au Zéphir, Les Souper de la Cour, ou L'art de travailler toutes sortes d'alimens, pour servir les tables*, Louis François Henri de Menon, 1755.

PLATE 6 Macaroni toast with stewed cheese, *The New Experienced English Housekeeper*, Sarah Martin, 1795.

PLATE 7 French-style macaroni and cheese as it might have been prepared in the late eighteenth century, based on the recipe for macaroni (pasta) that Jefferson recorded.

PLATE 8 Macaroni pudding, Broadside recipe leaflet, Louis (Lewis) Fresnaye, 1802.

PLATE 9 Bajan macaroni pie. Composite recipe.

PLATE 10 Macaroni a la Royale, *The Modern Cook*, Charles Elmé Francatelli, 1846.

PLATE 11 Baked macaroni, *The Cook Book by "Oscar" of the Waldorf*, Oscar Tschirky, 1896.

PLATE 12 Macaroni croquettes in cheese sauce, *Kentucky Cook Book*, Emma Hayes, 1912.

PLATE 13 Peanut macaroni and cheese, *How to Grow the Peanut: And 105 Ways of Preparing It for Human Consumption*, George Washington Carver, 1917.

PLATE 14 Chicken and macaroni supreme, *Friends of Lyndeborough Central High School Charity Cookbook*, ca. 1950.

PLATE 15 Vegan macaroni and cheese, original recipe, Carla Hall, 2024.

PLATE 16 Four-Cheese Macaroni and Cheese, adapted from New York Times Cooking, Melissa Clark.

There was a place indeed for these works in the years leading up to the Panic of 1837. Unrest festered as the divided country locked horns over abolition, the Missouri Compromise straining at the seams. As the young republic's appetite for land grew insatiable, wagonloads of newly minted Americans pushed on into the Midwestern territories. Concurrently, the Indian Removal Act of 1830 forcibly relocated many Native American tribes from their ancestral homelands, resulting in widespread suffering and loss of life. The fertile soil pioneers encountered promised limitless bounty, particularly for wheat cultivation. High dividends lured farmers and speculators alike into a frenzy of overproduction and financial gambles that went unchecked, causing the market to bottom out. With no precedent to guide them, these pioneers navigated the uncertainty by improvising solutions and clinging to hope as their compass. As they forged ahead and the economy grew, the bubble of prosperity swelled to dangerous proportions.

State-chartered banks, heavily invested in the land grab, recklessly issued paper currency and offered unsustainable credit, outstripping their actual reserves. Fallout was inevitable and the reckoning merciless. A wave of bank failures set off a chain reaction that left farmers struggling to repay debts, defaulting on their loans, and eventually losing their holdings.

It was in this climate of economic uncertainty that Leslie's *Directions for Cookery, in Its Various Branches* emerged. First published in 1837, it would become the bestselling American cookbook of the century. *Directions* became a such a household standard in a nation seeking stability that it was referred to simply as "Miss Leslie."

Within its pages, Leslie offered up "Rich Macaroni Soup," lifted from Rundell—the one where the thickener is made with liquified macaroni, and "To Dress Macaroni," a layered macaroni and cheese with butter, much like Mary Randolph's. Despite its excruciating simplicity, Leslie explains the procedure in hairsplitting detail—perhaps to disguise its lack of originality. Her only personal touch is that the last layer is macaroni, not cheese, a regrettable innovation that made for bony macaroni. Although her cookbooks garnered accolades and financial success, Leslie hoped that her reputation as a novelist would assure her legacy. But her exertions in that genre would be all but forgotten.

Unlike Leslie, who was primarily a working cook, authors such as Lettice Bryan, who wrote *The Kentucky Housewife* (1839), approached domestic life with a different perspective. Bryan emphasized the distinction between being a mere wife and the more esteemed role of a housewife: "Never make your husband blush to own that you are his wife; but by your industry, frugality, and neatness, make him proud, and happy to know that he is in possession of a companion who is a complete model of loveliness and true elegance."[9]

Bryan asserted that the housewife who had efficiently and effectively carried out her duties—governing the servants and slaves and ticking tasks off a routine checklist—should be free for other pursuits by midday. Such delineations served a dual purpose: it fostered a sense of purpose and control within the gendered hierarchy while distinguishing the housewife's role from that of her subordinates. Housewives of Bryant's stripe rarely had a direct hand in food preparation. While they may have been capable cooks if necessity demanded, delegating the servile, manual tasks to other hands defined their authority. The shared female experience between mistress and enslaved domestics was not a basis for empathy but rather a reason to sharpen boundaries.[10]

This complex relationship raises questions about who contributed the nuances of recipes ostensibly written by women who did not cook. Bryan claimed to have adapted the recipes to the "wants, conveniences, and pleasures of her country," specifically Kentucky, expressing confidence that they will be pleasing to all.[11] Yet the identity of those who actually developed these dishes remains obscured. Here is the Bluegrass State of affairs in 1839.

TO DRESS MACCARONI

1 lb (450 g) macaroni
2 cups (500 mL) milk + same amount of water
1/2 lb (225 g) sharp cheddar
1/2 lb (225 g) butter, melted
Salt to taste

Preheat the oven to 350°F (180°C). Bring the liquid to a boil and add the macaroni. Remove the macaroni with a slotted spoon and, in a buttered baking dish, create three layers with butter and cheese, sprinkling each layer with salt as you proceed. Bake for 25 minutes, watching that the top does not brown too much. Serve hot.

The slump of the 1830s saw only brief glimmers of recovery and bled into the downturn known as the Hungry Forties. Amid this prolonged downturn, Leslie put out a sequel to her bestseller: *The Lady's Receipt-Book* (1847). It featured "Cauliflower Maccaroni," an excellent recipe for macaroni and cheese—except that there is no macaroni. Here's the basic recipe.

CAULIFLOWER MACARONI

One head cauliflower, cut into florets
4 1/2 cups (1 L) milk
2 Tbsp (30 mL) butter
1 tsp salt
One stick (115 g) butter
1/2 cup (125 mL) light cream
3 oz (100 g) mild white cheddar, finely grated
1/2 tsp cayenne

Put the cauliflower in boiling milk with butter and salt. Cook until soft. Drain.

Put the stick of butter into a medium saucepan with the cream, half the cheese, salt, and cayenne. Add the cauliflower and cook five minutes longer, stirring occasionally. Place the mixture in a baking dish and cover with the rest of the cheese. Place under a broiler and cook until the top is browned.

"This," Leslie says, "will be found very superior to real macaroni." So, why call it macaroni at all? Evidently, the mere reference was powerful enough to entice readers, who might otherwise have breezed past a cauliflower recipe, to take notice.[12] Leslie's usage implies that macaroni and cheese had become a method of preparation whose key ingredient was interchangeable. Given the economic climate, one might presume that this was intended as a money-saving recipe, but that is doubtful. Leslie explicitly targets "families who possess the means and the inclination to keep an excellent table, and to entertain their guests in a handsome and liberal manner."[13] Notably, in her menu suggestions, actual macaroni is reserved for elegant occasions. Macaroni was still dressed to impress.

PASS THE GRAVY

On a parallel track, macaroni was entering a revolutionary phase.

THE GREAT MACARONI SCHISM: *IL RAGÙ ALLA NAPOLETANA* AND TOMATO SAUCE

While the marriage of fowl and macaroni had a long and distinguished history in Italy, that culinary coupling did not extend to beef. The combination debuts in 1773 in the Neapolitan chef Vincenzo Corrado's "Timballo di maccheroni al sugo." Here, *sugo* refers to a coulis or concentrated beef gravy, derived from a hunk of meat, vegetables, and herbs cooked to the nth degree and strained. Gravy was the point of the exercise; the meat was an afterthought. While both the gravy and the *timballo* were arguably drawn from the French tradition,[14] the Roman chef Francesco Leonardi wrested that pasta and gravy from its encasement and reclaimed it outright as "Maccaroni alla Napolitana." But it was Leonardi's suggestion in the 1807 edition of his work *Apicio moderno* that would prove revolutionary. In a literary wave of the hand, he concedes that the beef gravy could be *made with tomato sauce*. It was a fusion that would shape Italy's gastronomic identity both at home and abroad but was also a reminder that even the most iconic traditions have complex, hybrid origins.

English authors in the early nineteenth century noted these Neapolitan dishes. In her memoir, "A Lady of Rank" reminisced about the incomparable macaroni in Naples, typically served with the famous *cacio cavallo* cheese "when not cooked with sughilio [*sic*], the extract of stewed beef in wine, with all kinds of spices and herbs"—*sughillo* being the archaic dialect word for meat sauce.[15] An 1827 cookbook, *Domestic Economy, and Cookery, for Rich and Poor* included a recipe for "Sughlio, or Extract of Beef with Wine for dressing Macaroni," noting that the Neapolitans use it "to dress their fine pipe macaroni, which is simmered in it without being broken. . . . The beef, whatever piece it is made of, is inimitably good."[16]

Why Hadn't We Thought of This Before?!

Italy's slow embrace of the tomato spanned nearly three centuries before settling into the culinary scheme of things. Once again, it was Leonardi who sparked the revolution with "Catalan Soup with Fine Pasta," again in the 1790 *Apicio moderno*. It holds the coveted title of first pasta recipe with tomato, even though, as the name implies, tomatoes were still synonymous with Spain. But once the seed was sown, it crescendoed and in due time elevated the American fruit to iconic status in Italian cuisine.

An early mention of the tomato and macaroni pairing can be found in the 1806 memoires of Bartolommeo Nardini, a French sympathizer during Naples's power struggles at the turn of the nineteenth century. He observes, "You can't take ten steps down the street without encountering large pots filled with ready-made macaroni sprinkled with cheese, and garnished with small bits of tomato."[17] This vivid account captures the scene of a city where the tomato had firmly established itself, transforming from a foreign novelty to an indispensable staple.

Tomato sauce for vermicelli was deemed newsworthy enough for a write-up in Grimod de La Reynière's authoritative French guide *Almanach des gourmands* of 1807, praising it as having "a very agreeable acidity, enjoyed by nearly everyone who is used to it."[18] However, it wasn't until 1837 that the first pasta and tomato sauce recipe, one that explicitly belonged to the Neapolitan tradition, would be published in Italy. Perhaps it escaped mention because the combination was so self-evident.

A blush of plain tomato sauce became the daily default, while the versions enriched with meat were reserved for special occasions—that is, for those who could afford pasta. It was a revolution in taste that quickly laid deep roots, relinquishing macaroni and cheese to the foreigners. While medieval echoes of the milk, butter, and parmesan genre lingered, such as Leonardi's "Maccaroni al fior di latte," or "Fituccie al fior di latte," they no longer defined *italianità*.[19]

The French Seal of Approval

As we have seen, the umami rich flavor combination of meat broth or a final flourish of gravy had long been part of the macaroni and cheese story. But it was André Viard's coauthor, Fouret, who brought those elements together under the name "Macaroni à la Napolitaine"

(*continued on next page*)

(*continued from previous page*)

in *Le cuisinier royal: ou l'art de faire la cuisine* (1820). The gravy was a French *jus d'étouffade* ladled over macaroni layered with parmesan (*sans* tomato), which crowned the embattled beef top round with a regal finish. In England, a simpler version was listed in *The Cook's Dictionary and House-keeper's Directory* (1830), reprinted verbatim two years later in the American copycat compilation *The Cook's Own Book*. Beef gravy poured over the layered macaroni and cheese with an overkill dose of melted butter was an age-old favorite, rebaptized here as "Macaroni Napolitaine."[20]

When France's illustrious Carême gave his nod of approval with "Potage de macaroni à la Napolitaine" (1833), it cinched the deal. His rendition had a foot in both camps. Despite the allusion to Naples, it remained firmly grounded in France. It starts with a mixed *estouffade* base: two pounds of beef, veal knuckle, and two chickens are browned then slow-cooked for five hours with a host of vegetables and herbs in a mere pint of consommé. A mornay-esque sauce, crafted from butter, parmesan, egg yolks and double cream, is then combined with the precious liqueur from the braise and mixed into the cooked macaroni. Stir carefully while thickening so as not to break the liaison. Finish with extra cheese. It was an exhibitionist display, but it certainly showed up his rival Viard and Italian contemporaries. And yet, still no tomato.

Team France again makes a good showing in 1836 with *Côtelettes de cochon à la milanaise*. The chef Chevrier takes aim with braised pork chops in *Italian* tomato sauce served on macaroni and cheese but misses the mark with his choice of meat and the town of origin.

The blessing of France's culinary luminaries ushered macaroni with stewed beef into foreign kitchens. It was developing at the same time in Italy, but ultimately the French decided which Italian dishes would and wouldn't be sanctioned. This persistent French influence would later spark the ire of Ada Boni (1881–1973), a staunch Italian nationalist. She blamed the French stranglehold for foreign ignorance about Italian cuisine. "Foreigners have absolutely no idea what Italian cuisine is and think our gastronomic patrimony is limited to two or three specialties headed up by macaroni." The sauces are wrong, the cooking times too long. "All these concoctions get grouped into two categories: *macaroni à la napoletaine* and *nouilles fraîches à l'italienne*"—pasta with meat sauce and our classical French-style macaroni and cheese.[21]

ELIZA ACTON

Eliza Acton (1799–1859) chartered new territory in the anglophone world introducing a Neapolitan macaroni recipe in her book *Modern Cookery in All Its Branches*. It came off the presses in both London and Philadelphia in 1845, the American edition edited by Sarah Josepha Buell Hale (1788–1879)—author of *Mary Had a Little Lamb* and tireless campaigner for the establishment of Thanksgiving as a national holiday.

Macaroni was difficult to place in a cookbook. Acton tucks her three recipes into the Soufflés, Omlets, &c. section, evidently qualifying as etcetera. She advises against the English practice of soaking the macaroni for an hour in milk and water before cooking. What you gain in visual appeal, you lose in texture. Her preference was for the continental mode of dropping it in salted boiling water with just a bit of butter. After forty-five minutes to an hour, it will be perfectly cooked—be warned that less than this would provoke indigestion. Four ounces (113 g) of dried macaroni per person is the proper amount, but double that for enthusiasts. Her recipe is a simple, layered white-sauce version, but she advises her readers to feel free to substitute the usual parmesan with any "well-flavoured dry white cheese" that is less expensive and locally available.

The French, she observes, may add jellied meat gravy reduction, whereas the Italians "toss it in a rich brown gravy, with sufficient grated cheese to flavour the whole strongly. . . . We think that the rich brown gravy is also a great advantage to the dish, which is further improved by a tolerably high seasoning of cayenne. These, however, are innovations on the usual modes of serving it in England."[22]

Acton inserts a recipe for this novel preparation of serving macaroni in the Beef section, calling it "Stufato (*A Neapolitan Receipt*)" and crediting a friend at whose table it had been successfully served to Italian diplomats. To prepare, deep cuts are made in a six-pound doorstop of beef and filled with a mince of herbs, garlic, and ham. The whole is bound in string, then stewed confit-style in four pounds of butter for five to six hours. After skimming off the butter, half a pint of olive oil and a pot of tomato paste are mixed with the dark meat juices settled at the bottom of the pot. The sauce is mixed with cooked macaroni and given a generous sprinkling of parmesan cheese before serving. As an Englishwoman, Acton was rather puzzled about the role of the meat and shocked by the quantity of macaroni: "From our own slight experience of it, we should suppose that the excellence of the beef is quite a secondary consideration, as all its juices are drawn out by the mode of cooking, and appropriated to the maccaroni, which we must observe that 3 pounds, would make too *gigantic* a dish to enter well, on ordinary occasions, into an English service."[23] One wonders if the Italian diplomats were simply being . . . diplomatic.

CHARLES ELMÉ FRANCATELLI

Charles Elmé Francatelli (1805–1876), arguably the leading voice in the English culinary sphere, prepared to set everyone straight. He had studied classical French cookery under Carême and was influenced by his Italian gastronomic heritage but is quick to add, "Although bearing a foreign name, is happy in being an Englishman."[24] Francatelli's career was marked by prestigious appointments. He replaced chef Ude (who was let go after demanding an exorbitant salary, his ego getting the better of him) and would go on to become steward and chief cook to Queen Victoria.

His magnum opus was *The Modern Cook* (1846), a treatise approaching cookery "as an art by which refined taste is to be *gratified* rather than a coarse appetite *satisfied*," distancing himself from the "hackneyed terms employed in 'Guides' and 'Oracles' for economical makeshifts."[25] In one fell swoop, Francatelli disses the entire output of the penny-pinchers and takes a direct potshot at Kitchiner, who must surely have been a source of perpetual irritation for a chef of Francatelli's standing. *The Modern Cook* contains several recipes for macaroni, which built upon inspiration from his illustrious mentor, Carême, elevating them to new heights. One recipe "sometimes designated *à l'italienne*" is more of a thick cheese soup with macaroni in a creamy lemony French liaison, exemplifying technique, originality, and cosmopolitan sophistication. See recipe: "Macaroni Soup a la Royale

Francatelli assumes the lead in the macaroni and beef movement with two "a la Milanaise" preparations—a beef roulade and a braised fillet—both served on a bed of macaroni and cheese. Notably, his "Braised ribs of beef, a la Piemontaise," takes the bold step of adding a touch of tomato paste to the macaroni and cheese as it cooks in the braise gravy.

It is curious that the tomato finish was added to the northern dish, while his southern "Fillet of beef, a la Napolitaine," also served with macaroni, does not include it at all. Francatelli's interpretation of this

MACARONI SOUP A LA ROYALE

10 oz (300 g) long-form macaroni (candele, ziti, mezzani)

2 oz (60 g) butter

1 tsp pepper

2 Tbsp salt

2 quarts (1.9 L) rich chicken broth

6 large egg yolks

1 cup (250 mL) heavy cream

2 oz (60 g) Parmesan, grated

2 Tbsp (30 mL) fresh lemon juice

Boil the pasta in water, butter, salt, and pepper until al dente. Remove and cut into 1/2-in. (1 cm) bits. Put the bits into boiling broth for 5 minutes. Mix the rest of the ingredients together and, off heat, slowly add them to the pot, stirring. Return to the stove and thicken for 3 minutes. Serve hot.

dish well exemplifies the interplay of his English, French, and Italian grounding. Here we have a classic French braise in white wine with bay leaf, thyme, clove, and mace. Owing to the prime cut of meat, it is given a compassionate two-hour braise. He takes ample poetic license in finishing the meat sauce, adding a pot of red-currant jelly and horseradish. The macaroni and cheese is to be made in "the usual manner" then tossed with wine-soaked raisins. The prepared pasta is plated with the beefy centerpiece posited on top then promptly doused with the glaze. The braised meat is adorned with three ornamental skewers (hatelets), piercing it at either end and in the center. Each skewer holds a turnip that has been carved into a cup and dyed red with cochineal. These cups are filled with grated horseradish, while the remaining sauce is put into a gravy boat for diners to use at their discretion. Though it strains the imagination, the essence of *ragù alla napolitana* lurks somewhere in there. As can be gleaned from the recipe titles, these are conceptually meat forward with macaroni in the supporting role, reflecting the centrality of beef in the English tradition.

Familiarity with standard French and English stewing techniques would seamlessly ease the macaroni and beef pairing into the American repertoire. Americans were at an advantage, having no qualms about eating tomatoes, reputably "one of the most wholesome and valuable esculents of the animal kingdom."[26] In *The Carolina Housewife* (1847), they were stewed, baked, fried, omeletted, bottled, pickled, and condensed into tomato paste—and a main ingredient in "Macaroni a la Napolitana."

SARAH RUTLEDGE

Sarah Rutledge (1782–1855), the compiler of *The Carolina Housewife*, was cut from quite a different cloth than her American contemporaries. Writing under the nom de plume "A Lady of Charleston," she was posthumously revealed to be a member of one of Charleston's wealthiest families. As such, her claim that the recipes were for "families of moderate income" was a question of perspective, and it was unlikely that she had much, if any, hands-on experience in the kitchen. She barely acknowledges the source of the recipes, merely boasting that the dishes "have been successfully made by our own cooks," an inadequate acknowledgment of the enslaved women who actually prepared the meals.

In the "Eggs, Cheese, etc." section we find "To dress macaroni a la sauce blanche." Despite the Frenchy title, she tags it an "Italian receipt." Like Acton's version, it is a layered white sauce-cheese-repeat baked macaroni. The trendsetting Neapolitan macaroni is also layered and given the same tag of Italian authenticity.

MACARONI A LA NAPOLITANA

4 lb (1.8 kg) beef (chuck or other)

2 Tbsp salt

1 Tbsp butter

4 large onions, quartered

4 carrots, sliced

2 bay leaves

1 bunch thyme, bound

1 bunch parsley, bound

1 cup (250 mL) water
6 large tomatoes, diced, or 16 fl. oz (475 mL) tomato sauce
7 oz (200 g) pipe macaroni
1/4 lb (115 g) parmesan cheese, grated

Put the beef, salt, and butter in a pot and brown the meat well on high heat. Lower the heat to medium, add the onions, and cook until they start to brown. Add the carrots, bay leaves, the herbs, and the water. Cover and braise on low for 1 hour. Add the tomato and braise, covered, for 3 hours, turning the meat once.

Pass the sauce through a colander and keep it warm in a saucepan. Cook the macaroni until soft and then drain. Spoon the macaroni into a serving dish, layer one-third of the cheese over it, then the sauce, and finish with the rest of the cheese. Serve immediately.

Interestingly, she says nothing about the eventual fate of the meat.

In the 1855 edition of *The Carolina Housewife*, the recipe title would step away from its Italian pretense, favoring the chic French "Maccaroni à la Napolitaine." This shift in nomenclature reflected the enduring influence of French cuisine on American culinary culture. However, the interpretation of Neapolitan-style macaroni would evolve in vastly different directions over time. The invention of the meat grinder, first patented in Germany in 1845, would eventually lead to a phasing out of this particular trend, paving the way for new variations on the classic dish. But that is a story for another day.

HUNGER AND SOCIAL ADVOCACY

The period called the Hungry Forties is best remembered for the Irish Potato Famine (1845–1852), but the crisis fanned out into widespread food shortages and rampant infectious disease. The blight ignited the search for a solution to filling the empty stomach of the populace, and sights would turn increasingly to wheat-based solutions. In 1848, food insecurity aggravated the discontent among the working class and peasants in Europe, sparking a series of revolts collectively referred to as the Springtime of the Peoples. It was an era of uprisings and revolution, with crowds shouting for political reform, economic relief, and greater social equality. The potential for the unrest to spiral into violence and even war loomed large.

Inevitably, parallels were drawn between the struggles in Europe and the ongoing strife over workers' rights and slavery in the United States. Immigrants, referred to as the "Forty-eighters," sought refuge in the United States, bringing their ideologies in tow. They contributed to the growth of cities, the expansion of industry, and the diversification of American culture. As such, they played a significant role in shaping debates about democracy, labor rights, and social justice. Among the tide of immigrants was Antoine Zerega, who hailed from Lyon, France, a major hub for pasta manufacturing. He settled in New York, where his descendants claim he founded the first American macaroni company of the industrial age in 1848. Zerega's sons would go on to play a crucial role in shaping the future of macaroni in the country.

In the shifting socioeconomic climate, the middle classes emerged as one of the most powerful voices advocating for reform. Many of these people had risen from the ranks of the working class or had daily dealings with them, making them acutely aware of the hardships faced by the less privileged. The momentum stirred a sense of international solidarity, uniting struggles on various fronts as part of a broader movement for social and political change. Francatelli's *A Plain Cookery Book for the Working Classes* (1852) spearheaded the cookbooks aimed at assisting struggling families. It shows a genuine understanding of their socioeconomic condition and a sincere intention to provide a practical, useful text. "No. 8 Thick Milk for Breakfast" is a clear example: "To every pint of milk, mix a piled-up tablespoonful of flour, and stir the mixture while boiling on the fire for ten minutes; season with a little salt, and eat it with bread or a boiled potato. This kind of food is well adapted for the breakfast of women and children, and is far preferable to a sloppy mess of tea, which comes to more money." The nutritional needs of women and children were apparently indistinguishable. Contrary to Francatelli's upper crust publication, which abounded in macaroni, *A Plain Cookery* had none.

ALEXIS SOYER

Alexis Soyer (1810–1858) was perhaps the chef who was most personally invested in championing the poor. French by birth, he fled Paris in the revolts of 1830 to join his brother Philippe, who enjoyed a successful career as a chef in London. Alexis went on to become the head chef of the swank new Reform Club—a gathering place for politically progressive gentlemen. He could hardly have landed in a more fortuitous situation, given his own liberal-leaning views.[27] The kitchen over which he presided and helped design himself, was a sprawling state-of-the-art emporium of gastronomy (see fig. 6.1).

But as Soyer witnessed the devastation wrought by the Hungry Forties, he felt a moral calling to take an active role. At the behest of the British government, he took a leave of absence and traveled to Dublin to set up a network of soup kitchens, providing nourishment to the desperate masses. Right-wing detractors attempted to sabotage his efforts, claiming that soup was hardly sufficient for human sustenance. The accusation seemed to have struck a nerve as, while in Ireland, Soyer penned a vigorous apologia titled *Soyer's Charitable Cookery; or, The Poor Man's Regenerator* (1847).

In this work, he turned his focus to inexpensive, filling farinaceous foods like dried peas, barley, and Indian corn—the latter perhaps inspired by Eliza Leslie's recently published *The Indian Meal Book* (1846), which debuted first in London and Dublin before crossing the Atlantic. Macaroni was conspicuously absent from the economical solutions Soyer proposed,

FIGURE 6.1. Chef Alexis Soyer's kitchens in the Reform Club, London. *Source*: Public domain.

which suggests that it had not yet achieved a price point for it to be considered viable charity fare.

Back in England, Soyer next turned his sights toward the mainstream middle class with *The Modern Housewife* (1849; American edition, 1850). Framed as a fictional exchange of letters between two housewives, Hortense and Eloise, the book allowed Soyer to address the concerns of English homemakers grappling with food costs and budgets. Happily, macaroni falls within the ladies' means.

Soyer gives us three recipes that exemplify the tight control the French culinary authorities exerted over the dissemination and preparation of macaroni dishes. "*Macaroni à l'Italienne*" is the creamy French standard issue, with a touch of cayenne, finished with "strong gravy." What he dubs "*Macaroni à la Napolitaine*" is a straight-up layered parmesan, macaroni, and butter version that is generously doused with gravy before heading to the oven.

He caps his macaroni trio with the boldly branded title "*The real Italian method* (called *à l'Estoufade*)." "Real" amounts to an admission that the other two were, in fact, not Italian. Indeed, *Italienne* had become wholly subsumed into the French culinary canon, while *Napolitaine* implied a gravy intervention. Nothing new in that, as Menon had already proposed it way back when. Soyer's "real Italian" recipe is actually an attempt at *maccaroni alla napolitana*, but he had already coopted that name. He says to prepare the macaroni "as before" and then "take 2 pounds of rump beef larded through, put in a small stewpan, with 1/4 of a pound of butter, fry gently for one hour, turning, almost continually; when, forming a glaze, add half a pint of broth, let simmer another hour, take the fat off, and use that gravy instead of that above described; a little tomato may be introduced, if handy. Serve the beef at the same time in a separate dish."[28] Unlike Francatelli, who pleases the English with a meat protagonist supported by macaroni, Soyer attempts to observe the Italian custom or separating meat and pasta, though not in separate courses.

Hortense and Eloise are called upon again in 1855 for *A Shilling Cookery for the People: Embracing an Entirely New System of Plain Cookery and Domestic Economy*—a shilling being the price of the book. Apropos of macaroni and vermicelli, Hortense is made to say, "Pray, Eloise, why should not the workman and mechanic partake of these wholesome and nutritious articles of food, which have now, in consequence of those restrictive laws on provisions, having been repealed, become so plentiful and cheap? It only requires to know how to cook them, in order that they should become as a favorite food in these northern climes, as they are in the southern."[29] "Plain" is a word that had played well with English since the time of Hannah Glasse. It carried the positive meaning of being without fuss or pretense, rather than merely dull or insipid. While macaroni could not be proposed for the destitute, its time had come for the People—and the People did not want to muck about.

The "restrictive laws" he mentions allude to the recent repeal of the English Corn Laws, which had regulated the import and export of wheat. This economic overhaul had prompted a more general revision of trade laws. With the removal of tariffs and restrictions, Britain could now more freely import not only wheat but also wheat-based products like macaroni from countries where they were produced in great abundance.

The successful lobbying efforts of reformers such as Soyer helped to level the playing field of macaroni (and cheese), making it more accessible to the People, much to the delight of Hortense and Eloise. Soyer eggs his readers on with an inviting footnote: "Macaroni is now selling in London at fivepence per pound, and makes four pounds of food when boiled, as in No. 463." This tidbit caught the attention of Charles Dickens, who reprinted it for his readers in an article about the "art of making good food out of unpromising material" in his weekly magazine *Household Words*.[30]

Dickens added that this inexpensive pasta "is almost unknown among our poor. Yet, seasoned with pepper and salt, and flavoured with grated cheese (which the poor can buy very cheap) . . . it makes a dish not to be despised, even by epicures."[31] His suggestion may have been drawn from Soyer's Recipe 463, a no-frills boiled macaroni thrown in a pot with cheese, butter, salt, and pepper, which ends with "It will be found light and nutritious, and well worthy of the notice of vegetarians."[32]

Vegetarians

One of the earliest vegetarian associations in England was the Bible Christians, an outreach organization affiliated with the Bible Christian Church, a utopian community founded in Salford by Reverend William Cowherd at the turn of the nineteenth century. Their mission to promote vegetarianism was religiously motivated, based on Cowherd's interpretation of scripture. A foundational tenet underpinning their beliefs came from Genesis 1:29: "And God said, Behold, I have given you every herb bearing seed, which is upon the face of all the earth, and every tree, in which is the fruit of a tree yielding seed; to you it shall be for meat."

In 1833, the society member Martha Brotherton published the morally assertive *Vegetable Cookery, with an Introduction, Recommending Abstinence from Animal Food and Intoxicating Liquors*. True to its title, the introduction gives an extensive biblical defense for what adherents would call the "temperance of both solids and fluids." The pairing of vegetarianism and teetotalism was common among the religious groups that proliferated with the Second Great Awakening—a period of potent religious revivalism that was sweeping through Europe and the United States.

Despite vegetarianism remaining a fringe concept in countries with an entrenched meat-eating tradition, the rising tides of social reform and Christian fundamentalism helped softened the public's reception to the vegetarian cause. While *Vegetable Cookery* was published under the reserved attribution "by a Lady," Martha's uncle, Joseph Brotherton, himself a member of both the Bible Christians and the British Parliament (1832–1857), used his position more vocally to raise awareness about the dietary and ethical principles underlying the vegetarian and temperance philosophies rooted in his religious convictions.

A colony of the parent church had emigrated to Philadelphia in 1817, hoping to find sympathetic converts among Americans. The ardent vegetarian crusader William Alcott (1789–1859), cited the sect as an example in his austere treatise *Vegetable Diet: As Sanctioned by Medical Men*, expecting to turn heads with the claim that the local phrenologist Mr. Fowler had declared one of their members the strongest man in Philadelphia.[33] However, in the recipe section of his book, Alcott snubs Martha Brotherton's cookbook as being for "those who live solely to eat . . . where they will find indulgences enough and too many." Alcott's sparse offerings, like Receipt 12, typify his own unsmiling gastronomic orientation—"Bread pudding: Take a loaf of rather stale bread, cut a hole in it, add as much new milk as it will soak up through the opening, tie it up in a cloth, and boil it an hour."

The fundamentalist leaning of the period also manifested as an ideological return to nature, seen in Romanticism, idolizing the purity and simplicity of the nature, and Transcendentalism, whose philosophy of living in harmony with nature included forays into vegetarianism. Alcott derides macaroni and vermicelli as "at best very indifferent dishes."[34] His stance was that nature added nothing extraneous to food; therefore, dressings and sauces—even salt—were an abomination against her. Foods should be left, as he put it, "unvarnished." Because the customs of society had rendered macaroni "agreeable to perverted appetites," he reluctantly conceded that it could be tolerated on occasion, as its departure from nature was only slight.[35] One might observe that his stale bread pudding had hardly sprung unvarnished from nature's bounty.

Guilty as charged, Martha Brotherton had indeed attempted to lure readers into the fold with sumptuous macaroni dishes—a rich savory pudding, two milk-based macaroni and cheese (one verbatim from Raffald—still going strong after sixty-five years), a sweet pudding, and even a macaroni custard tart. She turns to Ecclesiasticus 39:26 as her defense: "The basic necessities of human life are water, fire, iron and salt and wheat flour, milk and honey," conveniently omitting the verboten wine from that verse.

The chief promoter of vegetarianism on the US front was the Presbyterian minister and dietary reformer Sylvester Graham (1794–1851) of graham cracker fame. Public lectures having become a popular form of "infotainment," Graham took to the road in the 1830s with his rousing message of healthful living and moral hygiene—abstention from meat, alcohol, and sex—ideas that intersected with the Second Great Awakening revival. His efforts culminated in the collected work *Lectures on the Science of Human Life* (1839). Despite Graham's complete lack of formal scientific education, it became a foundational text for vegetarians and catapulted him into the public eye.

Lectures was a work of passionate appeal rather than empirical science, a litany of anecdotal evidence attributing extraordinary vitality, enhanced senses, longevity, and intellectual acuity to a bland, spartan, vegetable-based diet. Anything that stimulated the system, Graham claimed—be it alcohol, drugs, "heating" foods (eggs, chocolate, wine, spices, flesh), inordinate exercise, or passion itself was sure to shorten one's days.[36] These claims were couched in flagrantly distorted histories and pseudoscientific rationalizations, presenting supposition as foregone conclusion. Typical of his reasoning are these quotations about macaroni: "'Milton studied in Italy, where the diet is olives, macaroni, and ice-water, and there laid the plan of his Paradise Lost,' says Sir Everard Home. It is admitted that men, who ordinarily subsist on a mixed diet of vegetable and animal food, can possess great intellectual powers; but it is contended that they would have possessed still greater powers if they had always subsisted entirely on a pure vegetable and water diet."[37] And "'In all the world,' says a recent traveller in Italy, 'there is not to be found a more lively and mercurial population than the lazzaroni and laborers of Naples, whose diet is of the simplest kind, consisting mainly of bread, macaroni (a vegetable dish), or potatoes, or the fruits of the season, including a large supply of watermelons for their greatest luxury, with water for their drink. They are generally tall, stout, well formed, robust, and active men.'"[38]

This is worth comparing to an 1833 cover story in *Penny Magazine of the Society for the Diffusion of Useful Knowledge*, a weekly intended to enculturate the working classes.[39] What Graham fails to mention is the lack of choice and preference in conditions of abject poverty: "The maccaroni thus sold in the streets is merely boiled in plain water, and frequently eaten without any condiment whatever—sometimes, however, it is sprinkled with some grated *caccia cavallo*, for which additional luxury a proportionate charge is made. The mere mention of "*quattro maccheroni con zughillo*," or "some maccaroni with meat gravy," will make your lazarone's mouth water, as *that* is a luxury which rarely comes within his means."[40]

Looking closer, the *Penny Magazine* article (see fig. 6.2) might have been the very source from which Graham cherry-picked his information: "For three *grani* more, he can indulge in a *carafa* or bottle of common wine, or in summer time, for the same sum, he can procure a large glass of deliciously iced-water, and half of a huge melon."[41] But he skipped over the next bit: "Your genuine lazarone despises to use a wine-glass or even touch the bottle to his lips—he drinks like the New Zealander, holding the bottle almost at arm's length, he pours a continuous stream from its neck into his mouth. This is a feat in which they take pride."[42]

In *Sketches of Naples*, Alexandre Dumas paints quite a different picture of the lazzaroni: "Other people rest when they are tired of working; the lazzarone works when he is tired of resting." He also asserts that macaroni is in fact *not* the food of the lazzarone but has been fully appropriated by Europeans: "The impression has gone out into the world that the lazzarone

THE PENNY MAGAZINE

OF THE

Society for the Diffusion of Useful Knowledge.

87.] PUBLISHED EVERY SATURDAY. [August 10, 1833.

NEAPOLITAN MACCARONI-EATERS

[The Maccaroni Seller of Naples.]

FIGURE 6.2. Macaroni cover story on this 1833 issue of the weekly *Penny Magazine*. *Source*: Courtesy of the Smithsonian Archive Center, Museum of American History. Public domain.

lives upon macaroni; this is a great mistake, which it is time to correct. The macaroni is, it is true, a native of Naples; but at the present time, it is a European dish, which has traveled, like civilization, and which, like civilization, finds itself very far from its cradle. The macaroni, moreover, costs two sous a pound; which renders it inaccessible to the purse of the lazzarone; except upon Sundays and holidays."[43]

Cookbook authors through the ages had variously filed macaroni and cheese among soups, puddings, pies, or cheese dishes. But, coinciding with rising vegetarian awareness, it was ever more frequently relegated to the vegetable section. For example, Catharine Beecher (sister to Harriet Beecher Stowe), author of *Miss Beecher's Domestic Receipt Book* (1846), situated macaroni and cheese squarely between a recipe for boiled cucumbers on buttered toast and instructions for washing lettuce. Mrs. Bliss, in *The Practical Cookbook* (1850), has it in the Vegetables, Salads and Garnishes section, stating clearly, "Macaroni is very generally used as a vegetable."[44]

The vegetarian evangelists were served a formidable pushback by the eminent Scottish physician Andrew Combe (1797–1847), who had attended no less than Queen Victoria herself. In his scholarly work *The Physiology of Digestion* (1849), Combe elaborated an extensive argument against vegetarianism in a section titled "Ought we to live on vegetable food alone?" Here he meticulously dismantled the assertions of Graham and Alcott as being utterly devoid of empirical evidence.

Combe's conclusion challenged the notion that dyspepsia—"the malady that under different names has decimated the inhabitants of civilized countries in which man is a 'cooking animal' "—arose from meat consumption.[45] Rather, he proposed that the modern frenetic lifestyle was the true culprit; the logical prescription was eating slowly and in moderation. Satisfying human dietary needs from vegetables alone, Combe argued, would require overconsumption, thus further taxing the organism. But there was one particular point in his concluding remarks that caught newspapers' attention, which they quickly seized upon and ran with: "It may be well to bear in mind, also, that England is the most flesh-consuming country in Europe, while its mortality is the smallest; the duration of life, being about a third longer than in Italy, where macaroni, and other farinaceous substances formed the staple diet."[46]

One of the journals that republished the incendiary citation was the *Vegetarian Advocate*, (transitioning from its clunky original title *Truth Tester, Temperance Advocate, and Man's Healthian Journal*), the official voice of the newly consecrated American Vegetarian Society (1850). An unnamed correspondent "favorable to progress" challenged the *Advocate* to respond to Combe's statement. Dropping the typically preachy rhetoric, the editor delivered a staid rebuttal underscoring the numerous factors contributing to human longevity: "Climates, social, political and religious Institutions, have often more influence on health and long life that mere dietetic habits. . . . Greek, Russian, Irish and Scotch labourers, who live on Vegetable food, are quite as healthy and long-lived as those who live on a mixed diet in this country."[47] He conveniently avoids mentioning Italians. Both Combe and Alcott died of tuberculosis before their time, but the vegetarian debate would rage on.

Oddly, the *Advocate* refused outright to endorse macaroni as a staple. In a scathing article critiquing Combe's *The Physiology of Digestion*, the writer rehashes the well-worn example of how Europe's peasantry are the fittest people on earth, despite eating less flesh than other classes—*except for the Italians*. "Italians living chiefly on maccaroni cannot be instanced as a fair example of vegetarians, because macaroni is objectionable on the score of concentration of nutriment."[48]

The mothership of the American Vegetarian Society was the Vegetarian Society of England, whose leading founder Joseph Brotherton recognized that he could garner wider support for the vegetarian crusade by reproposing it as an ethical, secular movement. The group launched the *Vegetarian Messenger*, riding the wave of a broader movement to popularize knowledge in an increasingly more educated and literate society. The *Messenger* mimicked the *Advocate*'s reservations about macaroni but with a caveat: "We consider the concentration of nutriment which macaroni presents, to be little adapted for the *principal* article of diet, although being more coarsely ground than the wheat flour in common use in this country, and unfermented, it is probably more wholesome and digestible than that which is sold as the "best white bread" in England."[49] Perhaps they hadn't got the memo that was circulating about a highly nutritive substance that would put macaroni on par with meat: gluten.

THE DISCOVERY OF GLUTEN

In the 1745 introduction to his treatise "On Wheat," Iacopo Bartolomeo Beccari (1682–1766) echoed the lament of scholars across the ages—that all significant discoveries had already been made, leaving contemporaries merely to split hairs over the insights of past geniuses. The hair Beccari set out to split involved separating the fundamental essences of wheat itself.

The road had, in truth, been partially paved, as the process for extracting the starchy component of flour had been known since antiquity, mentioned even in the writings of Pliny the Elder. But then, Beccari applied the scientific method to the gluey residual material, which had hitherto been ignored. His eureka moment came in realizing that wheat contained both a "vegetable substance"—starch—and an "animal substance"—the protein now known as gluten.

To Beccari, this discovery laid bare the nutritive value that wheat held for humans and explained how herbivores could build muscle mass without consuming meat. His hypothesis that gluten and animal material were the self-same stuff arose from the observation that vegetable matter fermented over time, while animal matter putrefied—as did gluten—yielding a "urineacious spirit. . . . Most stinkingly, it putrefies after the manner of a cadaver."[50] This perhaps accounted for the oft-mentioned admonitions in cookbooks about reeking pasta. Beccari further established that different wheat varieties contained more and less of this essential substance, with durum semolina being among the most enriched.

Scientists continued theorizing, albeit inconclusively, about how animals converted plants into flesh—but Beccari's groundbreaking wheat research lay dormant and underappreciated. At a public lecture titled "On Flesh-Forming Foods," chemist the E. R. Lankester marveled, "A curious thing about this discovery was that he described it very accurately, stated that it produced compounds precisely similar to the flesh of animals, and that in decomposition it gave out precisely the same smell; and yet no one until lately even suspected there was the slightest identity between this substance and the tissues of the animal."[51]

The "lately" breakthrough Lankester referred to was the work of the Dutch chemist Gerardus Johannes Mulder. In 1837, Mulder published analyses detailing the striking similarities between protein-based substances extracted from diverse plants and animals. Finding them composed of nearly identical elemental makeups, he proposed these "albuminous" substances all contained a common "protein" radical at their core. Mulder's work catalyzed significant interest in the emerging field of "animal chemistry" among his scientific contemporaries.

The concept of foods being divisible into vital essential nutrients—protein, carbohydrates, fats—that could be isolated and studied discretely emerged alongside the gradual demise of ancient humoral theories and the advancement of chemistry, physiology, and nutritional science. Leading this vanguard was the flesh-forming wheat protein Beccari had identified: gluten.

As the chemical structures of these macromolecules became better understood, the word "protein"—from the Greek *proteios*, meaning "of primary importance"—solidified in the scientific literature and vernacular. Though carbohydrates were present in the wheat kernel, gluten's "flesh-forming" properties dominated the discussion.[52] The high gluten content in durum wheat macaroni would, in due time, propel the food into a new sphere of prominence.[53]

The marriage of science and religion was joined together in Mary Tyler Peabody Mann's *Christianity in the Kitchen: A Physiological Cookbook* (1858), whose cover quotation "There's death in the pot" (2 Kings 4:40), could only have appealed to a very niche readership. Why Christian per se? Sickness was a moral failure, a sign that one had gone against God's natural laws. When man fell ill from indulging his appetites beyond nature's prescription, it was no less shameful than the drunkard suffering delirium tremens. Even the great guru Sylvester Graham had fallen ill after succumbing to gastronomic temptation but subsequently published an apology in a newspaper for his shortcoming. Mann's book was a remedial resource, offering temperate guidance for wholesome eating. She does not disdain macaroni, but in accordance with proper hygiene, the stolen recipe she presents as her own recommends carefully inspecting the tubes for insects.[54] The macaroni is thoroughly sanitized with a half-hour boil in water followed by another fifteen minutes in milk. By then, any ungodly threat will surely have cooked off.

Educating the Masses

The *Messenger* later softened its stance and devoted a full page to reprinting the *Penny Magazine* spread about macaroni but not before subjecting it to surgical edits to weed out references to meat and alcohol.[55] Though the tone verged on condescending, it provided a stark description of the fatigue and danger workers faced in a pasta factory in Naples.

Kneading the great quantities of stiff dough required men to exert their full bodyweight on one end of a lever balanced on a fulcrum, with a heavy block attached to the other that pounded the dough in a seesaw motion, an image that gives us pause to recall the root word for macaroni—*maccare*—to bruise, batter, or break. "The effect produced by a large manufactory, where several of these machines and the number of sturdy fellows, nearly naked, are all bobbing up and down, has something ludicrous in it to the eye of the stranger."[56]

The public was entranced by the manufacture of the exotic Italian staple. A colorful 1858 travel piece from Dickens's *Household Words*, recounting the spectacle of "macaroni-making" in Amalfi, opened with a description that had changed little since the 1833 *Penny* predecessor: "A crowd of men and boys, half-blind with flour, and as white as cauliflowers, sat on a lever, bumping up and down; and making it describe the arc of a circle. Grinding, sifting, mixing, kneading and pressing, were all going on in the same place; the manufactured article being taken to another place to dry."

He enters into detail about the process, the sight of the near-naked men still making a striking impression:

> The flour is well mixed in a large tub, in the proportion of twenty-four *caraffa* of water (a *caraffa* being about a pint and a-half), to a hundred and fifty Neapolitan pounds of flour. The quantity thus used, goes by the name of a Pasta, and is put on a large kneading-board. At the farther end of the board a long lever moves horizontally by a swivel; and, on the other extremity of it, sit three or four half-naked girdled men, who, for three quarters of an hour, move backward and forward on a kind of horizontal see-saw describing diminutive arcs of circles. In this way the lever is brought to bear upon the dough, kneading and cutting it till it is ready for pressing. The men remind one of figures in Egyptian drawings; stiff and unnatural. 'Tis hard work, however, and there is always a relief party to take the place of the exhausted men.

While the French proved more open to adopting the new hydraulic technology for macaroni production, the Neapolitans vehemently resisted—not out of a dedication to quality per se but fear that the technology posed a threat to jobs and economic stability. In the 1840s, one enterprising maverick set up a factory in Gragnano with hydraulic presses that minimized the backbreaking labor, cranking out ten times more pasta than local competitors. In response, those competitors banded together and succeeded in forcing the company to shutter.[57]

ISABELLA BEETON

The English cookbook author Isabella Mayson Beeton also sought to enlighten her readers with curiosities, history, culture, and a dash of politics. She believed that as the eldest of twenty children, between siblings, half-siblings and step-siblings, she was a natural domestic organizer. Her mother and stepfather were financially comfortable enough to send her to Heidelberg for part of her schooling, where she received a cultural education deemed proper for a young lady of their standing—including her first forays into formal instruction in pastry-making.

Shortly after her nineteenth birthday, Isabella Mayson became Mrs. Beeton, assuming the roles of editor and writer for one of her husband's publications, *The English Woman's Domestic Magazine*. Her contributions were mainly household management tips and recipes, of which none were her own creations. As one of England's most popular women's magazines, many of the recipes came via reader correspondence. What Beeton may have lacked as an innovator, she made up for as a skillful curator and compiler. She published a popular series of inserts for the magazine of recipes and tips. These were later bound into the 1861 volume *Beeton's Book of Household Management*, later lovingly referred to simply as *Mrs. Beeton*. The recipes were pulled from the long lineage of renowned English and French cookbooks stretching from Glasse to Carême to Francatelli, none of whom she acknowledged, of course. But to her credit, she and her team tested and tweaked each recipe until they met with her approval, effectively making them her own originals.

The underlying inspiration for writing the book, besides the guaranteed sales, was to educate young women in the *culture* of domesticity that they might become capable and informed curators of their domestic sphere. In so doing (sigh), they could create a home that would keep husbands from defaulting to the club, tavern, and dining-houses for solace, thus avoiding the main source of familial discontent: "a housewife's badly cooked dinners and untidy ways."[58] The only remedy to keep them home was for the mistress to be "thoroughly acquainted with the theory and practice of cookery, as well as perfectly conversant with all the other arts of making and keeping a comfortable home."[59]

Three recipes for macaroni and cheese are placed in the "Milk, butter, cheese and eggs" section, under the subheading "MACARONI as usually served with the CHEESE COURSE," the last course of the British meal. She provides a concise description of pasta manufacturing in Naples, taken from an 1844 domestic encyclopedia.[60] Though rather dated, little had changed in the state of the art since then, but Beeton was a better conduit, as she commanded a wider, more captive audience. She bypasses the seesaw kneading and focuses more on the pressing process: "It is put through a hollow cylindrical vessel, pierced with holes of the size of tobacco pipes at the bottom. Through these holes the mass is forced by a powerful screw bearing on a piece of wood made exactly to fit the inside of the cylinder. Whilst issuing from the holes, it is partially baked by a fire placed below the cylinders and is, at the same time, drawn away and hung over rods placed about the room, in order to dry."[61] Her closing comment is a clear and laudable statement about dietary reform for the masses: "As it is both wholesome and nutritious, it ought to be much more used by all classes in England than it is."[62] Parmesan cheese is the choice of the wealthy, she says, but her recipe makes concessions with the cheaper cheshire option.

The reform movement with macaroni in the frontline had made it all the way to colonial Australia, and so had the word on gluten. Edward Abbott's (1801–1869) recipe in *The English and Australian Cookery Book: Cookery for the Many, as Well as for the "Upper Ten Thousand"* (read "for the masses and the rich") is an English-style milk-based bake, with this serving tip: "Let the consumer use either pepper or cayenne, according to fancy; put none in the dish." He covers some background details about the Italian pasta industry and semolina, adding, "There is nothing more nutritious to adults and children than macaroni or vermicelli, as they are both made from the gluten of the best Southern wheat."

WHEAT, SLAVERY, AND WAR

As it had been in ancient Rome, the nation that controlled the wheat trade wielded immense power in the Western world—and Americans wanted in. Windows of opportunity opened on several fronts where they could position themselves as a threat to Russian dominance. The rise of American metalworking industries led to agricultural advancements in the United States well ahead of Russia. Railroads, the transport arteries shuttling wheat eastward, expanded rapidly thanks to the cheap labor of Irish immigrants fleeing starvation, freed and runaway slaves, and the cooperation of some Native American tribes. Innovations in naval technology also gave Americans a leg up in the global wheat trade.

Europeans were already uneasy about their dependance on Russian wheat, but when prices doubled during the Crimean War (1853–1856), trade with Americans became a very attractive alternative. As US wheat was not durum wheat, it could not be channeled directly into the macaroni industry—except for those who did not adhere to that stricture of quality. Nevertheless, it still significantly impacted European markets. Between 1840 and 1860, many European cities doubled in size owing to the cheap, plentiful supply of grain.[63] The surge in the grain supply also improved the quantity and the quality of cheese and butter, resulting in products that were both superior and more economical. Yesterday's wheat was today's petroleum, and cheap US wheat not only disrupted the balance of world power, it would also do so at home, causing a drop in cotton prices and forcing the question of the abolition of slavery.

Whatever the moral sentiments of abolitionists may have been, slavery in the Midwestern territories clashed with the capitalistic designs of the so-called "railroad barons". As Scott Reynolds Nelson points out, "Inequality in slaveholding regimes was so extreme that slavery's expansion into free territories posed an existential threat to profitable railroad settlement of the prairie lands of the Midwest." A robust flow of goods both east and west required a consumer base in the west with purchasing power. Empty westbound trains were a cash bleed, and the eastbound grain cargo shipped at the fourth-class rate, which encouraged farmers to plant wheat as their primary crop.[64] Western settlers who worked the land and populated the small towns had to believe they were building a future. Expansion of the plantation economy in the west would keep the railroad men from making money. Railroad magnates and grain traders saw Southern cotton growers

(*continued on next page*)

(*continued from previous page*)

and political divisiveness as the greatest threat to their ambitions.[65] "The success of railroads depended on stable balanced back and forth trade that gave them access not only to raw materials but also to a large, stable class of consumers for the products they sold."[66]

It was a heated topic among Southern powerbrokers and government officials. These gentlemen regularly convened for dinner in hotels or dining clubs to forge alliances over a good meal, referred to as a "mess." Mess comes from the Old English and French word "mes," indicating equally distributed portions, a term retained by the military. The F Street Mess was particularly influential in the lead-up to the War Between the States. Regular political discussions were held over dinners at the Willard Hotel in Washington, DC, in the mid-nineteenth century, fomenting plans to block emigration to the Midwest, which they rightly perceived as a direct threat to the power of the slave states.

Through their coordinated efforts, in 1852, the so-called "Committee of Nine" managed to block railroad expansion into the plains.[67] The stranglehold continued to intensify, and tensions escalated. Their alignment with proslavery interests in Kansas exacerbated the conflict and violence in the territory. Shots were exchanged between slaveholders and nonslaveholders in a period that would be called Bleeding Kansas (1854–1859)—the lead-in to the Civil War.

The nation was morally gripped and further polarized by the Dred Scott Decision of 1857. This landmark ruling declared that African Americans, whether enslaved or free, were not US citizens. It was a large brushstroke decision that concomitantly struck down the Missouri Compromise, which had prohibited slavery in the northern territories of the Louisiana Purchase above the 36°30′ parallel. Americans readied themselves to resolve these issues through armed conflict, both sides believing it would be short and decisive, neither of them able to afford prolonged warfare.

The American Civil War was fought between from April 12, 1861, and April 9, 1865, with an estimated eight hundred thousand dead.

Toward the conclusion of the War Between the States, the US Department of Agriculture embarked on a venture to cultivate durum wheat on US soil. Russia's dominance as the greatest exporter of this grain—amassing substantial revenues and maintaining control of food corridors—was the impetus to muscle in. What was stopping the United States? They boasted superior technological prowess and vast expanses of fertile, untapped land. The Gold Rush had bolstered the economy, spurred the development of transport and communication networks, and pushed the border to the Pacific coast. Everything was primed to go—except for one crucial oversight—people hadn't quite cottoned on to what they were actually going to do with that hard wheat. It wasn't needed for bread, and US macaroni manufacturers had resigned themselves to making cheap pasta with softer wheat varieties. Grain elevator operators refused to store it, fearing it would jeopardize current sales or, worse, that they would end up with a silo full of spoiled wheat. Millers lacked the equipment to process hard wheat and the incentive to invest in the technology to do so. As things were still in the experimental stages, miscalculations in planting and cultivation sometimes rendered a measly crop, a setback that cast a shadow over the whole operation. Enthusiasm waned and with it funding, but the project left a legacy that would resurface later in the century under the name "Macaroni Wheats."

Chapter Seven

AMERICANS VIE FOR THEIR PIECE OF THE PIE

Mistaken Identity: A servant girl was once given some macaroni by her mistress to prepare for the table. Noting the girl's surprise, the lady asked: "Didn't you cook macaroni at your last place?" "Cook it? We used them things to light the gas with!"

—*BUFFALO EVENING NEWS*, MARCH 20, 1893

COOKING UP A NATION: CULINARY NATIONALISM IN PRE-CIVIL WAR AMERICA

Americans were raring to declare their culinary independence—and they were taking macaroni and cheese with them. In the decades leading up to the United States centennial, American cookbook titles began to assert a distinct culinary identity that reflected the nation's growing self-assurance and a shift toward a more defined national cuisine. The initial stirrings can be traced back to Amelia Simmons's *American Cookery* of 1796, the first cookbook by an American author published in the United States. However, it was in the mid-nineteenth century that the movement gained significant momentum. As Americans shook off their inferiority complex, they audaciously began "redeeming" European cookery for an American audience, mirroring the call of Manifest Destiny.

Some authors were more timorous, submissively sourcing from or imitating foreign publications, such as *The Great American Cook Book: Adapted to American Housewifery* (1850), whose macaroni and cheese defaulted to old reliable: the Raffald recipe. *The American Family Encyclopedia* (1856), was little more than a British publication with a new title, importing another worn-out favorite, the Rundell liquified macaroni.

But in the spirit of Walt Whitman, others yearned for a cookbook to match the American experience. The naively earnest *The Practical*

American Cook Book (1855) painted a portrait of the young nation: "To our whole people, rich and poor together, the world is open, with all its pleasures, its hopes, and its prizes." Not exactly "whole" as 13 percent of the population was enslaved. "An American home is the theatre of the highest hopes and the proudest pretensions." In her bosom, the greatest of men "are cradled and educated there, often amid moderate resources, not unfrequently with stinted and inadequate means, seldom in the abundance of superfluous wealth."[1] Probity was the American Way: "Frugality and order must be the corner-stones of our republican edifice. The extravagant follies and unmeasured expenditure of the European aristocracies are impossible and incompatible here." Accordingly, the author, "A Housekeeper," leaves us with two painfully parsimonious macaroni and cheese recipes. Rebecca Upton's 1856 *Home Studies* spoke poignantly of American women's resilience "whose life is often partly spent in cities, partly on Western prairies, and partly on Southern plantations—perhaps begun in affluence, to be finally shorn of all but health, hands, and unfailing courage."[2] These patriotic cookbooks championed the republican virtues of the day—self-improvement, industriousness, civic duty, freely chosen employment, and the promise of upward mobility.[3]

Cuisines are not born overnight. Susan Crowen's *The American Lady's System of Cookery* sought a happy medium.[4] Her take on the authentic American kitchen drew from European counterparts but reflected American sensibilities. Crowen pushed for artistry in simplicity over pretention for its own sake. She had no argument with style so long as it was fast and simple—get it done the American Way.

She also favored domestic products, suggesting pineapple cheese as an alternative to parmesan in her macaroni and cheese. Pineapple cheese contains no pineapple. It was something between a cheddar and parmesan but made with extra cream, which lent a richer flavor but with enough body that could be pressed into a pineapple mold.[5]

"Pine-apple cheese" was already a popular commodity by the onset of the American Revolutionary War period.[6] But in 1810, the process was patented by a cheesemaker in Goshen, Connecticut, and quickly became a prosperous business—the eye-catching appeal and distinctive taste had made pineapple cheese a delightful everyday food and trendy gift item. By midcentury, coinciding with Crowen's writing, production had spread to her home state of New York. So great was demand that English cheesemakers produced it and exported to the United States.[7] The cheese's popularity endured well into the twentieth century, with James L. Kraft eventually buying out the Goshen company and continuing to produce pineapple cheese until 1931.[8] Its use in macaroni and cheese upped the creaminess quotient, a quality that Americans relished.

Crowen's mission statement reveals the work's double purpose as a cultural compass for immigrant women needing an introduction into American foodways and customs. Rather than forcing conformity, she offered a primer to help women assimilate into their adopted homeland. In northeastern cities, where foreign-born women dominated domestic service, Crowen's guidance promised to boost their job prospects.[9] This inclusionary sentiment was also expressed in Hannah Peterson's *The National Cook Book*. Peterson was a member of the Society of Friends (Quakers) in the City of Brotherly Love, and part of the culinarily renowned Widdifield family. She, too, saw the kitchen as a gateway to a new identity. Macaroni and cheese was a standard feature in these books and presented to the tired, poor, and huddled masses alongside these American ideals.

William Vollmer's *United States Cook Book: With Particular Reference to the Climate and Productions of the United States* (1856) exemplified another facet of the evolving American identity. Vollmer came in with the wave of one million Germans who immigrated to the United States in the aftermath of the 1848 Springtime of the Peoples. As a European-trained chef and émigré, he brought a cosmopolitan sensibility but branded the cultural synthesis American. Vollmer's patriotic effort included two macaroni and cheese recipes, highlighting the active appropriation of Old World traditions as New World adaptations.

FROM CRACKERS TO COCKAIGNE: COOKBOOKS AS WAR NARRATIVES

The Civil War brought new meaning to the adage that an army travels on its stomach. Recognizing this, the Union Defense Committee published *Camp Cookery and Hospital Diet for the Use of the US Volunteers Now in Service* (1861), drawing heavily on the dietary regimen Alexis Soyer (see chapter 6) had developed while working alongside Florence Nightingale during the Crimean War. Nightingale observed, "Thousands of patients are annually starved in the midst of plenty for want of attention to the ways which alone make it possible for them to take food." Addressing both dietary and culinary needs, the cookbook included two macaroni recipes—albeit sweet versions without cheese. The inclusion of macaroni in this military cookbook, inspired by Nightingale's emphasis on nourishment, underscores its status as a versatile staple—not only nutritious and sustaining for soldiers in harsh conditions but also comforting amid the ravages of war.[10]

The war had not only divided the nation politically but also shattered the economic foundations of the Confederacy, bringing the once-prosperous South to its knees. At the heart of this economic ruin was the Union's naval blockade, which effectively choked off the South's lifeblood: cotton exports. With food imports from the North and Midwest barely trickling into the South, cotton became a conflict of interest to the more pressing need for edible crops. Meanwhile, the North's wheat trade flourished, filling the granaries of Europe and cementing crucial international alliances. Banking on British desperation, the Confederate government wagered that the so-called "Cotton Famine"—hitting Lancashire hard and sending shockwaves through communities across Britain—would bend the will of European powers in their favor.[11] To hasten the crippling effect, restrictions were issued to discourage cotton production—alas, to little effect.[12] Loyalists stopped planting cotton, but the greedy persisted, unable to resist high market prices. Regardless, most of it ended up languishing on the docks along with the Confederacy's international leverage. England and France stood resolutely behind the Union and the abolition of slavery.

The economic reversal manifested dramatically in the daily struggle for sustenance, forcing Southern households to adapt to unprecedented scarcity, a reality reflected in *The Confederate Receipt Book* in 1863. This compilation, born of necessity, proposed stopgap solutions to make do with dwindling resources. Through its pages, we glimpse a society struggling to sustain itself in the face of mounting privation, a testament to the far-reaching consequences of economic warfare.

Most of the recipes were for domestic utility—how to strengthen watery ink or make cement to repair broken teacups. To describe the cooking section as spare would be an understatement. The recipe "Apple Pie Without Apples" is a prime example: "To one small bowl of crackers, that have been soaked until no hard parts remain, add one teaspoonful of tartaric acid, sweeten to your taste, add some butter, and a very little nutmeg."[13]

It is oddly reminiscent of Mary Randolph's "Mock Macaroni": "Break some crackers in small pieces, soak them in milk until they are soft; then use them as a substitute for macaroni." And it would be conceptually revisited under "Macaroni" in the 1874 charity work *Tried and True Recipes. The Home Cook Book of Chicago; published for the benefit of the Home for the Friendless*: "Cook, macaroni in water until soft; then put in a deep dish, with alternate layers of grated crackers and cheese, a little salt; fill up the dish with milk and bake one hour."[14]

Power of the imagination was an important ingredient. In a compilation like *The Confederate Receipt Book*, where only twenty-one of the "receipts" were actually for cooking—and these primarily focused on making do with limited supplies—a dish like macaroni and cheese was unthinkable. A few blockade runners managed to slip through with luxury goods, though quantities would have been severely limited, as were people who could financially or morally afford them. Confederate currencies had lost their value and priority went to military and medical provisions.

The *Poetical Cook-Book* (1864) stood in stark contrast to the pragmatic Civil War publications of the time. Maria J. Moss had not written the whimsical book with the express intent of raising money for the Union cause, but as one of the organizers of the Great Sanitary [Health] Fair in her native city of Philadelphia, she dedicated it to that purpose:

> "I did not think it would be of service to my fellow-creatures, for our suffering soldiers, the sick, wounded, and needy. . . . With these few words I dedicate this book to the Sanitary Fair to be held in Philadelphia, June, 1864."[15]

Purchasers were delighted by the idea of cookbook sales to support charity work.[16] While *Poetical* is not a community cookbook in the classic sense, it planted a seed: Women could pool their collective culinary knowledge to raise money to effect change.[17] Short of actually having the power to vote, these cookbooks were a creative, albeit circuitous, way to have a voice that counted in their communities.

True to its name, the book pairs recipes with uplifting verse, offering sustenance for both body and spirit in the dark days of the conflict. Moss's macaroni and cheese recipe is headed by lines from Sir Thomas Moore's 1818 satirical epistolary poem "The Fudge Family in Paris," recalling Boccaccio's psychedelic dreamland, Bengodi (see chapter 2), under the name Cocaigne:

> After dreaming some hours of the land of Cocaigne,
> That Elysium of all that is friand and nice,
> Where for hail they have bon-bons, and claret for rain,
> And the skaters in winter show off on cream-ice;
> Where so ready all nature its cookery yields,
> *Macaroni au parmesan* grows in the fields;

Her macaroni is a variant served on toast, a practice carried on from Sarah Martin's 1795 recipe (see chapter 3). This simple but indulgent creation—bread, fried in either butter or drippings, topped with buttered macaroni, breadcrumbs, and a thick layer of parmesan, then baked to golden—was indeed the stuff of dreams in a time of austerity.

The optimistic *What to Do with the Cold Mutton: A Book of Réchauffés* (1865) signaled the beginnings of recovery as well as a sociological shift. This culinary lifeline targeted young ladies who had "married down" or whose fortunes had fallen because of the war. The art of repurposing leftovers, without defaulting to the "inevitable 'hash,'" had come of age. Macaroni is put to work with pork, mutton, veal, beef, rabbit, sausage, fish, even oysters—the latest American macaroni craze. The book also showcased what had become of the American trifecta: macaroni (and cheese), *macaroni à l'Italienne* (creamy cheese and often gravy), and macaroni with tomato sauce. Once a luxury, macaroni had transformed into the downwardly mobile housewife's secret weapon for stretching her food dollars—a far cry cheerier than default hash.

MACARONI CENTER STAGE IN THE DAWN OF AMERICAN RESTAURANT CULTURE

Mid-nineteenth century America had precious few restaurants, and those that existed predominantly served what is best described as Frenchified English fare. Both French and English visitors found the American accent on this cuisine unbearable, their snooty pens gleefully skewering the attempts at culinary refinement they experienced during their stateside sojourns.

What exactly were they coming up against? The historian Paul Freedman's quantitative analysis of the surviving menus of high-end dining establishments revealed some startling findings. Amid the pretentions of haute cuisine, macaroni and cheese, in its various guises, was not only a constant but also repeatedly ranked as the most frequently mentioned dish.

By way of example, here are the top-10 ranking of entrées featured on menus from New York's Fifth Avenue Hotel between 1859 and 1865 and the number of times they appeared:

Oyster patties a la Bechamel (178)
Baked beans and pork (165)
Macaroni au Parmesan (164)
Oysters baked in shell (160)
Macaroni au gratin (160)
Macaroni with cheese (159)
Fillet of beef, larded, with mushrooms (159)
Macaroni a la creme (152)
Haricot of mutton a la bourgeoise (145)
Apple fritters (137)[18]
Total for macaroni = 635
Total for oysters = 338

Compare with the 1862–1865 menus from Boston's Revere House Hotel (est. 1847):

Macaroni au gratin (183)
Escalloped oysters (156)
Oysters baked in shell (144)
Oyster patties (139)
Fricassee of chicken (115)
Macaroni and cheese (115)
Salmis of duck (104)
Baked macaroni (92)
Macaroni au Parmesan (88)
Baked beans and pork (87)[19]
Total for macaroni = 478
Total for oysters = 439

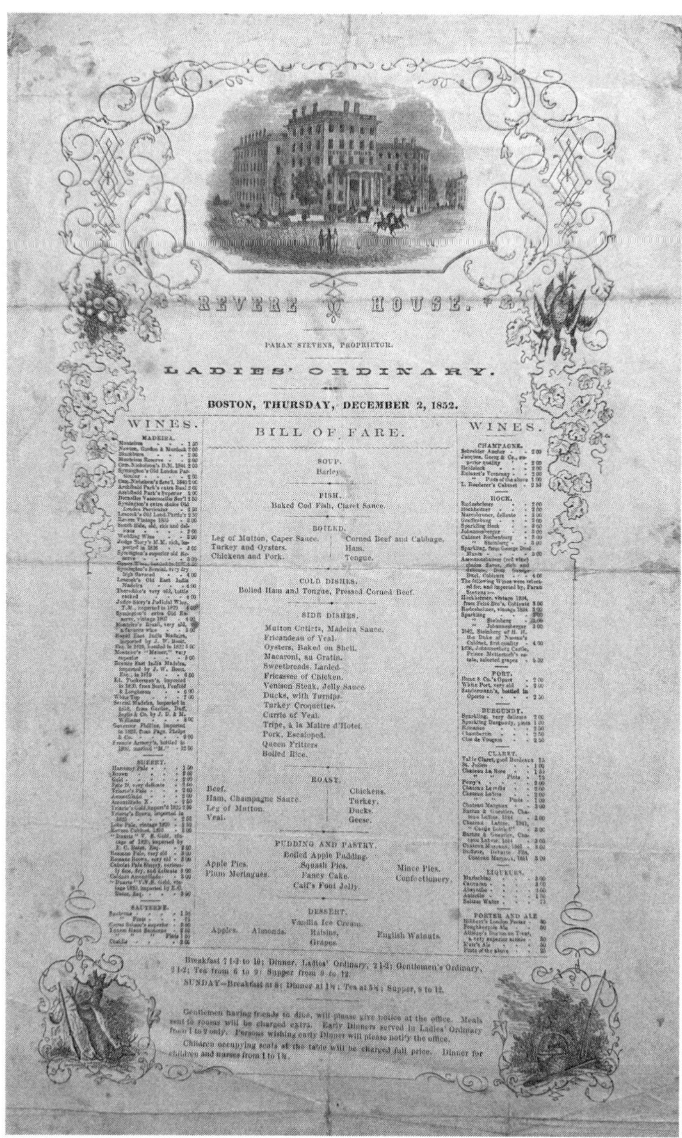

REVERE HOUSE.

PARAN STEVENS, PROPRIETOR.

LADIES' ORDINARY.

BOSTON, THURSDAY, DECEMBER 2, 1852.

BILL OF FARE.

SOUP.
Barley.

FISH.
Baked Cod Fish, Claret Sauce.

BOILED.
Leg of Mutton, Caper Sauce.
Turkey and Oysters.
Chickens and Pork.
Corned Beef and Cabbage.
Ham.
Tongue.

COLD DISHES.
Boiled Ham and Tongue, Pressed Corned Beef.

SIDE DISHES.
Mutton Cutlets, Madeira Sauce.
Fricandeau of Veal.
Oysters, Baked on Shell.
Macaroni, au Gratin.
Sweetbreads, Larded.
Fricassee of Chicken.
Venison Steak, Jelly Sauce.
Ducks, with Turnips.
Turkey Croquettes.
Currie of Veal.
Tripe, à la Maitre d'Hotel.
Pork, Escaloped.
Queen Fritters.
Boiled Rice.

ROAST.
Beef.
Ham, Champagne Sauce.
Leg of Mutton.
Veal.
Chickens.
Turkey.
Ducks.
Geese.

PUDDING AND PASTRY.
Boiled Apple Pudding.
Apple Pies.
Plum Meringues.
Squash Pies.
Fancy Cake.
Calf's Foot Jelly.
Mince Pies.
Confectionery.

DESSERT.
Vanilla Ice Cream.
Apples. Almonds. Raisins, Grapes. English Walnuts.

WINES.

WINES.

Breakfast 7 1-2 to 10; Dinner, Ladies' Ordinary, 2 1-2; Gentlemen's Ordinary, 2 1-2; Tea from 6 to 9; Supper from 9 to 12.

SUNDAY—Breakfast at 8; Dinner at 1½; Tea at 5½; Supper, 9 to 12.

Gentlemen having friends to dine, will please give notice at the office. Meals sent to rooms will be charged extra. Early Dinners served in Ladies' Ordinary from 1 to 2 only. Persons wishing early Dinner will please notify the office.

Children occupying seats at the table will be charged full price. Dinner for children and nurses from 1 to 1½.

FIGURE 7.1. This Revere House "Ladies' Ordinary" menu reflects the practice of separate dining spaces and meal service for women who were unaccompanied by men. Note how the offerings of this 1852 menu vary only slightly from those on the 1862 regular dinner menu. *Source*: Courtesy of the Smithsonian Archive Center, National Museum of American History. Public domain.

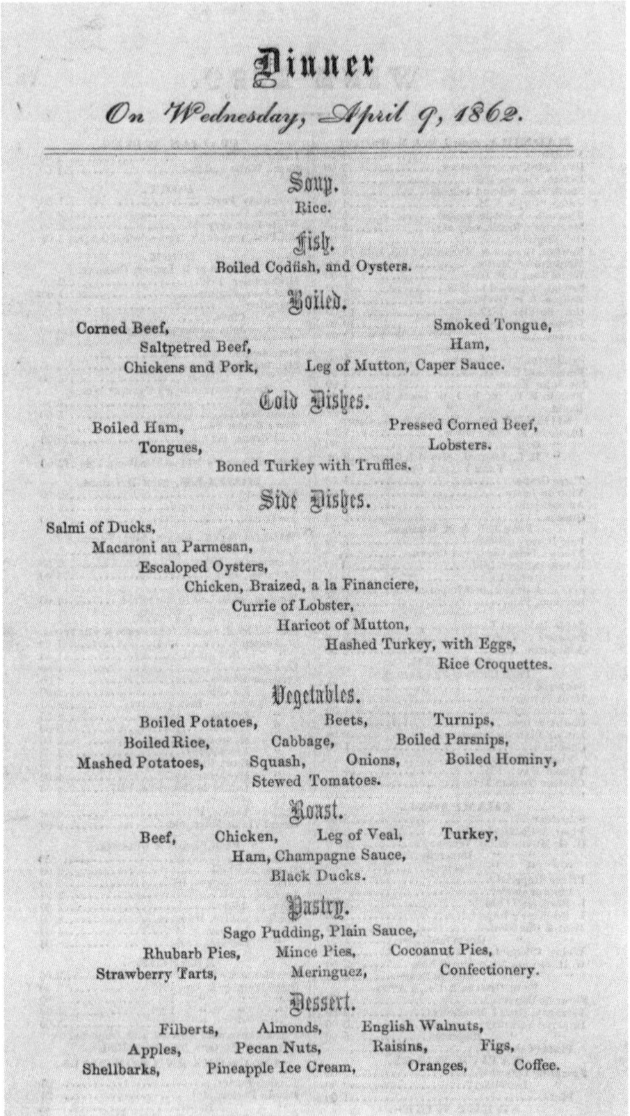

Dinner

On Wednesday, April 9, 1862.

Soup.
Rice.

Fish.
Boiled Codfish, and Oysters.

Boiled.
Corned Beef, Smoked Tongue,
Saltpetred Beef, Ham,
Chickens and Pork, Leg of Mutton, Caper Sauce.

Cold Dishes.
Boiled Ham, Pressed Corned Beef,
Tongues, Lobsters.
Boned Turkey with Truffles.

Side Dishes.
Salmi of Ducks,
Macaroni au Parmesan,
Escaloped Oysters,
Chicken, Braized, a la Financiere,
Currie of Lobster,
Haricot of Mutton,
Hashed Turkey, with Eggs,
Rice Croquettes.

Vegetables.
Boiled Potatoes, Beets, Turnips,
Boiled Rice, Cabbage, Boiled Parsnips,
Mashed Potatoes, Squash, Onions, Boiled Hominy,
Stewed Tomatoes.

Roast.
Beef, Chicken, Leg of Veal, Turkey,
Ham, Champagne Sauce,
Black Ducks.

Pastry.
Sago Pudding, Plain Sauce,
Rhubarb Pies, Mince Pies, Cocoanut Pies,
Strawberry Tarts, Meringuez, Confectionery.

Dessert.
Filberts, Almonds, English Walnuts,
Apples, Pecan Nuts, Raisins, Figs,
Shellbarks, Pineapple Ice Cream, Oranges, Coffee.

FIGURE 7.2. Revere House dinner menu, 1862. *Source*: Courtesy of the Rare Book Division, New York Public Library. Public domain.

The results of these menus make it clear why the prospect of combining macaroni with oysters so excited the American palate. There is no overstating the ravenous craze for oysters that lasted a good fifty years. While these samples represent just two restaurants, a remarkable conformity emerged as dining establishments began to crop up further west in later years. Even in Tombstone, Arizona, following the 1879 silver rush, *macaroni à l'Italienne* still headlined menus.[20] This uniformity also extended across seasons in an effort to maintain a reputable standard of elegance through consistent offerings for those indulging in this public act of leisure. Indeed, restauranteurs clung to the tried-and-true offerings until the 1890s, as if deviation might precipitate disaster.[21]

New York's Delmonico's was the gold standard in restaurants. Delmonico's maître d'hôtel, Oscar Tschirky, who would later take the helm at the rival Waldorf Astoria, though not a chef himself, compiled *The Cook Book by "Oscar" of the Waldorf* (1896). It included recipes from his years in the restaurant business, leaving posterity with a record of the butter-forward macaroni and cheese that set the bar for nineteenth-century restaurants. Most interesting is that the macaroni is left in its long form, for which bucatini could be used.

BAKED MACARONI

9 oz (250 g) long-form macaroni
Pepper and nutmeg to taste
1/3 cup (80 mL) bechamel sauce
1/4 lb (115 g) butter
2 oz (60 g) parmesan, grated
2 oz (60 g) gruyere, grated + more for topping

Bring a large pot of salted water to a boil and put in the macaroni sticks. Cook until done and drain. Put in a saucepan with pepper, nutmeg, and bechamel and warm it on the stove. Off heat add butter and the cheeses. Put the whole into a small baking dish, top with extra cheese, and bake thirty minutes in a preheated 350°F (180°C) oven.

The availability of macaroni in these inauspicious years is a curious constant, but supply apparently kept pace with demand. The ubiquity of macaroni and cheese on menus across the expanding landscape of American restaurants perpetuated its ritzy allure. As it had done for centuries, macaroni and cheese spread as an *aspirational* dish—one that diners sought out because of its prominence in upscale establishments. Yet its appeal in restaurants extended beyond sophistication and cosmopolitan taste. It was a dish that made practical sense: quick to prepare, amenable to advance cooking and reheating, made with nonperishable or routinely replenished staples, less expensive than meat, and required less culinary skill.

The mid to late decades of the nineteenth century were also the heyday of the "floating palaces"—luxury vacation steamboats, whose bills of fare replicated the most exclusive restaurant menus. The wait staff, who were primarily African American, were noted for their agility and professionalism.[22] A former waiter reminisced about the Golden Age: "We sho' live' high in dem days. Twenty-five stewhads we'd tote, an' the table, it would look jus' lahk it was spread fo' a weddin'"[23] Passengers raved about the lavish display of food, a "luxurious orgy" intended to leave them gaping in awe.[24] American tourists reveled in the grotesque abundance, but the leftovers did not go to waste.[25] As recounted by a Mississippi steamboat pilot, the crew were slopped with the daily cry of "Grub-pile!" Men descended upon the troughs of surplus food, hastily grabbing for the choicest bits before it was reduced to a general swill.[26] Thus, macaroni and cheese trickled down from fine china to crew tins, giving lower-deck diners a taste of upper-crust cuisine.

Paradoxically, as macaroni maintained its status on the tables of the elite, it was simultaneously entering American homes as a popular money-saving food. This dual identity—at once a symbol of refinement and a practical staple—propelled macaroni's ascent in American cuisine, bridging social classes and regional divides.

THE UNDERBELLY: NORTH, SOUTH, AND WEST IN THE WAKE OF THE CIVIL WAR

The Reconstruction era (1865–1877) ushered in a period of rapid economic change, but it was far from uniform across the nation. Northern factories that had once hummed with wartime efficiency transitioned to civilian production. Meanwhile, the South grappled with the dual challenges of physical reconstruction and the fundamental reinvention of its labor system in the absence of slavery. The West emerged as more than just a geographical frontier; it was an idea awaiting realization, open to the hopes and ambitions of a nation anxious to reinvent itself. Railroads, the symbol of progress and expansion, stitched disparate regions into an uneasy whole, connecting markets and facilitating the movement of goods, people, and dreams across the country.

Yet the apparent progress masked deep-seated inequalities. In urban centers, immigrant labor fueled industrial growth but often at the cost of exploitation and nativist backlash. African Americans, though legally free, found their economic opportunities severely constrained by both law and custom, a situation that worsened as Reconstruction policies waned. Native American communities faced further displacement as the nation expanded westward. The accumulation of vast fortunes among industrial magnates contrasted sharply with the poverty experienced by many workers, both in urban factories and rural fields. The term "Gilded Age" (1870s–1890s) aptly describes this later period: A thin veneer of genuine advancement overlaid the harsh reality of social tension, economic inequality, and political corruption. Understanding this era requires looking beyond the narrative of progress to examine the means to achieve this growth, who benefited from it, and who bore its costs.

The preservation of the Union through civil war instilled in many Americans a nuanced sense of national purpose, tinged with an air of moral superiority. This collective self-assurance, born of conflict and tempered by reunification rhetoric, manifested in various aspects of American life, including its approach to industry and innovation. The nation's demonstrated resilience and industrial might during the war years fed a growing conviction that American ingenuity could not only match but surpass Old World traditions. This belief in American exceptionalism increasingly manifested in dismissiveness toward European and other foreign cultures. As the country moved forward, an almost compulsive

(*continued on next page*)

(*continued from previous page*)

drive emerged to not merely imitate foreign practices but to appropriate and rebrand them in an American image. The Philadelphia Society for the Promotion of National Industry had long before zeroed in on macaroni's potential in America.[27] In an 1849 article detailing Italian manufacture of macaroni, *American Agriculturalist* magazine snooted, "The whole process of kneading, however, might be performed in a more cleanly manner, and greatly simplified by improved American machinery" (July 1849). Once it was invented, that is. Even the Lyonnais immigrant Antoine Zerega—whose descendants claim he set up the first American macaroni company in the United States in 1848—used a press that was literally "horse" powered, and dried his product in the open air.

The nascent sense of national stability, cultivated in the aftermath of the Civil War, was dealt a severe blow when the Vienna Stock Exchange collapsed in May 1873. This distant event exposed the intricate, often fragile connections of an increasingly global economy. In the United States, banks heavily invested in railroad expansion found themselves particularly vulnerable, their fates intertwined with speculative ventures that had once seemed unassailable. It culminated in the collapse of the New York Stock Exchange and precipitated the Panic of 1873.

On the ground, it resulted in mass unemployment; African Americans, still navigating the complex landscape of the post-emancipation United States, bore a disproportionate burden of economic hardship. Immigrants, too, found themselves at a crossroads, facing heightened discrimination and the difficult choice between sticking it out or repatriating. Job insecurity sparked the organization of labor unions, while radical ideologies of socialists and anarchists found fertile ground among the disillusioned. The steady stream of expansion westward slowed and even contracted as many were forced back east.

In time, this era would come to be known as "The Long Depression," a term that captures both its duration—persisting until 1879—and its profound impact on the national psyche. This designation would later serve as a point of comparison for future economic downturns, notably the Great Depression of the 1930s. The Panic of 1873 thus stands as a critical juncture in American history, a moment that challenged prevailing notions of progress and revealed the complex relationship between economic systems and social structures.

THE CENTENNIAL TABLE: SIZING UP AMERICAN DIVERSITY AND DISPARITY

As the Long Depression cast its shadow over the nation, the country's impending 1876 centennial celebration sparked a quest for its culinary identity. This introspective moment birthed several commemorative cookbooks, chief among them the *National Cookery Book*, a product of the Centennial Exposition in Philadelphia. The Women's Centennial Committees of the International Exhibition of 1876, the book's compilers, made it their mission to silence the incessant jab masquerading as curiosity from foreign visitors, who poked, "Have you no National Dishes?"[28]

The introduction, a window onto the compilers' worldview, harps on the wasteful ways in American households, a favorite criticism of foreigners. Yet in a revealing twist, it lays the blame squarely on "incompetent servants." "This evil," we are told, "bears heavily on the housewife." She is left with no choice but to "make the sacrifice of seeing more of her kitchen than suits her taste."[29] At the very least, a daily visit must be paid to the larder, compelling the mistress of the house to engage directly with the tiresome minutiae of domestic economy.

Revelatory comments like these expose the fraught, even spiteful relationship between the compilers and the unnamed, uncredited individuals whose familiarity with the recipes did not stem from genteel observation but from hard-earned experience. This centennial culinary portrait of the United States, for all its excellence, stands as a testament to bitter irony, since its very substance was drawn from the knowledge and labor of those it openly disparages: more often than not, African American women. In this significant historical moment, their contributions were not merely unacknowledged but deliberately obscured, a reflection of the deep-seated inequalities that had shadowed the nation since its founding and would continue to shape American society for generations to come.

The cookbook presents a concerted effort to represent a broad portrait of culinary Americana. It includes regional specialties: three recipes for gumbo, four chowders, and the emblematic Hoppin' John. Religious and ethnic diversity is reflected in Jewish and Catholic recipes, Middle Eastern dolma, Latin American fricadillo, West African–influenced gudinga, and Indian chicken curry. Quintessential American dishes like pork and beans,

Brother Jonathan, scrapple, and creamed chipped beef (the infamous "shit on a shingle") share pages with select picks like the "Idaho Method of Cooking a Deer Head." Native American influence is evident in recipes for preparing bear, woodchuck, muskrat, and succotash. Then, in the Vegetable section, right after "Pilgrim Dumplings (a dish used by our Forefathers in the place of Potatoes)," we find the old faithful, "To Dress Macaroni," celebrating the nation's hundredth anniversary, thereby galvanized as an American favorite.

TO DRESS MACARONI

14 oz (400 g) macaroni
1 cup (250 mL) milk or cream
Salt and cayenne pepper to taste
2 Tbsp butter
10 oz (300 g) cheddar cheese, grated
Butter toasted breadcrumbs to cover

Cook the macaroni in water until a fork goes through it. Drain and put back in the pot with the milk or cream, salt, cayenne pepper, and butter. Bring to a low boil and add half the cheese. Stir and pour out into a baking dish. Top with the rest of the cheese and the breadcrumbs. Bake in a preheated oven at 350°F (180°C) for 30 minutes until the top is golden.

THE HANDS OF HERITAGE: A RESTORATIVE HISTORY

From the very inception of macaroni and cheese in America, women of African descent labored in the kitchens of the landed gentry. Hollywood interpretations of how that played out in the South conjure standardized images that require no elaboration. However, it is owing to the immediacy of these projections that we must be reminded that *Gone with the Wind* plantations were very few. Landholdings came in all sizes and with varying setups. The number of people interacting in each setting and the interplay between them differed as much as the individuals themselves.

This diverse landscape of rural kitchens had its urban counterparts. In cities, cooking spaces ranged from modest homes to boardinghouses and grand hotels, while on the dining side there were caterers, cookshops, and restaurants, each with its own rhythms and hierarchies. Yet amid this diversity, shared cultural norms, entrenched beliefs, and behavioral expectations often persisted in ways seemingly impervious to change or challenge. Within this warp and weft, it was not uncommonly African American women who were "manning" these kitchens. Cooking was customarily relegated to women, and a prevailing belief held that African American women were innately endowed with culinary talent. This notion, while limiting, also placed them at the center of a culinary tradition that would profoundly influence American cuisine and propel macaroni and cheese into a new era of cultural significance and culinary innovation. A brief look back will help us trace the unbroken thread of this unexamined aspect connecting the past to the present, which illuminates the dish's enduring transformation.

Who's Cooking or Whose Cooking?

Not a single cookbook before Emancipation gives more than a barely discernable nod to the contribution of cooks. This omission is particularly striking in the South, given Southerners' pride in their cuisine and their eagerness to disseminate it. Granted, acknowledging cooks was not a common practice in cookbooks of the era, but given the role they played in shaping the region's legendary cuisine, such oversight represents a deliberate failure to acknowledge the hand African Americans had in Southern gastronomy and a willful perpetuation of a false narrative.

The assertion that Southern white women were mere satellites hovering superfluously in their own kitchens struck a raw nerve in Maria Massey Barringer. She channeled the energy of her ire into *Dixie Cookery; or, How I Managed My Table for Twelve Years* (1867). The introduction rings as a retort to northern smugness: "The common idea is that we are entirely destitute of practical knowledge in household affairs. This is a great mistake. The contrary is true."[30] The recipes she espouses are those she claims have been her "daily assistants for twelve years in the management of my house." While her words made it seem that the recipes cooked themselves, Barringer set out to show that wealthy housewives like herself were obliged to be well versed in cookery, as "cooks are not made to order and must be instructed in every particular."

She lays no claims to innovation; in fact, her recipe for macaroni and cheese is Eliza Leslie's, the one with the regrettable top layer of macaroni, not cheese. She clearly had not caught wind of the cautionary rhyme: "Grate gruyere cheese on macaroni; make the top crisp, but not too boney."[31] Is this the recipe Barringer's cook prepared, or she was she playing it safe by borrowing from a reputable source? Enslaved cooks were reputedly tight-lipped about their recipes, so Barringer may not have actually known how her cook made it. Macaroni and cheese isn't rocket science, yet something about this simple dish exerted an inexplicable pull on nineteenth-century cookbook authors. Volume after volume, it appeared with unfailing regularity. Some writers merely echoed well-worn recipes, while others daringly put their own spin on it. This raises the larger question of where, amid so many hands and voices, the tweaks and nuances shaping the South's culinary legacy arose.

Mrs. Shankland, in *Matron's Household Manual* (1875), seconds Mrs. Barringer's assertion that a cook's aptitude should not be taken for granted but questions the housewife's preparedness. Housekeeping manuals continued to serve a purpose owing to the "insane folly that has trained the American girl like a Princess, born to reign in some fairy land of music and art, when perhaps the future has nothing for her but to rule over and do all the work of a very humble and obscure household."[32] Certain young ladies shuddered when asked about the kitchen: "I can't bear to cook," they would say; "I let my girl attend to that."[33] Mistresses were also not "made to order," and there is no reason to assume that as a category they were able to instruct novice cooks or that they had any contribution of value to make to those with experience.

Cookbooks, written by and for white women, served as tools not just for self-education but for directing others in tasks they themselves didn't fully understand. The irony, then, was that these recipes, read aloud to the cooks, were often refined and adjusted in practice by the very people the mistress sought to instruct, only to find their way into future cookbooks. This dynamic—of unskilled but literate mistresses and knowledgeable cooks—was a defining feature of the Southern kitchen that went unacknowledged in cookbooks of the time. While women such as Barringer believed it was their responsibility to oversee every detail, convinced that their role was indispensable to the kitchen's success, in reality, the experienced hands of the cook often rendered such supervision unnecessary.

Each cook, upon hearing or reading a recipe, might alter it to suit their kitchen's specific needs, passing those changes along orally or jotting them down for others. The process was iterative, a quiet exchange of culinary knowledge that transcended race, class, and region. As a result, we can never be entirely sure to what degree the macaroni and cheese recipes in cookbooks were influenced by the innovations of Black cooks, relayed through layers of communication to white cookbook authors. What is certain, however, is that macaroni and cheese had by then become a staple of the Southern kitchen, its regular appearance at the table ensured by the labor, skill, and memory of the household cook.

The story of transmission cannot be reduced to a single, linear narrative as the contexts in which this happened were varied and intricate. The optimal, and historically traditional, path to culinary mastery was through apprenticeship, whether with an experienced cook mentoring a novice in the home or through a more structured kitchen setting. Cooks in these situations learned to master a repertoire of popular dishes along with general culinary skills that would give them a basis from which to experiment. In cooking, there's a constant push-me-pull-you dance between respect for traditional practices and the excitement of creative innovation. These layers of training, exchange, and a personal stamp shaped our dish over time and kept it evergreen on the menu.

Black Culinary Expertise and Its Reach

Eliza Seymour Lee's career exemplifies the complex and diverse culinary networks of the antebellum South. In 1847, Eliza and her husband, John Lee, free Blacks, purchased Jones Inn in Charleston. This establishment had a history of African American ownership, though it included reliance on slave labor. Eliza's own background reflects this complexity: Her mother, a former slave who became a slaveowner, ran a pastry shop where Eliza trained alongside enslaved workers, honing their skills to satisfy Charleston's aristocratic palates.

Under Seymour Lee's management, the inn's restaurant became renowned as one of Charleston's finest, still staffed by enslaved workers. Its reputation attracted white slaveowners seeking to improve their own kitchens, who sent their enslaved cooks to apprentice under her skilled staff. This arrangement highlights the paradoxical nature of culinary expertise in the South, where knowledge flowed across the boundaries of race and status, even as the institution of slavery persisted. David S. Shield, in *Southern Provisions*, contends, "The Seymour-Lee family did more than any other persons in the antebellum era to improve the quality of cooking available in Charleston, influencing elite domestic consumption through the pastry cooks they trained to expertise, as well as the public fare available in the city."[34]

In *High on the Hog*, the culinary historian Jessica B. Harris explores various other contexts in which dishes popular with high society—macaroni and cheese among them—circulated through a network of free and enslaved African Americans engaged in food service. She particularly highlights Philadelphia, where catering became one of the most lucrative businesses for free Blacks during this period.[35] With its bustling seaport and the largest population of free African Americans in the United States (about fifteen thousand in 1830), Philly served as a thriving hub for this culinary exchange.[36]

Robert Bogle's success there in catering inspired other free people of color to follow his path. As their numbers grew, they formed a union to protect their interests and assist other African Americans trying to make their way.[37] French Haitians, such as Peter Augustin and the Baptiste family, along with many of the city's West Indian diaspora, not only raised the bar but set standards for upper-class catering with their distinctive French flair. Their cooks and wait staff provided such refined service and were so attuned to the day's fashions that their services were requested up and down the East Coast. The respect these professionals commanded elevated the standing of food-service workers. W. E. B. Du Bois, the prominent sociologist and civil rights leader, commented on the dignity of these workers, who transformed "the Negro cook and waiter into the public caterer and restaurateur, and raised a crowd of underpaid menials to become a set of self-reliant, original businessmen, who amassed fortunes for themselves and won general respect for their people."[38]

That is not to imply that apprenticeships and learning from cookbooks were mutually exclusive. It is more than just a romantic notion that truly accomplished cooks do not need cookbooks, but literate cooks undoubtably had an extra iron in the fire. However one may have acquired her skills, the ideal cook kept abreast of the latest trends, blending novelty with tradition and personal style. These practitioners were well-positioned to propagate and proliferate traditions like macaroni and cheese—spreading its influence in ways that would resonate for generations to come.

Staking Cultural Claims: Access, Agency, Aspiration

The integration of macaroni and cheese into African American culinary heritage can be parsed through multiple historical contexts. Beyond the recorded evidence of regimented diets, gardening, and husbandry lies a more complex story of how this dish became not just possible but likely to be embraced.

Of all the refined dishes that skilled Black cooks had routinely prepared for white tables over two centuries, why was macaroni and cheese singled out and adopted? Let's approach this through a quote from Booker T. Washington's *Up from Slavery* (1901), where he offers a profound insight into this sociological phenomenon. Washington's mother had been an enslaved cook on a Virginia plantation, and as a child, he recalled watching the master's daughters and other women eating the ginger cakes she made for them. "At that time those cakes seemed to me to be absolutely the most tempting and desirable things that I had ever seen. I then and there resolved that if ever I got free the height of my ambition would be reached if I could get to the point where I could secure and eat ginger-cakes in the way I saw those ladies doing."[39] This quote powerfully illustrates how food served as a visceral symbol of racial inequality and power relations under slavery. Young Washington witnessed not just the consumption of his mother's labor but the casual privilege with which the master's children enjoyed what was denied to the very person who created it—and to her child. Aspirational foods in this context represent freedom, dignity, and self-determination. What ginger cakes were to Washington's childhood yearnings, macaroni and cheese was to countless enslaved: a dish that embodied privilege, prepared by many enslaved hands but enjoyed by few. In the same way, for free Blacks in the antebellum period, emulating fashionable foods symbolized social aspirations, as food often served as a marker of one's place in the social hierarchy. The ability to partake in certain dishes was more than a matter of taste; it conveyed a sense of acceptance within the social order.

Exposure to the pleasures of macaroni and cheese may have come about in various ways. In Southern households, where hospitality and abundance were highly valued, leftovers were common and may have been informally redistributed. Many cookbook authors of the period criticized what they saw as the "disgraceful" waste in American kitchens. Blame placed on servants may suggest willfully rather than carelessly preparing in excess to ensure trickle down so that they might claim their fair portion. Though the image of the sprawling plantation dominates popular imagination, the lives of enslaved Blacks unfolded across diverse settings, both rural and urban. They prepared food in various contexts, and in some cases, the same dishes they cooked were eaten by both the enslaved and their enslavers. In urban households, where they often shared a common table with their owners, popular dishes—including those in vogue within broader society—may have made their way onto everyone's plates.[40]

While enslaved cooks were reputed for their improvisational skills and typically "cooked by ear" rather than by recipe, mastery of the culinary arts was cultivated through trial and error—a method that required *tasting* to judge the results. Creativity was encouraged as excellence reflected on the owners. Indeed, the reluctance to give them the recipes reflected the value of expertise hard-won through this process of perfecting each dish. During holiday celebrations, the culinary mastery of these cooks could be shared more openly, as enslaved people were permitted to partake in foods typically reserved for the "big house," these festive occasions offering rare moments of culinary inclusion amid otherwise austere lives.

In more restrictive situations where generosity was seen as dangerously indulgent, enslaved individuals often faced severe privation—limited not only in quantity but in foods that provided comforting satisfaction or, as Charles Ball pointed out (see chapter 5), fulfilled the human desire for luxury. Under such conditions, stealing food outright became a natural response to both physical hunger and the spiritual denigration of being denied varied fare.[41] These quiet acts of defiance and resilience offered moments of self-determination and autonomy. Though such actions involved risk, especially given the extreme punishments meted out for perpetrators, it likely provided a sense of agency and equalization. Leftovers, perhaps, were more accessible than the pantry's locked ingredients, and easier to make disappear than raw materials.

In some contexts, the enslaved earned wages, made tips, or sold produce, wares, or services, enabling them to purchase improved clothing, furnishings, and food—possibly including, as noted by the Mount Vernon historian Mary V. Thompson, imported foods.[42] Others used their earnings to purchase food from the enslaver's own larder.[43]

LEARNING TO COOK FROM SCRATCH: THE INVENTION OF THE GOOD OLD DAYS

After Emancipation, cookbooks found a new purpose: providing guidance to women who were at their wits' end about how to make do without the help of their formerly enslaved cooks. Cookbooks romanticizing the Southern way of life, such as *Housekeeping in Old Virginia*, tried to boost the women's morale: "If persons without brains can accomplish this, then why not you?"[44] The desperation was real.

Another guide, the *Dixie Cook-Book* (1883), was specifically created "to meet the real needs of Southern matrons of to-day." It was dedicated to the "Mothers, Wives, and Daughters of the 'Sunny South' who have so bravely faced the difficulties which new social conditions have imposed on them as mistresses of Southern homes." They admit that most of it was selectively

FIGURE 7.3. "Love in a Cottage" (1875), a depiction of the trials of housewives fending for themselves in the kitchen. Engraving based on a drawing by the American illustrator Sol Eytinge Jr. *Source*: Public domain.

lifted from the bestselling cookbook at the time, *Practical Housekeeping* (originally *Buckeye Cookery and Practical Housekeeping*, published in 1877), a compilation with contributors from across the nation. To uphold their Dixie-themed title, they added "recipes handed down from generation to generation." Thus, we circle back to the intricate weave of culinary knowledge that passed through many hands, making the identification of provenance problematic. Macaroni and cheese was among the recipes skimmed from *Practical Housekeeping*. Its repositioning as a Southern specialty in the *Dixie Cook-Book* underscored the promiscuous nature of recipes, knowing neither borders nor attribution.

The title *Fifty Years in a Maryland Kitchen* (1873) sets up the expectation for a book by or at least about a lineage of African American cooks in what was then known as "The Oyster State," but the author is a white woman born into a wealthy family.[45] At seventy-two, she reflects on a lifetime of beloved recipes "tried and tested by the author in her own family." Among the dishes representing Old Time Maryland was a creamy layered macaroni and cheese. The pasta was cooked for an hour in water and another in milk, which was not discordant with prevalent tastes. The comfortingly soggy mass got a dash of cayenne and was layered with cheese. Top and bake—but not too long, as it might get tough. We wouldn't want that.

A contemporary critic praised the *Maryland Kitchen* and reminisced, "There are also the good-old-fashioned dishes, that bring up visions of the old and swiftly departing Maryland tables of the days when 'Aunt Chloe' ruled with iron severity in the kitchen, and 'Uncle Dan'l' stood behind old master's chair in sable dignity, and snuffed the candles and filled the glass with dry old sherry."[46] The critic's words encapsulate the post-Emancipation rebound, a shift in perspective that both paralleled and intertwined with the proliferation of cookbooks aimed at women thrust into managing households without slaves. Nostalgia for the "Good Old Days" germinates when imaginings about the past contrast starkly with contemporary reality. The longing for yesteryear is most acutely felt in times of discontent with the present, amplifying the gnawing fear that cherished traditions are inexorably slipping away.

Though Reconstruction was far from complete, it had formally ended, and the South was in a period of social regression. Jim Crow laws were asserting themselves in a desperate attempt to ossify the status quo. In the North, the unbridled excess of the Gilded Age was resisting the nascent restraints of the Progressive Era, while the siren call of "Westward Ho!" continued to beckon. The relentless march of urbanization, rampant consumerism, and the disruptive force of technological advancements—particularly electricity and the telephone—had society in a tailspin. The vaunted modernity of the Gay Nineties was experienced by social conservatives as nothing short of a moral unraveling. And rest assured that the next cataclysmic Panic would strike punctually in 1893. From our vantage point of hindsight, we may see these events as just more waves on the oceanic expanse of time—but to those navigating the waters, their force was overwhelming. The reimagining of the antebellum South as a pastoral idyll was the perfect antithesis to this rising tide of tension and uncertainty.

After a century of near invisibility in cookbooks, a peculiar nostalgia emerged beatifying the figure of "Mammy," or the "Old Negro Cook," and conjuring a sentimental vision of the Old South in general.[47] This revisionist perspective crystallized into a composite myth, epitomized by the Aunt Chloe musing. The repackaged "Mammy" was now placed on a pedestal for public consumption as the heart of a bygone way of life. It's a curious paradox: The very system that had stripped her of personhood now elevated her to an idealized status, laboring at the hearth as the embodiment of comfort and culinary heritage that could never be recovered. It was a bittersweet lament that concurrently saw her newfound freedom as precipitating the demise of the Old South, as if the very essence of Southern identity depended on her subjugation.

Notable among the Southern books to elaborate eulogistic introductions bemoaning the passing of an era were the New Orleans Creole cookbooks. *The Creole Cookery Book* (1885) was put out by the Christian Women's Exchange to raise funds for their venue where women could sell their handiwork and find employment—a lifeline to those left vulnerable by war, economic upheaval, or personal circumstances. They also ran a restaurant offering affordable, homestyle meals in a respectable setting where unaccompanied women could dine at a low cost without risking their reputations. The restaurant in turn provided employment opportunities for women as cooks and servers.

This charity cookbook, a first of its kind for New Orleans, was part of a new genre of deliberate nostalgia-making in the post–Civil War South. Similar to *Cooking in Old Virginia* (1877), cognizant of the passing era, it sought to halt the march of time by preserving a portrait of a reimagined social order. Central to this effort was the idealized Black woman cook—a figure used both as a symbol of the past and a way to anchor Southern identity in a rapidly changing world. The authors' declared aim was to infuse the "hereditary lore of our negro mammies" with the growing interest in the science of cookery so that Creole cuisine could finally take "its proper place in the gastronomical world." They would resuscitate Mammy in a way that would make her more marketable to white consumers. Among the listed contributors, a Miss Mary Pannell is given special recognition for her years spent collecting recipes from the colored "Aunties" of Virginia.[48] Pannell's efforts to collect from the source promised quality and authenticity, the real deal.

Fifteen years later, with the passing of women who had cooked under the bond of slavery, the nostalgia reached a fevered pitch. The introduction to *Picayune Creole Cookery* (1900) develops the narrative in its entirety: There was a time when no one in New Orleans would have thought that a Creole cookbook was necessary, coasting as they had been doing for two hundred years with the status quo of the Creole Negro cook in the kitchen, "carefully instructed and directed by their white Creole mistresses, who received their inheritance of gastronomic lore from France."[49] They were appreciative and quick to learn and, out of a desire to please, they "improvised and improved upon the products of the cuisine of Louisiana's mother country."[50] But the Civil War changed all that and "here, as elsewhere, she who had ruled as the mistress of yesterday, became her own cook today." The saddest part was "the passing of the faithful old negro cooks—the 'mammies' [who] felt it a pride and honor" to stay on with their former masters and mistresses. But the 'bandana and tignon' are fast disappearing from our kitchens."[51] Once the last of the "old cooks from the antebellum days" had passed, it would only be through these cookbooks that the "matchless recipes" from the "lips of the old Creole negro cooks" would be known to the "new colored woman" and the "new white woman."[52]

Macaroni and cheese is not the first thing that springs to mind at the mention of Creole cookery, and yet it was once an integral part of their culinary heritage, as New Orleans had "long been a favored point of migration for the sons of sunny Italy," owing to the bustling citrus import trade.[53] A robust macaroni manufacturing business developed as a consequence. *Picayune* devotes an entire section to macaroni, boasting, somewhat ironically, that it is only in New Orleans that the famous dish *Macaroni à l'Italienne* is cooked "in real Italian style." Well, yes and no. They start with a classic French roux made with butter, flour, and pasta water, but they use only parmesan, and heaps of it. To their credit, they warn readers not to overcook the pasta. The au gratin version was cooked until soft, which meant just short of falling apart, about a half hour. It is layered with parmesan, doused with bubbling hot white sauce, then topped with loads of cheese and nibs of butter. Bake until brown. In New Orleans this was considered "the nicest way of preparing Macaroni."[54]

Cooking in Old Creole Days (1904) concurs that a death knell sounded after the surrender at Appomattox, marking the imminent disappearance of the "colored" cook, "usually a fat woman of middle age, with a gay bandana kerchief about her head—proud of her art, somewhat despotic, and usually known as Aunty."[55] Her cooking acumen is referred to as black magic and incantations, "never written, save in some old-time receipt book, and was literally handed down from one generation to another." And it is one of those books that formed the basis of *Old Creole Days*. The only way to preserve and proliferate their fading culinary culture was by committing it to paper: "We [white people] are certainly not gifted with culinary talent."[56]

The Articles of Surrender at Appomattox bore no signature from Southern kitchens. Yet many conflated Emancipation with culinary extinction, mourning the imagined loss of Black culinary expertise. This myopic view ignored a simple truth: Traditions didn't dry up when Grant and Lee met, nor did culinary mastery evaporate just because Black cooks had gained the power to negotiate their worth. Whether they chose to stay in kitchens or pursue new opportunities, their recipes and know-how would remain an enduring legacy.

WE DON'T NEED YOUR DIRTY MACARONI

In early 1873, the pithy *Sunday Times* exposé "Macaroni Making" made international headlines with its scathing depiction of macaroni production in Naples. It walks us past the Ponte della Maddalena, to find row after row of trestles supporting canes with yellowish macaroni hanging in the sun to dry: "The flies know it very well and dot it in thousands, and the little boys know it very well, and crawl under the fringe, and just pinch the ends and pick up stray morsels that may drop. I saw it hanging just so while the ashes from Vesuvius were still blowing about. Nothing seems to harm it, neither boys, nor dust, nor flies; they add to the flavor."[57]

The author is treated to a tour of the macaroni-making process, but the Neapolitans are wary of Americans stealing their secrets to set up a rival industry in the United States. "Never fear," our author chides, "in America we have not got the Neapolitan water, and that is no great loss." He can't fathom what all the fuss is about. "Macaroni is only flour and water, it can't be the substance, . . . it must be the form."

Even among Italians, the Neapolitans felt sure that their pasta was superior to all others, but sensationalist reports conjuring up images of sweaty men mixing the flour and water with their bare feet, teams of hairy unclothed workers kneading and handling the dough, insects buzzing, dust flying, and street urchins pawing at it with their grubby mitts threatened the industry. But what could be done? Even the prestigious medical journal *The Lancet* had pronounced that pound per pound, macaroni contained more of that flesh-forming gluten than bread, and it would be regrettable if some bad press turned the public away from it.[58] Rather than deterring the consumption of pasta, the repelling reports inspired efforts to domesticate and "improve" it by importing the manufactory lock, stock, and barrel—Italian foremen, workers, and even flour but also the steam-powered machinery that Italians had been rejecting. *The Food Journal* spoke of unmatched care and cleanliness in these Anglo-Italian factories, assuring readers that the "purity and freedom from acidity, render it even more agreeable as an article of diet than that which is imported from the shores of the Mediterranean."[59] This narrative of improvement and adaptation of foreign cuisines would become a recurring theme in American culinary history as it aligned with the country's broader ethos of progress and innovation.

THE PEOPLE'S PASTA IN THE GILDED AGE

American women had caught wind of Charles Buckmaster's lectures on the burgeoning field of domestic science. As a popular, influential figure, he was in a better position than *The Lancet* to broadcast the gospel that macaroni was more nutritious than bread. He even went a step further and placed it on par with meat.[60] An 1874 *New York Times* article quotes him as saying now that it was cheaper "there is no good reason why it should not enter more largely into the food of the people." Juliet Corson latched onto this idea and became a true macaroni crusader for the working class.

Juliet Corson

Corson had been sickly as a child but received a notable education at home. Her mother died when she was sixteen, and her new stepmother forced her to leave home at eighteen and make her own way in the world. Corson found employment at the Working Woman's Library, earning four dollars per week, but, as she was unable to support herself on such a wage, she was allowed to sleep on the library sofa. Being thrust into the clutches of poverty at such a young age left a lasting impression on her. However, Corson also found meaning and purpose in her work, and her health improved. When a position opened to teach nutrition and cooking at the Women's Educational and Industrial Society in New York, she boned up on her skills and started what would be a lifelong career as an educator. In her spare time, she also did charity work, but when the Great Railroad Strike of 1877 hit, the devastation from broadscale layoffs stemming from the Panic of 1873 led her to write her first book, *Fifteen Cent Dinners for Workingmen's Families*.[61] She published it out of pocket with a warning in all caps on the title page: "All persons are cautioned not to pay for this book. This edition of 50,000 copies is published for free circulation only."

In it, Corson speaks at length about macaroni, reiterating the clarion call of Pasta for the People but through a medium that would reach a very different sort of public. Most of the railroad workers in the area were unskilled Irish and German immigrants. In smaller numbers, there were also African Americans and an ever-increasing population of Italians. "No hungry man will spend money on what he knows will not satisfy his appetite."[62] Macaroni, Corson preached, "is generally known as a rather luxurious dish among the wealthy; but it should become one of the chief foods of the people for it contains more gluten, or the nutritious portion of the wheat, than bread."[63] She realized that the laboring class may be unfamiliar with macaroni but implored them to try it, as they staved off hunger far too often with less wholesome starches such as rice, bread, and potatoes. She gives explicit directions for boiling macaroni then offers a clever kitchen hack: If you've made too much macaroni, "it can be kept perfectly good by laying it in freshwater which must be changed every day."[64]

Her "Macaroni with cheese" uses a parsimonious quarter-pound of cheese with a half-pound of macaroni that has been boiled enough to quadruple in weight. A spartan amount of butter is added before topping with a dusting of breadcrumbs. After a light browning in the oven, it is ready to feed a family of six. She promises, "It will make just as heavy and strengthening a meal as meat and will cost about twelve cents."

The *New York Times* applauded Corson on her efforts to educate the "poorer and more ignorant classes." The word "ignorant" was not a slip of the pen. The reviewer continues, "To a natural stupidity as to how food ought to be cooked so as to render it wholesome, our people are thoroughly unconscious as to the wicked waste they are daily committing" (December 28, 1877). Such was the parlance and perspective of the day.

By the time Corson wrote her last book, *Family Living on $500 a Year* (1888), she had become a noted authority on cooking and food reform. Her efforts to promote macaroni had not been in vain, and she was pleased to report that "within the past 10 years it has become a favorite American food."[65] That encouraged her to step up the macaroni evangelism. She devoted an entire chapter to it, convinced that it was the most important resource for healthy, economical meals.

Macaroni's American ascendancy owes much to an unlikely hero: the Hungarian roller mill. When the first of these techno-marvels touched down in Wisconsin in 1874, it revolutionized flour production. Faster, more consistent, and yielding a whiter product with an impressive shelf life, these mills were a game changer. American macaroni industrialists, ever resourceful, turned to the bountiful supply of cheap, hard winter wheat grown in Kansas, Minnesota, and North Dakota. They found that a coarse grade—farina—could stand in for traditional semolina, mimicking its texture and glutinous qualities, if not quite its pedigree.

As production soared, so did accessibility. Our highbrow dish was now poised to grace tables across the social spectrum, satisfying not only the cravings of Italian immigrants but also the culinary curiosity of the broader American populace. Yet, for all this progress, a debate simmered. Purists argued that American macaroni, born of softer wheat varieties, could never hold a candle to its Italian counterpart. Importing durum wheat might have settled the score, but such a move was both politically thorny and economically impractical. And so, American macaroni moguls forged ahead—a testament to stubborn determination and pragmatism, knowingly flooding the market with their inferior product in the relentless march of progress.

By 1888, Corson's view on American pasta had shifted dramatically. Once barely mentioned, it now earned her confident endorsement. She argued that selective use of farina could yield a product rivaling Italian imports—without risking the deleterious effects of overseas transit.[66] While not discouraging Italian macaroni outright, Corson's cautionary tale of fatalities in Philadelphia linked to Genoese pasta adulterated with yellow chrome likely gave readers pause.

In the decade between Corson's initial plea and macaroni's rise to staple status, Sarah Tyson Rorer—dietician and prolific cookbook author—was building her reputation. Through Philadelphia's New Century Club Cooking School, she orchestrated an impressive event: a sumptuous, nutritious meal for thirty-one invitees at nine cents a plate. Here are the total prices for the gala dinner:

Pea Soup	15¢
Veal Croquettes	25¢
Irish Stew	20¢
Pork and Beans	30¢
Curly Potatoes	6¢
Cold Slaw	15¢
Stewed Lentils	5¢
Macaroni and cheese	18¢
Rice Pudding	26¢
Apple Dumplings	30¢
Coffee with Milk	23¢
Parker House Rolls	12¢
TOTAL	$2.25

This banquet for Philly's elite drew full coverage in the *Philadelphia Inquirer*. The reviewer of "How to Live" couldn't resist a patronizing quip: "To the rich, their system of cookery shows how to get more than ever out of their wealth, and to the poor, by simple and easy methods, how to get out of what they have what they never got before."[67] Macaroni and cheese put in a good public showing alongside these money-saving dishes. Rorer gave a public follow-up lecture and demonstration a few nights later.[68] As her career unfolded, she would become a veritable bullhorn for American-made macaroni.

In the mid-1880s, San Francisco, Chicago, and New York stood as the main hubs of American macaroni production. All of them relied on winter wheat farina—more akin to grits than semolina—though Made in the USA was touted as superior to Italian imports. The *San Francisco Bulletin* needled the old anxieties: "Imported macaroni very often, indeed generally deteriorates by the ocean voyage. It is liable to be wormy and moldy." Their parting shot is a classic in food-scare journalism: "It may be moldy and not be detected by the unskilled.[69]

But after a century of cookbooks schooling readers that Italian pasta was superior to all others, the turnaround wasn't going to happen overnight. Enterprising Americans circumvented this bias by passing their products off as imports. Yet challenges persisted. With no duty on imported Italian macaroni, the domestic product often cost more due to higher labor costs. "We pay $8, $10, $12 for workmen. In Italy the best hands get sixty cents a day," they lamented. When confronted about US products mimicking Italian packaging—the same classic blue paper wrapping and the same style of box and labeling—the flimsy defense was "No, the Italian box is different wood; theirs is beech, ours is poplar."[70]

Other newspapers concurred that so long as sentimentalism about the foreign article persisted, US companies would be forced to "put goods up in packages counterfeiting the style and wording on imported brands. The manufacturers would much prefer to put out their goods in honest labels, but it becomes a question of bowing to the demands of the trade or going out of business. They hate the deception and feel that their goods are even better than those imported."[71]

During these transitional years of American manufacture of macaroni, the United States ramped up its xenophobic narrative. A cutting 1884 article, widely circulated in other newspapers, painted a grim picture of Naples's macaroni hawkers behind hot cauldrons, serving it up on unwashed tin plates as hungry hordes grasped the scalding food and stuffed it into their mouths. The rose-colored glasses had come off to

FIGURE 7.4. US trademark registration. Italian design and packaging were adopted by US manufacturers. The belief that pasta from Italy was higher quality coexisted alongside fears of contamination. *Source*: Public domain.

reveal a gruesome spectacle. Worse than the street vendors were the manufacturers who

> are very stupid to have immense establishments where foreigners can see the operation. If there is anything more filthy than a manufactory of macaroni we have not yet found it. . . . Their favorite location seems to be close to a tannery, the smell of which is only excelled in general ferocity by the odors of the alleys in the city.[72] Here is the tannery with its horrible odors, and in close juxtaposition is the macaroni factory, the odors of the one permeating and saturating the other.
>
> It was observable that those who were fondest of macaroni, after going through the macaroni regions declined the delicacy at table on their return, and it is safe to say that not one of them will ever eat a particle of it when they return unless they can be satisfied that it was not made in Italy.[73]

Cholera's relentless sweep through Italy in the 1880s, particularly ravaging the impoverished south, drove thousands to seek refuge across the Atlantic. While this desperate migration provided American macaroni factories with willing workers—some of whom later opened their own operations—Italian immigrants faced deep-seated prejudice, tragically branded as disease carriers in their new home.

The specter of contamination haunted food imports, too. When a cataclysmic cholera epidemic erupted in Naples in 1884, the alarm rang out through the food market. Neapolitan macaroni, the once prized import, now sparked fears of death-by-dinner-plate. Imports plummeted amid depictions of poorly sanitized production and handling processes (see fig. 7.5), along with Naples's economy and reputation. The *Trenton Gazette* was among many to echo the "plague" warning sounded in the London *Times*:

> I feel it be a duty I owe to the people of this country to caution them against the use of macaroni and other pastes made in Italy. Naples more especially. Every traveler who has ridden through the long, dusty road from Naples to Pompeii must have seen the large number of factories of macaroni on each side of the road and the unfinished macaroni hanging in the open air, amid clouds of dust, flies, and stench of all kinds, the locality being evidently one of the very poorest and dirtiest in this most beautiful city, and no doubt it is the stronghold of the dreadful scourge now devouring the poor inhabitants; then, without any stretch of the imagination, one has only to think of

FIGURE 7.5. The audacious title "Our Wholesome Macaroni Drying on the Dirty Streets of Naples" lays bare the American macaroni dilemma of the late nineteenth century. *Source*: Stereograph Courtesy of the Library of Congress Prints and Photographs division. Public domain.

> this important article of food, which is so much used, being manipulated by plague stricken workmen, who no doubt, sicken and die amid the macaroni which is being prepared under such horrible conditions, to be sent broadcast over the world and spread the pestilence.[74]

Their conclusion? "The best Italian macaroni to eat in the time of cholera—*or any other*—is that made in the United States, which is that most commonly sold."

The United States wasn't exactly a paragon of hygiene either. The *New York Sun* exposed a macaroni sweatshop where public washing tubs in a tenement building's second floor served as mixing bowls. Workers kneaded dough "as if death awaited their first stop to rest" then pounced on it with levers, echoing scenes from *Penny Magazine* half a century earlier. Here, too, manual force squeezed pasta through dies.

Jocular reports alluded to factories using the sweepings of warehouses and flour mills to make the popular treat "contributing largely to that 'peck of dirt' which is said must be eaten sooner or later by everyone."[75] Manufacturers, annoyed with the muckraking, began to refuse interviews.

But these weren't mere tabloid sensations. The Gilded Age's food industry, under laissez-faire policies, was rife with adulteration and filth, stoking fears of lurking health hazards. Reports of harmful additives and contamination amplified public anxiety. This mounting dread, coupled with glaring worker exploitation, would eventually fuel the Progressive Era's call for reform, demanding stricter rules to safeguard both laborers and consumers.

Contrary to today's veneration for artisan specialties, factory-made foods with their promise of minimal manual intervention offered reassurance of hygiene and purity. A flurry of articles trumpeted the superiority of the country's burgeoning macaroni industry over the squalor of tenement sweat shops. These new-age pasta palaces flexed their innovative might, pumping out such volumes that New Yorkers were no longer importing but *exporting* macaroni, "and the demand for the American article is growing."[76]

Chicago, one of the industry's nerve centers, observed that the "industry is solely in Italian hands and under Italian control." A mere fifteen years earlier, nine out of ten pounds sold were imports. By 1888, those figures had reversed. Credit went to the advent of roller mills "coupled with the fact that an Italian-American knows a profitable investment when he sees it."[77]

AMERICANS MUSCLE IN

Macaroni has taken a strong hold on the affections of food-eating Americans.

—*READING EAGLE*, JULY 31, 1892

When money talks, political heat rises. American manufacturers were incensed about the freewheeling, tariffless noodles and macaroni that were strong-arming the domestic product out of their own market. The sixty major US macaroni magnates were demanding action, casting themselves as patriots paying living wages while cheap European labor made competition impossible. The solution? A bill demanding a duty on all macaroni imports. This battle fit neatly into the long-standing tug-of-war between free traders and protectionists. As *The Pittsburg Press* colorfully put it, "The American noodle [macaroni] stands on the shore and weeps. Alongside of its big burly rival from France or Italy it must fight its way to get in at the kitchen doorway."

Ironically (or perhaps not) some of the loudest voices behind this complaint were first-generation Italian Americans. "If a tariff of 2 or 3 cents per pound is placed on the article, we would consume 3,000,000 more bushels of wheat and much less [macaroni] would be imported."[78] The pitch was simple: Competitive US prices meant more wheat sold, more pasta produced, and more jobs for American workers. This politically expedient idea caught the eye of the House Committee on Ways and Means, chaired by William McKinley, and the bill passed. American macaroni had its golden ticket.

In an economy where a decent hot meal could be had for ten cents, a two-cents-per-pound tariff was far from trivial. This move also signaled the government's recognition of the macaroni industry's potential to catalyze broader growth. They weren't fooled by the convenient excuse of higher labor costs. American advantages were clear: lower wheat prices, modern machinery churning out quantities inconceivable in Italy, and ready markets in Central and South America absorbing any domestic surplus.[79] The cogs of American exceptionalism were turning as the nation sought to establish itself as a powerhouse in yet another industry.

There was pushback from Democrats. A satirical piece came out in the *New York Times* wherein Henry has a conversation with his wife:

> "Confound it, Mary, this macaroni is awful!"
>
> "It is tasteless?"
>
> "I should say so."
>
> "Tough?"
>
> "That's not the word for it. Teeth make no impression on it. I'm swallowing mine whole. You've not been putting up a job on me, have you? This isn't rubber tubing cut into lengths with shears?"

Their friend, Jim, is over for "pot luck" (which in the 1890s meant "Sure, you can stay for dinner, but don't expect miracles") and plays the antagonist. Tariffs, he says, bar access to cheap, quality imported macaroni: "This I want not for the benefit of the rich, but for the good of the poor and those of moderate means, almost all of whom will buy inferior food rather than pay high prices for first-class goods." Henry is puzzled, so Jim continues. "You say it [American macaroni] is poor stuff, and yet you believe in putting a tariff tax of 2 cents on the only macaroni in the world that's fit to eat [imported macaroni]. Somebody went to McKinley and said: 'Can't you do a little something for the macaroni infant? The poor little flour-and-water thing is languishing. Give us some protection, so that folks will have to eat our product." Now, he says, you can only get the "good stuff" in "swell" stores. While politically slanted (the article concludes with Henry saying he is not going to vote Republican next time around), it makes a clear statement about the quality of American macaroni and the importance of the issue in the everyday American kitchen.[80]

But there was more going on than met the eye. Russia, the breadbasket for Italian and French macaroni producers, had suffered a series of poor harvests in the late 1880s. Severe droughts in 1890 and 1891 then plunged the country into crisis, with famine claiming hundreds of thousands of lives. The repercussions rippled far beyond Russia's borders. In a bizarre twist of fate, Italy and France—accustomed to sourcing from present-day Ukraine—found themselves in a predicament. The hard red winter wheat of the American heartland, previously considered unfit by European pasta makers, suddenly became the savior of Old World macaroni.[81] All good from the American perspective.

A political storm broke out over macaroni tariffs. The *New-York Tribune* accused Democrats of undermining the good works of McKinley by spreading false news about American manufacturers with trumped-up stories perpetuating the old tenement cellar reports. Industrialists, the paper argued, had created thousands of jobs, and tariffs had encouraged new factory openings. A spokesperson for Columbia Macaroni rebutted, "We've been in business one year and are making 3,300,000 pounds of macaroni a year. We expect to double the output next year."[82]

American newspapers relentlessly played the hygiene card, touting the superiority of fully mechanized US factories over their Italian counterparts. The *Newark Sunday Call*'s report on the new Moretto & Co. factory exemplified this narrative. The owners, once poor immigrants, had through perseverance joined "the better class of Italians"—a quintessential rags-to-riches tale. "The first thing that impresses the visitor on entering the place is the scrupulous cleanliness of everything used in the process of manufacture." From sifting to shaping, drying to packaging, hands-free processing became the ultimate selling point.[83] Industrial food meant uncontaminated food.

The public's fascination with the process of making macaroni remained evergreen as industrialization advanced and new bells and whistles were added. *Scientific American* (1893) dedicated a full spread to the modern New York process, contrasting sharply with what newspapers would start calling "primitive" Italian methods. This comparison, widely reprinted and emulated, set the tone for the next two decades.

In the meantime, another economic bubble burst. The Panic of 1893 sent wheat prices tumbling, devastating American farmers. Ironically, these low prices boosted wheat exports, as foreign buyers eagerly snapped up the cheaper grain. The strain on farmers fueled the rise of the Populist movement, as agricultural workers sought political solutions to their financial woes. This period marked a critical shift in US agricultural economics and politics, and macaroni would play a lead role in the unfolding drama.

The response grew angry and polarizing. Invoking Abraham Lincoln's protectionist wisdom about sourcing US raw materials for industry, the *Daily Reporter* railed that three million dollars' worth of macaroni had been purchased from a single district in Italy over the space of a year. They had no qualms with macaroni per se "if it is clean." What they found ludicrous was why a wheat-abundant nation supplying foreign pasta makers would turn around and import that same wheat back as macaroni.

American machine-made macaroni, they argued, was perfectly good and at the very least "cleaner than the Italian article, which, according to rumor, would revolt American stomachs if they could witness it."[84] Their manifesto: Keep those millions of macaroni dollars circulating in the United States. And for those still craving foreign pasta? Slap another tariff on it—which they did in 1897.[85]

Homegrown

Despite countless articles proclaiming that American macaroni was as good—or better—than Italian, an elephant remained in the room: the flour. Even pasta factories supplied by the famous Minnesota mill, Pillsbury (established in 1869), produced chalky-white macaroni that paled in comparison to the translucent golden semolina tubes. They had even gone so far as to patent a coarse grade of hard wheat flour dubbed "farinola." But there was no getting around science; the starch content made for pastier, stickier macaroni. It was undeniable: Semolina gave Italy an insurmountable edge.[86]

In the United States, durum wheat had been confined to small plots in upper Midwest immigrant communities, serving their needs and little else. But as the macaroni business gained momentum, enterprising exceptionalists set their sights on transforming this niche crop into a major player in the amber fields of grain.

The US Department of Agriculture (USDA) Macaroni Wheats project, spearheaded by the agronomist Mark Alfred Carlton, aimed to make a success of the fizzled 1864 pilot. The government was prepared to do whatever it took to have this potential goldmine take root on home soil. Domestic macaroni industrialists would have the best wheat possible at reasonable prices and, with Russia flailing on the sidelines from political strife and droughts, the United States stood a good chance of dominating the durum wheat trade abroad.

The program was a resounding success. Tasked with identifying durum wheat varieties suitable for the diverse climates of the United States, particularly the semiarid Great Plains, Carlton traveled to Russia and North Africa. This time the seed took to US soil as if it were its native land. It even flourished in soil where soft varieties had failed.[87]

By 1900, even Texas was staking its claim, sending samples of its durum wheat to France and Italy for approval for macaroni production—securing praise "beyond question."[88] Texans, always thinking big, were sure that if they could get their hands on the prized Taganrog seed from Russia, they alone could corner the export market to Italy and France.[89]

The news spread quickly in articles such as "Home-grown Macaroni," in the African American *Wichita Searchlight*, celebrating the development: "Domestic manufacturers of macaroni, who had been handicapped by lack of proper flour, are demanding all that can be produced now."[90] Meanwhile negative imagery about Italian macaroni continued unabated. The piece "A Day in Naples—A Graphic Description of a Pleasant Trip to the Italian Metropolis by Prominent American Negroes" was typical: "Poverty, squalor, dirt are on every hand. Our appetite for macaroni has vanished since seeing it suspended to dry in the streets amidst the filthy dust of moving vehicles and stonecutters' work."[91] Well, "pleasant" up to a point.

The nation was abuzz over the staggering results of this "tremendous cropper." Ads for wheat seed flooded newspapers, and even Theodore Roosevelt, in his address to the senate following the 1902 USDA report, was elated about the prospects of "macaroni wheat." This new wheat was a win-win. Not only could it revitalize the US industry, but the country also had the potential to be a significant competitor in the international durum wheat trade, supplying macaroni manufacturers in Europe, particularly in Italy.[92] In grasping the seriousness of the situation, the term "macaroni wheat" was officially abolished and replaced with the more respectable "durum wheat."[93] The data underscored the potential of keeping the macaroni business "in house." In 1900, the United States had imported a total of $717,510 worth of macaroni (in the broad sense of the term), equating to twenty-five million in 2023 dollars.[94] By 1929, Americans were producing over one billion dollars in today's terms of macaroni products—imports

FIGURE 7.6. Gennaro Cirillo, far left, in his International Macaroni Moulds Co. manufacturing facility, Brooklyn, New York, in the 1920s. *Source*: Courtesy of Nicholas Sambrato.

had decreased 92 percent.[95] Advertisers were emboldened to openly proclaim American-made macaroni "the best in the world".[96]

Production soared. Durum wheat had made a dignified debut with sixty thousand bushels in its first year, inspiring other farmers to take the leap. Then, pennies from heaven: World War I broke out, and US wheat found a ready market supplying the Allies. In spring 1917, when the country entered the war, Russia was teetering on the brink. When the Bolshevik Revolution hit that October, the country's monopoly was over. Between 1918 and 1922, Russia lost thirteen million citizens to war, starvation, disease, and emigration. With the Soviets out of the game, America gladly stepped up to fill the gap as the new grain powerhouse. In fewer than three decades, from 1900 to 1929, durum wheat production skyrocketed nearly 117,000 percent, leaping from sixty thousand bushels to an astounding seventy million bushels.

Pasta factories were cropping up across the country in those first decades of the century. With a reliable supply of durum wheat, macaroni was poised to become not just a favorite but a culinary identity marker, an indelible part of the US foodscape. The time was ripe for pasta industrialists to join forces to macaronize the nation rather than pitting themselves against each other. And so, in 1904, they formed the National Association of Macaroni and Noodle Manufacturers of America (NAMNMA).

Patent requests for brand names and technological upgrades flooded governmental offices. Frank Zerega, a founding member of the NAMNMA and son of the aforementioned Lyonnais emigrant Antoine, proudly patented his Glutaroni in 1906. But the association was nothing without the macaroni evangelists delivering veritable sermons in their cookbooks and cooking schools. Mrs. Rorer, the respected dietary authority and bestselling author, wrote extensively about macaroni. Her counterpart in Boston, the staid Mrs. Mary Lincoln of the renowned Boston Cooking School, was also an advocate. Even more fervent was Alice Gitchell Kirk. In *Practical Good Economy* (1917), Kirk acquaints homemakers with the recent history of durum wheat in the United States and thunders her message:

> Every man, woman, and child should know that macaroni furnishes a large quantity of gluten, which is one of the elements of food that the human system turns into blood, sinew, and muscle, and this macaroni made from durum wheat contains more gluten than any other wheat product. In this inexpensive food we have practically all the elements of bread and meat. It is quick, easy, and economical to prepare. If well cooked with varied seasoning, such as milk, meat, or cheese, the family will not tire of it, but ask for "more and oftener."[97]

By now, Americans had become creative with this staple foodstuff, but macaroni and cheese remained the go-to favorite. Fast, nutritious, filling, comforting, easy to prepare, and inexpensive, it still carried the air of elegance as one of the "seven delicacies of the world."[98] With durum wheat now flourishing in vast areas from north to south, American macaroni had pushed past the final obstacle.

The Midwest, the heartland of wheat, became a hub for pasta manufacturing. The Minnesota Macaroni Company established a state-of-the-art factory boasting full durum wheat pasta production. Their recipe pamphlet started with the heading "Macaroni: The Ideal Food" and reiterated the common household knowledge that macaroni was "much more nourishing than meat."[99] Children's health was at the forefront, emphasizing wholesomeness, digestibility, and its ability to grow strong bodies without being fattening (the concept of the calorie had recently gone mainstream, followed closely by the word "fattening"). Gluten was still hailed as a miracle nutrient—here spelled with a capital G. The first recipe was "Macaroni and cheese," calling specifically for "Minnesota CutRite macaroni"—the amusing elbow shape that appealed to children and would later become

FIGURE 7.7. Poster child for Minnesota Macaroni. Macaroni manufacturers increasingly targeted children by promoting the health benefits of semolina pasta. Such strategic advertising helped make macaroni and cheese the quintessential all-American kid food. *Source*: Public domain.

synonymous with macaroni itself, as well as the standard form for the dish throughout the country. the country.

What About Cheese?

As America was hurtling toward industrialization, cheese was brought into the arena. The year was 1851, and in the rolling hills of Rome, New York, the dairyman Jesse Williams hatched a plan that would forever change the industry. He applied his insight from past traditions of pooling the milk from local farmers to ensure consistent quality and applied it to industrial production methods, thus laying the foundation for the nation's first cheddar cheese factory.

William's vision extended beyond personal gain. He refused to patent his method, freely sharing his knowledge with others eager to follow suit. This decision accelerated the industry's growth dramatically. Americans had also adopted the streamlined procedure for cheddaring developed in England, and by the 1880s, there were over 2,500 cheese factories across the country, doubling production in just two decades.[100]

As the industry grew in New York, Wisconsin's lush pasturelands were positioned as a formidable rival. The advent of refrigerated railway cars, or "reefers," facilitated bulk trading, enabling cheese to travel vast distances without spoiling. Meanwhile, the 1890 McKinley and 1897 Dingley tariffs on foreign cheese fortified the industry's dominance at home, shielding cheesemakers from overseas competition. What had begun as a cottage industry swiftly transformed into a cornerstone of American enterprise.

Enter James Lewis Kraft (1874–1953). In 1903, he emigrated from his birthplace in Ontario, Canada, to Chicago, brimming with determination and an idea—a startup that would deliver cheese directly to grocers, sparing them the trek to the cheese market. But the path to success was far from smooth. Kraft lost three thousand dollars and his horse in the first year, but he carried on doggedly. His persistence paid off as business began to pick up. With prospects looking up, he convinced his brothers to make it a family venture, and by 1909, the J. L. Kraft & Bros. Company was born. Driven by relentless ambition and savvy publicity strategies, their business grew exponentially, even venturing into export markets.

The turning point came in 1914 when Kraft, drawing on his childhood on a dairy farm and years of experience in the cheese trade, decided to establish his own factory in Stockton, Illinois. With an uncanny knack for business, he set out to create a product that would make people wonder how they had ever lived without it: a consistently high-quality cheese that was economical, long-lasting without refrigeration, and uncontaminated. The Pure Food Act of 1906 had heightened public awareness of food safety, and Kraft was determined to meet this new standard. He recognized that while cheese was already a method of preserving milk, it was still perishable. To truly revolutionize the industry, his cheese would have to be shelf-stable and time-insensitive. Kraft secured his place at the forefront of the industry when he patented his pasteurized cheese process in 1916.[101] It was cheap, resisted the deleterious effects of summer, and in time, people would learn to love it. Indeed, processed American cheese went on to become the national favorite.

As the United States entered World War I, Kraft's timing proved uncannily well aligned with the nation's needs. Just as Williams' cheeses had sustained the Union Army, Kraft's product found a military market. He struck a deal with the government, selling twenty million quarter-pound tins of his cheese-like product to the US Army. After just sixteen years in the United States, James Kraft was living the American dream. And this was just the beginning.

Chapter Eight

MACARONI'S AMERICAN SOUL

Bringing It Home

> "The trouble with Gaelic is that it has no modern equivalents. For example, what would be the Gaelic word for Macaroni?"
> "I don't know. What's the English word for it?"
>
> —*SRUTH BILINGUAL NEWSPAPER* (1970)

THE RECKONING

Macaroni and cheese is now more than a millennium old. It has aged well. Its transmission across borders and oceans, and from cook to cook and book to book, has persisted through times of glut, dearth, war, and the whimsy of fashion without skipping a beat. And as we proceed into the twentieth century, it will continue chameleoning its way into a host of disparate situations.

The popular *Brides Cook Book* (1911) included it as a recipe to ensure marital bliss. Its reputation improved among vegetarians, ever seeking protein alternatives; *The Meatless Cookbook* (1912) boldly called its recipe "American macaroni." The brilliant new concept of workplace cafeterias that was spreading across the nation offered an ideal setting for macaroni and cheese to become a staple. Economical, satisfying, and suited to industrial-scale preparation, it was perfectly at home in the lunchrooms of factories, offices, stores, and hospitals. In the process, macaroni and cheese helped define—and homogenize—American food, shaped as it was by mass production, institutional dining, and the growing demand for efficiency. Prominent culinary institutions such as the Boston Cooking School propagated it in the curriculum, advising generations of students and homemakers that while macaroni was a cheap, wholesome food, it was "deficient in fat," requiring cream, butter, and cheese "to make a perfect food."[1]

Straight up "Macaroni and cheese" was the name Rufus Estes used in the dish's first appearance in an African American cookbook. *Good Things to Eat as Suggested by Rufus* (1911) was the culmination of decades of accrued expertise, with the discerning diner in mind. Much of Estes's experience had been honed as a chef on Pullman cars, luxury trains designed for long journeys. Their dining cars were bastions of impeccable service, featuring linen tablecloths, crystal glassware, and gourmet menus that included macaroni and cheese . . . as suggested by Rufus.

In its humble guise, it was served in charity-organized communal dining services, which had long provided cheap meals to those in need, especially destitute women and children. Despite the good intentions, this form of assistance drew criticism from clerics and cynics for harboring communist activities. The dish's reach penetrated even into specialized military divisions in *The A B C of Cooking: For Men with No Experience of Cooking on Small Boats, Patrol Boats, in Camps, on Marches, Etc.* (1912). The book was prepared as a companion package along with garments made by the Knitting Committee of the American Defense Society, hoping that both the recipes and the knitwear would provide comfort and warmth to the men serving their country.

As America entered World War I, the belt tightened on the home front. Citizens faced urgent calls to conserve meat, sugar, fats (including dairy products), and wheat for the war effort, yet macaroni was endorsed as a strategic, even patriotic, solution. In tandem with the slogan "Wheatless Wednesdays," Herbert Hoover, then director of the US Food Administration, bellowed "War Is Wheat," an alliterative reminder to consume less bread and eat more macaroni to conserve soft wheat flour for the troops (see fig. 8.1). Washington's *Evening Star* seized upon this theme with a propagandistic plug depicting macaroni as essential to victory, praising its ability to "supply the want of both bread and meat" while serving as "a vehicle for conserving other foods that would be wasted. . . . *Save Meat—Save Fat—Save Sugar* is the urgent appeal of our Government. Macaroni does all these things." The Cleveland Macaroni Company, which sponsored the piece, struck a notably selfless tone: "We do not ask you to eat our brand—but eat macaroni."[2] Others, such as the Skinner Manufacturing Company, introduced alternative products such as the short-lived "Kornroni."

Macaroni and cheese is known across the nation as a full-fledged American food. With hindsight, we know that three things have yet to transpire:

FIGURE 8.1. Promotional materials issued by the US Food Administration for public awareness of wheat during World War I. *Source*: Courtesy of the National Archives. Public domain.

its place secured as an American culinary icon, arguably surpassing even hot dogs or apple pie in cultural significance; its recognition as traditional fare of the southeastern United States, thereby adding a regional layer to its national presence; and, finally, as part of the Southern legacy, its elevation within the Soul Food tradition, transcending regional boundaries to become a culinary touchstone for African Americans across the nation.

REMAPPING SOUTHERN FOOD

Into the twentieth century's first decade, the stream of romanticized admiration attempting to immortalize Southern foodways of the Mammy era had become a torrent. *The Blue Grass Cook Book* exemplified this trend, devoting seven introductory pages of nostalgic prose before introducing a composite "Aunt Dinah." The author claimed these loyal Southern cooks had fortified the young men who served in the Confederacy, crooning, "There is not a Southerner who does not hold her, in spite of her faults, in loving remembrance." Outpourings like these resuscitating the Old South reached such a pitch that the printed page did not suffice. They wanted it in stone. In 1916, the United Daughters of the Confederacy proposed to erect a national monument to honor the "Faithful Colored Mammies of the South," a whitewashed enshrinement framing the ideal Black woman as consummate caregiver, covering historical truth with a commemorative statue.[3]

It had become clear, to borrow a phrase from Toni Tipton-Martin, that she who owned the cook did not own the recipes—but she was set on appropriating them. In *Aunt Caroline's Dixieland Recipes* (1922), we move a step forward, as the source is finally named in full: Caroline Pickett. The compilers, Emma and William McKinny, retain the antebellum flavor in the recipe titles: Massa's Cheese Croquettes, Aunt Jemima's Lemon Pie, Uncle Remus Mint Julep, Mammy's Sweet Potato Pudding, and Aunt Katy's Macaroni are listed among other carefully selected dishes that foreshadow a modern menu for Soul Food.[4]

In *Mammy's Cook Book* (1927), Katherine Bell's account leans beyond the typical platitudes toward more poignant and personal remembrances of her cook, Sallie Miller. Bell notes that most of the recipes in her collection were passed down by Miller, giving them the weight of authentic inheritance rather than a constructed vision of a bygone era.

The appearance of "Macaroni à la King" (see recipe) stands as a historical curiosity. This dish, a nod to upscale American restaurant trends that emerged in the late 1800s, diverged from the Old South repertoire. Miller, excluded from such dining establishments, could not have developed this recipe from direct experience. Its presence in Bell's cookbook reflects the complex flow of ideas and influences that shaped the evolution of macaroni and cheese—a dish that holds in tension aspiration and tradition, sophistication and inherited wisdom.

The tone takes a decided turn downward with *Mirations and Miracles of Mandy* (1929). Mandy, a demeaning caricature of African American women in popular culture, had gained notoriety with the 1918 Irving Berlin hit "Mandy," which was performed in minstrel-style blackface. Following suit, the author Natalie Scott refers to her servant Pearl as "Mandy" and to her friends' servants as interchangeable "Mandys". The minstrel show in

MACARONI A LA KING

3/4 cup (85 g) uncooked macaroni
1 cup (250 mL) scalded milk
3 egg yolks, beaten
1 cup (90 g) American cheese, grated
2 whole pimientos, chopped
1/3 cup (80 mL) melted butter
1 large onion, grated
1 tsp (5 mL) salt
1 Tbsp (15 mL) chopped parsley
1/8 tsp (1 mL) cayenne pepper
3 egg whites, beaten
2 cups cream sauce
1 small can button mushrooms

Cook and drain macaroni and then add the milk, yolks, and all the other ingredients other than the egg whites. As a last step, fold in the whites, put in a baking dish in a pan of hot water, and bake for 45 minutes. Make 2 cups rich cream sauce and add to it 1 small can of button mushrooms, the mushrooms halved.

When serving, pour about 2 Tbsp of sauce over each helping of macaroni. Serves 8.

cookbook form reached full bloom in *Aunt Priscilla in the Kitchen* (1929). Priscilla, portrayed as the sagacious Black cook, was the pseudonym of Eleanor Purcell, a white secretary at the *Baltimore Sun*. In her weekly cooking column, under the Priscilla guise, she answered a wide array of reader inquiries, dispensing her wisdom and cooking tips with what Tipton-Martin called "a pernicious slave dialect," with lines like "Folks dese days would sho' be broke if dey tried to keep up wid dem times."[5] Riding the wave of Priscilla's popularity, Purcell self-published a cookbook boldly signing it "*By* Aunt Priscilla, *herself*." The macaroni recipe captures the cultural distortion of the genre:

Macaroni au Gratin

Take 8 or 9 sticks of macaroni
1/4 pounds of good cheese
1 egg yolk
1 cup of milk
Butter de size of an egg
Salt an' pepper to taste

Break de macaroni into pieces two or three inches long an' put into yo' saucepan wid enough cold, salted water to cover well. Bring to de boil an' let boil for 20 minutes. Pour into yo' colander an' drain well. Grate de cheese. Put half de macaroni into yo' bakin' dish, sprinkle over it half de cheese, a few crackers or fine bread crumbs an' dot wid butter, seasonin' wid a little salt an' pepper. Put in de rest of de macaroni, de rest of de cheese, mo' seasonin', a layer of crumbs an' mo' bits of butter. Beat de yolk of de egg, stir into it de milk an' pour de mixture over de macaroni. Set in yo' oven an' let bake a nice rich brown.

Despite the research and effort Purcell invested in this work, it was by channeling the persona of Aunt Priscilla, the archetypal old-time Black cook, that she found her entry into food writing, gaining credibility that might otherwise not have been open to her as a white secretary.

The assumption that this "dying breed of cooks" would freely divulge their Old Southern recipes to other women who would profit from their experience ignored a crucial reality: Once freed from household bondage, these recipes were more than heirlooms—their very livelihoods depended on safeguarding their intellectual property. The resentment toward such entitlement rings clear in Marion W. Flexner's *Dixie Dishes*, where she recounts a typical scenario over biscuits:

"Lord, chile, Ah don' know. Ah jes' beats 'em up."
"But, surely you know how much flour you used."
"Yessum, Ah does."

When the information is not forthcoming, Flexner presses and gets swatted away: "Go way chile an' lemme finish ma dinner. You'se worrin' me. How

Ah gwine tell you how Ah mixes dat comcotion? Ah don' use no recipe. Ah jes' cooks by ear."[6] Flexner tells of her aunt confronting her cook, Molly, over a deliberately incorrect recipe. Molly shot back: "Effen Ah gives my receipts to everybody what axes for 'em, what Ah gwine ter hafe lef' ter surprise 'em wid? Ah'll give you a piece of advice from an ol' woman—always keep sumpin' in reserve what you kin do better'n ennybody else, and don' share dat secret wid no one."[7] Indeed, many of the recipes in *Dixie Dishes* were sourced from popular magazines.

CRAFTING A CULINARY INHERITANCE

Beyond white fantasies and commodified depictions, more empowering realities emerged. Exemplary among those is Emma Hayes, who asserted her authorship on the title page of *Kentucky Cook Book* (1912) as "By a Colored Woman," a pronouncement that her cookbook was a cut above those who were merely assembling the work of cooks.[8] After the brief introduction, she also reveals her name: Mrs. W. T. Hayes. It is a culinary coloratura, parading the accumulated mastery of "a colored cook of many years' experience." Her interpretation of the macaroni croquette presents something truly unique:

Macaroni croquettes, cheese sauce

> for the croquettes take enough cold boiled macaroni to make 2 cups when cut into small pieces add to this one teaspoon of lemon juice, half teaspoon of onion juice, a little celery salt and seasoning to taste. Mix with One Cup of white sauce made of 2 tablespoons of butter, 2 tablespoons of flour, seasoning and one cup of boiling milk. Let the mixture cool. Form in cone shape croquettes, roll in egg and bread crumbs and fry in deep fat until very light brown. Stick a small spray of parsley in the top of each croquette. Cheese sauce: to 1 cup of white sauce add 1/2 cup of grated cheese and one heaping tablespoon of walnut meats.

Macaroni in croquette form was part of the Franco-American tradition, thus in keeping with Southern foodways.[9] Hayes's other macaroni recipe was "Oysters and Macaroni," a combination whose appeal had still not worn thin.[10]

While intuition and impulse had their place in the kitchen, the Hampton Normal and Agricultural Institute, founded in 1868 in Hampton,

Virginia, recognized that formal training could set African and Native Americans on the path to economic independence (see fig. 8.2). By the 1880s, a domestic science curriculum was taking shape, emphasizing cooking, childcare, and household management—skills deemed crucial, in the context of the time, for female students' self-sufficiency and employability. The inclusion of macaroni and cheese in *A Book of Recipes for the Cooking School* (1921), the school textbook prepared by the white educator Carrie Alberta Lyford, would prove significant in these years, as Hampton-trained cooks may have been among the hopeful fleeing the South in the first wave of the Great Migration (1916–1940), carrying this dish, now part of both their professional repertoire and cultural heritage, to new territories across the nation.

Connecting with others and forging new communities is paramount for anyone relocating. For those first-wave African Americans escaping the harsh realities of Jim Crow laws and seeking employment opportunities in cities such as Chicago, Detroit, Philadelphia, and New York, solace was

FIGURE 8.2. African American women training in culinary arts at the Hampton Institute (1900). *Source*: Courtesy of the Library of Congress. Public domain.

often found in church activities, including potlucks, celebratory meals, and fundraising events. These gatherings not only offered a chance to cook together and share recipes but also served as incubators for establishing culinary identities. Social clubs, community centers, mom-and-pop eateries, and rent parties were other forums for bonding through food. As the Great Migration sounded the call northward, journeyers carried with them recipes and cooking methods that linked them to their Southern roots, including aspirational recipes—like macaroni and cheese—that many had learned as trained cooks or had eaten on occasion. In bustling urban neighborhoods, cooking transformed into a powerful means of preserving cultural identity amid the challenges of city life. Although the term "Soul Food" had yet to emerge, these cooks ingeniously adapted familiar dishes, utilizing locally sourced ingredients to create a distinctive culinary blend.

The reality of employment opportunities for African American women migrating north often mirrored the limited scope they faced in the South. Domestic service would remain the path of least resistance for years to come. As documented in W. E. B. DuBois's *The Philadelphia Negro* (1899), more than 91 percent of African American women in Pennsylvania were employed as domestics, and similar statistics held true for thirty-two of the forty-eight states.[11] The exceptions were in the South, where agricultural labor prevailed. This continuation of domestic roles influenced the spread of macaroni and cheese, fostering its evolution from a dish that had been reserved for special occasions on their own tables to its adoption as a regular staple, gradually embedding itself into the collective memory and identity of Black cuisine. This subtle yet decisive shift provided more grist for the mill that would raise the dish's status as a celebrated heritage food.

Other circumstances complemented the cultural assimilation of macaroni and gave it staying power. Dried pasta, particularly macaroni, was readily available in the urban hubs that attracted African American migrants, cities where Italians had established communities during their own mass exodus from 1880 to 1920. While Italian- and Italian American–influenced pasta dishes, especially spaghetti with tomato-based sauces, appeared frequently in African American and Southern cookbooks of the period—reflecting mainstream America's adoption of these cuisines—Italian gastronomy itself had long since moved beyond the pasta and cheese combo that had once been the only game in town.

Americans did not conceive of macaroni and cheese as Italian in the way they did spaghetti dishes. The Italians themselves had handed macaroni and cheese over to the French, offering it as *Maccheroni alla francese* in *Il Cuoco per tutti* (Everyone's Cook, 1917), which married butter, gruyere, parmesan, and long-form macaroni from Naples—ironically, what Americans called macaroni a l'Italienne. Their old noodle, butter, and cheese combo was downgraded to *pasta al burro*—mere buttered pasta—the cheese just a light customary dusting. While macaroni and cheese had become thoroughly Pan-American, its distinctive place in the African American culinary canon had sprung from the Southern experience and was encouraged further by the macaroni pie tradition brought by Afro-Caribbean immigrants, who arrived in significant numbers during the century's first decades.[12]

BATTLE OF THE CHEESEMONGERS

The dish's welcome into African American kitchens was also bolstered by the plentiful cheese supplies of the North and Midwest regions, whereas the South had always been wanting in that regard. Mass-produced processed American cheese in particular offered an affordable, shelf-stable option. There were many competitors muscling in on Kraft's monopoly, including Pabst—yes, the beer company. The brewer had turned to cheesemaking while waiting out the Prohibition years, and their in-house scientist developed a process not dissimilar to Velveeta, which had been patented by Emil Frey in 1923. The product dubbed "Pabst-ett" went on the market in 1926, but when it started making a sizable profit, the sideline business attracted attention. Kraft, who had taken out broad patents for cheese processing, sued for infringement and won.[13] Pabst could continue production but would have to pay royalties.[14] Kraft forged ahead, acquiring the rights to Velveeta in 1927. Natural cheesemakers derided such cheeses as "embalmed" or "renovated," but Kraft had the last laugh.[15] By 1930, 40 percent of all cheese sold in the United States bore the Kraft brand. Processed cheese was American cheese and American cheese was Kraft.

Kraft chose sanitation as the key attraction in early advertising, with men in lab coats and sterile factories that could double as hospitals, staffed by female workers dressed like nurses. The mouthwatering slogan was "The first hands to touch it are yours." Pabst followed suit with a scientist in a white lab coat with a neat goatee peering into a test tube, with the caption "Scientists have perfected the original whole milk cheese food."[16] Actual experts, however, raised caution: "The process of manufacture lends itself readily to abuses. Foreign fats and cheese of inferior quality can easily be incorporated and sold to the unsuspecting public." Thus, advertising language and images were warranted to circumvent fears of adulteration and contamination. As unpasteurized milk was associated with disease and even death, cheese that underwent processing to eliminate pathogens and was subjected to government quality controls was doubly reassuring and would revolutionize cheese consumption.[17]

The brewery rolled out their "Pabst-ett" on the popularity of macaroni and cheese. An early ad featured a fine silver chafing dish brimming with golden macaroni, bonding the brand name with the popular dish. The title "Pabst-ett macaroni—a triumph in the fine art of cooking" was followed by this awkward prose: "Pabst-ett has raised macaroni to a new favor on the menus of countless families. Now it's Pabst-ett Macaroni—a food of new deliciousness and even higher nutritive value. Children, elderly persons, even invalids may enjoy Pabst-ett to their heart's content. As a balanced regulative food, it is endorsed by many health authorities." Their catchy slogan was "More than cheese" (see fig. 8.3). The *Macaroni Journal* was thrilled about the prospects and ran a full-page article, concluding, "It's logical to presume that more macaroni will be consumed with Pabst-ett."[18]

Under the auspices of Kraft, Velveeta presented a nearly identical description but in hyperbolic overdrive: "a product that looks like cheese, tastes like cheese, but which because of its additional food value, many think should be termed a super cheese." The verbal gymnastics distracted

FIGURE 8.3. 1930s advertising slogan for the short-lived Pabst-ett processed cheese. *Source*: Public domain.

from the fact it did not meet the legal standards required to call it cheese. Kraft's Velveeta also boasted scientific backing, specifically citing the unlikely tastemakers at Rutgers University College of Pharmacy. Then, in lockstep with "Pabst-ett macaroni," Kraft's recipe booklet presented "Macaroni and Velveeta." The slogans "Digestible as milk itself," and "Everyone can eat it freely" needed tweaking, but the addition of melty Velveeta to macaroni was a dream pairing that would endure.

Quick and Easy the American Way

World War I had brought about many profound changes: As women entered the workforce in unprecedented numbers during wartime, America's mealtime practices shifted dramatically. The traditional rhythms of cooking, often dictated by time and labor-intensive methods, became increasingly impractical in the face of mounting responsibilities. After the war, many women remained in the workforce or sought a different balance in their home obligations, driving the demand for convenience foods to ease the burden. Manufacturers met the demand by producing new packaged and canned items that quickly gained traction in a society eager for speedy and efficient kitchen fixes in the postwar landscape.

The appetite for convenience played well in the casserole culture of the 1920s and 1930s, where social gatherings and household economy often converged. The glamourous chafing dish cast its aura onto casseroles—one-pot meals that took their name from the vessel they were cooked in. With the rise of home economics, the popularity of casseroles surged, transforming them into humble fare vehicles for thrift and sophistication. The influential *The Boston Cooking-School Cook Book* (1896) helped codify this shift and inclusion of a straightforward layered macaroni and cheese brought the dish into the larger trend. By 1914, the casserole was featured as a solo act in Olive M. Hulse's *Two Hundred Recipes for Cooking in Casseroles;* naturally, macaroni and cheese was a shoo-in. Among the many forces shaping American tastes during this period, few proved more enduring than Irma S. Rombauer's *The Joy of Cooking* (1931). It appealed to the times with the kind of unpretentious, no-fuss fare that had come to distinguish the national table. Macaroni and cheese held its place in its pages, emblematic of the sturdy, toothsome one-dish meals that resolutely bridged frugality and comfort.

As the decade wore on, the need for domestic convenience took on a new urgency. Although industrial canning had been around for some time, the demand for inexpensive, long-lasting foods heightened, and macaroni and cheese, ever primed for reinvention, would be recast for the can. Heinz capitalized on this demand in 1937, marketing their "Cooked Macaroni in a thick cream sauce with mellow cheese," with the slogan: "Fine eating just for the heating!" For added refinement, "turn it into a baking dish and shove oven-wards till the sauces bubble and the crust is flecked with gold." Franco-American muscled into the canned macaroni market in 1939, but withdrew with the onset of World War II. The Van Camp Packing Company had actually beat both of them to market back in 1898, with its canned "Macaroni and Cheese (prepared with tomato sauce)," but the innovation did not make it into the new century. The company found greater success in the 1930s with Tenderoni, their long, slender, quick-cooking macaroni—a welcome novelty for women with little time and even less room for error (see fig. 8.4). Tenderoni was not without fast-food rivals—Creamettes being chief among them—each brand promising ease and reliability in such uncertain times. Far from being stigmatized, these convenient innovations were widely embraced, particularly during the Great Depression, when they became valued allies in stretching food budgets. It was against this backdrop that someone came up with the brilliant idea to sell macaroni and cheese as a meal kit.

Depending on the source, the details of the origin story of the first boxed macaroni and cheese kit differ, but here's an amalgamation.[19] A Scottish immigrant named Grant Leslie devised a clever solution to increase sales of either Tenderoni or Kraft processed cheese.[20] Regardless, he is said to have strapped a small packet of grated Kraft cheese wrapped in cellophane to a box of macaroni with rubber band.[21] It was a simple but innovative idea, just the sort of convenience that thrifty housewives were looking for. In one version, Leslie presented his brainchild to Kraft, who hired him to follow through, and in another, Kraft had caught wind of the idea and ran with it independently. What is verifiable is that in 1937, the company launched its Kraft Dinner. Very lucky with timing, the product hit grocery stores the very same year that economic recovery was experiencing a downturn, renewing fears that the worst might not be over. At just nineteen cents for a box that would feed a family of four, the company sold an astronomical

Van Camp's
TENDERONI
A NEW and delicious treat for
MACARONI and SPAGHETTI lovers

TENDER, BUT NOT DOUGH-Y
cooks in 7 minutes

Distinctive flavor . . . tender . . . nourishing . . . everybody loves it . . . wins you praises from your family and friends . . . new and interesting recipes on every package . . . unlike ordinary macaroni or spaghetti because it's never pasty.

Get Van Camp's TENDERONI *at your grocer's today.*

TRY THIS EASY RECIPE

BAKED TENDERONI AND CHEESE: Cook 1 package Tenderoni as directed on the package. Mix with: 1 cup milk, 1 tablespoon grated onion (optional), and 1 cup grated American cheese. Turn into a greased casserole. Sprinkle with ¼ cup buttered, toasted crumbs. Bake in a moderate oven (350 degrees F.) 40 minutes. Makes 6 servings.

Another Van Camp's
quicker-easier-economical
"FEAST-FOR-THE-LEAST"

Made and distributed by the makers of the Famous Van Camp's Pork and Beans.

FIGURE 8.4. Van Camp's introduces its quick-cooking macaroni with a recipe that includes American cheese. The macaroni may have boiled up fast, but then it had to be baked for forty minutes. *Source*: Public domain.

eight million units in the first year in the United States and had equal success in Canada. Kraft was onto something big.[22]

Kraft Dinner was fast, cheap, and easy. The preamble to a 1938 advertisement laments that the "old-fashioned way" took an hour. In the accompanying vignette, a husband arrives home hungry from the office, dismayed to find his wife is just getting dinner on. Silly man, she's making the new Kraft Dinner with quick-cooking macaroni. In less than ten minutes (time for him to slide on his house slippers and pour a stiff drink), piping hot macaroni and cheese is steaming from a chafing dish. No baking required! Even better, with the New Deal electrification initiative (1935), more and more households were equipped to make Kraft Dinner on an electric stovetop.

Kraft was a master of publicity. His *Kraft Music Hall* radio show was initiated primarily as a marketing vehicle for Kraft Foods, effectively reaching millions of listeners during the 1930s and 1940s. Ratings soared when Bing Crosby took the helm as host in 1936. His suave voice, laid-back demeanor, and everyman appeal proved ideal for aligning products like Kraft Dinner with "wholesome" American values. The program not only reinforced Kraft's brand identity but also played a crucial role in embedding its products into American household routines . . . and hearts (see fig. 8.5).

MARKETING THE SOUTHERN KITCHEN: RACE, REGION, AND CULTURAL AUTHORITY

As millions of Black Americans chartered paths northward, the white South's arbiters of taste turned to curating their cultural identity by systematically codifying Southern culinary identity. This intentional regionalization standardized Southern heritage as a marketable product. Though macaroni and cheese graced tables nationwide, its strategic placement alongside dishes earmarked as "Southern"—in cookbooks, meals, and food writing—consolidated its meaning. Presented in this curated constellation, the dish itself became Southern. In this way, macaroni and cheese transcended mere geographic consumption patterns to become a performative symbol through which Southerners could affirm their cultural affiliation, distinguishing their foodways from the broader American gastronomic landscape.[23]

Exemplary works in the genre include Henrietta Stanley Dull's compilation *Southern Cooking* (1928) and *Two Hundred Years of Charleston*

FIGURE 8.5. Advertisement from the *Ladies Home Journal* (1948). *Source*: Public domain.

Cooking (1930), whose macaroni and cheese featured egg. The inclusion of eggs would become a point of division in Southern cookery that had cooks digging their heels in on either side of the fence, with Team Egg prevailing. The macaroni and cheese in *Virginia Cookery* (1930) was dully pragmatic and boiled down to three steps: throw cheese sauce on macaroni, top, and bake.[24] The luncheon menu suggestion lacked both local flair and inspiration: Macaroni and Cheese, Whole Wheat Muffins, Orange and Stuffed Date Salad, and Cup Cake with Hot Cinnamon Sauce. To their credit, these books were not wholly divorced from the living traditions of the South. While they paid homage to the past, they were not so much exhuming dead traditions as breathing new life into the vestiges.

The commodification of Southern cuisine reached a telling turning point when it attracted the attention of Northerners eager to profit from it. In 1935, Lillie S. Lustig, S. Claire Sondheim, and Sarah Rensel published *The Southern Cook Book of Fine Old Dixie Recipes*, which leaned heavily into stereotypes. Its "characteristic illustrations" depicted African Americans as ragtag men, decrepit old women, children eating watermelon, a man straining to haul a large bale of cotton, field laborers singing "Carry Me Back to Old Virginny," and an attractive maid serving at a candlelit dining table, along with a white-haired plantation owner, one hand raising a glass, the other clutching a fine walking stick. Its superficial engagement was also evident in omissions: While suggesting the tomato sauce recipe would pair well with baked macaroni and cheese, it failed to give a recipe for the emblematic dish. *The Southern Cook Book* was not a cooking manual per se but a voyeuristic, pseudo-anthropology. Despite the exploitative framing, one truth was evident: Southern cooking was indebted to African Americans.[25]

The dynamic of appropriation and exclusion transferred over into commercial spaces as well. The cover of *The Marigold Cook Book: A Practical and Useful Collection of Southern Recipes* (1938) depicts a smiling, bandana-clad African American woman holding a roasted chicken on a platter against a bright orangey background. The cookbook unveiled secrets of the Marigold cafeterias, a chain that made its name serving affordable home-style meals in casual settings. Cafeterias represented more than just a convenient dining option—they were reflective of the cultural patterns of the era. Their self-service model seemingly democratized dining: Office workers, students, and laborers could get a sit-down meal shared in the same dining hall. Women, too, could dine independently. Yet this veneer of inclusivity masked a bitter irony: African Americans, whose culinary contributions filled these pages and whose cheery image graced the cookbook's cover, were either segregated within or completely excluded from these spaces. The cafeteria's signature "Macaroni a la Marigold" was one of the staple comfort foods served at the restaurant that reverberated as a Southern culinary tradition while appealing to a broad customer base.

This fraught relationship between approbation, attribution, and appropriation persisted well into the twentieth century. Nearly a century after Emancipation, white women's unease with domestic duties still shadowed the well-heeled kitchens of the New South. A revealing glimpse of this persistent discomfort appears in *Recipes Collected by the Junior League of Charleston* (1950), where a prefatory poem masquerades as a light-hearted homage to the mammy figure while betraying deeper cultural tensions.

> There was a time when folks had cooks,
> Who never did depend on books
> To learn the art of cooking.
> The help knew all the tunes by ear,
> And no one dared to interfere;
> They brooked no overlooking.
>
> But times have changed, for worse we fear,
> Housewives handle the kitchen ware,
> And must learn how to cook,
> With that in mind, we've dug and delved,
> And unearthed treasures long been shelved,
> And placed them in this book.

WARTIME

Throughout the lean years of the Great Depression and into wartime, public health officials faced the challenge of widespread nutritional deficiencies that demanded immediate solutions. When the American Medical Association gave its stamp of approval in 1935, processed cheese was legitimized as a nutritional cornerstone. It spread throughout institutional America, showing up in school lunches, military messes, and the federal government's own relief programs. Paired with macaroni, it offered a protein-rich alternative to meat, its authority now grounded not in advertising promises but in professional validation and government distribution networks.

Even before official US involvement in World War II, the nation battened down to wartime conditions in support of the Allies, adopting a rationing system in 1940. When full-scale rationing followed in 1941, Kraft once again proved adept at turning crisis into opportunity, integrating Kraft Dinner into the program. A single ration ticket bought two boxes, supplying a family of four with two meals—compared to the same ticket's worth of just two portions of meat. But there is an underbelly to the story.

During the war, Kraft continued his interest in developing time-insensitive foods that could withstand the gauntlet of wartime logistics. Among the priorities was powdered cheese. While inventors had long explored the possibilities inherent in spraying and drying liquid cheese, it was under the pressure of war that the golden cheese dust found its true calling. It seemed to defy time itself, indestructible in its sealed packet. The innovation served both military necessity and civilian preparedness, finding enduring success as Americans developed an abiding affection for that strangely compelling orange macaroni.

The association with austerity measures put macaroni and cheese at risk for losing its cachet, but despite its new duties—getting schoolchildren fed and pulling families through tough times—the dish underwent a remarkable parallel transformation. While sales of Kraft's version rose steadily, housewives were busy giving the homemade classic a makeover. Charity and community cookbooks repositioned it squarely in the "Luncheon" section, conjuring visions of the archetypal "ladies who lunch": women's organizations, church socials, bridge and garden clubs, charity fundraisers, and department store restaurants. There, the humble casserole was tarted up with descriptors like "mousse," "divine," "ring," "deluxe," "delight," and "supreme," arriving at tables in chafing dishes, as garishly garnished casseroles, or as dainty individual timbales.[26] The National Macaroni Institute, the PR arm of the industry, ever vigilant to keep their product in the public eye from the 1930s through the 1950s, put out a steady stream of recipes. Their pièce de résistance, "Macaroni Ring Supreme," dotted with chopped pimento and filled with creamed chicken or seafood, was pitched as "perfect for bridge luncheons."

The fundraising cookbook by Friends of Lyndeborough Central High School (ca. 1950) offers a delightful recipe that unwittingly draws upon historical elements threading all the way back to seventeenth-century Europe—although the method is one-of-a-kind American.

CHICKEN AND MACARONI SUPREME

7 oz (200 g) macaroni
2 cups (500 mL) milk
2 cans (10 1/2 oz/295 mL) cream of mushroom soup, undiluted
1 onion, chopped fine
1 cup (120 g) diced Velveeta
15 oz (400 g) raw chicken, diced
150 g stuffed green olives, halved
4 hard-cooked eggs, sliced

Mix the macaroni, milk, soup, onion, Velveeta, chicken, and half the olives. Refrigerate overnight in a baking dish. Remove and bake one hour in a preheated oven at 350°F (180°C). Garnish with the eggs and remaining olives.

SOUL FOOD: THE WELCOME TABLE

> I'm not talking about small slivers of skinned chicken breasts surrounded by miniature carrots and radishes cut like roses. I'm about something to eat. Like a pan of macaroni and cheese, made with real cheese!
>
> —VERTAMAE SMART GROSVENOR

Adrian Miller poses the question "How Did Macaroni and Cheese Get So Black?" as the title to his chapter on the dish in *Soul Food: The Surprising Story of An American Cuisine* (2013). Much of the foundation in answer to that question has been laid over the course of this book, but now we are ready to bring it home.

World War II's grim paradox lay in how its devastation opened unexpected doors of opportunity. The conflict ignited the second wave (1940–1970) of the Great Migration, as wartime industries demanded labor. To preempt protests, the government moved to curb employment discrimination.[27] Meanwhile, the mechanization of Southern agriculture was making traditional farming jobs obsolete, pushing rural workers to seek opportunities elsewhere. Wages for the second wave were not just higher than on farms—they were higher overall, creating an unprecedented economic uplift. This migration was larger and geographically broader than the first, with about 5 million people relocating compared to 1.6 million in the first wave.

As Black veterans and their families settled in new cities, restaurants and food businesses became important community spaces. Despite discrimination in accessing full rights to GI Bill benefits, veterans were able to leverage them to pursue higher education, training, homeownership, or open small businesses, including restaurants. These spaces weren't just about food—they were safe havens for gathering, organizing, and celebrating their culture in a still segregated society.

Even in supposedly progressive areas, the influx of African Americans triggered a backlash as migrants competed for housing, jobs, and public resources. They were met with racial violence and hostility that belied the promise of freedom and prosperity outside the South. Yet this did not deter them. Determined not to return to prewar subjugation, they pressed on. Having fought for democracy abroad, they now demanded it at home. This newfound entitlement to equal rights fueled a wave of activism and heightened the call for systemic change.

Lena Richard

While the second wave of the Great Migration saw millions of African Americans seeking new lives in Northern and Western cities, not all chose to leave the South behind. In New Orleans, Lena Richard (1892–1950) charted her own course, building a culinary legacy within a region that often stifled Black ambitions. Having started her career as a domestic servant, Richard had left for a time to study at the Fanny Farmer Cooking School in Boston. But she returned to the South, leveraging her knowledge, talent, and determination to become a celebrated chef, restaurateur, and cookbook author at a time when few Black women were recognized in the culinary world.[28]

Richard opened a cooking school of her own, aimed at helping young African Americans enter a career track. Her opus, *Lena Richard's Cook Book* (1939), put her name front and center on a book that attracted the attention of notables such as James Beard. By 1940, it was marketed internationally as *The New Orleans Cook Book*, the first to celebrate the gastronomic heritage of New Orleans by an African American woman. It showcased her culinary prowess, ranging from modern trends to Southern classics, passed down through generations. The brief "Macaroni, Rice, Cheese" section is exemplary, headed up by "Macaroni and Cheese," where she introduces a novel thickening technique, mixing flour with the cheese before layering it with macaroni. It's then topped with cheese, doused in milk, and baked. It keeps company with jambalaya, fried grits, two methods of cooking rice, a soufflé ring called simply "Macaroni," and, finally, the centuries-old classic "Welsh Rarebit."[29] The book's success led to the local TV cooking show *Lena Richard's New Orleans Cook Book* in 1948.[30]

While Richard's legacy was distinct from the Soul Food movement that would emerge later, her public prominence helped establish a path for other Black culinary professionals to assert their voices. At a time when African American cooks were largely relegated to anonymous domestic work, Richard became a respected figure in the public eye. Her work demonstrated that Black chefs could claim recognition and influence in a predominantly white industry.

Freda De Knight

While Lena Richard was making her mark in New Orleans, Freda De Knight was carving out her own path in the North as one of the first African American women to gain national recognition in food journalism. As food editor for *Ebony* magazine, she provided a platform that celebrated African American culinary traditions while introducing innovative recipes to a growing Black middle class. She put a fine point on it in *Date with a Dish: A Cook Book of American Negro Recipes* (1948), a nonregional collection featuring recipes "from and by Negroes from all over America." She aimed not just to reach the inner circle but to compete on equal footing with any other cookbook—a bold and much needed leap forward.

De Knight answers a question that surfaced with Sallie Miller's "Macaroni a la King," recounting the story of an old woman from Tennessee recalling the days of slavery: "When I was a little girl the Mistress of the house came into my mother's kitchen and said, 'Rosa. I've just returned from New York, and at the hotel and restaurants I had the most wonderful food.'" After just a vague description, "the dish was perfected and became plantation talk."[31] This is the legacy of cookery that would proliferate with the migratory movements of African Americans. De Knight thoughtfully acknowledges "cooking by ear" and innate calling but also that not everyone is so gifted. Cookbooks served as the written expression of the "experiments and genius of the naturally endowed," collected and preserved to be passed down, not as museum pieces, but as a foundation to celebrate and build upon.[32]

However, hailing from the North, she was not interested in yoking herself to the Southern standard of fried chicken, greens, corn pone and the like, convinced that others, too, sought new horizons. Yet, in mapping her vision of the new Pan-American "Negro" kitchen, she signposted macaroni and cheese in the dedicated chapter "Macaroni, Spaghetti, Noodles." True to her belief that cooks should add some "special little twist" to keep traditional recipes current, she reimagined macaroni and cheese with a decisive seasoning mix of mustard, paprika, celery salt, garlic salt, and pepper. The choice of cheese, grated or chopped, is up to the discretion of the cook.

De Knight's work represents an essential yet often bypassed element in the Soul Food story in that it promoted awareness of a culinary collective with history and meaning at a time when African Americans were dispersing throughout the nation. It was intended as a unifying force across the vast internal American diaspora, binding scattered communities through shared foodways that preserved their strength and identity. This is part of a cultural pattern mirroring the larger story of the African diaspora, where displaced communities adapted while maintaining their cultural touchstones yet evolving to meet the challenges and opportunities of their new surroundings. As the Civil Rights Movement coalesced in the mid-1950s, food became intertwined with the rise in political consciousness, part and parcel of the manifesto of Black cultural autonomy.

In 1958, the National Council of Negro Women published *The Historical Cookbook of the American Negro*, a unique fundraising effort that was not just a collection of recipes but a companion to current events, most notably the challenge to segregation in schools and public spaces, the Civil Rights Act of 1957, and the systemic suppression of voting rights. Aimed at educating and uplifting African American women, the cookbook emphasized their significance in American history and culture. Given the white male dominance in the public-school curriculum, these authors used food as a means to integrate African American history into the larger American narrative, combating misinformation, disinformation, and the absence of Black history.

The *Historical Cookbook* was not a history of African Americans but an inclusive American history told through recipes. Structured as a calendar, each month features a different historically valued figure. January honors George Washington Carver, a pioneering agricultural scientist who empowered Black families to break free of their dependance on cotton through crop diversification, particularly peanuts, a crop with African roots. Carver developed hundreds of uses for the peanut, including this high-protein version of macaroni and cheese, originally published in his 1917 cookbook, and brought forth in the *Historical Cookbook* in recognition of Carver's achievements.

PEANUT MACARONI AND CHEESE

1 cup (100 g) broken macaroni
2 quarts (2 L) water
1 tsp salt
1/4 to 1/2 lb (115 to 225 g) cheese
1 cup (250 mL) rich milk
2 Tbsp flour

1 cup (150 g) coarsely ground peanuts
Dash of cayenne pepper
1/3 cup (70 g) breadcrumbs toasted in butter

Preheat the oven to 350°F (180°C).

Cook macaroni in salted water then drain and rinse in cold water. Mince cheese, and mix it with the milk, flour, peanuts, and cayenne pepper. Put the cheese sauce and macaroni in alternate layers in a well-buttered baking dish. Cover with buttered crumbs and bake 30 minutes. Tent with foil if crumbs become too brown.[33]

SOUL FOOD CAPSULE

Soul Food is much more than just a type of cuisine; it is a symbol of Black culture and history. It has become a way for African Americans to celebrate their shared heritage, resilience, and sense of community. The term "soul food" had existed for centuries, referring to spiritual nourishment or sustenance—something that fed the soul, rather than just the body.[34] This imagery resonated deeply with African Americans as the fight for civil rights intensified in the 1960s. At its core, the concept of "soul" represented profound, enduring connections that went beyond food or politics, reflecting collective strength and identity.

Even before the Civil Rights Movement, food was a foundation for community among African Americans. The Great Migration had brought Black communities together in Northern cities, where they came to see their everyday food not just as a carryover from the past or as Southern traditions, but as a statement of their identity and resistance in a new environment, shifting from "self-evident to self-conscious" awareness.[35]

As the Civil Rights Movement gained momentum, foods began to symbolize the shared struggles of the African American community. These were often foods that had been stigmatized or dismissed by the dominant culture—subsistence foods that had nourished and sustained African Americans in the South. Yet they encapsulated the will to thrive, lending meaning to their current plight. This became soul food in the truest sense: not just food to fill the stomach but food that fed the spirit and fortified the resolve for the ongoing fight for equality.

While some composed music, wrote poetry and prose, or crafted fashion and art, others constructed a representative culinary culture—not by inventing something new but by giving new meaning to what was already there. When community members partook of these dishes, they engaged in affirmation of their cultural bonds and historical consciousness, embracing the deeper cultural narrative these foods embodied. Soul food is a form of communion.

But one of these soul foods is not like the others. If this culinary genre is defined by dishes evolved from hardship, then isn't macaroni and cheese a conspicuous outlier alongside chitterlings, corn pone, catfish, and collards? Thus, we circle back to ask the question: How *did* macaroni and cheese get so Black? Or rather, how does it fit into the Soul Food canon?

The culinary historian Frederick Douglass Opie distilled "Soul" down to five cardinal guidelines. Point 4 gives us the in we are after:

1. Soul is a cultural mixture of various African tribes and kingdoms
2. Soul is adaptations and values developed during slavery and emancipation
3. Soul is the style of rural folk culture
4. Soul is the values and styles of planter elites in the Americas
5. Soul is spirituality and experiential wisdom that make black folk unique
6. Soul is putting a premium on suffering, endurance, and surviving with dignity[36]

Once an aspirational dish reflecting the values and style of planter elites, macaroni and cheese had become affordable and accessible. Its memory as an elite dish faded, supplanted by the warmth of familiarity and the new meaning that arose through emotional associations. Given sociocultural, political, and economic shifts over centuries, macaroni and cheese was not the odd one out but a historically integral part of the African American culinary culture.

It was a classic—if not iconic—Soul Food side dish, especially in "meat and three" offerings of African American restaurants. Its cultural significance solidified during the Civil Rights era, served at culinary landmark institutions like Dooky Chase's in New Orleans, Pascal's and Deacon's in Atlanta, Sylvia's in Harlem, and Princess Pamela's Little Kitchen in the East Village. Sylvia Woods had migrated from North Carolina in 1940 and opened her restaurant in 1962. Both she and Princess Pamela Strobel were enmeshed in a diasporic environment reaching a diverse clientele. Black New Yorkers developed a broader view of what Soul Food meant. The diaspora was more inclusive, moving beyond "downhome Southern" to embrace Caribbean and Latin American influences, reflecting New York's diverse Black community.[37] These restaurants were more than places to eat; they were community anchors for political discussions and strategy sessions, fueling not just bodies but also the movement for civil rights.[38]

As the twentieth century progressed, nearly every sizable city in the United States boasted a Black-owned Soul Food restaurant. Some of them had survived from the Great Migration and went on to be icons, like Sylvia Woods's restaurant on Malcolm X Boulevard in New York. When she died in 2012, her funeral was a major event drawing dignitaries such as the former president Bill Clinton and Reverend Al Sharpton coming to pay homage.

Years after soul food was a recognized culinary genre, it was institutionalized in cookbooks. Oddly, most of the foundational Soul Food cookbooks do not include macaroni and cheese: Ruth L. Gaskins's deep South cookbook *A Good Heart and a Light Hand* (1968), which Craig Claiborne called "far and away the best cookbook to deal with soul food"; Hattie Reinhart Griffin's compact and essential *Soul Food Cookbook* (1969); caterer to the stars, Bob Jeffries, *Soul Food Cookbook* (1969), where he asserts that "all soul food is southern food, but not all southern food is 'soul' food," and yet the dish was not among the elect;[39] and *Princess Pamela's Soul Food Cookbook* (1969), a whimsical combination of anecdotes, wisdom, and poetry with recipes ranging from traditional Soul Food staples to personal favorites but no macaroni and cheese. This absence doesn't imply that these authors didn't make, serve, or enjoy the dish, but we must wonder if its noninclusion was intentional.

These works were published during a crucial time, as Soul Food was being codified in print—establishing not only what it was but also why it mattered. If we entertain the omission of macaroni and cheese as a deliberate choice, it suggests that these authors aimed to define the genre more narrowly, possibly excluding dishes associated with broader, more commercialized American culture. This raises a compelling question: Was macaroni and cheese considered *Black enough* for the Soul Food canon? Despite its appeal to a broad demographic, might Kraft's white, middle-class advertisements in the 1950s and 1960s have cast it as something outside the cultural identity these cooks were shaping? Perhaps the overriding image was more emblematic of mainstream America, rather than the South or Black culinary heritage. While it may have had a curiously rough start, eventually the floodgates opened.[40]

The Embedding of a Cultural Icon

By 1970, when Pearl Bowser and Joan Eckstein's *A Pinch of Soul* came out, Soul Food had expanded beyond the inner circle to become "a very real and legitimate addition to the repertory of American cuisine."[41] As such, macaroni made a circuitous reentry into the mainstream via Soul Food, reclaiming its place in US kitchens—this time dressed in new culinary vestments. Bowser and Eckstein's generous concept of Soul Food brought macaroni and cheese into the fold, and others would follow suit. With an emphasis on cheese, they suggest blending sharp cheddar, American, Muenster, and garlic cheddar. Though cheeses may vary, for them a good mix makes or breaks the final outcome. Notably, they call it "Macaroni 'n' Cheese"—marking the first appearance of this term of endearment.

The dish gained star appeal when the "Queen of Gospel" included it in *Mahalia Jackson Cooks Soul* (1970). Jackson's prominence as an African American artist during the Civil Rights era aligned with cultural and social consciousness central to soul music. Similarly, Pearl Bailey, an indomitable singer and actress, showcased her confidence as cook in "Macaroni and Cheese If I Say So Myself."[42] "Nobody ever has a little bit of my macaroni and cheese," she says. "Each time it gets more divine."[43] In her conversational style she gives instructions on the cheese, starting with good-quality sharp cheddar: "I use *tons* of cheese. When the thing is done I know that I'm going to call it macaroni and cheese and not macaroni and macaroni."[44]

However, Bailey rejected the concept of Soul Food, and she was not alone. Any food that is made with care is "worthwhile no matter what his race or his nationality or station in life."[45] Many felt that the term burdened African Americans with a single narrative, locking their heritage in a perpetual loop with slavery and hardship stifling progress and overshadowing any potential for growth.[46] The Soul Food repertoire also faced criticism for its association with a slew of health issues—diabetes, heart disease, and cancer—drawing fire from various health experts. As far back as 1967, the guru Elijah Muhammad warned African Americans, "If you want to live a long time, do not eat [macaroni] at any meal," a message purportedly relayed from "God in person."[47] Experiences close to home told a cautionary tale, pushing people to reject those "traditional" foodways. In answer to the cultural misgivings, macaroni and cheese easily shifted into the more accommodating "heritage" category, but the health accusations were a bigger hurdle, requiring an in-depth rethink.[48] "Rather than yield to a call for complete abstinence," Opie maintained, "African Americans will continue to adapt soul food as they have done for centuries."[49]

The Neo-Soul Food movement put macaroni and cheese on the hit list, suggesting cold comfort alternatives like low-fat mac or macaroni and tuna salad. Vegans, too, wanted in. The celebrity chef Carla Hall took the question to heart. Under her Soul Food banner, she created a superlatively creamy stovetop mac and cheese and the self-assured "The Only Four Cheese Mac and Cheese Recipe You Need."[50] But as a nonpartisan health advocate she also created a vegan recipe and revised it specially for us:

BAKED VEGAN MAC & CHEESE

1 Tbsp vegan butter, melted
1 Tbsp extra-virgin olive oil
1/4 tsp kosher salt
1 cup (95 g) panko
1/2 cup (30 g) + 2 Tbsp nutritional yeast

8 oz (230 g) dried elbow macaroni

1 Tbsp white miso
1 Tbsp tamari soy sauce
1 Tbsp Dijon mustard
2 tsp white vinegar
2 oz (55 g) vegan butter
1/2 medium onion, roughly chopped
2 medium carrots, peeled and roughly chopped
1 tsp (5 mL) kosher salt
2 cloves garlic, smashed
1/2 tsp (5 mL) black pepper
1/4 cup (30 g) all-purpose flour
2 1/2 cups (625 mL) unsweetened plant-based milk
10 oz (230 g) vegan cheddar cheese, grated

Preheat the oven to 375°F (190°C).

Prepare topping: In a medium bowl, combine 1 Tbsp vegan butter, olive oil, and salt. Add the panko and toss to coat well. Stir in the 2 tbsp nutritional yeast and set aside.

Cook the macaroni: Bring a large pot of salted water, covered, to a boil over high heat. Add macaroni and cook, uncovered, just until translucent (about 2 minutes). Drain and rinse macaroni and set aside.

Make the sauce: In a small bowl, combine the miso, tamari, mustard, and vinegar; set aside.

Melt the 2 oz vegan butter in a large, wide pot over medium-low heat. Add the onions, carrots, salt, garlic, and pepper. Cook until the carrots are tender, about 5 minutes.

Stir in the miso mixture. Sprinkle the flour over the mixture and continue stirring to incorporate. Cook the flour, stirring constantly with a wooden spoon, about 4 minutes. Gradually add the milk alternative, whisking constantly to incorporate and make a smooth sauce. Increase the heat to medium-high and bring the sauce to a low boil, whisking constantly. Reduce to a simmer, whisking occasionally, and cook until it has thickened and coats the back of a spoon, about 3 minutes more. Stir in the vegan cheese just until melted. Pour the mixture into a blender, add the 1/2 cup nutritional yeast, and puree until smooth. Pour 4 cups of the sauce back into the pot or a large bowl (there may be a little left over). Add the drained macaroni and stir well to coat. Immediately transfer the macaroni mixture to the prepared baking dish. Sprinkle the panko topping evenly over the macaroni and bake for 15 to 17 minutes until the sauce is bubbly and the crumb topping is golden brown.

Sylvia Woods's grandson, Lindsey Williams, carried on her legacy in his own way. In his *Neo Soul: Taking Soul Food to a Whole 'Nutha Level* (2003), he speaks candidly about a lifetime of indulgence in traditional soul food only to find himself tipping the scales at four hundred pounds while he was still a young man. In the book, Williams advises neophytes on how to cut their cake so they can eat it, too, but in his catering business, Neo Soul means daring to challenge tradition and express individual style—no small task in the shadow of Soul Food royalty Sylvia Woods. Ultimately, Chef Williams shines with his signature macaroni and cheese, shared here for the first time. The note of sweetness harkens back to the Middle Ages, but also to his grandmother, who added a teaspoon of sugar for good measure.

NEO SOUL MAC AND CHEESE

Dedicated to Chef Nesty

2 lb (900 g) elbow macaroni
2 cups (200 g) each: monterey jack, mozzarella, yellow sharp cheddar, and smoked gouda
1/3 cup (80 mL) sweetened condensed milk
2 cups (500 mL) whole milk
2 tsp Lawry's® seasoned salt, or to taste
1 stick (115 g) salted butter, melted
4 eggs

Preheat oven to 350°F (180°C). Boil macaroni in salted water and cook until al dente. Drain and rinse with cold water. Mix the cheeses and set aside 2 cups. In a large bowl, mix the rest of the cheeses with the rest of the ingredients. Add macaroni to the mixture. Pour into a 9 × 13-inch (23 × 33 cm) greased baking dish. Cover with foil and bake 30–40 minutes until set but still creamy. Top with the reserved cheese mix. Bake uncovered 7–10 minutes until golden. Serve hot.

In interviews I conducted at the National Museum of African American History and Culture, participants agreed that health concerns around Soul Food are best dealt with by reserving it for special occasions—church functions, major holidays, Sunday dinner, or a night out—making it an infrequent indulgence rather than a dietary lifestyle.[51] For most African American families, homemade macaroni and cheese is a must at Thanksgiving, Christmas, and the week of Kwanza.[52] Jessica Harris features "Spicy Three-Cheese Macaroni and Cheese" as a representative potluck dish in *A Kwanzaa Keepsake and Cookbook* (2024).

Macaroni and cheese was not just a special dish but verged on the sacred: "The elaborated Sunday-gathering macaroni and cheese has attained such a hallowed status that one must present personal references from trusted family members before being allowed to cook it for an important occasion."[53] Even in households where not everyone is particularly fond of the dish, its presence at holidays is nonnegotiable—omitting it would break with tradition.[54] Kraft mac 'n' cheese is verboten on these occasions. The spiritual "Thanksgiving Anthem" makes it clear:

> If you're not serving macaroni and cheese,
> do not invite me.
> If the word "Kraft" is in your macaroni recipe,
> do not invite me.
> I thought we were friends.
> I thought you liked me.
> You must want to fight me.
> You just got demoted to bringing store bought cakes.
> Jesus didn't die so that you could put that on my plate.[55]

The fascinating conflation of the Crucifixion with Thanksgiving dinner in this passage underscores the sacredness of macaroni and cheese.

Getting Cheesy

> Mac and cheese is a food that makes people irrational, unpredictable, and irresponsible. In other words, they will drop everything and trample a baby kitten for good-quality mac.
>
> —JEANNIE CLOE, ORGANIZER OF THE 2009 SAN FRANCISCO FOOD WARS

While the historical underpinnings were distinctly different, the diet of poor whites and Blacks actually varied little in the South, but Ernest Matthew Mickler takes it down a notch in *White Trash Cooking* (1986), now available in a twenty-fifth anniversary edition. "Netty Irene's Macaroni & Cheese" is a Southern custard-style mac, putting three eggs, a cup of Carnation evaporated milk (no substitutes, please), and a cup of yellow cheese to four cups of cooked macaroni. While "yellow cheese" is a broad description, the economic conditions depicted in *White Trash* lead us to another influence in the ongoing popularity of our dish: government cheese.

The story of government cheese began as a way to stabilize milk prices during the Depression. Private contractors won bids to turn surplus milk into processed cheese in strict accordance with USDA specifications, resulting in a homogeneous product. The problem with a guaranteed buyer was that it became impossible to stanch the flow of greed. Dairies overproduced to the point that by the 1970s there were massive stockpiles of cheese. A plan was devised to offload the sheer tonnage of processed cheese through food assistance programs. The term "government cheese" was coined when millions of Americans started hauling home those distinctive boxes containing five-pound blocks of cheese from food banks, churches, and other local distribution points. While the idea of government cheese may not make you salivate now, people loved it at the time—and thought it made *the* best mac and cheese. As Jessica Harris phrased it, macaroni was "the delicious final resting place for more than one package of the infamous government cheese."[56]

"We used to call it 'welfare cheese,'" Delilah Winder said in our interview. "That cheese had a flavor that just hit the mark! When that cheese started disappearing, people started looking for other cheeses to fill the void for their macaroni because that cheese held its own by itself. I mean, I remember a time when people were scurrying to find that cheese!"[57]

Winder knows what she is talking about. In 2003, her macaroni and cheese received the Midas touch when Oprah Winfrey named it the best in America. Let's see what she did to fill the government cheese void in *Delilah's Every Day Soul* (2006):

MACARONI AND CHEESE

2 pounds (900 g) elbow macaroni
12 eggs
1 cup (115 g) cubed Velveeta cheese
1/2 pound (225 g) butter, melted
6 cups (1.5 L) half-and-half (10% milkfat cream)
4 cups (450 g) sharp yellow cheddar cheese, grated
2 cups (225 g) extra sharp white cheddar cheese, grated
1 1/2 cups (165 g) mozzarella cheese, grated
1 cup (115 g) Asiago cheese, grated
1 cup (115 g) Monterey Jack cheese, grated
1 cup (115 g) Muenster cheese, grated
1/8 tsp salt
1 Tbsp black pepper

Preheat the oven to 325°F (160°C).

Bring a large saucepan of salted water to a boil. Add the macaroni and cook until slightly al dente, about 10 minutes. Drain and set aside to keep warm.

Whisk the eggs in a large bowl until frothy.

Add the Velveeta, butter, and 2 cups of the cream to the eggs in the bowl and mix well. Add the warm macaroni, tossing until the Velveeta has melted and the mixture is smooth. Add the remaining cream, 3 cups of the yellow cheddar cheese, the remaining grated cheeses, salt, and pepper, tossing until completely combined.

Pour the mixture into a 9 × 13-inch (23 × 33 cm) casserole or baking dish and bake for about 30 minutes. Sprinkle with the remaining cup of the yellow cheddar cheese and bake until golden brown on top, about 30 minutes more. Serve hot.[58]

COMFORT ME WITH MACARONI

> Is that the feeling of a soul being soothed, or just the onset of a mac-and-cheese-induced food coma?
>
> — "WHY COMFORT FOOD COMFORTS" CARI ROMM

Few people would claim that their go-to comfort food is salad. For most people, comfort food means something high in fat and carbohydrates, and often soft and warm—so it should come as no surprise that 99 percent of all comfort-food cookbooks include macaroni and cheese, often as the first recipe and sometimes even as the cover photo. However, scientists say that it is not the composition of the food that kindles that cuddly contented feeling but the association with positive affective memories from the past. They strip the phenomenon of its metaphysical poetry as "social surrogacy and embodied cognition assume that cognitive associations with nonhuman stimuli can be affectively charged."[59] What we plebeians know is that comfort food promotes a sense of security and belonging and that macaroni and cheese is particularly potent.

In 2022, as the COVID-19 pandemic was winding down, Kraft put out a press release announcing it was changing its name from "macaroni and cheese" to the comfier "mac & cheese." A dripping, bright orange elbow smile rests on a royal blue background to "embody what positive comfort looks like: noodlefuls of delight that lift you up and make you happy inside and out." The brand manager continued, "We know that people aren't turning to comfort food as a guilty pleasure, they are positively embracing comfort, saying yes to feeling good, saying yes to caring for themselves. There is a familiar, craveable, positive comfort to Kraft Mac & Cheese that makes it so special and iconic to millions of people across the world and our new look is a reflection of what our brand means to our consumers."[60]

Whether your memories are of boxed mac & cheese, homey mac on toast, elaborate gooey casseroles at family gatherings, or elegant macaroni and cheese with lobster, most of us have some fond recollection of the dish from our past that rouses tender feelings when this nonhuman, affectively charged stimulus releases dopamine and activates the emotional processing modulator oxytocin—the love chemical.

The queen of Southern cuisine, Edna Lewis, shared her memories of flavors and traditions that shaped her childhood in Virginia in *The Gift of Southern Cooking* (2003). Born in 1916 to a family with deep roots in the South, Lewis was the granddaughter of an emancipated slave. At sixteen, she ventured to New York City, initially working at the Museum of Natural History. However, it was her passion for food that truly defined her path, leading to her first cookbook in 1972. In her later years, having moved back to the South, she wrote *The Gift of Southern Cooking* with her partner Scott Peacock, a young white chef from the South, aligning the resurgence of traditional Southern cooking with the Neo Soul movement.[61] In one particularly heartfelt headnote, Lewis reminisced about the macaroni and cheese of her youth—a dish that captures the warmth and essence of Southern comfort food.

> Everyone has childhood memories of macaroni and cheese. I remember that I developed my taste for really good, really sharp flavored macaroni and cheese as a child. My mother would take me to the butcher shop (which we called "the cold storage") to buy a wedge of sharp cheddar, freshly cut from a huge wheel of cheese with red wax rind, which we called "mouse cheese." At home, my mother and I would both nibble on little pieces of cheese while she prepared the macaroni and custard, and I would grate more for sprinkling over the top.
>
> This macaroni and cheese is creamier and richer than most: it will seem very loose when you take it from the oven but will thicken nicely after a brief rest.

Her recipe serves ten, enough to comfort and make memories with your intimate circle.

MACARONI AND CHEESE

1 3/4 cups (230 g) elbow macaroni
Salt
1 1/2 cups (150 g) extra sharp cheddar cheese cut into 1/2- inch (1.1 cm) cubes
2 Tbsp plus one tsp all-purpose flour
1 1/2 tsp salt
1 1/2 tsp dry mustard
1/4 tsp freshly ground black pepper
1/8 tsp cayenne pepper
1/4 tsp freshly grated nutmeg
2/3 cup (160 mL) sour cream
2 eggs, lightly beaten
1/3 cup (35 g) grated onion
1 1/2 cups (375 mL) half-and-half (10% milkfat cream)
1 1/2 cups (375 mL) heavy cream (36% milkfat cream)
1 tsp Worcestershire sauce
1 2/3 cups (180 g) extra sharp cheddar cheese, grated

Cook the macaroni in a large pot of boiling salted water until just tender. Drain well and transfer to a buttered 9 × 13-inch (22 × 33 cm) baking dish. Mix in the cubed cheddar cheese.

Preheat the oven to 350°F (180°C).

Put the flour, salt, mustard, black pepper, cayenne pepper, and nutmeg in a large mixing bowl and stir to blend. Add the sour cream, followed by the eggs, and stir with a wire whisk until blended and homogeneous. Whisk in the onion, half and half, heavy cream, and Worcestershire sauce until blended. Pour this custard over the macaroni and cubed cheese and stir to blend. Sprinkle the grated cheese evenly over the surface of the custard. Bake until the custard is set around the edges of the baking dish but still a bit loose in the center, about 30 minutes. Remove from the oven and cool for 10 minutes to allow the custard to thicken.[62]

When the tastemaker duo Yotam Ottolenghi and Helen Goh put their hand to mac and cheese for their cookbook *Comfort* (2024), they ultimately set it aside—not because it fell short but because, as Goh explained, similar flavor profiles were already well represented. They have graciously allowed me to include their recipe here, offering my readers an exclusive glimpse into the endless possibilities that have inspired creative cooks for centuries.

MAC AND CHEESE WITH BUTTERNUT, FETA, AND BURNT BUTTER CRUMBS

Serves 4–6

3 lb 5 oz (1.5 kg) butternut squash (1 large or 2 small squashes), peeled and seeds removed and cut into 1.2-inch (3 cm) chunks
2 Tbsp (30 mL) olive oil
Salt and black pepper
10 oz (280 g) macaroni pasta
1.8 oz (50 g) panko breadcrumbs
3 1/2 Tbsp (50 g) unsalted butter
15–20 fresh sage leaves
1 Tbsp unsalted butter, plus extra for greasing
2 banana shallots (120 g), finely chopped
2 large garlic cloves, crushed
1 Tbsp finely chopped rosemary leaves
2 tsp cumin seeds, lightly toasted and crushed
1 tsp chili flakes
2/3 cup (160 mL) double cream (48% milkfat cream)
4.2 oz (120 g) mature cheddar cheese, grated
1/2 tsp finely grated nutmeg
7 oz (200 g) feta cheese, crumbled into 1-in. (2 cm) chunks

Preheat the oven to 350°F (180°C).

Add the squash in one layer to a large parchment-lined tray, along with 1 Tbsp of oil, 1/2 tsp salt, and a good grind of black pepper. Mix well to combine and then roast for until light golden and a knife goes into the flesh with no resistance, about 45 minutes. Remove from the oven and, when cool enough to handle, remove 14 oz (400 g)of the roasted butternut and place it in the bowl of a food processor. Blitz until smooth and set aside. Keep the remaining chunks whole and set aside.

While the squash is roasting, prepare the other components. Bring a medium pot of salted water to a boil and add the pasta. Cook for 6 minutes until al dente then drain, saving about 1.5 cups (375 mL) of the cooking water. Rinse the pasta under cold water to stop the cooking process and then set aside.

To make the crumb topping, place the panko in a medium bowl and set aside. Place the butter in a small saucepan over medium-high heat and cook until it has melted and turned foamy, about 3 minutes. Add the sage and cook until the leaves are crispy and the butter turns golden brown, about 45 seconds. Using a slotted spoon, lift out the sage and transfer to a paper towel-lined plate. Pour the butter on the panko crumbs, toss to combine, and set aside.

Add the remaining tablespoon of oil and 1 tablespoon of the butter to a medium pan. Place on medium heat, add the shallots, and cook for about 5 minutes, stirring a few times, until softened. Add the garlic, rosemary, cumin, and chili. Lower the heat and cook for about 5 minutes more, stirring, until fragrant. Add the blitzed pumpkin, cream, 2.8 oz (80 g) of the cheddar, the reserved pasta cooking water, nutmeg, 3/4 teaspoon of salt and a good grind of black pepper. Crumble in 4 or 5 of the crispy sage leaves and stir until combined and warmed through. Take off the heat and fold in the cooked pasta and reserved roasted butternut chunks. Lightly fold in the feta so that it does not break up too much.

Grease a rectangular 8 × 12-in (20 × 30 cm) or 10-in. (26 cm) round baking dish with butter and pour in the pasta mixture. Mix the remaining 1.4 oz (40 g) of cheddar into the brown butter crumbs and scatter evenly over the pasta.

Bake for 20 minutes, until the top is golden brown. Remove from the oven and scatter the remaining sage leaves on top, crumbling the larger ones as you go. Leave for about 5 minutes, so it is not piping hot, and then serve.

As an antidote to the blues, mac 'n' cheese is so effective that there are single-subject cookbooks and monothematic restaurants dedicated solely to this revered dish, ensuring that everyone can get their fix.[63] Users should be warned: Self-medicating with comfort foods may lead to overindulgence, crossing the line from simple self-care to wanton guilty pleasure—but the scope of this book does not extend to the moral philosophy of macaroni.[64]

HEY, WHAT ABOUT THE ITALIANS?

The two ends of our journey come together full circle with the marriage of Italy and the United States. On the Italian side, we have Fettuccini Alfredo, a dish "invented" ca. 1908 by Alfredo di Lelio and served to Mary Pickford and Douglas Fairbanks in 1920 while they were honeymooning in Rome. They couldn't believe their tastebuds and recommended it to their VIP friends. Despite its clear antecedents in "Roman macaroni" (see chapter 2), one of the foundational dishes in Italian culinary history, Romans overwhelmingly reject the dish as an *Americanata*—a vulgar mangling, American style. The sarcastic quip "This dish is really quite famous in Rome; they serve it for lunch and dinner to hospital patients" is one of the kinder *scherzi*; the comparison with cat vomit, less so.[65] But abroad "Alfredo" became a multimillion-dollar business. Too bad the originator never patented it, though—he'd be laughing all the way to the bank.[66]

Macaroni and cheese is another *Americanata*—but one that is met with anthropological curiosity. From that safe distance, a few Italian bloggers have tried to replicate it for their adventurous compatriots, working around the challenges of finding cheddar cheese and elbow macaroni.[67] While readers are forewarned about it being an unhealthy "calorie bomb," the tiptoeing seems rather much given some version's similarity to the indulgent favorite *pasta ai quattro formaggi*. Indeed, culinary influences flow both ways. Melissa Clark, the food editor of the *New York Times*, riffs on that magic number, blending French, Italian, and American cheeses. While Clark tells me she fondly remembers being raised on the blue box stuff, she has definitely moved on a piece in this sophisticated reimagining of the dish.

FOUR-CHEESE MACARONI AND CHEESE

Adapted from the website *New York Times Cooking*

Butter for baking dish

1 lb (454 g) short pasta
6 oz (170 g) Brie, cut into chunks
4 oz (120 g) cream cheese, cubed and softened
3 large eggs, lightly beaten
1 cup (240 g) mascarpone, room temperature
3 oz (85 g) Parmigiano-Reggiano, grated
3/4 tsp (4 mL) freshly ground black pepper
1/4 tsp (1 mL) finely grated nutmeg

Preheat oven to 375°F (190°C). Butter a 2-quart (1.9 L) baking dish. Bring a large pot of salted water to a boil. Cook pasta to al dente; drain well. Transfer hot pasta to a large bowl and toss immediately with Brie and cream cheese until melted. In a separate bowl, whisk together the eggs, mascarpone, and Parmigiano-Reggiano. Stir the egg mixture into the pasta. Season with pepper and nutmeg. Turn into prepared pan. Bake until golden brown and bubbling, about 30 minutes. Serve immediately.[68]

ONWARD AND UPWARD

The days of yielding to Elizabeth Raffald and thickening sauces with liquified macaroni are long behind us. Macaroni and cheese has rebounded to become an international favorite. Modern recipe creators have since ventured in countless directions, each adding their signature to this timeless dish, pushing it to new heights while honoring its essential character. International interpretations are seen in Judy Joo's "Kimchi Mac and Cheese," the Australian "Mac 'n' Cheese Spring Rolls," the Krispy Boyz' "Mac 'n' Cheese Birria Taco," and the Anglo-Indian inspired "Tikka Masala Mac 'n' Cheese."[69] Here's my own version of this fragrant delight.

TIKKA MASALA MAC 'N' CHEESE BAKE

3 Tbsp ghee
3 cloves garlic, minced
1-inch (2.5 cm) piece of fresh ginger, minced
1 medium onion, thinly sliced
7 cardamom pods, crushed
1 Tbsp coriander seeds
1 tsp cumin seeds
1-in. (2 cm) stick cassia cinnamon
2 cloves
1 tsp black peppercorns
2 hot dried chilis
1/3 cup (80 mL) tomato puree
1/3 cup (80 mL) chicken broth
1/2 tsp (2 mL) salt
1/3 cup (80 mL) whipping cream (30% milkfat cream)
1 lb (450g) macaroni elbows
1/3 cup (80 mL) yogurt
7 oz (200 g) sharp cheddar, grated
5 oz (150 g) fontina, grated

Heat the ghee in a medium saucepan. Add the garlic and ginger and sauté on medium heat until softened. Then add the onions and cardamon pods. Cook until softened and browning. Grind the rest of the spices and add. Sauté one minute. Add the tomato puree and cook without stirring until it begins to stick. Add the chicken broth, salt, and cream. Cover and simmer for 10 minutes. Preheat oven to 350°F (180°C).

In the meantime, cook the macaroni in salted water until al dente. Drain and pour into a baking dish. Add the sauce, yogurt, and cheeses (except for a half cup). Mix well. Smooth the top, cover with the remaining cheese, and bake 30 minutes. Finish under the grill until crusty.

Though an epic history cannot but conclude in the present, the momentum of the past assures us that the annals of macaroni and cheese will continue well into the future. The United States has set aside July 14 as National Macaroni and Cheese Day, but perhaps the time has come to propose an international celebration to honor this versatile favorite that crossed oceans and endured generations. Macaroni and cheese is more than a dish; it is a cultural phenomenon, a testament to the enduring power of simple ingredients to bring joy, comfort, and connection to people everywhere. So long as cuisines, tastes, cultures, and technology continue to advance, so too will the story of macaroni and cheese—endlessly inventive, deeply cherished, and always, irresistibly delicious.

ACKNOWLEDGMENTS

This book has been a long journey, and I am deeply grateful for the countless acts of kindness and support I received along the way. So many people contributed to this project in so many ways, and I am honored to acknowledge them here.

First and foremost, I extend my heartfelt thanks to the many individuals who generously shared their time, expertise, and insights through consultations, interviews, and research assistance. Among them are Annette Gordon-Reed, Pulitzer Prize–winning author of *The Hemingses of Monticello*, who graciously offered to review the Jefferson-Hemings chapter; Psyche Williams-Forson, scholar of Black life, food, and foodways; Leni Sorensen, culinary historian at large of Monticello; Marcie Ferris and Liz Williams, experts in Southern foodways; the cookbook authors Delilah Winder, Carla Hall, and Lindsey Williams; Cynthia Greenlee, editor of *The Guardian* US; Thérèse Nelson, curator of Black culinary history; Dawn Davis, editor with Simon and Schuster; Ashbell McElveen, founder of the James Hemings Society; Manon Henzen, Dutch culinary historian; Franka Philip, Caribbean culinary expert; Josh Windsor, cheese expert; Andrew McGowan, scholar of food in early Christianity; Ivan Day, English culinary historian; Keja Valens, scholar of Caribbean literature; Peter Peter, professor of medieval studies; Jim Chevallier, French culinary historian; and the Little Falls Historical Society. I am indebted to Yotam Ottolenghi and Helen Goh, Carla Hall, and Lindsay Williams for generously sharing their unpublished macaroni and cheese recipes. A special note of gratitude goes out to Adrian Miller, whose unwavering belief in me and this project helped to transform it into a book. And finally, I extend my warmest thanks to culinary historian Jane Levi, whose wisdom and encouragement kept me on a steady course.

I'd like to thank Eric Wolfinger—friend, collaborator, and photographer extraordinaire—for the succulent cover photos. And also Nicole Litvack, who stepped in at the last moment to test and photograph the vegan mac.

In summer 2023, I was fortunate to receive a fellowship at the International Center for Jefferson Studies in Monticello. I am profoundly thankful to the staff there, especially Anna Berkes, who has been a steadfast supporter from the very beginning. My thanks also go to the (then) acting director Frank Cogliano and archaeologist Fraser Neiman for their invaluable contributions.

In 2024, the macaroni and cheese project was honored with a fellowship at the Lemelson Center of the Smithsonian's National Museum of American History—an experience of a lifetime. I am deeply grateful to my advisers, Alison Oswald and the stellar Eric Hintz, for their guidance, as well as to my cofellow Dan Stone, and to Joanne Hyppolite and Mary Elliott from the National Museum of African American History and Culture. Above all, I would like to thank the food history curator Paula Johnson, whose generosity, wisdom, patience, and kindness extended far beyond our weekly formal consultations. She and her husband, Carl Fleischhauer, opened their home on Capitol Hill to me for my two-month sojourn, providing a base of comfort and safety after long days of research.

While in DC on my fellowship, I spent countless hours at the Library of Congress, first under the wing of the legendary research librarian Constance Carter and later with Jennifer Harbster, Head of the Science Reference Section and the library's culinary expert. Jennifer was not only an extraordinary research consultant but also a kindred spirit in many an epic conversation about food. This book would not have been possible without the Library's outstanding staff and resources. Seeing Thomas Jefferson's original drawing of the "macaroni machine," brought out by early American manuscripts curator Julie Miller, was an unforgettable highlight.

And finally, in the spring of 2025, I completed this book while on fellowship at the George Washington Presidential Library at Mount Vernon.

Many thanks to the Library staff, and in particular to the immensely helpful Nell McCarty. I am also grateful to archaeologists Lily Carhart and Jason Boroughs, food historian Gail Cassidy, and Senior Interpretive Supervisor Anette Ahrens.

Last but not least, I am also deeply appreciative of my readers, Adrian Bregazzi, Katie Rodriguez, Sheila Crye, and Maria Louise Wagner, as well as partial readers Michelle Farkas, Josh Windsor, Lisa Rolen, and Lorenzo Alunni. Your insights and encouragement helped me stay motivated and on course.

And thanks to my infinitely patient husband Simone Nocchi—*sei buono come il pane.*

Finally, I would be remiss if I did not thank Columbia University Press and senior editor Jennifer Crewe for recognizing the potential of a book-length work devoted to macaroni and cheese.

NOTES

1. DIGGING IN: ANCIENT ANTECEDENTS

1. W. Warde Fowler, "Mundus Patet: 24th August, 5th October, 8th November," *Journal of Roman Studies* 2 (1912): 26.
2. Lucius Septimus Severius (145–211 BCE) wanted to erect a triumphal arch commemorating his achievements on the same spot, so the Umbilicus was moved and reassembled out of its ruins to rather inglorious effect.
3. Scott Reynolds Nelson, *Oceans of Grain: How American Wheat Remade the World* (Basic Books, 2022), 201.
4. Augustus was not formally deified until his death in 14 AD and had eschewed divine homage during his lifetime, although he was worshipped as godlike.
5. Cato, *De Agri Cultura* 5, 76.
6. Cato, *De Agri Cultura* 5, 78.
7. Cf. Charles Perry, "What Was Tracta?," *Petits propos culinaires* 12 (1982): 37–39, argues that this *tracta* is not pasta because when broken into pieces the bits would be irregularly sized, and thus, in his opinion, an unpleasant eating experience. He therefore concludes that *tracta* was a thickener.
8. One of the more confident distortions of this fabrication is from the alleged culinary historian Tindaro Gatani: "*Agli inizi del Milleduecento, Federico II di Svevia, che aveva unito sotto il suo Impero mezza Europa, stabilendosi nella sua sontuosa reggia di Palermo, era diventato, come ci racconta uno dei suoi biografi contemporanei, un tal Walter von der Vogelweide, grande amatore e consumatore di pasta e particolarmente di «maccheroni dal sugo dolce», conditi cioè con lo zucchero, come si usava a quei tempi* [At the beginning of the 1200s, Frederick of Swabia, who had united half of Europe under his empire, having settled into his sumptuous palace in Palermo, had become, as one of his contemporary biographers, a certain Walter von der Vogelweide tells us, a great lover and consumer of pasta and particularly

of 'macaroni with a sweet sauce,' that is, dressed with sugar, as it was done in those days.]" In *"Pasta e ancora non basta" Storia e fortuna di un alimento che è diventato una bandiera*, accessed November 22, 2022, https://cucinamk.files.wordpress.com/2014/12/storia-della-pasta.pdf.

9. A satchel made of woven palm leaves.
10. Museo delle Paste Alimentare, founded in 1958 as a private collection by Vincenzo Agnesi, and formally opened to the public in 1993. It is currently relocating; however, plans for reopening have been delayed.
11. *A Pocket Guide to Italy* (Armed Forces Information and Education, Department of Defense, 1964), 13.
12. Archivio di Stato di Genova, "Atti del notaio Ugo Scarpa," register 2, fol. 51.
13. Mark Wheelis, "Biological Warfare at the 1346 Siege of Caffa," *Emerging Infectious Diseases* 8, no. 9 (2002): 971–75.
14. Anthony Buccini, "The Merchants of Genoa and the Diffusion of Southern Italian Pasta Culture in Europe," in *Food and Markets: Proceedings of the Oxford Symposium on Food and Cookery 2014*, ed. Mark McWilliams (Prospect, 2015), 58–59.
15. Laura Galoppini, "L'isola Dei Maccheroni," *Medioevo* 9, no. 80 (2003): 44.
16. Mario Pei, *The Story of Language* (Lippincott, 1949), 214.
17. Cf. Andrew Dalby, *Food in the Ancient World from A-Z* (Routledge, 2003), 251.
18. *Codex Diplomaticus Cavensis*, Cava dei Tirreni, Salerno (I).
19. B. W. Mitchell, "Merlin and Macaroni," *Classical Weekly* 25, no. 5 (1931): 34.
20. Michael McCormick, "Rats, Communications, and Plague: Toward an Ecological History," *Journal of Interdisciplinary History* 34, no. 1 (2003): 14.
21. Anna Martellotti, *I ricettari di Federico II: Dal meridionale al liber de coquina* (Olschiki, 2007), 85.
22. Martellotti, *I ricettari*, 14.
23. Medieval convents were actually renowned for their culinary products, many of which demonstrated extraordinary mastery and creativity. The resulting donations that these generated were an important source of revenue.
24. Martellotti, *I ricettari*, 15.
25. C. B. Hieatt, "How Arabic Traditions Travelled to England," in *Food on the Move: Proceedings for the Oxford Symposium 1996*, ed. Harlan Walker (Prospect, 1996), 121.
26. See also Constance B. Heiatt and Sharon Butler, eds., *Curye on English* (Oxford University Press, n.d.), 204–5.
27. The word *ruayan* indicates milk from feedings on the second growth of grass, called "rowen." See also Hieatt and Butler, *Curye on Inglysch*, 211.

2. MACARONI ON PAPAL PLATES

1. Gene A. Brucker, " 'The Horseshoe Nail': Structure and Contingency in Medieval and Renaissance Italy," *Renaissance Quarterly* 54, no. 1 (2001): 1–19.
2. Luigi Ballerini, "Food for the Bawdy: Johann of Bockenheim's Registrum Coquine," *Gastronomica* 1, no. 3 (2001): 35. The date given by Bruno Laurioux is December 1, 1417, cf. " 'Le Registre de Cuisine' de Jean de Bockenheim, Cuisinier Du Pape Martin V," *Mélanges de l'Ecole Française de Rome: Moyen-Age, Temps modernes* 100, no. 2 (1988): 710.

3. Laurioux, "'Le Registre de Cuisine' de Jean de Bockenheim," 712.
4. From MS 7054 Bibliothèque nationale de Paris Laurioux, 738.
5. In fact, the culinary scholar Bruno Laurioux has expressed doubt about Bockenheim's presence at the Holy See, suggesting he may have acquired his experience from his many benefices, which would have kept him occupied in Germany. See Bruno Laurioux, "De Jean de Bockenheim à Bartolomeo Scappi : cuisiner pour le pape entre le XVe et le XVIe siècle," *Offices et papauté (XIVe-XVIIe siècle): charges, hommes, destins* (2004): 303–32.
6. Soup as a term did not necessarily indicate a liquidy food eaten in a bowl with a spoon. It is better understood as a preparation that involved a liquid like broth, as is the case here.
7. For more information on Martino's manuscripts, see Luigi Ballerini, *The Art of Cooking: The First Modern Cookery Book* (University of California Press, 2005); Terence Scully, ed., *Cuoco Napoletano: The Neapolitan Recipe Collection*, trans. Terence Scully (University of Michigan Press, 2015).
8. Ballerini, *The Art of Cooking*, 4.
9. A previous version attributed to Martino also includes yolks. See Scully, *Cuoco Napoletano*.
10. For a full discussion of taste in the hierarchy of the senses, see Carolyn Korsmeyer, *Making Sense of Taste: Food and Philosophy* (Cornell University Press, 2014).
11. Printed books were still expensive, which kept distribution to an exclusive clientele. Printed books met with criticism by those who valued the beauty of the handwritten manuscript and felt printing destroyed the quality of books as objects. A similar sentiment is mirrored in criticism of e-books in contrast to the feel and affective familiarity of paper books. The mass production potential of printed books also entailed a significant loss of control over the dissemination of ideas.
12. In the fifteenth century, Italy received sugar primarily from the Mediterranean regions of Cyprus, Crete, and Sicily, where production relied on local labor, indentured servants, and some enslaved people, but African slave labor had not yet become dominant. In the late fifteenth century, with the establishment of Portuguese sugar plantations on Atlantic islands, and later in the Americas during the sixteenth century, enslaved Africans became the primary labor force in sugar production, significantly influencing the European sugar trade.
13. Although this is set in Bologna and the pasta is lasagne, that does not indicate a tray of baked lasagna as is currently associated with Emilia-Romagna. These would be the pasta swaths the size of the palm of one's hand or wide noodles and cheese at this time still called macaroni.
14. Ortensio Lando, *Commentario delle più notabili, et mostruose cose d'Italia & altri luoghi Aramea in italiana tradotto* (Venice: Bartholomeo Cesano, 1548), 8. Since the Middle Ages, Italy had been the central trading hub of sugar in Europe. Sugar was cultivated in Sicily as well as the Venetian colony of Cyprus.
15. For an interesting article on the misquoted phrase, see Diana Cardenas, "Let Not Thy Food Be Confused with Thy Medicine: The Hippocratic Misquotation," *E-SPEN Journal* 8, no. 6 (2013): e260–62.
16. This sweet, bland pudding is made with almonds and fish. On meat days, it was made with chicken breast instead of fish. Whitedish, also known by the French

blancmange, originated in the Middle Ages and remained wildly popular in Europe for three centuries.

17. Madeleine Lazard and Gilbert Schrenck, eds., *Pierre de L'Estoile, Registre-journal du règne de Henri III*, vol. I (1574–1575) (Droz, n.d.), 171–72.
18. Loïc Bienassis and Antonella Campanini, "La reine à la fourchette et autres histoires. Ce que la table française emprunta à l'Italie: analyse critique d'un mythe," in *La table de la Renaissance. Le mythe italien*, ed. Florent Quellier and Pascal Brioist (Presses universitaires François-Rabelais, 2018), sec. 125.
19. He died in 1542 and is buried in Rome, evidence that he may have remained chef until that date. See Laurioux, "De Jean de Bockenheim à Bartolomeo Scappi."
20. The work would go through nine French editions between 1575 and 1579 and was translated into English, Latin, and German but notably not Italian.
21. In the original Italian the word is "paste," which in this context translates to "doughs" and not "pastas," which has led to misinterpretation.
22. Bienassis and Campanini, "La reine à la fourchette et autres histoires," sec. 27.
23. Bienassis and Campanini, sec. 36.
24. Adrien-Maurice de Mairault, *Observations sur les écrits modernes*, vol. XXVIII (Chaubert, n.d.), 157.
25. Dennis Diderot, *Encyclopédie ou dictionnaire raisonné des sciences, des arts et des métiers*, vol. 1 (Briasson, 1751), 765.
26. This was part of a larger work on the social history of France, commissioned by Marquis de Paulmy (Antoine-René de Voyer d'Argenson).
27. Pierre-Jean Baptiste Le Grand d'Aussy, *Histoire de la vie privée des Français* (Ph.-D. Pierres, 1782), 230.
28. The books were later donated to Louis XV two centuries later. See Bruno Laurioux, *Le règne de Taillevent: Livres et pratiques culinaires à la fin du Moyen Âge* (Éditions de la Sorbonne, 1997).
29. Antonella Campanini, "The Illusive Story of Catherine de' Medici," *The New Gastronome* (blog), December 18, 2018, https://thenewgastronome.com/caterina-de-medici-a-gastronomic-myth/.
30. Gasterman, "Introduction à l'histoire de la gourmandise," *Journal des gourmands et des belles ou l'Épicurien français*, May 1807, 118.
31. Campanini, "The Illusive Story of Catherine de' Medici."
32. Bienassis and Campanini, "La reine à la fourchette et autres histoires," 130.

3. THE FRENCH CONNECTION AND ENGLISH REFLECTION

1. Cited in Ewoud Sanders, *Woorden met een verhaal* (Prometheus, 2004), 76.
2. Anne Wilson, *The Cookbook Library* (University of California, 2012), 93.
3. François Pierre de La Varenne, *La Varenne's Cookery*, ed. and trans. Terence Scully (Prospect, 2005), 58.
4. Pottage had long indicated a thick peasant soup more or less on a constant boil. Foods were added according to their availability. In the seventeenth century, the term more generically denoted soup and crossed class distinctions, although the ingredients and preparation reflected one's status.
5. Of note in the Lenten section of *Le cuisinier françois*, the flesh of turtles, ducks, and frogs did not register as meats.

6. Susan Pinkard, *A Revolution in Taste: The Rise of French Cuisine* (Cambridge University Press, 2009), 66.
7. There is a culinary chauvinism inherent in the idea that "natural flavors," interpreted as herbs and delicate sauces, represent good taste and that spices are not also natural, in addition to the dismissal of those who use spices indiscriminately, broadcasting them across food like whitewash.
8. By comparison, see *A True Gentlewoman's Delight: Wherein Is Contained All Manner of Cookery* (1653), by Elizabeth Grey, Countess of Kent.
9. Digby would later recount that Queen Marie de Medici was so enamored of him that he was forced to feign his death and flee France incognito.
10. The title echoes the 1665 book purportedly by Queen Henrietta Maria, containing her medical and culinary secrets, *The Queen's Closet Opened*.
11. Gilly Lehmann, "The Cook as Artist?," in *Food in the Arts: Proceedings of the Oxford Symposium on Food and Cookery*, ed. Harlan Walker (Prospect, 1998), 129.
12. Tobacco and smoking became refined because of the finely crafted accessories, including distinctive boxes made of silver, gold, porcelain, and ivory.
13. It is unclear whether the young ladies were given manuscript copies or blank books into which they transcribed recipes from the class. The handwriting differs, but the quality of the script indicates a professional hand. The pagination also varies somewhat, supporting the idea that sheets were inserted as completed.
14. For an example, see Leeds University, Brotherton Library, MS 75.
15. More precisely, the first edition was printed from engraved script.
16. One example was Sarah Harrison's *The House-keeper's Pocket-book, and Compleat Family Cook* (1733). See David Potter, "Some Notes on Edward Kidder," *Petits propos culinaires* 65 (2000): 11. Plagiarism became a legally punishable offense in 1710.
17. Katherine Harbury, *Colonial Virginia's Cooking Dynasty* (University of South Carolina Press, 2004), 250.
18. Cited in Barbara Ketcham Wheaton, *Savoring the Past: The French Kitchen and Table from 1300 to 1789* (Touchstone, 1996), 167.
19. The assumption is that the pie is covered with a top crust and baked, details that are absent on nearly all of La Chapelle's pie recipes.
20. Elizabeth Robins Pennell, *My Cookery Books* (Houghton Mifflin, 1903), 39.
21. Pennell, *My Cookery Books*, 40.
22. Not until 1778 did editors adjust the spelling to vermicelli.
23. This is an offshoot of *The Whole Duty of a Woman, or, A Guide to the Female Sex, from the Age of Sixteen to Sixty* etc., by Lady Marry Cressy (1695). The updated 1737 title positions cookery as the main thrust of the book. Meanwhile, under the original title, another edition came out in 1753, retaining only the moral guidance, by William Kendrick, reputedly a depraved drunk, using the anonymous signature "by A Lady." It was reprinted in over twenty editions, including in Boston and Philadelphia.
24. This list would be stolen verbatim in Lydia Honeywood's *The Cook's Pocket-Companion and Complete Family-Guide: Being a Collection of the Very Best Receipts* (1758).
25. Giorgio Riello, "A Taste of Italy: Italian Businesses and the Culinary Delicacies of Georgian London," *London Journal* 31, no. 2 (2006): 209.
26. Similarly, the 1737 Dutch cookbook manuscript *Heele goeje remedien, en resepte om te koken te bakken en te confijten* by Jacob and Isabella Scott also separates

sweet and savory recipes for macaroni and cheese. Fine food boutiques and apothecary spice shops in the Netherlands sold macaroni in bulk from wooden barrels. Research assisted by Manon Henzen, Dutch culinary historian, by email, August 15, 2023.

27. Louis XV's second mistress (in the mid-1760s), Jenne du Barry, was a member of the bourgeoisie and made a point of hiring a woman as her chef du cuisine, setting a trend. A French male chef in 1795 commanded a wage that was six times higher than of a female counterpart. See J. J. Hecht, *The Domestic Servant Class in 18th Century England* (Routledge and Kegan Paul, 1956), 142, 147.
28. This is the dish I served at Monticello in July 2023 as part of my fellowship presentation. I've included the recipe here upon request.
29. Thanks to Matt Preston @mattscravat, who shared this recipe from his family's heirloom collection.
30. Robert Chambers, *The Book of Days: A Miscellany of Popular Antiquities*, vol. 2 (London: W. & R. Chambers, 1832), 32.
31. The club was founded in 1735 by John Rich, an actor-manager at Covent Garden Theatre, and the artist William Hogarth. Membership included prominent figures from the arts, theater, and politics, such as Samuel Johnson, the Prince of Wales (later King George IV), and notable actors, playwrights, and artists.
32. Chambers, *The Book of Days*, 2:32.
33. The proverb is English but in Italian. The English quite admired Italian culture, and many learned to speak Italian, Queen Elizabeth herself was fluent. Their opinion of Italian people, however, was at best mixed.
34. George B. Parks, "The First Italianate Englishmen," *Studies in the Renaissance* 8 (1961): 214.
35. Documentation dates back to the 1760s. See Arthur S. Marks, "Angelica Kauffmann and Some Americans on the Grand Tour," *American Art Journal* 12, no. 2 (1980): 5–24.
36. Early evidence in New York for macaroni imports: *New-York Gazette and Weekly Mercury*, May 11, 1772 (and onward); the *Royal Gazette* (New York), June 5, 1780 (and onward); the *Independent Journal* (New York), November 17, 1783 (and onward). The trend would spread to other cities.
37. Mary V. Thompson, *"The Only Unavoidable Subject of Regret": George Washington, Slavery, and the Enslaved Community at Mount Vernon* (University of Virginia Press, 2019). Harriott Horry Pinkney, A Colonial Plantation Cookbook: The Receipt Book of Harriet Pinckney Horry, 1770, ed. Richard J. Hooker (University of South Carolina, 1984), 191. Kelley Fanto Deetz, *Bound to the Fire: How Virginia's Enslaved Cooks Helped Invent American Cuisine* (University Press of Kentucky, 2017), 50. Harriott Pinckney Horry, *A Colonial Plantation Cookbook: The Receipt Book of Harriet Pinckney Horry*, 1770, ed. Richard J. Hooker (University of South Carolina, 1984), 2. Primary source: Mary Hooker Cornellius advises her readers to teach illiterate servants to read in *The Young Housekeeper's Friend* (1845). This claim contrasts with numerous literacy bans decreed in slave codes. See also Catherine Clinton, *The Plantation Mistress: Woman's World in the Old South* (Pantheon, 1982), 184.
38. Jane Carson, *Colonial Virginia Cookery: Procedures, Equipment, and Ingredients in Colonial Cooking, Williamsburg* (Colonial Williamsburg Foundation, 1985). The earliest documentation of Raffald's *Experienced* in Virginia dates to 1772, owned by Hannah Lee Corbin.

39. For example, the following authors used close versions of her recipe: John Farley (1783); Richard Briggs (1788); W. A. Henderson (1791; American edition [1847]); *The Young Woman's Companion* (1811); Elizabeth Alcock (1812); and Colin MacKenzie (1822); (American edition [1825]).
40. Bruno Rosada, *Il Settecento veneziano. La letteratura* (Corbo e Fiore, 2007), 231.

4. JEFFERSON, HEMINGS, AND THE MACARONI MYTHOLOGIES

1. "Guided Primary Source Analysis: Jefferson's Pasta Machine," Primary Source Nexus, April 13, 2012, https://primarysourcenexus.org/2012/04/guided-primary-source-analysis-jefferson-pasta-machine/; *Spaghetti Dinner* (Coachwhip, 2018); "Mac and Cheese Is Truly the Pinnacle of Black American Dishes, Culture," AFRO, May 21, 2021, https://afro.com/mac-and-cheese-is-truly-the-pinnacle-of-black-american-dishes-culture/.
2. *Jefferson and Monticello: The Biography of a Builder* (Holt, 1990).
3. "7 Things Invented or Popularized by Thomas Jefferson," Interesting Engineering, July 20, 2023, https://interestingengineering.com/lists/7-things-you-wont-believe-thomas-jefferson-invented; "Thomas Jefferson: A Man of the Pasta | Timeless," Library of Congress Blogs, December 2, 2019, blogs.loc.gov/loc/2019/12/thomas-jefferson-a-man-of-the-pasta; "10 Modern Variations on Macaroni and Cheese," Mental Floss, August 20, 2013, https://www.mentalfloss.com/article/52313/10-modern-variations-macaroni-and-cheese; *Jefferson and Monticello*; "Guided Primary Source Analysis."
4. "Jefferson's House on the Hill," *Cosmopolitan*, March 1963; "Marvelous Macaroni and Cheese," *Smithsonian* magazine, https://www.smithsonianmag.com/arts-culture/marvelous-macaroni-and-cheese-30954740/; *The Geometry of Pasta* (Quirk, 2010); "The Origins of Macaroni and Cheese," YouTube, https://www.youtube.com/shorts/6Lm_HMbkA1A, accessed June 2, 2025.
5. "Mac and Cheese Is Truly the Pinnacle of Black American Dishes"; "How Mac and Cheese Became an All-American Dish," Weird History Food, https://www.youtube.com/watch?v=o19R-OrKq2A&t=329s, accessed June 2, 2025.
6. "5 Foods Thomas Jefferson Introduced or Made Popular in America," Mental Floss, March 9, 2016, https://www.mentalfloss.com/article/62565/5-foods-thomas-jefferson-introduced-or-made-popular-america; *Thomas Jefferson's Cookbook* (Garrett & Massie, 1938); "How Mac and Cheese Became an All-American Dish"; "The Origins of Macaroni and Cheese."
7. "James Hemings Mac and Cheese Recipe," October 10, 2024, https://www.andrewpriorfabulously.com/post/james-hemings-mac-and-cheese-recipe.
8. "Mac and Cheese Is Truly the Pinnacle of Black American Dishes"; "You Can Thank James Hemings, the Enslaved Chef of Thomas Jefferson, for the Mac and Cheese on Your Table," Today, November 23, 2022, https://www.today.com/food/people/james-hemings-mac-and-cheese-enslaved-chef-thomas-jefferson-rcna58226; "Please Raise Your Fork for James Hemings, Founding Father of Mac and Cheese," Medium, February 14, 2022, https://medium.com/of-pasta-and-plagues/please-raise-your-fork-for-james-hemings-the-man-who-brought-macaroni-and-cheese-to-america-21b4beca6802.
9. Katherine Harbury, *Colonial Virginia's Cooking Dynasty* (University of South Carolina Press, 2004).

10. The exclusive circle included luminaries such as George Wythe, signatory of the Declaration of Independence.
11. Philip Mazzei, *Philip Mazzei: My Life & Wanderings*, ed. Margherita Marchione, trans. Eugene Scalia (American Institute of Italian Studies, 1980), 141.
12. Rayford W. Logan, ed., *Memoirs of a Monticello Slave / as Dictated to Charles Campbell in the 1840's by Isaac, One of Thomas Jefferson's Slaves* (University of Virginia Press, 1951), 35.
13. The fire was apparently caused by a careless soldier during the American Revolution years.
14. Logan, *Memoirs*, 13.
15. Jupiter was born into slavery on Peter Jefferson's plantation, Shadwell, in 1743 and grew up alongside Thomas Jefferson.
16. Norton Mason Frances, *John Norton & Sons, Merchants of London and Virginia: Being the Papers from Their Counting House for the Year 1750–1795* (Augustus M. Kelley, 1968).
17. Dunmore became governor of the Bahamas in 1787.
18. As early as 1611, Italians started coming to Virginia, not as the hungry hordes that characterized nineteenth-century immigration, but as craftsmen and tradesmen. They also settled in Catholic Maryland mid-century. A formal declaration was made in 1649 that guaranteed they would be given lands under the same stipulations accorded with persons of English and Irish descent.
19. A. J. Morrison, ed., *Travels in Virginia in Revolutionary Times* (J. P. Bell, 1922), 55.
20. George Washington, diary entry, April 26, 1786.
21. Annette Gordon-Reed, *The Hemingses of Monticello: An American Family* (Norton, 2008), 109.
22. Letter to Thomas Jefferson from Henry Martin, May 15, 1784.
23. Thomas Jefferson, The Papers of Thomas Jefferson**, vol. 17,** 1 July to 12 November 1790, ed. Julian P. Boyd (Princeton University Press, 1965), 229. In a letter to Washington dated December 15, 1789, Jefferson expresses ambivalence but also an inclination to defer to his sense of duty to the president and the nation. Washington's reply, written from the seat of government in New York on January 21, 1790, offers a clearer description of the role of Secretary of State, while respectfully acknowledging that "it must be at your option to determine relative to your acceptance of it, or continuance in your Office abroad." Thomas Jefferson, *Papers*, vol. 16, 34, 116–17.
24. Jefferson's youngest daughter, Lucy, would die beforehand. Maria (Polly) would make the trip with James's sister Sally Hemings.
25. Jefferson, The Papers of Thomas Jefferson**, vol. 8,** 25 February to 31 October 1785, **ed**. Julian P. Boyd (Princeton University Press, 1953), 437.
26. François Jean de Chastellux, *Voyages dans l'Amérique septentrionale dans les années 1780, 1781 & 1782*, 2nd ed., vol. 2 Paris: Prault, Imprimeur du Roi 1791, 1221–22.
27. *The Papers of Thomas Jefferson: The Memorandum Books*, vol. 2, *1777–1782*, ed. James A. Bear, Jr., and Lucia C. Stanton (Princeton University Press, 1999), 607.
28. *Memorandum Book*, 570, footnote 22.
29. *Memorandum Book*, 649.
30. *Memorandum Book*, 650.
31. In 1790, 39 percent of the population of Virginia was of African descent.

32. Mazzei, *Philip Mazzei.*
33. Letter to James Madison from Jefferson, March 16, 1784.
34. The word in the original is "allievo," which in eighteenth-century Italian indicates a person who has followed the teachings of a master and been brought to proficiency through the guidance of a skilled professional. It carries a different meaning from *studente* or *alunno.*
35. Letter to Jefferson from Philip Mazzei, April 17, 1787.
36. Letter to Jefferson from Mazzei, April 4, 1787.
37. Gordon-Reed, *Hemingses*, 203.
38. Letter to Jefferson from Mazzei, April 4, 1787.
39. Letter to Mazzei from Jefferson, May 6, 1787. The word "antient" is taken from the French *ancien chef des cuisines*, meaning senior.
40. Thomas Jefferson, "Notes of a Tour into the Southern Parts of France, &c.," journal entry April 23, 1787, *The Papers of Thomas Jefferson*, vol. 11, *1 January–6 August 1787*, ed. Julian P. Boyd (Princeton University Press, 1955), 415–64.
41. *Lloyd's* was an important British newspaper that was imported and reprinted in major cities of the American colonies and played a role in shaping public opinion during the American Revolutionary War.
42. Letter to Charles Clay from Jefferson, October 14, 1799.
43. Fredrick Accum, *A Treatise on the Adulteration of Food and Culinary Poisons* (J. Mallett, 1820), 290.
44. *Memorandum Book*, 673, footnote 80.
45. Enclosure: Jefferson's Instructions for Procuring Household Goods, April 6, 1790.
46. Silvano Serventi and Françoise Sabban, *Pasta: The Story of a Universal Food*, trans. Anthony Shugaar (Columbia University Press, 2002), 98.
47. Edwin Wolf and Kevin J. Hayes, *The Library of Benjamin Franklin* (American Philosophical Society, 2006).
48. Paul-Jacques Malouin, *Description et détails des arts du meunier, du vermicelier et du boulenger, avec une histoire abrégée de la boulengerie et un dictionnaire de ces arts*, Paris: Académie Royale des Sciences, 1767, 101.
49. Letter to William Short from Jefferson, March 16, 1789.
50. Ephraim Chambers, *Cyclopedia: Or Universal Dictionary of Arts and Sciences*, vol. 2 (W. Innys, 1728), 478.
51. Letter to Short from Jefferson, March 24, 1789. Letter to Jefferson from Short, April 3, 1789. *Papers*, vol. 17, 229.
52. Gordon-Reed, *Hemingses*, 474.
53. Gordon-Reed, *Hemingses*, 576.
54. Letter to Tobias Lear from George Washington, September 9, 1790.
55. Mary V. Thompson. *"The Only Unavoidable Subject of Regret": George Washington, Slavery, and the Enslaved Community at Mount Vernon* (Univerisity of Virginia Press, 2019), 194.
56. Interview with Frank Cogliano, historian and acting president of the International Center for Jefferson Studies, July 20, 2023. See *A Revolutionary Friendship: Washington, Jefferson, and the American Republic* (Harvard University Press, 2024).
57. Letter to George Gilmer from Jefferson, March 15, 1793.
58. *Moule* means a cast, mold, or die, whereas *moulin* means mill.
59. *Memorandum Book*, vol. 2, 907.

60. Between 1795 and 1800, Jefferson and Mussi exchanged fifteen letters, none of which survive. Given Mussi's line of business, it is reasonable to speculate that some of that correspondence might have included orders for food imports from Italy.
61. Letter to James Monroe from Jefferson, May 12, 1795.
62. Letter to Mary Jefferson from Thomas Jefferson, May 1, 1797.
63. Letter to Jefferson from Francis Say, February 23, 1801.
64. Letter to William Evans from Jefferson, February 22, 1801.
65. Letter to Jefferson from Evans, February 27, 1801.
66. Letter to Evans from Jefferson, March 31, 1801.
67. Harriott Pinkney Horry, *A Colonial Plantation Cookbook: The Receipt Book of Harriet Pinckney Horry, 1770*, ed. Richard J. Hooker (University of South Carolina, 1984) 22. For evidence that Honoré Julien prepared macaroni and cheese while employed at the President's House in Philadelphia, see "Washington's Household Account Book, 1793-1797 (Continued)," *Pennsylvania Magazine of History and Biography* 31, no. 2 (1907): 176–94. http://www.jstor.org/stable/20085380, 10.
68. Letter to Evans from Jefferson, November 1, 1801.
69. Letter to Jefferson from Evans, November 5, 1801.
70. Gordon-Reed, *Hemingses*, 731.
71. William Parker Cutler and Julia Perkins Cutler, *Life, Journals and Correspondence of Rev. Manasseh Cutler, LL. D. By His Grandchildren*, vol. 2 (Robert Clark, 1888), 71–72.
72. Letter of presentation to Jefferson from the Committee of Cheshire, Massachusetts, December 30, 1801.
73. Royet, J. P., D. Meunier, N. Torquet, A. M. Mouly, and T. Jiang, "The Neural Bases of Disgust for Cheese: An fMRI Study," *Frontiers of Human Neuroscience* 10, no. 511 (2016).
74. According to the food historian Leni Sorenson, Edith Fossett Hern likely served as a scullion from a young age and is documented as having been a baby-minder for Sally Hemings's daughter Harriet. Interview January 2, 2024.
75. "Honoré Julien Advertisement," *National Intelligencer*, June 25, 1814, https://link.gale.com/apps/doc/GT3017468736/NCNP?u=smithsonian&sid=bookmark-NCNP&xid=7b9bf928.
76. This is known because one unwilling boy who had been sent to him ran away. Honoré Julien, "Six Cent Reward," *National Intelligencer*, January 27, 1815, https://link.gale.com/apps/doc/GT3017473001/NCNP?u=smithsonian&sid=bookmark-NCNP&xid=e98e62a7.
77. Lucia Stanton, *Those Who Labor for My Happiness: Slavery at Thomas Jefferson's Monticello* (University of Virginia Press, 2012), 204.
78. There is no documentation to confirm it, but Jefferson may have been ordering macaroni for more than just his own household.
79. W. Edward Farrison, "The Origin of Brown's Clotel," *Phylon* 15, no. 4 (1954): 347–54.
80. Fleming, Tom, and Alice Fleming. "Jefferson's House on the Hill," *Cosmopolitan* 154, no. 3 (1963): 28–32.
81. Leonard E. Roberts, *The Negro Chef Cookbook* (Vantage, 1969), 16.
82. Karen Hess, "Jefferson, Thomas," in *The New Encyclopedia of Southern Culture*, vol. 7, ed. John T. Edge, n.d., 189–90.

5. THE NEW WORLD ORDER: MACARONI'S TRIANGULAR TRANSFORMATION

1. Approximately 14 1/2 fl. oz (425 mL).
2. Macaroni manufacture in Edinburgh is documented in the 1833 *Twopenny Post Directory* under the name Thomas Newstead. Ben Mervis intimates that today macaroni pie served on a soft buttered bap is a favorite Scottish indulgence in the wee hours of the morning. *The British Cookbook* (Phaidon, 2022), 207.
3. See, for example, "Essence of Ham," in *Domestic Economy, and Cookery, for Rich and Poor—by a Lady* (1827), 174.
4. Maria Eliza Rundell, *A New System of Domestic Cookery: Formed Upon Principles of Economy, and Adapted to the Use of Private Families* (New York: R. McDermut & D. D. Arden, 1814), 128.
5. Carême also explored the potential of long-form tubular pasta as the construction medium for the timbale crust itself, painstakingly coiling strands round and round a baking mold greased with crayfish butter for his "Timbale à la Parisienne" or in alternating rows of saffron-dyed and plain macaroni to create the casing for the curry-filled "Timbale à la indienne."
6. Thomas Hood, ed., "French Cooks and Cookery," in *The New Monthly Magazine and Humorist* 2 (Henry Colburn, 1842), 7.
7. "Vermicelli & Macaroni," *Aurora General Advertiser*, 1802.
8. "Vermicelli & Macaroni."
9. United States Congress, *Journal of the House of Representatives of the United States, at the Second Session of the Tenth Congress, Begun November 7, 1808 – March 3, 1809* (Washington, D.C.: A. & G. Way, printers, 1809).
10. "Manufacture of Vermicelli and Macaroni, in the U. States," *Richmond Enquirer*, June 30, 1809.
11. "Manufacture of Vermicelli and Macaroni, in the U. States."
12. "Manufacture of Vermicelli and Macaroni, in the U. States."
13. Eliza Acton, *Modern Cookery, in All Its Branches: Reduced to a System of Easy Practice, for the Use of Private Families* (Longman, Brown, Green, and Longmans, 1845), 5.
14. E. B. O'Callaghan, *Documents Relating to the Colonial History of the State of New York*, vol. 1 (Albany, 1856).
15. The cows from Barbados and the Bermudas were Spanish in origin. In 1494, Columbus returned to the West Indies with livestock; by 1512, stock-raising had become a lucrative industry. These cows were used primarily for hides, secondarily for meat, and provided less milk in comparison to the English cows.
16. William Hilton's *Relation* (1664), cited in G.A. Bowling, "The Introduction of Cattle into Colonial North America," *Journal of Dairy Science* 25, no. 2 (1942): 149.
17. Thomas Newes (1682), cited in Bowling, 150.
18. Jessica B. Harris, *Sky Juice and Flying Fish: Traditional Caribbean Cooking* (Simon & Schuster, 1991), 19.
19. Psyche Williams-Forson, *Building Houses out of Chicken Legs* (University of North Carolina Press, 2006), 16.
20. Interview with the Caribbean Studies professor Keja Valens, March 12, 2024.
21. Mary Randolph, *The Virginia House-Wife*, ed. Karen Hess (University of South Carolina Press, 1984).

22. Cited in Malcolm Thick, "Sir Hugh Plat's Promotion of Pasta as a Victual for Seamen," *Petits Propos Culinaires*, vol. 40 (1992), 47.
23. Most are loyal to the New Zealand brand Anchor, although independent local cheesemakers are now making inroads.
24. Conversation with the Trinidadian culinary expert Franka Philip, December 19, 2023.
25. Andrew F. Smith, *Pure Ketchup: A History of America's National Condiment, with Recipes* (University of South Carolina Press, 1996), 18.
26. Haitian Creole, or *kreyòl ayisyen*, refers to the language and the people of Haiti. The term "Creole" denotes the unique cultural identity that emerged from the blending of African, European, and Indigenous influences during Haiti's colonial period. Haitian Creoles are descendants of African slaves, French colonizers, and Taíno people. Part pf their rich cultural heritage is reflected in their food; Smith, *Pure Ketchup*, 19.
27. The original source has remained elusive. Most of Hunter's recipes are traceable to other cookbooks, including his macaroni recipes (from Raffald and Mollard, among others), but in the introduction, he merely says that they came to him via professional practitioners.
28. In the same year, Honoré Julien advertised "Tomata catsup" at his shop in Washington, DC. "Honoré Julien Advertisement," *National Intelligencer*, June 25, 1814.
29. Sophie D. Coe, *America's First Cuisines* (University of Texas Press, 1994), 63.
30. Coe, *America's First Cuisines*, 64–65.
31. "Scots in the Caribbean," National Library of Scotland, accessed February 4, 2024, https://www.nls.uk/collections/scotland-and-the-slave-trade/caribbean/.
32. Thomas Young, *Narrative of a Residence on the Mosquito Shore*, 2nd ed. (London: Smith, Elder and Co, 1847), 107.
33. See, for example, *The Pennsylvania Packet and General Advertiser*, December 6, 1783.
34. The same ad appears in the *Philadelphia Gazette & Universal Daily Advertiser*, October 17, 1795.
35. Louis (Lewis) Fresnaye, "To Make Soup of Vermicelli, Maccaroni and Other Kinds of Paste," (The Library Company of Philadelphia, 1802).
36. Murray ended up buying her out for a sizable sum, but he more than made his money back.
37. See, for example, Elizabeth Hammond in *Modern Domestic Cookery, and Useful Receipt Book* (1816).
38. A Lady, *Domestic Economy, and Cookery, for Rich and Poor, Containing an Account of the Best English, Scotch, French, Oriental, and Other Foreign Dishes* (London: Longman, Rees, Orme, Brown, and Green, 1827), 16.
39. Charles Estienne, *Caroli Stephani, De Nutrimentis* (1550), 15; Alexander Hunter, *Culina famulatrix medicinae: Or, Receipts in Cookery by Ignotus* (York: T. Wilson and R. Spence, 1804), 27.
40. Andrew Valentine Kirwan, *Host and Guest: A Book About Dinners, Dinner-Giving, Wines, and Desserts* (London: Bell and Daldy, 1864), 41.
41. Letter to Thomas Jefferson from Martha Jefferson Randolph, January 2, 1808. Mary Randolph took out an ad in the *Virginia Gazette and General Advertiser* to announce vacancy at her boardinghouse, March 4, 1808.

42. Randolph, *Virginia Housewife*, xliv.
43. Interview with the culinary historian Leni Sorensen, February 11, 2024.
44. Christian Isobel Johnstone (writing as Margaret Dods). *The Cook and Housewife's Manual: A Practical System of Modern Domestic Cookery and Family Management.* Edinburgh: Oliver & Boyd, 1826., 31.
45. Letter to Jefferson from Mary Randolph, March 17, 1825.
46. Letter to Randolph from Jefferson, March 30, 1825.
47. Letter to Randolph from James Madison, March 26, 1825.
48. Catherine Clinton, *The Plantation Mistress: Woman's World in the Old South* (Pantheon, 1982), 19.
49. From a very young age, however, children, including girls, were given slaves so that they might learn how to manage human property. See chapter 1 of Stephanie E. Jones-Rogers, *They Were Her Property: White Women as Slave Owners in the American South* (Yale University Press, 2019). A Swedish visitor to the South, Federika Bremer, leaves the following account: "The young girls, I should like to see a little move active in the house and more helpful to their mothers in various ways. But it is not the custom; and the parents, from mistaken kindness, seem not to with their daughters to do anything except to amuse themselves." From *America in the Fifties: Letters of Fredrika Bremer*, ed. Adolph B. Benson (American-Scandinavian Foundation, 1924), 130.
50. Charles Ball, *Fifty Years in Chains: Or, The Life of an American Slave* (University of North Carolina Press, 1997), 218.
51. Ball, *Fifty Years in Chains*, 219.
52. These details have been parsed by numerous authors. For examples, see Barbara Christian, *Black Women Novelists* (Praeger, 1980), 11–12, and Melissa V. Harris-Perry, *Sister Citizen* (Yale University Press, 2013).
53. By 1820, 12 percent of the Black population was African-born; by 1840, it had decreased to 4 percent (Robert William Fogel and Stanley L. Engerman, *Time on the Cross* [Boston, 1974]). As such, in the period under examination, the handing down of African foodways would have been several generations removed from direct transmission, learned from others who had learned in the diaspora.
54. In early nineteenth-century advertising or descriptive language, the word "tolerable" generally meant adequate, competent, or decent—not exceptional, but good enough to meet expectations. It did not have the faintly negative or grudging connotation it carries today. At the time, it was often used in a neutral or even mildly positive sense.
55. Williams-Forson, *Building Houses*, 29.
56. Rebecca Sharpless, *Cooking in Other Women's Kitchens: Domestic Workers in the South, 1865–1960* (University of North Carolina Press, 2010), xxiii.

6. PASTA, POWER, AND PROGRESS: FROM THE ELITE TO THE EVERYDAY

1. Prior to this in Canada, Menon, *La cuisinière bourgeoise: précédée d'un manuel prescrivant les devoirs qu'ont à remplir les personnes qui se destinent à entrer en service dans les maisons bourgeoises* (Quebec: Augustin Germain, 1825), had been published in French.

2. Oddly, Leslie acknowledges neither the author, Louis-Eustache Audot, nor the title of the cookbook. She credits Chef Sulpice Barué, who was taken on as editor in 1827. "Maccaroni pie" predates Barué, while "Maccaroni" is from the revised edition. The revised edition was also published in Belgium in 1829 only under Suplice Barué's name.
3. Jan Longone, "From the Kitchen," *American Magazine and Historical Chronicle* 4, no. 2 (1988): 48.
4. Lydia Maria Child, *The Frugal Housewife. Dedicated to Those Who Are Not Ashamed of Economy* (Boston: Marsh & Capen, 1829), 8.
5. Donna Gabaccia and Jane Aldrich, "Recipes in Context Solving a Small Mystery in Charleston's Culinary History," *Food, Culture & Society* (April 29, 2015): 213.
6. Gabaccia and Aldrich, "Recipes in Context," 207; Caroline (A Lady of Charleston) Gilman, *The Carolina Receipt Book or Housekeeper's Assistant* (Charleston: James S. Burges, 1832), 3.
7. Gilman, *Carolina Receipt Book*, 4.
8. Child would later write the fiercely abolitionist *An Appeal in Favor of That Class of Americans Called Africans* (1833).
9. Lettice Bryan, *The Kentucky Housewife* (Cincinnati: Shepard & Stearns, 1839), vii.
10. Rebecca Sharpless, *Cooking in Other Women's Kitchens: Domestic Workers in the South, 1865–1960* (University of North Carolina Press, 2010), 130.
11. Bryan, *Kentucky Housewife*, vi.
12. For a modern version, see Ali Slagle's "Cauliflower 'Mac' and Cheese," New York Times Cooking, March 26, 2020, https://cooking.nytimes.com/recipes/1020969-cauliflower-mac-and-cheese.
13. Eliza Leslie, *The Lady's Receipt-Book* (Philadelphia: Carey and Hart, 1847), 3.
14. See for example "*Sugo di Manzo*" in *L'economia della città e della campagna, ovvero, Il nuovo cuoco italiano secondo il gusto francese* (1772), 20.
15. A Lady of Rank, *Venice Under the Yoke of France and of Austria* (London: G. and W. B. Whittaker, 1824), 231.
16. A Lady, *Domestic Economy, and Cookery, for Rich and Poor, Containing an Account of the Best English, Scotch, French, Oriental, and Other Foreign Dishes* (London: Longman, Rees, Orme, Brown, and Green, 1827), 285.
17. Bartolommeo Nardini, *Mes perils pendant la révolution de Naples* (Paris: A. Égron, 1806), xvij.
18. Grimod de La Reynière, *Almanach des gourmands*, 5th ed. (Paris: L'imprimrie de Cellot, 1807), 106.
19. *Fior di latte* here means good, whole milk, not to be confused with the fresh string cheese *fiordilatte*.
20. Both of these books were collected works. The original source of the recipe has not yet surfaced.
21. Ada Boni, *Talismano della felicità*, 4th ed. (Rivista "Preziosa," 1934), 12.
22. Eliza Acton, *Modern Cookery in All Its Branches: Reduced to a System of Easy Practice, for the Use of Private Families* (Philadelphia: Lea and Blanchard, 1845), 422–23.
23. Acton, *Modern Cookery in All Its Branches*, 188.
24. Charles Elmé Francatelli, *The Modern Cook: A Practical Guide to the Culinary Art in All Its Branches* (London: Richard Bentley, 1846), vii.
25. Francatelli, *The Modern Cook*, vi.

26. "The Tomato," *The Fredericksburg News*, August 12, 1852, sec. Miscellaneous, 1.
27. Soyer's eccentric reputation and culinary talents may have inspired the character of Alcide Mirobolant in William Makepeace Thackeray's novel *The History of Pendennis*. As a member of the Reform Club, Thackeray would have been familiar with the chef's flamboyant personality.
28. Alexis Soyer, *The Modern Housewife or Ménagère* (New York: Appleton & Company, 1850), 266.
29. Alexis Soyer, *A Shilling Cookery for the People: Embracing an Entirely New System of Plain Cookery and Domestic Economy* (London: G. Routledge, 1855), 10.
30. Charles Dickens, "Common Cookery," *Household Words* 13, no. 305 (1856): 42.
31. Dickens, "Common Cookery," 43. The wording indicates that this may have been written by Dickens's young editor of household matters, Mary Hooper, who would go on to champion the macaroni cause in her own later publications.
32. The English novelist William Makepeace Thackeray and Charles Dickens would parody the figure of the French chef in works such as *Vanity Fair*, *The History of Pendennis*, and *Little Dorrit*.
33. William Andrus Alcott, *Vegetable Diet: As Sanctioned by Medical Men*, 2nd ed. (New York: Fowlers and Wells, 1851), 227.
34. Alcott, *Vegetable Diet*, 306.
35. William Andrus Alcott, "What We May Eat," *American Vegetarian and Health Journal*, (January 1854): 98–99.
36. Sylvester Graham, *Lectures on the Science of Human Life* (Marsh, Capen, Lyon & Webb, 1839), 195–96.
37. Graham, *Lectures on the Science of Human Life*, 158.
38. Graham, *Lectures on the Science of Human Life*, 165.
39. *Penny Magazine* was also distributed in the United States, and newspapers there frequently republished the content, including this article. See the *Phenix Gazette* and *Albany Daily Advertiser* (1833).
40. Charles Knight, "Neapolitan Maccaroni-Eaters," *Penny Magazine of the Society for the Diffusion of Useful Information* 87 (1833): 307.
41. Knight, "Neapolitan Maccaroni-Eaters," 307.
42. Knight, "Neapolitan Maccaroni-Eaters," 307.
43. Alexandre Dumas, *Sketches of Naples*, trans. A. Roland (Philadelphia: E. Ferrett, 1845), 29. Dumas goes on at length about watermelon and ice water, saying, however, that the lazzaroni do not drink water in the summer as the aristocrats do.
44. Mrs. Bliss, *The Practical Cook Book: Containing Upwards of One Thousand Recipes* (Philadelphia: Lippincott, Grambo & Co., 1850), 93.
45. Mrs. N. K. M. Lee, *Cook's Own Book: Being a Complete Culinary Encyclopedia* (Boston: Munroe & Francis, 1832), v.
46. Andrew Combe, *The Physiology of Digestion*, 9th ed. (Edinburgh: Maclachlan and Stewart, 1849), 149.
47. "Notices," *Vegetarian Advocate* (1850): 132.
48. Nairategeva, "Combe on Digestion," *Vegetarian Advocate* 2, no. 7 (1850): 84.
49. "The Vegetarian Treasury—Macaroni," *Vegetarian Messenger* (September 1851): 18.
50. Beccari cited in Eliot F. Beach, "Beccari of Bologna: The Discoverer of Vegetable Protein," *Journal of the History of Medicine and Allied Sciences* 16, no. 4 (1961): 363.

51. Sir Edwin Ray Lankester, *On Food: Being Lectures Delivered at the South Kensington Museum* (London: Robert Hardwicke, 1861), 130.
52. Andrew B. McGowan, "True Bread: Medieval Patriarchs, Ancient Rabbis, and the Modern Magisterium on Leavening, Fermentation, and Gluten," in *On Earth as in Heaven: Liturgy, Materiality, and Economics*, ed. Melanie C. Ross (Liturgical Press Academic, 2025), 282.
53. This is a specific reference in a scientific document to the high gluten content in Italian macaroni: Isaac Burney Yeo, *Food in Health and Disease* (Philadelphia: Lea Brothers, 1890), 81.
54. The original source is Mary Hooker, *The Young Housekeeper's Friend: Or, a Guide to Domestic Economy and Comfort by Mrs Cornelius* (Boston: C. Tappan, 1846), 126.
55. The *Messenger* had actually used the 1851 reprinting in *Pictorial Half-Hours* as its source, a periodical owned by the same publisher, C. Knight, as *Penny Magazine*.
56. "The Vegetarian Treasury—Macaroni," 18.
57. Silvano Serventi and Françoise Sabban, *Pasta: The Story of a Universal Food*, trans. Anthony Shugaar (Columbia University Press, 2002), 129.
58. Isabella Beeton, *Beeton's Book of Household Management* (London: S. O. Beeton, 1861), iii.
59. Beeton, *Beeton's Book of Household Management*, iii.
60. Thomas Webster, "Farinaceous Substances Which Are Used in Various Parts of the World Instead of Bread," in *An Encyclopaedia of Domestic Economy: Comprising Such Subjects as Are Most Immediately Connected with Housekeeping* (London: Longman, Brown, Green and Longmans, 1844), 766.
61. Beeton, *Beeton's Book of Household Management*, 72.
62. Beeton, *Beeton's Book of Household Management*, 72.
63. Scott Reynolds Nelson, *Oceans of Grain: How American Wheat Remade the World* (Basic Books, 2022), 71.
64. Nelson, *Oceans of Grain*, 93.
65. Nelson, *Oceans of Grain*, 88.
66. Nelson, *Oceans of Grain*, 99.
67. Nelson, *Oceans of Grain*, 95.

7. AMERICANS VIE FOR THEIR PIECE OF THE PIE

1. Housekeeper, *The Practical American Cook Book, or, Practical and Scientific Cookery* (New York: D. Appleton and Company, 1855), 6.
2. Rebecca A. Upton, *Home Studies* (Boston: Crosby, Nichols, and Company, 1856), iii.
3. "Republican" here refers to civic virtues promoting the public good—not partisan Republican Party politics.
4. I was able to consult the enlarged edition from 1860, but there is no extant copy of the 1847 copyright edition.
5. J. G. Davis, *Cheese*, vol. 3 (Churchill Livingstone, 1972), 648–49. It has also been suggested that the name is derived from the criss-cross markings left by the flax netting used to hang the bulbous forms as they aged.
6. Harriet Horry Ravenel, *Eliza Pinckney* (New York: Charles Scribner's Sons, 1896), 253.

7. Attested in an import document from London to Philadelphia, October 1871, Box 26, folder 13, NMAH Archives.
8. "The Story of Pineapple Cheese: Connecticut History, June 4, 2022, https://connecticuthistory.org/the-story-of-pineapple-cheese/.
9. Mrs. L. G. Abell, *Woman in Her Various Relations: Containing Practical Rules for American Females* (Holdrege, 1851), 60.
10. See Alexis Soyer, *Soyer's Charitable Cookery; or, The Poor Man's Regenerator* (Simpkin, Marshal & Co., 1847), 520. Sugar was also considered an important food for maintaining health and energy.
11. Plea example "Advertisement," *Southern Cultivator*, January 1861, 58.
12. Andrew F. Smith, *Starving the South* (St. Martin's, 2011), 18.
13. Apples were largely imported from the North. See Smith, *Starving*, 14.
14. Another book of the same title for the same charity appeared in 1876 out of Toledo, Ohio; however, the content differs as these were local compilations.
15. Zach Klitzman and Susan Reyburn, *American Feast: Cookbooks and Cocktails from the Library of Congress* (Library of Congress, 2023), 27.
16. Klitzman and Reyburn, *American Feast*, 27.
17. Cf. introduction, Andrew F. Smith, ed., *Centennial Buckeye Cookbook* (Ohio State University Press, 2000), xliii.
18. Paul Freedman, "American Restaurants and Cuisine in the Mid-Nineteenth Century," *New England Quarterly* 84, no. 1 (2011): 20–21.
19. Freedman, "American Restaurants," 14.
20. Freedman, "American Restaurants," 27.
21. Freedman, "American Restaurants," 40.
22. Robert Gudmestad, *Steamboats and the Rise of the Cotton Kingdom* (Louisiana State University Press, 2011), 62.
23. Herbert Quick and Edward Quick, *Mississippi Steamboatin'* (Holt, 1926), 253.
24. Quick and Quick, *Mississippi Steamboatin'*, 254.
25. Harvey Levenstein, *Revolution at the Table: The Transformation of the American Diet* (University of California Press, 2003), 7.
26. George Byron Merrick, *Old Times on the Upper Mississippi: The Recollections of a Steamboat Pilot from 1854–1863* (Arthur H. Clark Co., 1909), 29.
27. Mathew Carey, *Addresses of the Philadelphia Society for the Promotion of National Industry* (Philadelphia: C. & Son, 1819), 26.
28. Women's Centennial Committees, *National Cookery Book: Compiled from Original Receipts* (Philadelphia: Henry B. Ashmead, 1876), vi.
29. Women's Centennial Committees, *National Cookery Book*, xv.
30. Though the book was prepared before the Civil War, the introduction was likely written just before publication; Maria Massey Barringer, *Dixie Cookery; or, How I Managed My Table for Twelve Years* (Boston: Loring, 1867), 3.
31. Adolphe Meyer, "Culinary Hints from an Old Cookbook," *International Culinary Magazine*, January 4, 1915, 109.
32. Mrs. E. R. Shankland and Sue W. Hetherton, *The Matron's Household Manual* (Debuque: Palmer, Winall & Co., 1875), 5–6.
33. Shankland and Hetherton, *Matron's Household Manual*, 6.
34. David S. Shield, *Southern Provisions: The Creation & Revival of a Cuisine* (University of Chicago Press, 2015), 114.

35. Jessica B. Harris, *High on the Hog* (Bloomsbury, 2011), 117.
36. The 1840 census recorded only sixty-four slaves in the entire state of Pennsylvania; they were most likely elderly individuals born before 1780.
37. Harris, *High on the Hog*, 118.
38. Harris, *High on the Hog*, 120–21.
39. Booker T. Washington, *Up from Slavery*, ed. William L. Andrews (Oxford University Press, 1995), 6.
40. Adrian Miller, *Soul Food: The Surprising Story of an American Cuisine* (University of North Carolina Press, 2013), 19.
41. Psyche Williams-Forson, *Building Houses out of Chicken Legs* (University of North Carolina Press, 2006), 28. Dorothy Schneider and Carl Schneider, *Slavery in America: From Colonial Times to the Civil War*. Facts on File, 2000, 84. Mary V. Thompson, *"The Only Unavoidable Subject of Regret"*: George Washington, Slavery, and the Enslaved Community at Mount Vernon. (Charlottesville: University of Virginia Press, 2019), 235–37.
42. Thompson, *"The Only Unavoidable Subject of Regret,"* 194.
43. According to Thompson, this showed "a more fluid exchange between master and slave than many contemporary Americans would probably think possible. Thompson, *"The Only Unavoidable Subject of Regret,"* 232.
44. Marion Cabell Tyree, ed., *Housekeeping in Old Virginia* (Louisville: J. P. Morthon & Co., 1878), 19.
45. The oyster industry was at its peak in the Chesapeake Bay during this period as recent innovations in dredging technology had greatly increased oyster harvests.
46. Undated single page from the National Museum of American History Archive Center.
47. Karen L. Cox, *Dreaming of Dixie* (University of North Carolina Press, 2011), 3. Recommended reading this for a thorough discussion of the packaging of the South for popular consumption.
48. This appellative of familiarity commonly applied to African American women, an honorific title from Africa that rang with condescension outside its cultural context.
49. Introduction to the 1900 edition in *The Picayune's Creole Cook Book* (The Picayune, 1910), 5.
50. *The Picayune's Creole Cook Book*, 5.
51. *The Picayune's Creole Cook Book*, 6.
52. By the 1816 edition, they stopped including this introduction.
53. *The Picayune's Creole Cook Book*, 183.
54. *The Picayune's Creole Cook Book*, 185.
55. Célestine Eustis, *Cooking in Old Creole Days* (R. H. Russell, 1904), 6.
56. Eustis, *Cooking in Old Creole Days*, 6.
57. "Making Macaroni," reprinted in *The Sidney* (Ohio) *Journal*, May 21, 1873.
58. "Macaroni," *Food Journal*, no. 37 (1873): 8.
59. "Macaroni," 8.
60. John Charles Buckmaster, *Buckmaster's Cookery* (London: George Routledge, 1874), 114.
61. There are two title pages for this book; the other calls it *Fifteen-Cent Dinners for Families of Six*.

62. Juliet Corson, *Fifteen Cent Dinners for Workingmen's Families* (New York, 1877), 14.
63. Corson, *Fifteen Cent Dinners*, 24.
64. Corson, *Fifteen Cent Dinners*, 25.
65. Juliet Corson, *Family Living on $500 a Year: A Daily Reference Book for Young and Inexperienced Housewives* (New York: Harper & Brothers, 1888), 37.
66. Corson, *Family Living on $500 a Year*, 38.
67. "How to Live," *Philadelphia Inquirer*, March 4, 1881.
68. Such efforts drew criticism for encouraging the poor to accept their lot and absolving governments of the responsibility to address systemic poverty.
69. *San Francisco Bulletin*, January 30, 1884.
70. *San Francisco Bulletin*, January 30, 1884.
71. *Dupuyer Acantha*, June 9, 1898.
72. Tanneries in the nineteenth century were infamous for their overpowering stench, largely due to the use of ammonia-rich urine, which was essential for softening hides and removing hair during the tanning process.
73. D. R. Locke, "Italian Macaroni," reprinted from the *Toledo Blade* in the *Clinton Evening News*, February 6, 1884.
74. *Trenton Gazette*, October 9, 1884.
75. "Succulent Macaroni—Sunny Italy's National Dish," *Baltimore American*, October 26, 1886.
76. *New York Mail and Express*, reprinted in the *Turner Falls Reporter* May 9, 1888.
77. *Maine Farmer*, November 15, 1888.
78. *Pittsburg Press*, February 9, 1890.
79. 53rd Congress, first session, 1893.
80. "Even Macaroni," *New York Times*, October 14, 1892.
81. *New-York Tribune*, November 2, 1892.
82. *New-York Tribune*, November 2, 1892.
83. "Making Macaroni," *Newark Sunday Call*, October 2, 1892.
84. *Daily Reporter*, May 2, 1895.
85. The price of imported macaroni decreased following the Wilson-Gorman Tariff Act of 1894, a Democratic effort to lower protective tariffs; however, tariffs were raised again under the Republican-backed Dingley Tariff Act of 1897, reflecting a return to protectionist policies aimed at shielding US industries from foreign competition.
86. Cf. Mary Elizabeth Green, *Food Products of the World*, 6th ed. (Chicago: Frazer, 1896), 172–76. Strong claims to the contrary were frequently voiced.
87. "West Finds Wealth in Macaroni Wheat," *Colorado Springs Gazette*, December 11, 1905.
88. James B. Simpson, "France, Italy, Texas," *Wisconsin Weekly Advocate*, April 19, 1900.
89. "American Macaroni Industry May Be Supplied Soon by Wheat from Texas," *Washington Bee*, April 28, 1900; "Wheat for Macaroni" *Afro-American Advance*, May 12, 1900. By this time, macaroni and cheese was well embedded in the culinary culture of Texas, as seen in *The First Texas Cook Book* (1883).
90. "Home-grown Macaroni," *Wichita Searchlight*, December 21, 1901.
91. Prof. W. S. Scarborough, "A Day in Naples," *Freeman*, December 28, 1901.
92. Durum wheat exports for 1906 in bushels: Italy 6,208,095; France 2,803,518; Germany 1,007,116;. "Our Macaroni Wheat Exports," *Wisconsin Weekly Advocate*, June 27, 1907.

93. "New Kind of Wheat," *Bismark Daily Tribune*, September 8, 1904.
94. Robert P. Skinner, *Manufacture of Semolina and Macaroni* (Government Printing Office, 1902), 31.
95. George Julian Carr, *International Trade in Macaroni Products*, Bulletin 788 (Government Printing Office, 1932), ii. These figures included other pasta shapes that were still under the broader umbrella term—with the exception of spaghetti and vermicelli.
96. Cecil Salmon and J. Allen Clark, *Durum Wheat*, farmer's bulletin 534 (Government Printing Office, 1913), 15.
97. Alice Gitchell Kirk, *Practical Food Economy* (Little, Brown, 1917), 113.
98. *New-York Tribune*, January 24, 1904.
99. The printing was ca. 1910. The extant ca. 1916 version is the fifth edition.
100. Henry Stewart, *American Cheese and Cheese-Making* (Philadelphia: J. B. Lippincott Company, 1898), 3. Exports increased from 10,000 lb in 1830 to 129,584,981 lb in 1880.
101. Others were working on the same project. The Swiss dairymen Walter Gerber and Fritz Stettler patented their own process in 1911.

8. MACARONI'S AMERICAN SOUL: BRINGING IT HOME

1. Fannie Merritt Farmer, *The Boston Cooking-School Cook Book* (Boston: Little, Brown, 1896), 86. It was an immediate classic. Publication continues to this day.
2. "Food and This Nation's Fate," *Evening Star*, January 10, 1918.
3. When the formal proposal was brought before Congress in 1923, it met with a decided backlash from the NAACP and was ultimately rejected.
4. Toni Tipton-Martin, *The Jemima Code* (University of Texas Press, 2015), 37.
5. Tipton-Martin, *The Jemima Code*, 46.
6. Marion W. Flexner, *Dixie Dishes* (Hale, Cushman & Flint, 1941), x.
7. Flexner, *Dixie Dishes*, 125–26.
8. This may have been a self-published work; as such, the choice may have been her own.
9. See, for example, Felix Délée, *The Franco-American Cookery Book; or, How to Live Well and Wisely Every Day in the Year* (1884).
10. Of the two cookbooks published by African American women in their own name that predate this, Malinda Russell's *A Domestic Cook Book* (1866) and *What Mrs. Fisher Knows About Old Southern Cooking* (1881), neither has a recipe for macaroni and cheese.
11. Isabel Eaton, "Special Report on Negro Domestic Service in the Seventh Ward Philadelphia," in W. E. B. DuBois, *The Philadelphia Negro: A Social Study* (University of Pennsylvania Press, 1996), 427–28.
12. There was a significant wave of West Indians from 1900 to 1930, particularly during World War I and following the completion of the Panama Canal, which had brought in two hundred thousand Afro-Caribbean immigrants, many of whom relocated to North America, later curtailed by the Johnson-Reed Immigration act of 1924. Damani Davis, "Ancestors from the West Indies," National Archives, September 6, 2024, https://www.archives.gov/publications/prologue/2013/fall-winter/ancestors-from-west-indies.

13. Unlike Kraft's 1916 processed-cheese patent, which relied on emulsifying salts to stabilize the product and prevent separation, Velveeta's 1923 process used a unique blending technique that retained whey proteins, allowing for a creamy, shelf-stable texture without relying on Kraft's emulsification method. The Pabst process was based on the same principle as Velveeta.
14. "In Days Gone Dry," *Pabst Mansion Newsletter*, September 2020, 3.
15. Lucius L. Van Slyke and Walter V. Price, *Cheese* (Orange Judd, 1927), 206.
16. Van Slyke and Price, *Cheese*, 206.
17. The most popular dish in *Modernist Cuisine at Home* honors Kraft by adding sodium citrate as an emulsifier, creating creaminess without the need for starchy binders.
18. "Pabst-Ett Macaroni: Instead of Macaroni and Cheese," *Macaroni Journal*, December 15, 1927, 30.
19. The Kraft Heinz Company ignored my initial emails and then denied my request for an interview. The information available is all undocumented hearsay, each one feeding off the other's unsubstantiated claims.
20. A spokesman for Kraft Inc. reported the cheese sales version to the *Northwest Herald* of Illinois, March 4, 1987.
21. Cellophane was invented in 1908 by the Swiss chemist Jacques Brandenberger and gained popularity throughout the 1920s and 1930s, especially in food packaging. It is logical that he would have used cellophane, as plastic wrap and baggies had not yet been invented, but this is my own supposition.
22. A commemorative marker on the Skinner Macaroni Building states that in 1927 the company "introduced Cheesroni, one of the first macaroni and cheese products." But further details about the product were unavailable. "Skinner Macaroni Building 1914–1915," hmdb.org, https://www.hmdb.org/m.asp?m=83293, accessed June 9, 2025.
23. An analogous discussion related to chicken and the African American culinary identity is discussed in Psyche Williams-Forson, *Building Houses out of Chicken Legs* (University of North Carolina Press, 2006).
24. This austere recipe appeared again in Alice Bradley's 1943 *The Wartime Cookbook*.
25. Paul Freedman points out that *Louisiana's Fabulous Foods and How to Cook Them* (1930) acknowledges French, Italian, Spanish, and Native American influence but African Americans are never mentioned. *American Cuisine and How It Got That Way* (Liveright, 2019), 44.
26. Many thanks to Jennifer Harbster, Head of the Science Reference Section at the Library of Congress, who allowed me access to the Constance Carter Room of uncatalogued historical charity and community cookbooks.
27. America was preparing for possible entry into World War II, and the prospect of such a massive protest highlighting racial discrimination at home while fighting overseas deeply worried the Roosevelt administration. Eleanor Roosevelt in particular recognized the gravity of the situation. A. Philip Randolph strategically used this leverage, refusing to back down until President Roosevelt issued Executive Order 8802, which banned racial discrimination in defense industry hiring and created the Fair Employment Practice Committee to enforce it.
28. Richard's fame earned her a cooking show on a local TV channel—the first Black woman to host her own show, in an era when few even owned televisions. Sadly, no footage survives, so it's unknown if macaroni and cheese ever made an appearance.

29. Kraft's Cheez Whiz was originally created as a way to make Welsh rarebit quickly and easily but was later fashioned as Macaroni and Cheeze Whiz.
30. The start date is uncertain and may be 1949. For an in-depth contextual analysis of Lena Richard's contribution, see Ashley Rose Young, "Nourishing Networks: The Public Culture of Food in Nineteenth-Century America," (PhD dissertation, Duke University, 2017), 338–58.
31. Freda DeKnight, *Date with a Dish* (Hermitage, 1948), 2.
32. DeKnight, *Date with a Dish*, 2.
33. George Washington Carver, *How to Grow the Peanut: And 105 Ways of Preparing It for Human Consumption* (Tuskegee Normal and Industrial Institute, 1917), 18.
34. Southern food traditions had made purchase in Paris from the very first nightclub, Ida Smith's Bricktop. The Kentuckian Leroy Haynes opened Haynes' Soul Food Restaurant in 1949. Soul food was eaten in the South during segregation, "a good meal [that] will put you in the religious faith," but for Southerners, it was not a distinct category. It was just food. From an interview with Ashbell McElveen, founder of the James Hemings Society, September 15, 2024.
35. Sheila Bock, "'I Know You Got Soul': Traditionalizing a Contested Cuisine," in *Comfort Food: Meanings and Memories*, ed. Michael Owen Jones and Lucy Long (University Press of Mississippi, 2017), 166.
36. Fredrick Douglas Opie, *Hog and Hominy: Soul Food from Africa to America* (Columbia University Press, n.d.), 137.
37. Opie, *Hog and Hominy*, 150.
38. Jessica B. Harris, *High on the Hog* (Bloomsbury, 2011), 203.
39. Bob Jeffries, *Soul Food Cook Book* (Bobbs-Merrill, 1969), vii.
40. Of note in the genre are Sheila Ferguson, *Soul Food: Classic Cuisine from the Deep South* (1989); Kathy Starr, *The Soul of Southern Cooking* (1989); Leah Chase *The Dooky Chase Cookbook* (1990); Sylvia Woods, *Sylvia's Soul Food* (1992); Joyce White, *Soul Food: Recipes and Reflections from African American Churches* (1998); Sylvia Woods and family with Melissa Clark, *Sylvia's Family Soul Food Cookbook* (1999); and Robbie Montgomery, *Sweetie Pie's Cookbook: Soulful Southern Recipes, from My Family to Yours* (2015).
41. Pearl Bowser and Joan Eckstein, *A Pinch of Soul* (Avon, 1970), 12.
42. Patti LaBelle, the "Godmother of Soul," follows suit with "Over the Top Top Top Macaroni and Cheese" in *Recipes for the Good Life* (2008).
43. Pearl Bailey, *Pearl's Kitchen: An Extraordinary Cookbook* (Harcourt Brace Jovanovich, 1973), 145–46.
44. Bailey, *Pearl's Kitchen*, 147.
45. Bailey, *Pearl's Kitchen*, 40.
46. Interview with the culinary historian Thérèse Nelson, September 8, 2024, blackculinaryhistory.com.
47. Elijah Muhammad, *How to Eat to Live, Book One* (Secretarius MEMPS Ministries, 1967), 31.
48. See, for example, Joe Randall and Toni Tipton-Martin, *A Taste of Heritage: The New African American Cuisine* (1998), and Jessica Harris, Albert Lukas, and Jerome Grant, *Sweet Home Café Cookbook: A Celebration of African American Cooking* (2018).
49. Opie, *Hog and Hominy*, 172.

50. Carla Hall, "The Creamiest Stovetop Mac and Cheese," January 24, 2024, https://carlahall.com/the-creamiest-stovetop-mac-and-cheese/; Carla Hall, "The Only Four Cheese Mac and Cheese Recipe You Need," November 18, 2022, https://carlahall.com/the-only-four-cheese-mac-and-cheese-recipe-you-need/.
51. From interviews carried out October 1–4, 2024, at the Smithsonian's National Museum of African American History and Culture.
52. Kwanzaa, created in 1966 by Dr. Maulana Karenga, is a week-long celebration honoring African American culture and heritage. *Karamu* is a festive communal meal held on December 31 during Kwanzaa, focusing on unity and gratitude.
53. Karima Moyer-Nocchi and Adrian Miller, "The Fascinating History of Mac and Cheese, America's Favorite Comfort Food," Epicurious, September 26, 2022, https://www.epicurious.com/ingredients/who-invented-mac-and-cheese.
54. Cf. Williams-Forson, *Building Houses*, 199.
55. "Thanksgiving Song," https://www.youtube.com/watch?v=FT7CorlMqVc. Thank you, Jessica Harris, for sending this on.
56. The quotation is in the reissue of the 1995 edition (with a new foreword by Carla Hall): Jessica B. Harris, *A Kwanzaa Keepsake and Cookbook* (Scribner, 2024), 83.
57. Interview with Delilah Winder, October 2, 2024. To curb the mounting surplus of dairy products, the government lowered price supports in the 1980s, reducing incentives for farmers to overproduce. This was followed by the Dairy Termination Program (1986–1987), which paid farmers to cull their herds and halt milk production for five years. These measures gradually shrank the stockpiles of government cheese, and by the early 1990s, the large-scale distribution to low-income families ceased as surpluses dried up and the program was no longer necessary.
58. Delilah Winder, *Delilah's Everyday Soul* copyright © 2006. Reprinted by permission of Running Press Adult, an imprint of Hachette Book Group, Inc.
59. Jordan D. Troisi and Shira Gabriel, "Chicken Soup Really Is Good for the Soul: 'Comfort Food' Fulfills the Need to Belong," *Psychological Science* 22, no. 6 (June 2011): 747–53.
60. "Kraft Macaroni and Cheese Is Changing Its Name and Iconic Blue Box Introducing . . . Kraft Mac & Cheese," Kraft Heinz, June 22, 2022, https://news.kraftheinzcompany.com/press-releases-details/2022/Kraft-Macaroni-and-Cheese-Is-Changing-Its-Name-and-Iconic-Blue-Box-Introducing . . .-Kraft-Mac--Cheese/default.aspx.
61. Harris, *High on the Hog*, 232.
62. "Macaroni and Cheese" from *The Gift of Southern Cooking: Recipes and Revelations from Two Great American Cooks: A Cookbook* by Edna Lewis and Scott Peacock with David Nussbaum, copyright © 2003 by Edna Lewis and Scott Peacock. Used by permission of Alfred A. Knopf, an imprint of the Knopf Doubleday Publishing Group, a division of Penguin Random House LLC. All rights reserved.
63. Joan Swartz, *Macaroni & Cheese: 52 Recipes from Simple to the Sublime* (2001); Marlena Spieler and Noel Barnhurst, *Macaroni & Cheese* (2005); (my pick) Stefanie Stiavetti and Garrett McCord, *Melt: The Art of Macaroni and Cheese* (2013); Allison Arevalo and Erin Wade, *The Mac + Cheese Cookbook: 50 Simple Recipes from Homeroom, America's Favorite Mac and Cheese Restaurant* (2013); Malachi Jenkins and Roberto Smith, *Trap Kitchen: Mac N' All Over The World: Bangin' Mac

N' Cheese Recipes from Around the World (2022); and Ivory Ray, *Mac & Cheese Cookbook: The Ultimate Collection for Mac & Cheese Recipes* (2024).

64. Michael Owen Jones and Lucy Long, eds., *Comfort Food: Meanings and Memories* (University Press of Mississippi, 2017), 5.
65. *Fettuccine Alfredo: La ricetta originale delRristorante Alfredo alla Scrofa*, accessed November 14, 2024, https://www.youtube.com/watch?v=Sk9HCxfIREo.
66. The current owner, Matteo Mozzetti, explained to me in a 2018 interview the history of the decision not to patent and that it is not a product that one can simply put into a jar; it is a technique, not a sauce. He had changed his mind by 2020: "La Salsa Alfredo arriva a casa in barattolo. Idea del mitico ristorante romano delle Fettuccine," Gambero Rosso, May 9, 2020, https://www.gamberorosso.it/notizie/la-salsa-alfredo-arriva-a-casa-in-barattolo-idea-del-mitico-ristorante-romano-delle-fettuccine/.
67. There is an Italian pasta called *gomiti*, which means elbows, but it is a tiny soup pasta.
68. Melissa Clark, "Four-Cheese Macaroni and Cheese," New York Times Cooking, accessed June 9, 2025, https://cooking.nytimes.com/recipes/1014635-four-cheese-macaroni-and-cheese.
69. Judy Joo, "Kimchi Mac and Cheese," https://www.judyjoo.com/recipes/kimchi-mac-and-cheese-42/, accessed December 1, 2024; Lucy Nunes, "Mac 'n' Cheese Spring Rolls," Taste.com.au, https://www.taste.com.au/recipes/mac-n-cheese-spring-rolls-recipe/bzmgqd7r, accessed December 1, 2024; "Mac 'n' Cheese Birria Taco," Krispy Boyz, https://www.thekrispyboyz.com/, accessed June 9, 2025.

BIBLIOGRAPHY

SECONDARY SOURCES

Ballerini, Luigi. "Bockenheim Revisited." *Gastronomica* 3, no. 2 (2003): 50–63.

——. "Food for the Bawdy: Johann of Bockenheim's Registrum Coquine." *Gastronomica* 1, no. 3 (2001): 32–39.

——. *The Art of Cooking: The First Modern Cookery Book*. University of California Press, 2005.

Beach, Eliot F. "Beccari of Bologna: The Discoverer of Vegetable Protein." *Journal of the History of Medicine and Allied Sciences* 16, no. 4 (1961): 354–73.

Bienassis, Loïc, and Antonella Campanini. "La reine à la fourchette et autres histoires. Ce que la table française emprunta à l'Italie: analyse critique d'un mythe." In *La table de la Renaissance. Le mythe italien*, ed. Florent Quellier and Pascal Brioist, 29–88. Presses universitaires François-Rabelais, 2018.

Bock, Sheila. " 'I Know You Got Soul': Traditionalizing a Contested Cuisine." In *Comfort Food: Meanings and Memories*, ed. Michael Owen Jones and Lucy Long. University Press of Mississippi, 2017.

Bower, Anne L. *African American Foodways*. University of Illinois Press, 2007.

Bowling, G.A. "The Introduction of Cattle Into Colonial North America." *Journal of Dairy Science* 25, no. 2 (February 1, 1942): 129–54.

Brucker, Gene A. " 'The Horseshoe Nail': Structure and Contingency in Medieval and Renaissance Italy." *Renaissance Quarterly* 54, no. 1 (2001): 1–19.

Buccini, Anthony. "The Merchants of Genoa and the Diffusion of Southern Italian Pasta Culture in Europe." In *Food and Markets: Proceedings of the Oxford Symposium on Food and Cookery 2014*, ed. Mark McWilliams, 54–64. Prospect, 2015.

Campanini, Antonella. "The Illusive Story of Catherine de' Medici." *The New Gastronome* (blog), December 18, 2018. https://thenewgastronome.com/caterina-de-medici-a-gastronomic-myth/.

Cardenas, Diana. "Let Not Thy Food Be Confused with Thy Medicine: The Hippocratic Misquotation." *E-SPEN Journal* 8, no. 6 (2013): e260–62.

Carson, Jane. *Colonial Virginia Cookery: Procedures, Equipment, and Ingredients in Colonial Cooking, Williamsburg*. Colonial Williamsburg Foundation, n.d.

Cesari, Luca. *Storia della pasta in dieci piatti*. Il Saggiatore, 2021.

Clinton, Catherine. *The Plantation Mistress: Woman's World in the Old South*. Pantheon, 1982.

Coe, Sophie D. *America's First Cuisines*. University of Texas Press, 1994.

Cogliano, Francis D. *A Revolutionary Friendship: Washington, Jefferson, and the American Republic*. Harvard University Press, 2024.

Cox, Karen L. *Dreaming of Dixie*. University of North Carolina Press, 2011.

Cross, John A. "Changing Patterns of Cheese Manufacturing in America's Dairyland." *Geographical Review* 102, no. 4 (2012): 525–38.

Dalby, Andrew. *Food in the Ancient World from A-Z*. Routledge, 2003.

Davis, Angela Y. *Women, Race and Class*. Random House, 1983.

Davis, Damani. "Ancestors from the West Indies." National Archives, September 6, 2024. https://www.archives.gov/publications/prologue/2013/fall-winter/ancestors-from-west-indies.

Davis, J. G. *Cheese*. Vol. 3. Churchill Livingstone, 1972.

Diner, Hasia R. *Hungering for America: Italian, Irish, and Jewish Foodways in the Age of Migration*. Harvard University Press, 2023.

Edgar, Gordon. *Cheddar: A Journey to the Heart of America's Most Iconic Cheese*. Chelsea Green, 2015.Egerton, John. *Southern Food*. University of North Carolina Press, n.d.

Fanto Deetz, Kelley. *Bound to the Fire: How Virginia's Enslaved Cooks Helped Invent American Cuisine*. University Press of Kentucky, 2017.

Farrison, W. Edward. "The Origin of Brown's Clotel." *Phylon (1940–1956)* 15, no. 4 (1954): 347–54.

Ferris, Marcie Cohen. *The Edible South*. University of North Carolina Press, 2014.

Fleming, Tom, and Alice Fleming. "Jefferson's House on the Hill." *Cosmopolitan* 154, no. 3 (1963).

Fowler, W. Warde. "Mundus Patet. 24th August, 5th October, 8th November." *Journal of Roman Studies* 2 (1912): 25–33.

Freedman, Paul. "American Restaurants and Cuisine in the Mid-Nineteenth Century." *New England Quarterly* 84, no. 1 (2011): 5–59

——. *American Cuisine and How It Got That Way*. Liveright, 2019.

Gabaccia, Donna, and Jane Aldrich. "Recipes in Context Solving a Small Mystery in Charleston's Culinary History." *Food, Culture and Society* (April 2015): 197–221.

Galoppini, Laura. "L'isola dei maccheroni." *Medioevo* 9, no. 80 (2003): 42–49.

Ganeshram, Ramin. *The General's Cook: A Novel*. Arcade Publishing, 2018.

"Golden Ray Margarine." https://www.youtube.com/watch?v=zrHJcy_7730, accessed June 9, 2025.

Gordon-Reed, Annette. *The Hemingses of Monticello: An American Family*. Norton, 2008.

Gudmestad, Robert. *Steamboats and the Rise of the Cotton Kingdom*. Louisiana State University Press, 2011.

Harbury, Katherine. *Colonial Virginia's Cooking Dynasty*. University of South Carolina Press, 2004.

Harris, Jessica B. *High on the Hog*. Bloomsbury, 2011.
Haulman, Kate. "Fashion and the Culture Wars of Revolutionary Philadelphia." *William and Mary Quarterly* 62, no. 4 (2005): 625–62.
Hecht, J. J. *The Domestic Servant Class in Eighteenth-Century England*. Routledge and Kegan Paul, 1956.
Henzen, Manon. "Early Dutch Cookbook: 1737 Jacob and Isabella Scott," August 15, 2023.
Hess, Karen. "Jefferson, Thomas." In *The New Encyclopedia of Southern Culture*, ed. John T. Edge. Vol. 7: Foodways, n.d.
Hieatt, C. B. "How Arabic Traditions Travelled to England." In *Food on the Move: Proceedings of the Oxford Symposium 1996*, ed. Harlan Walker. Prospect, 1996.
Hieatt, Constance B., and Sharon Butler, eds., *Curye on Inglysch: English Culinary Manuscripts of the Fourteenth Century (Including the Forme of Cury)*, Oxford University Press, 1985.
Hieatt, Constance B., and Robin F. Jones. "Two Anglo-Norman Culinary Collections Edited from British Library Manuscripts Additional 32085 and Royal 12.C.Xii." *Speculum* 61, no. 4 (1986): 859–82.
Hildebrand, Caz, and Jacob Kennedy. *The Geometry of Pasta*. Quirk, 2010.
Holmes, Frederic L. "Elementary Analysis and the Origins of Physiological Chemistry." *Isis* 54, no. 1 (1963): 50–81.
Jones, Michael Owen, and Lucy Long, eds. *Comfort Food: Meanings and Memories*. University Press of Mississippi, 2017.
Ketcham Wheaton, Barbara. *Savoring the Past: The French Kitchen and Table from 1300 to 1789*. Touchstone, 1996.
Kimball, Marie Goebel. *Thomas Jefferson's Cookbook*. Garrett & Massie, 1938.
Klitzman, Zach, and Susan Reyburn. *American Feast: Cookbooks and Cocktails from the Library of Congress*. Library of Congress, 2023.
Koger, Larry. *Black Slaveowners: Free Black Slave Masters in South Carolina*. University of South Carolina Press, 1995.
Korsmeyer, Carolyn. *Making Sense of Taste: Food and Philosophy*. Cornell University Press, 2014.
"Kraft Macaroni and Cheese Is Changing Its Name and Iconic Blue Box Introducing . . . Kraft Mac & Cheese." Accessed February 21, 2025. https://news.kraftheinzcompany.com/press-releases-details/2022/Kraft-Macaroni-and-Cheese-Is-Changing-Its-Name-and-Iconic-Blue-Box-Introducing . . .-Kraft-Mac--Cheese/default.aspx.
La Varenne, Françios Pierre de. *La Varenne's Cookery*. Ed. and trans. Terence Scully. Prospect, 2005.
Laurioux, Bruno. " 'Le Registre de Cuisine' de Jean de Bockenheim, Cuisinier Du Pape Martin V." *Mélanges de l'Ecole française de Rome: Moyen-Age, Temps modernes* 100, no. 2 (1988): 709–60.
——. *Le règne de Taillevent: Livres et pratiques culinaires à la fin du Moyen Âge*. Éditions de la Sorbonne, 1997.
——. "De Jean de Bockenheim à Bartolomeo Scappi : cuisiner pour le pape entre le XVe et le XVIe siècle." *Offices et papauté (XIVe-XVIIe siècle) : charges, hommes, destins* (2004): 303–32.
Lazard, Madeleine, and Gilbert Schrenck, eds. *Pierre de L'Estoile, Registre-Journal du règne de Henri III*. Vol. I (1574–1575). Droz, 1992.

Lear, Tobias, and Bartholomew Dandridge. "Washington's Household Account Book, 1793–1797 (Continued)." *Pennsylvania Magazine of History and Biography* 31, no. 2 (1907): 176–94.

Lehmann, Gilly. "The Cook as Artist?" In *Food in the Arts: Proceedings of the Oxford Symposium on Food and Cookery*, ed. Harlan Walker. Prospect, 1998.

Levenstein, Harvey. *Revolution at the Table: The Transformation of the American Diet.* University of California Press, 2003.

Longone, Jan. "From the Kitchen." *American Magazine and Historical Chronicle* 4, no. 2 (1988): 47–55.

Marks, Arthur. "Angelica Kauffmann and Some Americans on the Grand Tour." *American Art Journal* 12, no. 2 (1980): 4–24.

Martellotti, Anna. *I ricettari di Federico II: Dal meridionale al liber de coquina.* Olschiki, 2007.

McCormick, Michael. "Rats, Communications, and Plague: Toward an Ecological History." *Journal of Interdisciplinary History* 34, no. 1 (2003): 1–25.

McLaughlin, Jack. *Jefferson and Monticello: The Biography of a Builder.* Holt, 1990.

M'Clure, W. Frank. "The Manufacture of Macaroni." *Scientific American* 92, no. 1 (1905): 5.

McGowan, Andrew B. "True Bread: Medieval Patriarchs, Ancient Rabbis, and the Modern Magisterium on Leavening, Fermentation, and Gluten." In *On Earth as in Heaven: Liturgy, Materiality, and Economics*, ed. Melanie C. Ross. Collegeville, MN: Liturgical Press Academic, 2025.

McMillan, Brenda F. "Soul Food She." *American Poetry Review* 28, no. 5 (1999): 15.

Medearis, Angela Shelf. *The African-American Kitchen: Cooking from Our Heritage.* Dutton, 1994.

Miller, Adrian. *Soul Food: The Surprising Story of an American Cuisine.* University of North Carolina Press, 2013.

Mitchell, B. W. "Merlin and Macaroni." *Classical Weekly* 25, no. 5 (1931): 33–39.

Morrison, A. J., ed. *Travels in Virginia in Revolutionary Times.* J. P. Bell, 1922.

Moses, Marissa, and Pathmanathan Umaharan. "Genetic Structure and Phylogenetic Relationships of Capsicum Chinense." *Journal of the American Society for Horticultural Science* 137, no. 4 (2012): 250–62.

Moyer-Nocchi, Karima, and Adrian Miller. "The Fascinating History of Mac and Cheese, America's Favorite Comfort Food." Epicurious, September 26, 2022. https://www.epicurious.com/ingredients/who-invented-mac-and-cheese.

Nelson, Scott Reynolds. *Oceans of Grain: How American Wheat Remade the World.* Basic Books, 2022.

nettles, kimberly d. "'Saving' Soul Food." *Gastronomica* 7, no. 3 (2007): 106–13.

Nicholls, William H. "Post-War Concentration in the Cheese Industry." *Journal of Political Economy* 47, no. 6 (1939): 823–45.

Nystrom, Justin A. *Creole Italian: Sicilian Immigrants and the Shaping of the New Orleans Food Culture.* University of Georgia Press, 2018.

O'Callaghan, E. B. *Documents Relating to the Colonial History of the State of New York.* Vol. 1. Albany, 1856.

Opie, Fredrick Douglas. *Hog and Hominy: Soul Food from Africa to America.* Columbia University Press, n.d.

Pabst Mansion Newsletter. "In Days Gone Dry." September 2020.

Parks, George B. "The First Italianate Englishmen." *Studies in the Renaissance* 8 (1961): 197–216.

Pei, Mario. *The Story of Language*. Lippincott, 1949.
Pennell, Elizabeth Robins. *My Cookery Books*. Houghton Mifflin, 1903.
Perry, Charles. "What Was Tracta?" *Petits propos culinaires*, no. 12 (1982): 37–39.
Horry, Harriott Pinkney. *A Colonial Plantation Cookbook: The Receipt Book of Harriet Pinckney Horry, 1770*, ed. Richard J. Hooker. University of South Carolina, 1984.
Pinkard, Susan. *A Revolution in Taste: The Rise of French Cuisine*. Cambridge University Press, 2009.
A Pocket Guide to Italy. Armed Forces Information and Education, Department of Defense, 1964.
Prezzolini, Giuseppe. *Spaghetti Dinner*. Greenville: Coachwhip, 2018.
Quick, Herbert, and Edward Quick. *Mississippi Steamboatin'*. Holt, 1926.
Resurgam in Chicago Herald. "How Macaroni Is Made." *Atchison Daily Champion*, January 8, 1890. Nineteenth Century U.S. Newspapers.
Riello, Giorgio. "A Taste of Italy: Italian Businesses and the Culinary Delicacies of Georgian London." *London Journal* 31, no. 2 (2006): 201–22.
Romm, Cari. "Why Comfort Food Comforts." *The Atlantic* (blog), April 3, 2015. https://www.theatlantic.com/health/archive/2015/04/why-comfort-food-comforts/389613/.
Rosada, Bruno. *Il Settecento veneziano. La letteratura*. Corbo e Fiore, 2007.
Royet J. P., D. Meunier, N. Torquet, A. M. Mouly, and T. Jiang. "The Neural Bases of Disgust for Cheese: An fMRI Study." *Frontiers in Human Neuroscience* 10, no. 511 (2016).
"Safeguarding Cheese." *Canadian Journal of Public Health* 37, no. 1 (1946): 28–30.
Sanders, Ewoud. *Woorden met een verhaal*. Prometheus, 2004.
Scully, Terence, ed. *Cuoco Napoletano: The Neapolitan Recipe Collection*. Trans. Terence Scully. University of Michigan Press, 2015.
Serventi, Silvano, and Françoise Sabban. *Pasta: The Story of a Universal Food*. Trans. Anthony Shugaar. Columbia University Press, 2002.
Sharpless, Rebecca. *Cooking in Other Women's Kitchens: Domestic Workers in the South, 1865–1960*. University of North Carolina Press, 2010.
Shield, David S. *Southern Provisions: The Creation & Revival of a Cuisine*. University of Chicago Press, 2015.
Schneider, Dorothy and Schneider, Carl. *Slavery in America: From Colonial Times to the Civil War*. Facts On File, 2000
Smith, Andrew F. *Pure Ketchup: A History of America's National Condiment, with Recipes*. University of South Carolina Press, 1996.
——. *Starving the South*. St. Martin's, 2011.
Smith, Andrew F., ed. *Centennial Buckeye Cookbook*. Ohio State University Press, 2000.
Stanton, Lucia. *Free Some Day: The African-American Families of Monticello*. University of North Carolina Press, 2000.
——. *Those Who Labor for My Happiness: Slavery at Thomas Jefferson's Monticello*. University of Virginia Press, 2012.
"Story of Pineapple Cheese, The." June 4, 2022. https://connecticuthistory.org/the-story-of-pineapple-cheese/, accessed June 29, 2024.
"Thanksgiving Song." https://www.youtube.com/watch?v=FT7CorlMqVc, accessed June 9, 2025.
Thick, Malcolm. "Sir Hugh Plat's Promotion of Pasta as a Victual for Seamen," *Petits Propos Culinaires* Vol. 40 (1992). 43–50.
Thompson, Mary V. *"The Only Unavoidable Subject of Regret" : George Washington, Slavery, and the Enslaved Community at Mount Vernon*. University of Virginia Press, 2019.

Tipton-Martin, Toni. *The Jemima Code*. University of Texas Press, 2015.

Troisi, Jordan D., and Shira Gabriel. "Chicken Soup Really Is Good for the Soul: 'Comfort Food' Fulfills the Need to Belong." *Psychological Science* 22, no. 6 (2011): 747–53.

Van Slyke, Lucius L., and Walter V. Price. *Cheese*. Orange Judd, 1927.

Wade, Richard C. *Slavery in the Cities: The South 1820–1860*. Oxford University Press, 1964.

Washington, Booker T. *Up from Slavery*. Ed. William L. Andrews. Oxford University Press, 1995.

Wheelis, Mark. "Biological Warfare at the 1346 Siege of Caffa." *Emerging Infectious Diseases* 8, no. 9 (2002): 971–75.

Williams-Forson, Psyche. *Building Houses out of Chicken Legs*. University of North Carolina Press, 2006.

Wilson, Anne. *The Cookbook Library*. University of California, 2012.

Witt, Doris. *Black Hunger: Soul Food and America*. University of Minnesota Press, 2004.

Wolf, Edwin, and Kevin J. Hayes. *The Library of Benjamin Franklin*. American Philosophical Society, 2006.

Wright, Clifford A. "The History of Macaroni." *Clifford A. Wright Archive*. https://mbarchives.blogspot.com/2006/09/history-of-macaroni-by-clifford-wright.html, accessed June 10, 2021.

Young, Ashley Rose. "Nourishing Networks: The Public Culture of Food in Nineteenth-Century America." PhD dissertation, Duke University, 2017.

COOKBOOKS AND HISTORICAL TEXTS

A B C of Cooking: For Men with No Experience of Cooking on Small Boats, Patrol Boats, in Camps, on Marches, Etc., The. Moffat, Yard, and Company, 1917.

A Lady. *Domestic Economy, and Cookery, for Rich and Poor, Containing an Account of the Best English, Scotch, French, Oriental, and Other Foreign Dishes*. London: Longman, Rees, Orme, Brown, and Green, 1827.

A Lady of Rank. *Venice Under the Yoke of France and of Austria*. London: G. and W. B. Whittaker, 1824.

Abbott, Edward. *The English and Australian Cookery Book: Cookery for the Many, as Well as for the "Upper Ten Thousand."* London: Sampson Low, Son & Co.,1864.

Abell, Mrs. L. G. *Woman in Her Various Relations: Containing Practical Rules for American Females*. New York: Holdrege, 1851.

Accum, Fredrick. *A Treatise on the Adulteration of Food and Culinary Poisons*. London: J. Mallett, 1820.

Acta Sanctorum. Vol. 9. Antwerp: Society of Bollandists, 1675.

Acton, Eliza. *Modern Cookery, in All Its Branches: Reduced to a System of Easy Practice, for the Use of Private Families*. London: Longman, Brown, Green, and Longmans, 1845.

——. *Modern Cookery in All Its Branches: Reduced to a System of Easy Practice, for the Use of Private Families*. Philadelphia: Lea and Blanchard, 1845.

Alcock, Elizabeth. *The Frugal Housekeeper's Companion*. Liverpool: J. Smith, 1812.

Alcott, William Andrus. *Vegetable Diet: As Sanctioned by Medical Men*. 2nd ed. New York: Fowlers and Wells, 1851.

——. "What We May Eat." *American Vegetarian and Health Journal* (January 1854).
An English Physician. *French Domestic Cookery: Combining Economy with Elegance and Adapted for the Use of Families of Moderate Fortune*. London: Thomas Boys, 1825.
Audot, Louis Eustache. *La Cuisinière de La Campagne et de La Ville*. Paris: Audot, 1823.
Aurora General Advertiser. "Vermicelli & Macaroni." 1802.
Bailey, Pearl. *Pearl's Kitchen: An Extraordinary Cookbook*. Harcourt Brace Jovanovich, 1973.
Bailey Thurman, Sue, ed. *The Historical Cookbook of the American Negro*. Corporate Press, 1958.
Baldwin, Mary H., and Evelyn G. Hinds. *The Marigold Cook Book. A Practical and Useful Collection of Southern Recipes*. Doubleday, Doran, 1938.
Ball, Charles. *Fifty Years in Chains: Or, The Life of an American Slave*. University of North Carolina Press, 1997.
Barringer, Maria Massey. *Dixie Cookery; or, How I Managed My Table for Twelve Years*. Boston: Loring, 1867.
Beauvilliers, A. B. *The Art of French Cookery*. 3rd ed. London, 1827.
Beecher, Catharine Esther. *Miss Beecher's Domestic Receipt Book*. New York: Harper & Brothers, 1846.
Beeton, Isabella. *Beeton's Book of Household Management*. London: S. O. Beeton, 1861.
Beverley, Robert. *The History and Present State of Virginia*. Book IV. London: R. Parker, 1705.
Bliss, Mrs. *The Practical Cook Book: Containing Upwards of One Thousand Recipes*. Philadelphia: Lippincott, Grambo & Co., 1850.
Boni, Ada. *Talismano della felicità*. 4th ed. Rivista "Preziosa," 1934.
Bowser, Pearl, and Joan Eckstein. *A Pinch of Soul*. Avon, 1970.
Bradley, Alice. *The Wartime Cook Book*. World, 1943.
Briggs, Richard. *The New Art of Cookery, According to the Present Practice; Being a Complete Guide to All Housekeepers, on a Plan Entirely New*. London: G.G.J. and J. Robinson, 1788.
——. *The New Art of Cookery, According to the Present Practice*. Philadelphia: Spotswood, Campbell, Johnson, 1792.
Brotherton, Martha. *Vegetable Cookery, with an Introduction, Recommending Abstinence from Animal Food and Intoxicating Liquors*. 4th ed. London: Effingham Wilson,1833.
Bryan, Lettice. *The Kentucky Housewife*. Cincinnati: Shepard & Stearns, 1839.
Buckmaster, John Charles. *Buckmaster's Cookery*. London: George Routledge, 1874.
Callaghan, E. B. O. *Documents Relating to the Colonial History of the State of New York*. Vol. 1. Albany, 1856.
Camp Cookery and Hospital Diet for the Use of the U.S. Volunteers Now in Service. New York: Fredric A. Brady, 1861.
Campbell, Tunis G. *Never Let People Be Kept Waiting: A Textbook on Hotel Management: A Reprint of Tunis G. Campbell's Hotel Heepers, Head Waiters, and Housekeepers' Guide*. Ed. Doris Elizabeth King. Doris Elizabeth King, 1973. Reprint of the original nineteenth-century manual.
Carême, Marie-Antoine. *Le pâtissier royal parisien*. Paris: Chez Barba,1815.
——. *L'art de la cuisine française au dix-neuvième siècle*, 1833.
Carey, Mathew. *Addresses of the Philadelphia Society for the Promotion of National Industry*. Philadelphia: M. Carey and Son, 1819.
Carr, George Julian. *International Trade in Macaroni Products*. Bulletin 788. Government Printing Office, 1932.

Carter, Charles 1730 The Complete Practical Cook: Or, A New System of the Whole Art and Mystery of Cookery. London: W. Meadows, 1730.

Carter, Susannah. *The Frugal Housewife, or Complete Woman Cook*. Boston: Edes and Gill, 1772.

Carver, George Washington. *How to Grow the Peanut: And 105 Ways of Preparing It for Human Consumption*. Tuskegee Normal and Industrial Institute, 1917.

Casteau, Lancelot de. *Ouverture de cuisine*. Liege: Leonard Streel, 1604.

Cavalcanti, Ippolito. *Cucina Teorica-Pratica*. Naples: Luigi Marotta, 1837.

Chambers, Ephraim. *Cyclopedia: Or Universal Dictionary of Arts and Sciences*. Vol. 2. London: W. Innys, 1728.

Chambers, Robert. *The Book of Days: A Miscellany of Popular Antiquities*. Vol. 2. London: W. & R. Chambers, 1832.

Chase, Leah. *The Dooky Chase Cookbook*. Pelican, 1990.

De Chastellux, Françoise Jean. *Voyages dans l'Amérique Septentrionale dans les années 1780, 1781 & 1782*. Vol. 2. 2nd ed. Paris, 1791.

Chevrier, A. *Le Cuisinier National et Universel*, 1836.

Child, Lydia Maria. *The Frugal Housewife. Dedicated to Those Who Are Not Ashamed of Economy*. Boston: Marsh & Capen, 1829.

Christian Women's Exchange of New Orleans, ed. *The Creole Cookery Book*. New Orleans: T. H. Thomason, 1885.

Clark, Melissa. "Four-Cheese Macaroni and Cheese Recipe." New York Times Cooking. Accessed December 1, 2024. https://cooking.nytimes.com/recipes/1014635-four-cheese-macaroni-and-cheese.

Collingwood, Francis, and John Woollams. *The Universal Cook: And City and Country Housekeeper*. London: J. Scatcherd and J. Whitaker, 1792.

Collins, Angelina Maria. *The Great Western Cook Book : Or, Table Receipts, Adapted to Western Housewifery*. New York: A. S. Barnes, 1857.

Combe, Andrew. *The Physiology of Digestion*. 9th ed. Edinburgh: Maclachlan and Stewart, 1849.

Confederate Receipt Book. *A Compilation of Over One Hundred Receipts Adapted to the Times*. West & Johnston, 1863.

Corrado, Vincenzo. *Il cuoco galante*, Naples:1773.

Corson, Juliet. *Fifteen Cent Dinners for Workingmen's Families*. New York, 1877.

———. *Family Living on $500 a Year: A Daily Reference Book for Young and Inexperienced Housewives*. New York: Harper & Brothers, 1888.

Crowen, Mrs. T. J. *Mrs. Crowen's American Lady's System of Cookery: Comprising Every Variety of Information for Ordinary and Holiday Occasions*. New York: Dick & Fitzgerald, 1860.

Cutler, William Parker, and Julia Perkins Cutler. *Life, Journals and Correspondence of Rev. Manasseh Cutler, LL. D. by His Grandchildren*. Vol. 2. Robert Clark, 1888.

DeKnight, Freda. *Date with a Dish*. Hermitage, 1948.

Déliée, Felix. *The Franco-American Cookery Book; or, How to Live Well and Wisely Every Day in the Year*. Putnam, 1884.

Dickens, Charles. "Common Cookery." *Household Words* 13, no. 305 (1856): 42–43.

Diderot, Dennis. *Encyclopédie ou dictionnaire raisonné des sciences, des arts et des métiers*. Vol. 1. Paris: Briasson, 1751.

Digby, Sir Kenelm. *The Closet of the Eminently Learned Sir Kenelme Digbie Kt. Opened*. London: E. Cotes, 1669.

Dods, Margaret. *The Cook and Housewife's Manual*. Edinburgh, 1826.

Dolby, Richard. *The Cook's Dictionary, and House-Keeper's Directory*. London: Henry Colburn and Richard Bentley, 1830.

Dumas, Alexandre. *Sketches of Naples*. Trans. A. Roland. Philadelphia: E. Ferrett, 1845.

Eaton, Isabel. "Special Report on Negro Domestic Service in the Seventh Ward Philadelphia." In W. E. B. Du Bois, *The Philadelphia Negro: A Social Study*. University of Pennsylvania Press, 1899.

Estienne, Charles. *Caroli Stephani, De Nutrimentis*, Paris: 1550.

Eustis, Célestine. *Cooking in Old Creole Days*. R. H. Russell, 1904.

Evening Post. "Joseph Anastasi Advertisement." March 22, 1813.

Farmer, Fannie Merritt. *The Boston Cooking-School Cook Book*. Boston: Little, Brown, 1896.

Ferguson, Sheila. *Soul Food: Classic Cuisine from the Deep South*. Weidenfeld & Nicolson, 1989.

Fettuccine Alfredo: La ricetta originale del ristorante Alfredo Alla Scrofa. Accessed November 14, 2024. https://www.youtube.com/watch?v=Sk9HCxfIREo.

Fisher, Abby. *What Mrs. Fisher Knows About Old Southern Cooking: Soups, Pickles, Preserves, Etc*. Ed. Karen Hess. Applewood, 1995.

Flexner, Marion W. *Dixie Dishes*. Hale, Cushman & Flint, 1941.

Florio, John. *A Worlde of Wordes, or Most Copious, and Exact Dictionarie in Italian and English*. London: Arnold Hatfield for Edward Blount, 1598.

Food of Working Women in Boston, The. Wright & Potter, 1917.

Forme of Cury, The, 1390.

Fredericksburg News, The. "The Tomato." August 12, 1852, sec. Miscellaneous.

Fox, Minnie C. *The Blue Grass Cook Book*. Fox, Duffield & Company, 1904.

Francatelli, Charles Elmé. *The Modern Cook: A Practical Guide to the Culinary Art in All Its Branches*. London: Richard Bentley, 1846.

——. *A Plain Cookery Book for the Working Classes*. London: Routledge, Warne, and Routledge, 1852.

Frances, Norton Mason. *John Norton & Sons, Merchants of London and Virginia: Being the Papers from Their Counting House for the Year 1750–1795*. Augustus M. Kelley, 1968.

Franklin, Benjamin. "Manner of Making the Parmesan Cheese, as Observed by Dr. Leith, and by Him Communicated to B. Franklin, Esq." *Lloyd's Evening Post*, December 20, 1773.

Frazer, Mrs. *The Practice of Cookery, Pastry, Pickling, Preserving, &c*. Edinburgh: Peter Hill, 1791.

Fresnaye, Louis (Lewis). "To Make Soup of Vermicelli, Maccaroni and Other Kinds of Paste." The Library Company of Philadelphia, 1802.

Frugoli, Antonio. *Pratica e scalcaria d'Antonio Frugoli Lucchese*. Rome: Francesco Caualli, 1638.

Gaige, Crosby. *Crosby Gaige's Macaroni Manual*. M. Barrows, 1947.

Gasterman. "Introduction à l'histoire de la gourmandise." *Journal des gourmands et des belles ou l'Épicurien français*, May 1807.

Gilman, Caroline (A Lady of Charleston). *The Carolina Receipt Book or Housekeeper's Assistant*. Charleston: James S. Burges, 1832.

Glasse, Hannah. *The Art of Cookery Made Plain and Easy*. London, 1747.

Graham, Sylvester. *Lectures on the Science of Human Life*. Boston: Marsh, Capen, Lyon & Webb, 1839.

Grey, Elizabeth, countess of Kent. *A True Gentlewoman's Delight*. London: G. D., 1653

Green, Mary Elizabeth. *Food Products of the World*. 6th ed. Chicago: Frazer, 1896.

Hall, Carla. "The Only Four Cheese Mac and Cheese Recipe You Need," November 18, 2022. https://carlahall.com/the-only-four-cheese-mac-and-cheese-recipe-you-need/.

——. "The Creamiest Stovetop Mac and Cheese," January 24, 2024. https://carlahall.com/the-creamiest-stovetop-mac-and-cheese/.

Hammond, Elizabeth. *Modern Domestic Cookery, and Useful Receipt Book*, London: John Booth, 1819.

Harris, Jessica B. *Sky Juice and Flying Fish: Traditional Caribbean Cooking*. Simon & Schuster, 1991.

——. *A Kwanzaa Keepsake and Cookbook*. Scribner, 2024.

Harris, Jessica B., Albert Lukas, and Jerome Grant. *Sweet Home Café Cookbook: A Celebration of African American Cooking*. Smithsonian, 2018.

Harrison, Sarah. *The House-Keeper's Pocket-Book, and Compleat Family Cook*. London: R. Ware, 1733.

Harrison, William. "Description of Elizabethan England, 1577." In *Holinshed's Chronicles*, 1577.

Hayes, Emma, Mrs. W. T. *Kentucky Cook Book*. J. H. Tomkins, 1912.

Heiatt, Constance B., and Sharon Butler, eds. *Curye on Inglysch*. Oxford University Press, 1985.

Henderson, W. A. (William Augustus). *The Housekeeper's Instructor; or, Universal Family Cook: Being a Full and Clear Display of the Art of Cookery in All Its Various Branches*. London: W. & J. Stratford, 1791.

Honeywood, Lydia. *The Cook's Pocket-Companion and Complete Family-Guide: Being a Collection of the Very Best Receipts*. London: C. Henderson, 1758.

Hood, Thomas, ed. "French Cooks and Cookery." In *The New Monthly Magazine and Humorist* 2: 6–12. London: Henry Colburn, 1842.

Hooker, Mary. *The Young Housekeeper's Friend: Or, a Guide to Domestic Economy and Comfort by Mrs. Cornelius*. Boston: C. Tappan, 1846.

Hooper, Mary. *Hints on Cookery and Management of the Table (Ma Cuisine)*. London: Spencer Blackett, 1891.

Hopkisk, James. *Dictionnaire portatif de cuisine, d'office, et de distillation*. Paris: Chez Lottin le jeune, 1772.

Housekeeper. *The Practical American Cook Book, or, Practical and Scientific Cookery. Practical and Scientific Cookery*. New York: D. Appleton and Company, 1855.

Howard, Mrs. B. C. [Jane Grant Gilmore]. *Fifty Years in a Maryland Kitchen*. Baltimore: Turnbull Brothers, 1873.

Hulse, Olive M. *Two Hundred Recipes for Cooking in Casseroles*. Hopewell, 1914.

Hunter, Alexander. *Culina Famulatrix Medicinae: Or, Receipts in Cookery by Ignotus*. York: T. Wilson and R. Spence, 1804.

Il cuoco di tutti. Adriano Salani, 1917.

Jeffries, Bob. *Soul Food Cook Book*. Bobbs-Merrill, 1969.

Johnson, Ben. *Cynthia's Revels, or the Fountain of Self-Love*. London, 1600.

Johnstone, Christian Isobel (writing as Margaret Dods). *The Cook and Housewife's Manual: A Practical System of Modern Domestic Cookery and Family Management*. Edinburgh: Oliver & Boyd, 1826.

Joo, Judy. "Kimchi Mac and Cheese." Judy Joo. Accessed December 1, 2024. https://www.judyjoo.com/recipes/kimchi-mac-and-cheese-42/.

Jr. League of Charleston. Ed. Mary Vereen Huguenin. Walker Evans & Cogswell, 1950.

Julien, Honoré. "Six Cent Reward." National Intelligencer, January 27, 1815. https://link.gale.com/apps/doc/GT3017473001/NCNP?u=smithsonian&sid=bookmark-NCNP&xid=e98e62a7.

Kemble, Fanny. *Journal of a Residence on a Georgian Plantation in 1838–1839*. London: Longman, Green, Longman, Roberts & Green, 1863.

Kidder, Edward. *Receipts of Pastry and Cookery for the Use of His Scholars*. London, 1702.

Kirk, Alice Gitchell. *Practical Food Economy*. Little, Brown, 1917.

Kirwan, Andrew Valentine. *Host and Guest: A Book About Dinners, Dinner-Giving, Wines, and Desserts*. London: Bell and Daldy, 1864.

Kitchener, William. *Apicius Redivivus: or, The Cook's Oracle: Wherein Especially the Art of Composing Soups, Sauces, and Flavouring Essences Is Made So Clear and Easy, by the Quantity of Each Article Being Accurately Stated by Weight and Measure, That Every One May Soon Learn to Dress a Dinner, as Well as the Most Experienced Cook; Being Six Hundred Receipts, the Result of Actual Experiments Instituted in the Kitchen of a Physician, for the Purpose of Composing a Culinary Code for the Rational Epicure . . . [Etc.]*. London, 1817.

——. *The Cook's Oracle : Containing Receipts for Plain Cookery on the Most Economical Plan for Private Families Etc.*, 4th London ed. A. Constable, 1822.

——. *The Cook's Oracle: Containing Receipts for Plain Cookery, on the Most Economical Plan for Private Families*. 2nd American ed. Munroe & Francis, 1823.

Knight, Charles. "Neapolitan Maccaroni-Eaters." *Penny Magazine of the Society for the Diffusion of Useful Information* 87 (1833).

La Chapelle. *The Modern Cook*. Vol. 2. London, 1733.

La Reynière, Grimod de. *Almanach des gourmands*. 5th ed. L'imprimrie de Cellot, 1807.

La Varenne, François Pierre de. *Le cuisinier françois*. Paris: Pierre David, 1651.

Labat, Jean Baptiste. *Voyages du P. Labat en Espagne et en Italie*. Vol. 2. Paris: J. B. Delespine, 1730.

LaBelle, Patti. *Recipes for the Good Life*. Simon & Schuster, 2008.

Ladies Association of the First Presbyterian Church, ed. *The First Texas Cook Book*. Houston, 1883.

Lando, Ortensio. *Commentario delle più notabili, et mostruose cose d'Italia & altri luoghi Aramea in italiana tradotto*. Venice: Bartholomeo Cesano, 1548.

Lankester, Sir Edwin Ray. *On Food: Being Lectures Delivered at the South Kensington Museum*. London: Robert Hardwicke, 1861.

Latini, Antonio. *Lo scalco alla moderna, overo L'arte di ben disporre li conviti*. Vol. 2. Naples: Parrino e Mutii, 1694.

Le Grand d'Aussy, Pierre-Jean Baptiste. *Histoire de la vie privée des Français*. Paris: Ph.-D. Pierres, 1782.

L'economia della città e della campagna, ovvero, il nuovo cuoco italiano secondo il gusto francese. Vol. 1. Florence: Stecchi Giovanni Battista & Antonio Giuseppe Pagani, 1772.

Lee, Mrs. N. K. M. *Cook's Own Book: Being a Complete Culinary Encyclopedia*. Boston: Munroe & Francis, 1832.

Leonardi, Francesco. *Apicio moderno*. Rome, 1807.

——. *L'Apicio moderno*, 1790.

L'École parfaite des officiers de bouche. Paris: Ian Ribov, 1662.

Leslie, Eliza. *Domestic French Cookery*. Philadelphia: Carey & Hart, 1832.

——. *Directions for Cookery, in Its Various Branches*, Philadelphia: Carey, Lea & Blanchard, 1837.

——. *The Indian Meal Book: Comprising the Best American Receipts for the Various Preparations of That Excellent Article*. London: Smith, Elder and Co., 1846.

——. *The Lady's Receipt-Book*. Philadelphia: Carey and Hart, 1847.

Lincoln, Mary Johnson (Mrs. D. A.). *Mrs. Lincoln's Boston Cook Book: What to Do & What Not to Do in Cooking*. Boston: Roberts Brothers, 1884.

Logan, Rayford W., ed. *Memoirs of a Monticello Slave / as Dictated to Charles Campbell in the 1840's by Isaac, One of Thomas Jefferson's Slaves*. University of Virginia Press, 1951.

Lustig, Lillie S., S. Claire Sondheim, and Sarah Rensel. *The Southern Cook Book of Fine Old Dixie Recipes*. Culinary Arts, 1935.

Lyall, W. R. "Art. IX. The Fudge Family in Paris Edited by Thomas Brown the Younger. Author of the Twopenny Post-Bag." *The British Critic* 9 (1818): 496–501.

Lyford, Carrie Alberta. *A Book of Recipes for the Cooking School*. Hampton Normal and Agricultural Institute, 1921.

"Macaroni." *The Food Journal* 37 (February 1, 1873): 7–8.

MacKenzie, Colin. *Five Thousand Receipts in All the Useful and Domestic Arts*. London: G. and W. B. Whittaker, 1822.

——. *Five Thousand Receipts in All the Useful and Domestic Arts: Constituting a Complete and Universal Practical Library and Operative Cyclopædia*. Philadelphia: Abraham Small, 1825.

Macaroni Journal, The. "Pabst-Ett Macaroni: Instead of Macaroni and Cheese." December 15, 1927.

Mairault, Adrien-Maurice de. *Observations sur les écrits modernes*. Vol. XXVIII. Paris: Chaubert, 1742.

Malouin, Paul-Jacques. *Description et détails des arts du meunier, du vermicelier et du boulenger, avec une histoire abrégée de la boulengerie et un dictionnaire de ces arts*. Vol. 40. Paris: Académie Royale des Sciences, 1767.

Mann, Mary Tyler Peabody. *Christianity in the Kitchen: A Physiological Cook-Book*. Boston: Ticknor and Fields, 1858.

Martin, Sarah. *The New Experienced English Housekeeper*. Doncaster: D. Boys, 1795.

Mazzei, Philip. *Philip Mazzei: My Life & Wanderings*. Ed. Margherita Marchione. Trans. Eugene Scalia. American Institute of Italian Studies, 1980.

McAllister, Ward. *Society as I Have Found It*. New York: Cassell, 1890.

M'Clure, W. Frank. "The Manufacture of Macaroni." *Scientific American* 92, no. 1 (1905): 5.

McKinney, Emma and McKinney, William. *Aunt Caroline's Dixieland Recipes*. Laird & Lee Inc., 1922.

Mendes, Helen. *The African Heritage Cookbook*. The Macmillan Company, 1971.

Menon. *La cuisiniere bourgeoise*. Suivie de L'Office a l'usage de tous ceux qui se mêlent de dépenses de maisons. Paris: Guillyn, 1748.

Menon, Louis Francois Henri de. *Les soupers de La cour; ou L'art de travailler toutes sortes d'alimens pour servir les meilleures tables, suivant les quatre saisons*. Paris: Guillyn, 1755.

Merrick, George Byron. *Old Times on the Upper Mississippi: The Recollections of a Steamboat Pilot from 1854–1863*. Arthur H. Clark, 1909.

Messisbugo, Cristoforo di. *Banchetti, composizione di vivande, et apparecchio generale.* Ferrara: Giovanni de Buglhat et Antonio Hucher, 1549.Meyer, Adolphe. "Culinary Hints from an Old Cookbook." *International Culinary Magazine*, January 4, 1915.

Mickler, Ernest Matthew. *White Trash Cooking*. Ten Speed, 1989.

Mitchell, B. W. "Merlin and Macaroni." *The Classical Weekly* 25, no. 5 (1931): 33–39.

Mollard, John. *The Art of Cookery Made Easy and Refined: Comprising Ample Directions for Preparing Every Article Requisite for Furnishing the Tables of the Nobleman, Gentleman, and Tradesman*. London: 1801.

Mollard, John. *The Art of Cookery Made Easy and Refined*. 2nd ed. London, 1802.

Montgomery, Robbie. *Sweetie Pie's Cookbook: Soulful Southern Recipes from My Family to Yours*. HarperCollins, 2015.

Moss, Maria J. *A Poetical Cook-Book*. Philadelphia: Caxton, 1864.

Muhammad, Elijah. *How to Eat to Live, Book One*. Secretarius MEMPS Ministries, 1967.

Nairategeva. "Combe on Digestion." *Vegetarian Advocate* 2, no. 7 (1850): 83–84.

Napier, Mrs. Alexander. *A Noble Boke off Cookry Ffor a Prynce Houssolde or Eny Other Estately Houssholde: Reprinted Verbatim from a Rare Ms. in the Holkham Collection*. London: Elliot Stock, 1882.

Nardini, Bartolommeo. *Mes périls pendant la révolution de Naples*. Paris: A. Égron, 1806.

National Intelligencer. "Honoré Julien Advertisement." June 25, 1814. https://link.gale.com/apps/doc/GT3017468736/NCNP?u=smithsonian&sid=bookmark-NCNP&xid=7b9bf928.

Nourse, Mrs. *Modern Practical Cookery, Pastry, Confectionary, Pickling and Preserving*, 1813.

Nunes, Lucy. "Mac 'n' Cheese Spring Rolls Recipe." Taste.com.au. Accessed December 1, 2024. https://www.taste.com.au/recipes/mac-n-cheese-spring-rolls-recipe/bzmgqd7r.

Ottolenghi, Yotam, Helen Goh, Verena Lochmuller, and Tara Wigley. *Ottolenghi Comfort: A Cookbook*. Penguin, 2024.

Parkes, Mrs. William, and Thomas Webster. *The American Family Encyclopedia of Useful Knowledge*. Ed. David Meredith Reese. New York: Derby & Jackson, 1856.

Peterson, Hannah Mary Bouvier. *The National Cook Book: By a Lady of Philadelphia*. Philadelphia: T. B. Peterson, 1866.

Picayune's Creole Cook Book, The. The Picayune, 1910.

Plat, Sir Hugh. "Certaine Philosophical Preparations of Foode and Beverage for Sea-Men, in Their Long Voyages," London: 1607.

——. *The Jewel House of Art and Nature*.London: Peter Short, 1594.

Purcell, Eleanor. *Aunt Priscilla in the Kitchen*. Aunt Priscilla Publishing, 1929.

Radcliff, M. *A Modern System of Domestic Cookery: Or, The Housekeeper's Guide*. Manchester: J. Gleave, 1824.

Randolph, Mary. *The Virginia House-Wife*. Ed. Karen Hess. University of South Carolina Press, 1984.

Ravenel, Harriet Horry. Eliza Pinckney. New York: Charles Scribner's Sons, 1896.

Ray, John. *Observations Topographical, Moral, & Physiological Made in a Journey through Part of the Low-Countries, Germany, Italy, and France*. London: John Martyn, 1673.

"Receipts in Cookery, M. S. Book Belonging to Mrs. White of Stoney Lane." England, 1700s. https://digital.lib.uiowa.edu/islandora/object/ui%3Acookbooks_13656.

Recueil de planches de l'encyclopédie: Encyclopédie mèthodique arts et métiers méchaniques. Vol. 8. Paris: Panckoucke, 1787.

Rhett, Blanche S., and Lettie Gay. *200 Years of Charleston Cooking*. J. Cape & H. Smith, 1930.

Richard, Lena. *Lena Richard's Cook Book*. Rogers, 1939.

Richmond Enquirer. "Manufacture of Vermicelli and Macaroni, in the U. States." June 30, 1809.

——. "Wednesday, Nov. 23, 1808." November 28, 1808.

Roahen, Sara, and John T. Edge, eds. *The Southern Foodways Alliance Community Cookbook*. University of Georgia Press, 2010.

Roberts, Leonard E. *The Negro Chef Cookbook*. Vantage, 1969.

Rombauer, Irma S. *The Joy of Cooking: A Compilation of Reliable Recipes with a Casual Culinary Chat*. A. C. Clayton Printing Co., 1931.

Romoli, Domenico. La singolare dottrina di M. Domenico Romoli sopranominato Panunto. Venice: Michele Tramezzino, 1560.

Rose, Giles, trans. *A Perfect School of Instructions for the Officers of the Mouth*. London: Bently and Magnes, 1682.

Rossetti, Giovan Battista. *Dello Scalco*. Ferrara, 1584.

Rundell, Maria Eliza. *A New System of Domestic Cookery: Formed Upon Principles of Economy, and Adapted to the Use of Private Families*. Philadelphia: Benjamin C. Buzby, 1807.

——. *A New System of Domestic Cookery : Formed upon Principles of Economy, and Adapted to the Use of Private Families*. London: John Murray, 1810.

Rundell, Maria Eliza (A Lady). *A New System of Domestic Cookery: Formed Upon Principles of Economy and Adapted to the Use of Private Families throughout the United States* (New York: R. McDermut & D. D. Arden, 1814.

Russell, Malinda. *A Domestic Cook Book*. Paw Paw, MI: Published by the author, 1866.

Rutledge, Sarah. *The Carolina Housewife*. Charleston: W. B. Babcock, 1847.

Salmon, Cecil, and J. Allen Clark. *Durum Wheat. Farmer's bulletin 534*. Government Printing Office, 1913.

Scappi, Bartolomeo. *Opera*. Venice: Michele Tramezzino, 1570.

Scott, Jacobus Elias. *Heele goeje remedien, en Resepte om te kloken te bakken en Confijten*, 1737.

Shankland, Mrs. E. R., and Sue W. Hetherton. *The Matron's Household Manual*. Dubuque: Palmer, Winall & Co., 1875.

Simmons, Amelia. *American Cookery; or, The Art of Dressing Viands, Fish, Poultry, and Vegetables, and the Best Modes of Making Pastes, Puffs, Pies, Tarts, Puddings, Custards, and Preserves, and All Kinds of Cakes, from the Imperial Plum to Plain Cake: Adapted to This Country, and All Grades of Life*. Hartford, 1796.

Skinner, Robert P. *Manufacture of Semolina and Macaroni*. Government Printing Office, 1902.

Smith, Eliza. *The Compleat Housewife: Or, Accomplish'd Gentlewoman's Companion*. Williamsburg: William Parks, 1747.

Smith, Jacqueline Harrison, ed. *Famous Old Receipts Used a Hundred Years and More in the Kitchens of the North and the South*. J. Winston, 1908.

Smith, Mrs. *The Female Economist, Or, A Plain System of Cookery for the Use of Families*. London: Mathews and Leigh, Strand, 1810.

Society of Gentlemen, A. *The Universal Receipt Book: Being a Compendious Repository of Practical Information in Cookery, Preserving, Pickling, Distilling, and All the Branches of Domestic Economy*. Philadelphia: M. Carey & Son, 1818.

Southern Cultivator. "Advertisement." January 1861.
Soyer, Alexis. *Soyer's Charitable Cookery; or, The Poor Man's Regenerator*. London: Simpkin, Marshal & Co., 1847.
——. *The Modern Housewife, or Ménagère*. London: Bradbury and Evans, 1850.
——. *The Modern Housewife or Ménagère*. New York: Appleton & Company, 1850.
——. *A Shilling Cookery for the People: Embracing an Entirely New System of Plain Cookery and Domestic Economy*. London: G. Routledge, 1855.
——. *Soyer's Culinary Campaign*. London: G. Routledge, 1857.
Spencer, E. *The Modern Cook: And Frugal Housewife's Compleat Guide to Every Branch in Displaying Her Table to the Greatest Advantage*. Newcastle upon Tyne: T. Saint, 1782.
Starr, Kathy. *The Soul of Southern Cooking*. University Press of Mississippi, 1989.
Stewart, Henry. *American Cheese and Cheese-Making*. Philadelphia: J. B. Lippincott, 1898.
Sulley, P. K. *What to Do with the Cold Mutton: A Book of Réchauffés*. New York: Bunce and Huntington, 1865.
Tipton-Martin, Toni, and Joe Randall. *A Taste of Heritage: The New African American Cuisine*. Macmillan, 1998.
Tried and True Recipes—The Home Cook Book of Chicago—from Recipes Contributed by Ladies of Chicago and Other Cities and Town: Published for the Benefit of the Home for the Friendless. Chicago: J. F. Waggoner, 1874.
Tschirky, Oscar. *The Cook Book by "Oscar" of the Waldorf*. New York: Werner, 1896.
Twamley, Josiah. *Dairying Exemplified, or, The Business of Cheese-Making*. Warwick: Sharp, 1787.
Tyree, Marion Cabell, ed. *Housekeeping in Old Virginia*. Louisville: J. P. Morthon, 1878.
Ude, Louis Eustache. *The French Cook*. London: 1813.
——. *The French Cook*. Philadelphia: Carey, Lea and Carey, 1828.
Upton, Rebecca A. *Home Studies*. Boston: Crosby, Nichols, and Company, 1856.
Vegetarian Advocate. "Notices." 1850.
"The Vegetarian Treasury: Macaroni." *Vegetarian Messenger*. "The Vegetarian Treasury: Macaroni." September 1851.
Verral, William. *Complete System of Cookery*. London: Andrew Millar, 1759.
Viard, André. *Le cuisinier royal: ou, L'art de faire la cuisine et la pâtisserie, pour toutes les fortunes*. Paris: Barba, 1817.
Voelcker, Augustus. *Agricultural Chemistry: Four Lectures*. London: Ridgway, 1857.
Vollmer, William. *The United States Cook Book*. Philadelphia: Schaefer & Koradi, 1856.
Webster, Thomas. "Farinaceous Substances Which Are Used in Various Parts of the World Instead of Bread." In *An Encyclopaedia of Domestic Economy: Comprising Such Subjects as Are Most Immediately Connected with Housekeeping*. London: Longman, Brown, Green and Longmans, 1844.
Whole Duty of a Woman, or, An Infallible Guide to the Fair Sex: Containing Rules, Directions, and Observations, for Their Conduct and Behavior through All Ages and Circumstances of Life, as Virgins, Wives, or Widows, The. London: T. Read, 1737.
Winder, Delilah. *Delilah's Everyday Soul: Southern Cooking with Style*. Running Press, 2006.
Wittenmyer, Annie. *A Collection of Recipes for the Use of Special Diet Kitchens in Military Hospitals*. St. Louis: U.S. Christian Commission, 1864.
Women's Centennial Committees. *National Cookery Book: Compiled from Original Receipts*. Philadelphia: Henry B. Ashmead, 1876.

Woods, Sylvia, with Melissa Clark. *Sylvia's Family Soul Food Cookbook*. HarperCollins, 1999.

——. *Sylvia's Soul Food*. Hearst, 1992.

Yeo, Isaac Burney. *Food in Health and Disease*. Lea Brothers, 1890.

Young, Thomas. *Narrative of a Residence on the Mosquito Shore*. 2nd ed. London: Smith, Elder and Co., 1847.

Young Woman's Companion: or, Frugal Housewife. Containing the most approved methods of pickling, preserving, potting, collaring, confectionary . . . Also the art of cookery, carving, and household arts. Manchester: Russell & Allen, 1811.

Zacchia, Paulo. Il vitto quaresimale di Paulo Zacchia medico romano. Rome: Piero Antonio Facciotti, 1637.

INDEX

Page numbers in *italics* indicate illustrations.